The Argentine Silent Majority

Sebastián Carassai

The Argentine Silent Majority

Middle Classes, Politics, Violence, and Memory in the Seventies

Duke University Press   Durham and London   2014

Printed in the United States of America on acid-free paper ♾
Text designed by Courtney Leigh Baker and
typeset in Quadraat by Tseng Information Systems, Inc.

Library of Congress Cataloging-in-Publication Data
Carassai, Sebastián.
The Argentine silent majority : middle classes, politics, violence,
and memory in the seventies / Sebastian Carassai.
pages   cm
Includes bibliographical references and index.
ISBN 978-0-8223-5596-0 (cloth : alk. paper)
ISBN 978-0-8223-5601-1 (pbk. : alk. paper)
1. Middle class—Political activity—Argentina—History—20th century.
2. Argentina—Politics and government—1955–1983. 3. Political
violence—Argentina—History—20th century. 4. Argentina—History—
1955–1983. I. Title.
HT690.A7C37 2014
305.5′50982—dc23
2013048706

I have laboured carefully, not to mock, lament, or execrate, but to understand human actions; and to this end I have looked upon passions, such as love, hatred, anger, envy, ambition, pity, and the other perturbations of the mind, not in the light of vices of human nature, but as properties, just as pertinent to it, as are heat, cold, storm, thunder, and the like to the nature of the atmosphere, which phenomena, though inconvenient, are yet necessary, and have fixed causes, by means of which we endeavor to understand their nature.—Baruch Spinoza

Contents

Acknowledgments

Funds from Bernardo Mendel Endowment and the Center for Latin American and Caribbean Studies (CLACS) at Indiana University enabled me to carry out the first trips to Buenos Aires, Correa, and San Miguel de Tucumán, between 2006 and 2009. Its completion was possible thanks to the Paul V. McNutt and Kathleen McNutt Watson Graduate Fellowship and the Louise McNutt Graduate Fellowship, granted me by the College of Arts and Sciences (COAS) of Indiana University. In 2011, my entry as a researcher into the National Scientific and Technical Research Council of the Argentine Republic (CONICET) allowed me to finish the fieldwork and devote the time to writing this book. The University of Buenos Aires, meanwhile, gave a UBACYT subsidy to the research group I lead that made it possible to extend this research to new issues.

I thank the disinterested collaboration that I received from all of the people I interviewed throughout my research. I omit their real names because their testimonies are a fundamental part of the subject studied in this book. Every one of them knows, however, that without their sincere disposition to speak with me extensively about Argentine history and their own personal histories over the span of three years, my book would lack one of the basic elements that sustains it. I am equally indebted to those who gave me many hours of their time to speak about the politics, journalism, humor, theater, movies, music, and literature of the 1970s, and who were, at the time, protagonists of one or more of these realms. Among these were Abrasha Rottemberg (former editor of the *La Opinión* newspaper), Alberto Monti (former mayor of Correa), Antonio Guerrero (former political activist), Arturo Álvarez Sosa (poet and journalist), Arturo Blatezky (founding member of the Ecumenical Movement for Human Rights), Beto Ponce (musician), Carlitos Balá (actor and humorist), Carlos Diez (journalist), Carlos Páez de la Torre (historian), Carmen Zayuelas (founder of the IPSA consulting firm), Chicha Chorobik de Mariani (founder of the Abuelas de la Plaza de Mayo), Dardo Nofal (writer and journalist), David Lagmanovich (literary critic and literature professor), Eduardo Rosenzvaig (historian), Enrique Alé (journalist), Enrique Fogwill (writer), Fabián Cejas (mayor of Correa), Frederick Turner (sociologist), Harry García Hamilton (former editor of La Gaceta), Héctor Pessah (former director of A&C consulting firm), Horacio González (sociologist), Hugo Marcantonio (musican), Humberto Rava (former political activist), Inés Aráoz (poet), José Enrique Miguens (sociologist, former director of the CIMS consulting firm), José María Roch (former political activist), Juan Carlos Di Lullo (journalist), Juan Carlos Gené (playwright), Juan José Sebreli (writer), Juan Tríbulo (playwright), relatives of Julio Aldonate (poet), Julio Ardiles Gray (journalist and writer), León Rozitchner (philosopher), Luis Giraud (journalist), Maximiliano Burckwarat (journalist), Miguel "El Griego" Frangoulis (bookseller), Nené Marcatto (director of the folkloric music restaurant El Amanecer), Roberto Pucci (historian), Renzo Bicciuffa (musician), Ricardo Monti (playwright), relatives of Roberto Champi (poet), Roberto Galván (former mayor of Correa), Rogelio Signes (poet), Rubén Rodó (journalist), Ruth Andrada (former director of the Burke consulting firm), Santiago Varela (humorist), Silvia Rolandi (journalist), Susana Pérez Gallart (founding member of the Asamblea Permanente por los Derechos Humanos), Tony Arnedo (journalist), Tuqui Bragalenti (musician), Vides Almonacid (journalist and humorist), and Walter Ventroni (journalist).

I also give thanks for the friendship of those that took me into their homes, introduced me to their acquaintances, and facilitated my access to data or information about the three sites considered in my research. These were Mauro Gatti, Luis Abrach, and Pancho Nadal in Tucumán, Cacho and Nancy Galdo in Correa, and my parents and friends in Buenos Aires. In Correa, I accessed valuable information thanks to the officials of various town institutions, such as the Regional Museum and Historical Archive of Correa, the popular library Caja de Créditos Correa, and School No. 254 Bartolomé Mitre. Gerardo Álvarez allowed me to consult the archives of the Cañada de Gómez Museum. Pablo Cribioli and Juan Carlos Altare, in Rosario, and Mario Rodríguez and the officials of the Wayra Killa foundation and those of the Archive of the Historical House [Casa Histórica] in Tucumán facilitated my access to the archives of La Capital in Rosario and La Gaceta and Noticias in Tucumán. In Buenos Aires, I thank the staff of the National Archive and the newspaper archives of the Congress of the Nation, the National Library, and the Buenos Aires legislature that, not always without difficulties, managed to allow me to consult the materials that I needed. I also thank the staff of the Center for the Documentation and Investigation of Left-Wing Culture in Argentina [Centro de Documentación e Investigación de la Cultura de Izquierdas en Argentina] (CeDInCI) and the Estudio PRISMA. Edgardo Sampaolesi of the Ministry of Education of the Nation, Roberto Moreyra of the Circulation Verification Institute [Instituto Verificador de Circulaciones], Lila Magdalena of the Argentine Chamber of Advertisers [Cámara Argentina de Anunciantes], Silvana Piga of University of San Andrés, and Luis González, Latin American bibliographer. Indiana University efficiently assisted me by providing data. Marilyn Milliken, from the Roper Center for Public Opinion Research at the University of Connecticut, helped with the identification of statistics unprocessed until today. Nathaniel Birkhead, from Indiana University, helped me to decipher them.

Finally, I extend my gratitude to those who accompanied me in the ordinary and exhausting task of conducting research and writing a book. In Bloomington, Indiana, I was lucky to meet good friends to share, among other things, our passion for Latin American history. I owe special thanks to Alfio Saitta, Matthew Van Hoose, and David Díaz. With no less passion, I benefited from conversations with my Argentine friends Ariel Lucarini, Cecilia Derrigo, Jack Nahmías, Rodrigo Daskal, and Lisandro Kahan, in whose home in Northampton, Massachusetts, we discussed over the course of many weeks some of these ideas. Filmmaker Silvina Cancello enthusiastically edited the documentaries with archival material that I produced for my interviews. At different times, María Sol Alato and Laura Smit helped me in my search for material and journalistic information. Andrew Lyubarsky efficiently worked on the translation of the original work. Jeffrey Gould, Peter Guardino, Arlene Díaz, and Alejandro Mejías-López, all from Indiana University, were among the first readers of this work. Improved through their feedback, I later benefited from the reading of Carlos Altamirano and Hugo Vezzetti. Between 2011 and 2013, specific sections and chapters were discussed in several meetings with students and colleagues. I thank Eric Sandweiss and Patrick Dove, both from Indiana University, the members of the Open Seminar coordinated by Lila Caimari at the University of San Andrés, attendees to my talk at the Center for the Study of History and Memory at Indiana University, directed by John Bodnar and Daniel James, my colleagues of the Centre for Intellectual History, directed by Adrián Gorelik, at the National University of Quilmes, and Eva-Lynn Jagoe and my extraordinary friend Kevin Coleman, from University of Toronto, whose cooperation and intelligence have been invaluable to my work. More thanks: María Paula Ansolabehere believed I could take this project forward even when I doubted. My parents, Helvecia Frías and Hugo

Carassai, beside me unconditionally, even in the distance. Lynn Di Pietro, my young mother in North America. My greatest debt will always be to Daniel James, my advisor and friend. Like a thief, I took the spoils of his uncomfortable questions, incisive reading, intellectual talent, and a willingness to talk at undisturbed length about history and everything else.

"Our middle class is a joke. That's why we laugh at it. . . . If we are not indulgent with ourselves, we cannot have pity for the Argentine middle class, for our class," wrote David Viñas in 1972, prefacing a play critical of the Argentine middle-class family.[1] Viñas's sentence was not a phrase written in passing. It condensed a pejorative judgment about the middle class, quite prevalent in the early 1970s among intellectuals, artists, progressive journalists, and politically committed youth that already had a long history and would also have a considerable future. During the first half of the 1970s, a broad sector of the Argentine intelligentsia, especially in Buenos Aires, devoted articles in newspapers and magazines, plays and films, to questioning the middle class.

The same year that Viñas wrote this phrase, the journalist Tomás Eloy Martínez published a series of articles entitled The Ideology of the Middle Class in the daily La Opinión. According to Martínez, after having arrived in the country from Europe in the late nineteenth century with greater desires to return than to stay, the Argentine middle class had no problems submitting to a variety of governments, indifferent to the electoral fraud that they practiced. Decades later, obsessed by consumption and without having any other goals than buying a car and a house that the neighbors would envy, the middle class acquired the characteristics that would define it: resistance to change, fear of losing comfort and security, distrust of any communitarian ideology, disposition to accept the social leaders that are imposed upon it, adherence to the values propagated by mass-circulation newspapers and traditional currents of thought, reluctance to discuss history, sexual repression, and the cult of appearance.[2] In their desperation to be accepted, according to Martínez, the middle class adhered to the interests of the ruling classes and imitated their customs, style of dress, and food.[3] In summary, in its docile adaptation to society, the Argentine middle class was a creature without ideology.[4]

However, in the turbulent early 1970s, it was this very quality that made the middle class a bounty to fight over for many of its critics. Because even if, unlike the working class, the middle class was strongly criticized, it was never deemed "unrecoverable"—unlike other groups such as the economic elites or the military. The darts thrown against it took the form of prescriptions for the sick, as if the goal were to attempt to awaken a sleepwalker. The middle class might be a joke, but Viñas and others still felt a duty to criticize it mercilessly; this was not because it was a social sector closed to any dialogue. In other words, these criticisms were accompanied by a hope, tacit or explicit, for its transformation.

This hope was clearly presented in film and theater. In *Las venganzas de Beto Sánchez* (1973)—a film directed by Héctor Olivera, based on Ricardo Talesnik's book—a middle-class youth decides to avenge himself, revolver in hand, against a series of people he considers responsible for his personal failures: the teacher who gave him a conventional education, the priest who instilled taboos in him, the girlfriend who repressed his sexual instincts, the military official who humiliated him during his conscription, the boss who condemned him to a boring routine, and the friend who taught him to aspire for "status." The film, while demonstrating the dead end that this individual reaction leads to, sought to arouse the spectator. "Beto Sánchez strives to individualize the culprit," a film critic wrote, "until he understands that the real culprit is not a person or several people, but rather that elusive mechanism called the System." [5] The frustrations of the middle class should not lead its members to individual rebellion, but rather to questioning the established order.

There is perhaps no clearer example of this pedagogical mission than the play entitled *Historia tendenciosa de la clase media argentina, de los extraños sucesos en que se vieron envueltos algunos hombres públicos, su completa dilucidación y otras escandalosas revelaciones*, by Ricardo Monti.[6] With a title that emulated the works of Peter de Vries, the play was influenced by the Brechtian atmosphere that permeated one of the ways of conceiving art in those years.[7] Written in 1970, and released the following year, *Historia tendenciosa* parodied the behavior of the Argentine middle class from the 1920s until the early 1970s. The criticism combined denunciation with a call for change. Although the middle class was again found guilty (of being cowardly, complacent, stingy, and racist), the play appealed to its conscience, forcing it to confront its supposedly miserable qualities. It also aspired to change the middle class's attitude, inviting it to cease tipping the balance of history in favor of imperialism and the oligarchy, both allegorical characters represented in the plot. At the end of the plot itself, the actors refused to leave the stage, resisting the idea that everything must end as it always does, and asked themselves if there was any other solution besides repeating their historically subservient behavior. Meanwhile, behind them a new being was being born, the Child, "a white and pretty young man, made beautiful by pure light," as a theater critic put it, who rose up slowly with a machine gun in his hand.[8] As the same critic noted in his commentary, the Child was "an allegory for the possible, the possible answer," the armed struggle as a solution.[9]

The discourse that aspired to question and challenge the middle class, criticize it and teach it where history was going, appropriately introduces this book's object of study. This book deals with the enormous general public that did not hear or ignored this discourse. I study the middle classes that were not directly involved in the political struggle of the 1970s, principally focusing on two subjects key to understanding this period, politics and violence.

If it was judged necessary to denounce the "middle class" in the worlds of theater, film, journalism, and essay, this was because the majority of those who formed this class did not get involved in the political struggle, at least not in the form that was demanded. In all of history, even during great revolutions or epic periods, different actors can be distinguished by the level of their participation in the events that brought them about. Studies of this period of Argentine history (1969–1982) have generally concentrated on its protagonists: the military or civilian authorities, labor union, political party, or ecclesiastical leaders, the mobilized sectors of the workers' movement, politicized youth, armed groups of the Left, and military and security forces. Without a doubt, these actors occupied the center of the political stage, and "made history," as is typically said. However, countless anonymous stories unfolded in the background, playing less of a leading role but still influencing, and at the same time suffering the influence of, the course that the events took.

The Argentine Silent Majority

This book adopts an analytical distinction that determines the scope of study. The heterogeneous universe that made up the middle classes in the 1970s is divided into two segments. On one side are the activists, composed of university youth and cultural and intellectual elites, characterized by a strong political commitment and direct participation in the social struggles that included, although were not limited to, the path of armed insurrection. On the other side are the nonactivists, made up of the majority of the middle classes that kept their distance from the type of commitment and mode of participation that characterized the activists. This distance, however, did not necessarily imply a lack of interest in politics. Those who formed this middle-class silent majority may not have been the protagonists of history, but they were no mere spectators.

For Argentina, the 1970s has passed into history as the decade of political violence and repression. In no other period of the twentieth century were both so intense. The memories of my interviewees have led me to grant even greater centrality to violence in order to understand this period. The people interviewed remember the devaluations, the adjustments, the fall of real wages or economic liberalization more diffusely than they do a guerrilla attack or the disappearance of someone they knew. This is why the analysis of violence occupies a central place in this study.

Numerous works have already been devoted to this problem. Adding to the analysis studying the groups and institutions that exercised some form of violence in the 1970s, the last twenty years have seen the appearance of essays, biographies, and autobiographies based on oral testimonies or participant memories. A majority of these works have been oriented toward recovering the memories of those who were directly affected (relatives, friends, fellow activists, or the authors themselves) by state terrorism. In this book, however, I will consider documentary sources and oral testimonies together, and concentrate my analysis on the life stories of people who were not reached by state terror—a slant that both complements and needs to be complemented by the mentioned studies. For its part, the literature on the middle classes in Argentina during the 1970s has privileged the study of radicalized youth, political groups, revolutionary movements, and intellectual elites. The less politicized people, certainly the majority, have remained largely on the margins of their analysis.

In chapter 1, about the political culture of the middle classes, I focus on their relationship with Peronism. Since its emergence in the mid-1940s, this political movement created stark divisions within Argentine society. In that context, the middle classes mostly joined the resistance to the regime, mainly on the grounds that, in Peronism, they saw a threat to their self-perception as autonomous beings and freethinkers. Although toward the 1970s their anti-Peronism softened, their memories of historical Peronism decisively shaped the ways in which these sectors read Perón's return to Argentina in 1973 and the fall of his government three years later.

The rest of the book focuses on the issue of violence. After a brief preliminary excursus about this topic, in chapters 2, 3, and 4 I attempt to elucidate how the rise in violence was perceived by the nonactivist middle classes, and what role they themselves played in this process. In chapter 2, I analyze social violence, specifically referring to uprisings and the radicalization of student activism. Gradually weary of the military regime of the Argentine Revolution (1966–1973), by 1969 part of the middle classes endorsed anything that posed a challenge to that government. However, it would be wrong to confuse the solidarity that middle classes felt with the protest movements, especially those featuring students, with ideological agreement. The attitudes of the middle classes toward social violence were linked less to the political than to the affective dimension.

In chapter 3, I explore the perception that the middle classes had about armed violence, specifically related to the guerrillas. The sympathy they generated within the middle classes was concentrated in youth vanguards, who were mostly at the universities. The guerrilla phenomenon offered, in fact, an opportunity for a majority of the middle classes to reaffirm how far their positions were from a global questioning of the capitalist order. Contrary to what scholars have assumed, from the beginning these sectors massively disapproved of the attempts made by the guerrillas. In this disapproval, we can trace much of the middle classes' moral vision of the world, including the political world.

In chapter 4, I offer an analysis of how these sectors coexisted with state violence. The arrival of the military dictatorship, in March 1976, added death and imposed order to this process, multiplying and monopolizing violence. The feeling of the return of the state, as well as the civil superstition that ascribed an ultimate knowledge to it, played a decisive role in how the middle classes decoded state violence. However, the discourse of memory cannot take responsibility in the first person for the actions and omissions of those years, a point that opens up questions about the responsibility that these social sectors share in that history.

After a second excursus, in which I try a different way to explore the complexity of speech that usually characterizes memory, I turn to examine, in chapter 5, some of the representations of violence in the symbolic realm, taking the analysis from the conscious to the unconscious scope, from the real to the imaginary world. The positive valuation of weapons in the social space of Argentina, the proliferation of metaphors and images of violence in advertising art and humor, help us to understand that the 1970s were lived against a background in which violence was tacitly accepted as a way of resolving social conflicts and that "common sense" went far beyond the political-ideological.

Researchers have noted the absence of studies about the behavior of Argentine society during the years of the last dictatorship (1976–1983) that went beyond focusing on its major corporative groups.[10] In my understanding, there is in fact a broader, double absence. It is broader because it also encompasses the previous years (1969–1976), frequently approached only through the history of their (political, labor union, intellectual, or artistic) vanguards. And it is double because, generally, it does not just study the period's protagonists but also privileges the big cities, such as Buenos Aires or Córdoba, extending the validity of any conclusions made about them to the entirety of the country. To counter the first absence, in this work I study the years between 1969 and 1982. To counter the second absence, I consider three very different locations. In selecting them, I took into account not only strictly sociological considerations (see appendix 1) but also the presence of middle-class sectors and the heterogeneity between each of the three sites. These locations were the city of Buenos Aires, the center of political events and the most influential metropolis for the entire national territory; the city of San Miguel de Tucumán, the capital of a northwestern province that was characterized by a turbulent political life from the middle of the 1960s on; and Correa, a town of five thousand inhabitants in the province of Santa Fe in the country's rich region, which did not experience great upheavals during those years.

In terms of the sources consulted (see appendix 2), I would like to emphasize the methodology employed to collect the oral testimonies. I conducted two hundred interviews with a variety of people, ranging from middle-class families who did not participate in activism in the 1970s to journalists, politicians, historians, actors, writers, playwrights, and musicians who were active in the period. I interviewed a smaller number of people who belonged to two groups that were not my object of study: former middle-class activists and members of the working class. These testimonies are partially included in my argument. Nevertheless, in addition to providing me with valuable information, they played the role of what sociologists call the "control variable." What I call a nonactivist middle-class "sensibility" in this study can at the very minimum be distinguished from that of two other groups, those who were activists, and, for other reasons, those who belonged to the working class.

I developed a specific methodology to carry out the interviews with members of the nonactivist middle class. I created a documentary called COMA 13: Del Cordobazo a Malvinas: Trece años de historia en imágenes, which I used to trigger discussions. This documentary does not feature any sort of off-screen narration.[11] It shows images and plays audio that provide a glimpse of each of the years studied in chronological order, juxtaposing news shows; popular songs; political speeches; comedy sets; famous movies; cartoons; newspapers; magazine and book covers; advertisements; images of labor unions; political, military, guerrilla, and religious leaders; protests; rebellions; electoral rallies; scenes of repression; news of bombings and kidnappings—in other words, history in images. All images and audio come from those years (none come from later productions filmed about the period), so that the footage could have been seen or heard by the interviewees at the time they were initially broadcast. I conducted a minimum of three interviews with each subject over the course of two and a half years, between June 2007 and January 2010. The method that I used consisted of a first interview in which I collected a typical life history, and second and third meetings where, after watching both parts of the documentary (1969–1974 and 1975–1982), we conversed about the memories that the images and audio awoke for the interviewee. This methodology allowed me to access memories that would not have come up otherwise, to hear accounts linked to what Walter Benjamin, following Proust, called the "involuntary" memory instead of the voluntary, conscious, deliberately reasoned memory.[12] The images of the past enriched the interviews, provoking diverse and sometimes surprising memories. The excursus that appears in this book proves that without the documentary, the interviews would not have been enough to awaken some memories that were not always readily accessible.

The Middle Classes: Concepts and Characteristics

I use the concept "middle classes" in the plural, because it translates the intrinsic heterogeneity that characterizes these sectors better than the singular "middle class."[13] Drawing on Pierre Bourdieu's sociological perspective, I define the middle classes as a theoretical construction based on the objective existence of differences and differentiations that in turn are expressed in different dispositions or habitus. In other words, people can be aggregated together in "classes" or "groups" because, in order to exist socially, they distinguish themselves from one another. They exist as groups or classes because they differentiate themselves from others. This means that some practices and not others, some tastes and not others, some goods and not others, and even some ways of seeing the world and not others are associated with particular social positions. For example, the working and middle classes tended to have different practices that are in turn distinctive. Consumer goods, primarily cultural goods, affirm the class status of their consumers and help each person tacitly affirm what they are and what they are not.[14] The habitus is the product of these social positions that are not only different but also differentiating. Thus, for the researcher, according to Bourdieu, in the space of differences that constitute any social world, "classes exist in some sense in a state of virtuality, not as something given but as something to be done."[15] The middle classes studied here were cut out or "dotted," to use Bourdieu's expression, based on the relative positions that, in each case, made the definition of an intermediate social stratum differentiated from other strata possible. In many Argentine social environments, social differentiation translates into a neat geographical division. In the case of Correa, for example, it is expressed in the division between those that lived on one side of the railroad, those that lived in "the center," and those that lived on the other side of the road, in "the north."

This does not mean that the middle classes make up a homogeneous conglomerate. On the contrary, they typically differ according to their economic and cultural capital. The intensity of this heterogeneity, however, has not always been the same. Socioeconomic data demonstrate that, during the period studied in this book, the Argentine middle classes, while heterogeneous per se, were relatively homogeneous compared to both prior and later periods.[16] At the beginning of the 1980s, Argentina had not yet experienced high rates of unemployment, the pronounced impoverishment of her middle classes, or the dismantling of her modest welfare state (which guaranteed acceptable levels of education and health care for a majority of the population).[17]

National censuses show that the middle class in the 1970s continued with the expansionary phase that had began in the 1940s. Once constituting 40.6 percent in 1947 and 42.7 percent in 1960, it came to represent 44.9 percent in 1970 and almost half of the population in 1980 (47.4 percent).[18] Although its independent/self-employed sector decreased relative to its salaried sector,[19] a comparison of the 1970 and 1980 censuses shows that during these ten years, the composition of the middle class remained stable; in general terms, 26 percent was independent and 74 percent salaried.

In conclusion, although certain long-term processes that would end up modifying Argentina's social structure had already begun in the 1970s, the middle-class structure did not change significantly. This allows us to consider them jointly but also invites us to explore often overlooked heterogeneous elements, such as those linked with age (the generation that subjects belong to), social environment (if they belong to a university or not), and, less decisively, geographic area (a small town, a mid-size city, or the Capital Federal). Thus, socioeconomically the condition of the middle classes in 1980 was much more similar to their condition ten years earlier than to their much-diminished condition ten or twenty years later. The most profound transformation the decade (1970–80) produced, which was destined to last until the present, was that tied to the question of violence and its relation with politics, to which analysis this book is dedicated.

I am repelled by the idea that a person allows someone to tell him "Perón, Perón, how great you are!" This person is either crazy or a fool. If someone told me: "Mr. So and so, how great you are!" I would tell him "Ok, look, my friend, let's change the subject. . . ."—Jorge Luis Borges

One   Political Culture

In June 1943, a military revolution put an end to the conservative cycle that began with the overthrow of Hipólito Yrigoyen thirteen years earlier. The young officers of the armed forces developed an increasingly significant rule in the new government, occupying positions and helping shape its political orientation. One of these officers, Juan Perón, soon became the strategic head of the revolution. When he was the Labor and Welfare Secretary, Perón granted unions long-awaited concessions that quickly earned him the sympathy of a majority of the nation's workers. This fact, coupled with the incentives that Perón gave to working-class protests, turned him into a potential threat for the traditional political parties and, above all, for his military comrades in the government, who decided to arrest him in October 1945. On October 17, thousands of workers marched to the Plaza de Mayo to the presidential palace and demanded his release. A political identity that persists until the present day was born.

Perón deepened and extended state intervention beyond the economic realm, implementing a populist program that transformed Argentina's social landscape in a matter of years. His first two terms (1946–1955) left an indelible mark on both supporters and detractors. His fall, provoked by another military revolution in September 1955, reopened a cycle of institutional instability that would only multiply over the two following decades. Whether Peronism was rising or in crisis, whether it was legitimate or prohibited, whether Perón was in power or in exile, the society reacted dividedly. The question of whether one was with Peronism or against it defined much of Argentina's twentieth century.

In this chapter, I explore the political culture of the middle classes. I analyze experiences, memories, and responses to Peronism and propose continuities and notable fractures, for example around the figure of Evita, in middle-class views of Peronism. In particular, I challenge recent accounts that have portrayed the middle class as turning to the left, and toward Peronism, in the 1970s. At the same time, I examine a largely unexplored hypothesis regarding Perón's strategy toward the middle class in this key period. To grasp what is at stake, however, we must begin with a deeper examination of what the first Peronist administrations had meant to the middle classes.

Anti-Peronism and Enlightenment

The years of the first Peronist government (1946–1955) stained the prism through which the new political juncture created in 1973 by the return of a democratic regime without prohibitions was read. In that period, the middle class developed the sensibility that would later serve to decode important events of the 1970s, Peronism's triumph in March 1973, Perón's definitive return to the country in June of that year, and even the March 24, 1976, coup. Whether the memories of the Peronist decade were their own or inherited from their family, they tell us something fundamental about the political identity of the middle classes, as well as allowing us to understand their future behavior.

From the rise of Peronism, the political identity of most of the middle classes was conditioned by a sensibility that structured itself as a reaction to this movement.[1] What was traditionally called "anti-Peronism" was at the heart of this sensibility. From 1945 on, various political identities (radicals, conservatives, liberals, socialists, communists) came together in their anti-Peronism and were mobilized by this sensibility.[2] This fact did not make a middle-class Peronist vote impossible. As shall later be seen, Peronism was a multiclass movement from its origins, and, both at midcentury and in the 1970s, enjoyed the support of a fraction of the middle classes.

However, when a sector of the armed forces put an end to almost ten years of the Peronist regime in 1955, the multitude that celebrated the rise of the so-called Liberating Revolution (1955–1958) was largely composed of the middle classes. From this coup to 1973, the various political actors in conflict demonstrated, on the one hand, their inability to impose their own political project and, on the other, their ability to impede those of their rivals. This "hegemonic tie" resulted in military and civilian governments with limited legitimacy due to the banning of Peronism, who sooner rather than later were able to corroborate the persistence of the Peronist political identity.[3] In 1973, in the epilogue of another military coup, the Argentine Revolution (1966–1973), the de facto government assumed the failure of its project to "de-Peronize" the country and called for the first election in eighteen years that allowed the Peronist party to present candidates, while proscribing Perón himself. The Peronist ticket of Héctor Cámpora and Vicente Solano Lima were elected with a large majority.

Although the intensity of anti-Peronism weakened after the regime's fall in 1955, a majority of the middle classes remained "not Peronist" in the two following decades; the furious anti-Peronism of the 1950s gave way to a more nuanced "non-Peronism." This should not, however, lead us to lose sight of the fundamental issue: the political identity of much of the middle classes remained conditioned by that sensibility, organized around their distinction from Peronism.[4]

An ambivalence emerges in the memories of Peronism's return to power in 1973 that members of the middle class evoke today. For some, this return represented the hope for a peaceful and orderly solution to the political crisis. For others, it represented the fear that the dark days of the first Peronism would return. Ricardo Montecarlo, a young man from Tucumán who in 1973 was finishing his studies of medicine at the Universidad Nacional de Tucumán, speaking about Perón's return, stated:

> I, at least, had some hope, despite not being a Peronist. Perón was the element that—Perón the person, Perón the individual—was the element that could have united people with different ideas. His famous pendulum swing, from left to right, from right to left. [. . .] When he

died, the bell tolled. Everything fell apart [. . .] I knew that Perón had come back to die. But I felt sorry and disappointed to lose hope, because I knew that everything was falling apart. He was the only one that, perhaps, could have united the Argentine people. And everything fell apart, as you see later, because then came the big mess.

Memories like Ricardo's contrast with those who remember having felt hopelessness and even fear at the return of Peronism. Many questions that I posed about 1973 were answered with references to the first Peronist decade, especially by those who were young people or adults in the earlier period. In the first interview with Jorge Van der Weyden, who was born in 1928, the issue of Perón's return led to the following dialogue:

SC: My question is how you saw Peron's return at that moment. Not the reflection that you have today, but in that moment, if you remember, did it make you feel . . . ?

JORGE: Fear, yes, yes. That man's return, for all of us who lived through his first period, one said: "well, now we're going to return to the same old stuff." Fortunately it wasn't like that. But the fear was present. It was present. Not because of ideology or anything like that, because that's all "verse." It was because of the methods, and because of what could happen [. . .] People don't know what the first Peronist period was like. Now, people talk about Peronism— I'm sorry that I'm getting to this, but for me it's a fundamental part of the country's skeleton, right?—All the first Peronist period was a dictatorship with all of its letters capitalized. We couldn't have this conversation in a bar, nothing. Not even with your family, or it would depend with whom and behind closed doors. Not in a subway, not in a train. This is how far we had gotten with that fine gentleman. Maybe he changed later, he came back [in 1973], seemed like a nice old man, people are left with that image, or the young people that didn't live through [the first Peronist period], see that and are left with that. But I knew the reality. You would pick up a newspaper, any newspaper, eh? And all of the pages, all of them said, "Perón" and "Perón." The province of Chaco was called Perón, Retiro [the train terminal] was called Perón, everything, everything: "Perón," "Perón," "Perón." It was unbearable. And everything was like that: the kids in school, studying Evita's virtues. [. . .] There were the block captains, which meant that each block had an informant that could point you out. Look, that was really serious! The famous 1970s that everyone talks about, it was a wild time for those that were in the activist movements. Those of us that weren't involved in that, well, we lived through the World Cup [of soccer, in 1978], and everyone was content and happy. In that period, [during the first Peronist government], no. That was universal, universal.

By 1973, after several years of political party inactivity, the vast majority of the middle classes (which by that point included generations that did not have direct memories of the first Peronist government) were not affiliated with radicalism, developmentalism, socialism, or communism. Many of their members sympathized with some of these political currents, and, in that sense, these sympathies separated them. However, they were united by what they had in common: whether they inherited it from their parents or whether it was their own, they maintained that non-Peronist sensibility that was the child of the anti-Peronism cultivated during the ten years of the regime. Thus, although by the 1970s the party sympathies of the middle classes were dispersed, their political identity was defined less by what they supported than by what they opposed. And what they opposed continued to be Peronism.

The memories of anti-Peronism are filtered through the generational variable. However, the driving force of the different generations only differs in its intensity, not in its nature. Maurice Halbwachs taught us that collective memory is neither global nor homogeneous.[5] Collective memory never reflects the beliefs of "society" as a whole, viewed as a totality; instead, it is a product of the standards, values, and social experiences of particular groups and classes. Social memory has limits, and these limits correspond, with some flexibility, to the symbolic framework and representations of defined social classes. The memories of the Peronist regime that I will now present can be, with some flexibility, assigned to the "nonactivist middle class in the 1970s."

The grounds for anti-Peronism (or of the more tolerant non-Peronism) can be organized around four types of elements attributed to the regime: that it was fascist, that it was dictatorial or authoritarian, that it was immoral, and that it was hostile to culture or "anticulture." In the fascist category are mentioned the ubiquity of Perón and Evita and of government propaganda in the mass media and the school books that were required reading; the replacement or introduction of curricular content oriented to glorifying the regime; the compulsory membership in the party to have access to or maintain a job in the public sector (including health and education); the obligation to attend and participate in the emblematic days associated with Peronism (such as wearing mourning clothes after Evita's death); the great demonstrations of people to cheer the leader on; and the persecution, torture, and jailing of opponents. To present it as dictatorial or authoritarian, they mention the police-style surveillance over the population, primarily over those nicknamed "*contreras*" (those contrary to Peronism), put into place through a network of informers and groups like the Nationalist Liberation Alliance (Alianza Libertadora Nacionalista), the verticalism and the total submission to the leader (and its counterpart, the obsequiousness of his followers); its antidemocratic character (a democracy defined less in terms of votes than in the freedoms and spaces for citizen autonomy permitted). The immoral elements tended to emphasize the corruption that, while not new, had achieved scandalous levels for the first time in the political history of the twentieth century (the enrichment of both Perón and many regime officials); the state manipulation of those who did not have cultural or material resource to refuse state favors; and Perón's own sexual degeneracy in his relationship with adolescents of the Secondary Students Union (Unión de Estudiantes Secundarios). Finally, the elements relating to Peronism's "anticultural" imprint tend to cite the old slogan at the regime's beginning, "yes to sandals [alpargatas], no to books"; the incorporation of illiterate people or those lacking in formal instruction to the legislature; anti-intellectualism, evidenced by the unanimous opposition of universities to the regime[6]; the stoking of emotional and passionate tendencies of the masses to the detriment of their rationality; and the incitement to mediocrity or even vagrancy through the improvement of the population's standard of living through demagogic actions that discredited personal effort, merit, and education.

These memories tend to emerge together with anecdotes in which they, or people close to them, had to elude the impositions of the regime or attempted to do so. Perhaps it is not unreasonable to postulate that the middle classes, between 1946 and 1955, exercised a spontaneous and disorganized resistance to what they perceived to be excesses or abuses to their dignity, a resistance which, while also political and social, was above all cultural. It is thus relevant to ask, What nerve of the middle class's subjectivity was irritated by the serious restructuring of social life that Peronism implied, so that these memories persist so vividly? Is it as simple as affirming that they felt attacked by those that they had always considered to be inferior? In the argument that follows I attempt to respond to both questions, starting with the latter.

There are racist elements present in the discourse of some of the members of the middle class, visible in the allusion to working-class and "popular" sectors using terms such as "blacks," "bums" (*gronchos*), and "browns." This contrasts with the romanticism with which middle-class activist youth in the 1970s viewed the poor in general and the working class in particular, a conception that led to "proletarianization" as a tactic to obtain a greater closeness with the "objectively" revolutionary subject. However, the young middle-class activists in the 1970s, whether they were Peronists or Marxists, assigned themselves the role of the political vanguard of the working and popular classes, and in so doing denied to these sectors sufficient knowledge to construct for themselves a politics commensurate with their interests. Therefore, even if it is true that a majority of the nonactivist middle classes tended to express themselves as if they had belonged and continue to belong to a social and cultural world that was hierarchically situated above that inhabited by the working and lower classes, this self-declared superiority cannot be attributed exclusively to the sector that kept its distance from activism or middle-class anti-Peronists. On the contrary, everything indicates that this feeling of superiority corresponded more to a class perception than one associated with political identity.[7] In other words, if the middle classes that are the object of my study (their nonactivist sectors in the 1970s) or those analyzed in this section (their anti-Peronist members) had and conserve a dual and hierarchical vision of society—where they situate the lower-class and working-class sectors at the bottom and place themselves above them— this is not related to either of the two groups mentioned but rather with a more general class habitus. Both in the past and today, they feel and think themselves to be superior not because they are anti-Peronists or because they were not activists but because they are "middle class," for having accumulated enough cultural and economic capital to distinguish themselves qualitatively from the poor and the working class. This trait seems to evoke a resemblance with, as opposed to differentiating them from, the various sectors of the middle classes, regardless of their political identity or degree of politicization.

The answer to the first question should thus be looked for elsewhere. I propose to analyze carefully a component of their sensibility that I call "enlightened." This is the middle classes' self-perception (neither activists nor Peronists in the 1970s) as being autonomous and freethinking subjects; in other words, not determined by anything other than their free will to think and to act in the way that they think and act. The anti-Peronist memories, no matter which of the four types they belonged to, often emphasize this "enlightened" element. Peronism, experienced as a fascist, dictatorial, immoral, or anticultural regime, challenged this self-perception by either taking away or threatening to take away this autonomy.

The following excerpts belong to two Correa residents from different generations. The first is from Luis Martino, born in 1953, and the second is from Linda Tognetti, born eleven years before. In the first case, his anti-Peronism was inherited from relatives and acquaintances. In the second case, it was a combination of inheritance and her own personal experience.

LUIS: In my generation, there wasn't so much Peronism and anti-Peronism. In the older generations, there was. I remember, for example, when Perón returned in 1973, when I was twenty years old — and I'm talking about people that were doing their military service in the period of the Liberating Revolution — [there were people that] had a mortal hatred [of Perón]. When Evita died, they were forced to go to kneel down in the church, they forced them and those that did not kneel down were punished, all those things . . .

SC: And they told you these stories?

L: Yes, but people who lived through them, people who lived through them. For example, my wife's father, in Carcarañá. They had suspended him from his job because he hadn't gone to the mass to remember Evita, and such things! I didn't like these things, there was no free thought. I have a book here, one of Perón's books that were handed out in schools in that period, right? *The First Worker* and all those things . . . Like they were trying to get the kids to think that [Peronism] was always best. I saw a lot of demagoguery in these things . . .

LINDA: I never liked totalitarian governments, nor those that tried to direct my thoughts, and I was always very rebellious. I always wanted to "go against." When I was young I didn't realize . . . I do know that [in Perón's period] there were people who received toys, who received books . . . Not me, never. And they used to say: "let's go to the railroad, where Eva will be passing" [. . .]. But it always hurt me that they throw things at you or they just give them to you. I always thought that one has to earn them. So, nobody had to throw some sweet bread and cider at me, or send me a toy, no. Without ever having anyone teach me this, even when I was a little girl I always thought that one needs to have the means of having something. That was born with me. Or because I was rebellious, what do I know? [. . .] And I do remember one of my youngest brother's books, that said, "Mama loves me. Papa loves me. I love . . . Perón." That annoyed me a lot. [. . .] How am I going to teach my brother to read that? [. . .] Here in the house, we had our ideas: no matter who rises or who falls, we never got anything through politics, nothing. Everything was done with effort. Because I never got a job because of politics, because I had a pretty face or an ugly face. You see, when you don't owe anything to anyone? Maybe it is because I love freedom . . .

The excerpts cited allude to three of the four types of anti-Peronist memories. Luis evokes memories that correspond to the fascist type, such as the obligation to worship the symbols of the regime (kneeling in church when Eva Perón died or being suspended from work for missing a commemorative mass). Linda invokes memories of both the fascist type (the books of indoctrination) and the immoral (the gifts "thrown" by Eva Perón to the population) and anticulture types (the discrediting of one's own effort, the attainment through favors of what should be achieved by merit). What they perceive as being incompatible with their lifestyle is, in all cases, the quashing of individual autonomy. In 1973, Luis did not vote for Peronism because "he did not like" these memories that had been transmitted to him, because there was "no free thought" under Peronism. Linda did not vote for Peronism either, because "totalitarian governments" or the fact that they "wanted to direct [people's] thinking" clashed with her nature to "go against" things. According to Linda, she "was born with" this tendency to reject everything that violated her freedom of judgment. Her "love for freedom" was directly associated with her anti-Peronist view when, in our following meeting, she said: "I will tell you: I wasn't and I'm not a Peronist. I was free." Freedom and Peronism appear as incompatible terms.

Something similar occurs with non-Peronists' ideas about education and culture. When explaining their opposition to Perón's movement, they defended their character as freethinkers. When in our first interview I asked Ángela and Sergio Caballero from Tucumán (born in 1940 and 1935, respectively) if they came from Peronist families, they answered:

SERGIO: No, no, my dad was a sugar engineer and my mom was a doctor of pharmaceutics and biochemistry, and a professor at the university.

ÁNGELA: In my house we've always been freethinkers. In my house, there wasn't. . . . We were anti-Peronists. But I'll tell you, my father, during Perón's first government, he was a rabid Peronist. Of course, because he said, "What a great guy! He supports the working people, gives them vacations, bonuses" and everything else. And then, when the second government came, he said: "[Perón] tricked me, because everything he did was the means to an end and he's not continuing that." In other words, "there's not a clear line of conduct" and from then on, he became anti-Peronist. Because really, Perón changed completely in his second presidency [1952–1955].

Some anti-Peronists such as Ángela had older relatives who were originally Peronists, at least at some point in their lives. These family members, in most of the cases working-class people, adhered to Peronism because they experienced the concrete improvements that the regime produced in the working world, especially during its first years (1946–1949). As some families consolidated their status or ascended to the middle class in the late 1940s, their children—born in the 1930s and early 1940s—began to acquire what I have called an anti-Peronist sensibility as they grew older (the opposite of what would occur in the 1970s with the younger generations). Ángela, who attended university, was anti-Peronist because they were "freethinkers" in her house. Additionally, her husband's response adds an important issue, also evident in several interviews. He did not tell what political sympathies there were in his house; instead, he mentioned his parents' professions. His mother was not a Peronist, she was a "doctor of pharmaceutics and biochemistry, and a professor at the university." Education and culture are perceived as conflicting with this political identity.

As I have mentioned, the testimonies of those who lived through the first Peronist government as youth or adults tended to condemn more strongly what the regime meant. In the account of Jorge Van der Weyden, twelve years older than Ángela, both the issue of freethinking and how Peronism was experienced as a threat to this self-perception can be seen with greater intensity. Born in the 1920s, Jorge was studying at the Universidad de Buenos Aires during the Peronist regime. After watching the first part of the documentary (1969–1974), we had the following dialogue:

SC: I asked about Cámpora, what memories do you have of him?

JORGE: A total good-for-nothing. Cámpora is like if I said [naming a current official whom he describes as being obsequious]. Peronism functioned like that: there's someone above you, whatever his name might be, the one below him sucks up to him, and the one that sucks up the most is the one that is closest to the top. That is Peronism in its pure essence. [. . .] But this was born from the military mentality that he [Perón] imposed. Peronism is "leadership" [*conducción*] [he is referring to the typical way that Peronist candidates promote themselves]. "So-and-so leadership," a third-rate mayor: "[Names a current mayor] leadership." What is he leading us to? I don't need to be led! I'm a thinking being! Why "leadership"? Are they going to pull me by the ear like that? And the Peronists like that. One of their party locals is a barracks where everyone is; the party locals of the Socialists were libraries, there's a difference.

The indignation produced by the loss of autonomy and the renouncement of freedom, which these social sectors link with Peronism, is not primarily political. In another part of the interview, Jorge explicitly stresses that he did not distance himself from Peronism because of a political-ideological problem ("with the Peronist program that Perón took from socialism I can agree with 99 percent"). The problem is, instead, moral: "it's very sad to show society how I use these human slaves, I use them and I have them so that they come and go, come and go." Jorge feels that the typical appeal of the Justicialist leaders to the idea of "leadership" is offensive to his condition as a thinking being and degrades his autonomous capacity. It is striking that this element appeared again at the moment when the middle classes explained why they did not join the activism of the 1970s. Later on, when I examine perceptions of violence and political activism, there will be occasion to return to other testimonies that confirm the "enlightened" element as a primordial component of their self-perception.

The paradox in this extreme valorization of freedom of thought and autonomy of the will is that, in both the 1950s and the 1970s, it was compatible for support for or indifference toward ruptures in the constitutional order. Opposing the fascism, authoritarianism, immorality, and/or anticulturalism of the regime, in 1955 these anti-Peronist middle classes positioned themselves with the coup plotters. They resisted a regime that they judged to be de facto dictatorial, by supporting an actual dictatorship. Twenty-one years later, when in 1976 the armed forces deposed the government of Isabel Perón (who occupied the presidency after her husband's death in 1974), it would be primarily their desire for order, but also the necessity to end the immorality, corruption, and indecency of this government, that would once again push them on the side of the military. In both cases, this anti-Peronist sensibility, lived or inherited, favored the idea that nothing could be worse than the prolongation of Perón's despotism in 1955 or Isabel's decadence in 1976. If much of the middle class appeared to be explicitly or silently allied with these military revolutions, the reason is not to be found in their militarism or in their love for uniforms and hierarchical orders (easier to find in the Peronist ranks) but rather in what these revolutions opposed. In other words, these middle classes were not primarily promilitary but rather anti-Peronist in both 1955 and 1976.

During the 1960s, a combination of events, including Cuba's joining the socialist camp, the death of Che Guevara in 1967, the May 1968 protests in Paris, and local social uprisings, seemed to indicate to many that the world was veering to the left. At the same time, Perón's prolonged exile, his party's proscription, the loyalty of the workers' movement to their leader, and the nature of some of his enemies created the necessary conditions for revising earlier condemnations of Peronism. However, a "leftward shift" and/or "Peronization" did not occur evenly among the middle classes, essentially affecting numerous university youth and progressive groups of the church.[8]

Along with the rise of working-class sectors more inclined to struggle than dialogue within the world of trade unions, the explosive growth of left-wing activism and the rise of guerrilla groups both within and outside Peronism, such as the Montoneros and the People's Revolutionary Army (Ejército Revolucionario del Pueblo) were important factors of the political situation. However, although the majority of these young activists were of middle-class origin, the excessive emphasis that is often given to this phenomenon risks tinging the entire past with its intense color, impeding rather than contributing to an understanding of the ideological sympathies and electoral behavior of the middle classes in the early 1970s. Before taking on both topics, I will briefly return to the late 1960s and analyze the political humor of the society in those days.

From the late 1950s on, a certain consensus regarding the necessity of implementing a modernizing, developmentalist program existed in various sectors of Argentine society. The democratic governments of Arturo Frondizi (1958–1962) and Arturo Illia (1963–1966) attempted to orient their politics in this sense, each in its own way. By 1966, in a context of fierce criticism of the slow pace of change that the institutional processes of a state of law demanded, many political and social sectors agreed that this program could be implemented better, with haste and without interruption, by an authoritarian government. General Juan Carlos Onganía then began a new military regime, the Argentine Revolution (1966–1973), which aimed to modernize the economy by postponing the political debate and domesticating Peronism through agreements with the union movement.

Little more than a year after the regime's installation, the bulk of the support for the government of the Argentine Revolution was concentrated in the "upper class" and "upper-middle class," among which 60.2 percent approved of the military regime. On the other side of the social spectrum, only 34.3 percent of the "lower class" had a favorable opinion of Onganía's government, while the two other segments established by the poll, the "intermediate" and "lower" middle classes, situated themselves between the two extremes.[9] Hostile positions toward the government were tied inversely to wealth: the lower the social level, the greater the negative opinion of the government. Therefore, the report of the Centro de Investigaciones Motivacionales y Sociales (CIMS; Center of Motivational and Social Research), which carried out the study, indicated that "support for the revolution depended on social class."[10] In terms of age, endorsement of the Argentine Revolution was more common among older respondents. Among people over fifty-one years old, 52.3 percent supported President Onganía. In contrast, only 40.6 percent of youth (eighteen to thirty years old) expressed favorable opinions of Onganía. In terms of the country's regions, in November 1967 Onganía garnered greatest support in Capital Federal (48.8 percent) and the least in Córdoba (37.5 percent).[11] What this report makes clear is that, from the beginning, the Argentine Revolution enjoyed greater support among the upper and middle classes than among the working class, and greater support from adults than from youth.

The next year (1968), another consulting firm, Analistas de Empresas y Consultores de Dirección (A&C; Business Analysts and Management Consultants), conducted a survey for *Primera Plana* magazine. The percentages of support had decreased. However, one conclusion remained intact: "the survey once again demonstrated that opinions were fundamentally influenced by the real position occupied in the social hierarchy."[12] The discontent was much greater in the lower class than in the upper, and once again the middle classes were situated between the two. Despite the initial support that the revolutionary government obtained from labor union leaders, the lower class, as CIMS informed President Onganía, "did not give [him] their trust." However, a large part of the middle class had indeed given the government theirs. In conclusion, the dissatisfaction with his government that would be made evident by the social uprisings of 1969 only reflected disappointment in the middle class (and the statistically irrelevant upper class).

This disenchantment, however, had very little to do with an ideological shift. The nonactivist middle classes in the first half of the 1970s were not radically different from what they had been earlier or from what they would be in the immediate future. There is no doubt that they changed their sympathies toward some political actors (such as Onganía, for example), but these changes were less related to ideological transformations than to the judgment that they made about the capacity of those actors to modernize the country. By 1969, a large section of the middle classes had already withdrawn the expectations they had for the government at the beginning of the Argentine Revolution. This did not, however, make them allies of the militant workers' movement or the radicalized student sectors, which would shortly thereafter struggle for a socialist revolution.

Various authors have emphasized that, from the 1960s on, Argentine society, and especially its middle classes, underwent a process of "shifting to the left" and/or "Peronization." However, both the surveys available from the period and the analysis of the electoral results run counter to this vision.[13] In the first several months of 1973, a few days before the elections, CIMS conducted surveys that showed that left-wing groups represented small minority sectors that were unrepresentative of the urban bourgeoisie.[14]

The generational question is key to understanding this period, given that 45 percent of the population in 1970 was over thirty years old (and 35 percent was under eighteen years old).[15] A great part of middle-class youth political activity had the university as its epicenter, and only a minority of youth had access to this institution. Considering the university-age population (eighteen to twenty-five years old), in 1970 only 8.22 percent of these youth had attended or were attending a university or other institution of higher education.[16] The sympathy for the Left that was detected by CIMS declined notably as the age of the population increased. Only 5 percent of those who were forty-seven years old or older sympathized with it, while the level of sympathy reached 13 percent among those under twenty-six. The enthusiasm for left-wing currents, far from being a majority phenomenon, was concentrated in a rather specific strip of the population: youth of the "upper-middle class" and the "upper class," the two sectors who proportionally had the greatest access to the universities. However, even in these two segments these sympathies represented a minority. The electoral results of March 11, 1973, confirmed that the openly leftist options—I will soon consider the Peronist vote—did not enjoy great support.[17]

CIMS's surveys also proved that Peronism maintained an extremely high level of support (60 percent) in the working class and in the "popular sectors" (categorized as "lower class") and that the sympathy for Peronism reduced significantly as one rose in socioeconomic class. Perón's movement, after eighteen years of proscription—and having created during the failed Argentine Revolution a situation whose resolution rested on the figure of Perón, at least for much of the press—did not manage to convert the sympathy that it had traditionally awoken among the middle classes into a majority sentiment. The political sympathies of the middle classes were largely oriented toward the Radical Civic Union (UCA) or other non-Peronist currents of the center or center-right.

The radicalized youth were without a doubt quite numerous in 1973, and this was clear in the multitude of people that marched to Ezeiza to welcome

Perón on June 20, which included Peronists of a variety of social extractions, ideological tendencies, and age groups, but with a strong youth presence. On this occasion, the Peronist youth demonstrated not only their numbers but also their high capacity for mobilization. However, as an analyst wrote that year, the Peronist youth may be "more visible than the non-Peronist youth"; this "does not indicate, however, that there are really more of them."[18] This affirmation was also valid for radicalized middle-class youth in general, regardless of their closeness to Peronism: the radicalized youth were more visible, but not more numerous than the nonradicalized youth, or those that did not mobilize. Indeed, university youth were a social minority. In the mid-1970s, the total of the students of the Universidad de Buenos Aires represented 1 percent of the country's population, and that of all the national universities reached only 2 percent.[19] These facts help us to measure the weight that the middle-class activist youth had. The political importance that they acquired in the early 1970s has tended to overshadow how relatively little significance they had in the demographic and electoral structure of the population.

By 1973, Peronism had become a signifier for a plethora of political and social meanings. In the March elections, its electoral formula (Cámpora–Solano Lima) attracted almost half of the votes.[20] All types of voters, although not in equal proportions, cast their ballot for this formula, moved by different and even antagonistic political aspirations. The 49.56 percent that the Justicialist Liberation Front [Frente Justicialista de Liberación, FREJULI] obtained (a heterogeneous front formed by Peronism and minority parties of the center and center-right: the Popular Conservative [Conservador Popular] party; the Integration and Development Movement [Movimiento de Integración y Desarrollo]; the Popular Christian Party [Partido Popular Cristiano]; and some provincial parties) was fed by votes that came from different extractions.[21] Their electoral weight was also, in part, a manifestation that reflected more a disgust with the military government among a part of the citizenry than ideological conviction, something that *La Opinión*, two days after the elections, commented on and exaggerated, affirming that "the vote was against the Argentine Revolution."[22] The temporary rise of sectors of the Peronist left to positions of power in Cámpora's government has led some analysts to conclude that the electorate sympathized with left-wing positions. Nevertheless, the influx of leftists reflected alliances and agreements within the Peronist movement more than an expression of the will of the electorate.[23]

Four indicators support the assertion that the Peronist left's influence on the reasons that motivated people to vote for FREJULI was significant only within the realm of the Peronized youth activists. First, the electoral platform of the front did not differ ideologically from the traditional Peronist programs of the past.[24] Cámpora's running mate recognized that "an important part" of its voters "did not vote for the FREJULI candidates," but rather "voted for the FREJULI program, voted for its programmatic proposals."[25] Second, the FREJULI electoral formula was associated with Perón's plans, which guaranteed it the support of traditional working-class and lower-class Peronist voters. For the great majority of the working class, what was important was the return of their leader to power (and all that the workers associated with him) and not conjectures about his conversion to a Left that, in a not-so-distant past, Perón viewed as foreign if not hostile.[26] In regard to this, it is revealing that the most effective indicator to predict the results of the 1973 elections was voters' evaluation of the first Peronist government (1946–1955).[27] Third, the society had an inclination toward the less rebellious positions among the internal currents of the movement led by Perón, even considering only Peronist sympathizers.[28] Finally, the even more overwhelming Peronist victory in the September 1973 elections retrospectively cleared up questions about the place that the Left played for Perón in his movement. If the Peronist electoral base had been mainly mobilized by left-wing aspirations in March 1973, it is difficult to explain that only six months later, an even larger number of voters would have voted for the Perón-Perón formula, which, after the Ezeiza massacre and the strengthening of López Rega's influence in the government, could only be voted for from the Left by denying reality. It is true that many young middle-class Peronist activists offered the Perón-Perón ticket a tactical support, working to achieve an overwhelming victory to later pressure the leader from within. However, the quantitative weight of these groups was relatively small in the composition of the Peronist vote.

Thus, the middle classes did not Peronize in the 1970s. In 1973, the Peronist movement continued to be, as it was in 1946 and to a greater degree than in 1955, a force that was primarily supported by working- and lower-class sectors. What did change was the electoral composition of the opposition. A comparison of the Peronist and non-Peronist votes in 1946 and 1973 showed not only that Peronism had maintained the same proportion of working-class support, but also that, had the relationship between the working-class and non-working-class population remained unchanged, Perón's electoral force would have become even more homogeneously proletarian. If this did not occur, this was because in 1973 the working class was proportionally smaller than it was in 1946 (a fact that is compatible with the growth of the middle classes that the 1970 census established). Furthermore, the comparison showed that the non-Peronist vote had become much more homogeneously non-working-class than it was in 1946.[29] An analysis of the Radical vote in Capital Federal, for example, revealed that in 1973, this portion of the electorate presented "marked levels of association with the middle sectors," coming primarily from professional, technical, white-collar, self-employed, and highly educated people.[30] In summary, in 1973 the non-Peronist parties were mainly (and in some cases, exclusively) composed of the middle classes and statistically irrelevant upper class, and Peronism, a multiclass movement from its origin, enjoyed support from all social sectors but primarily from the popular sectors, both working class and non-working class—in a proportion that practically did not vary in thirty years.[31]

Studies of the Peronist vote in March 1973 demonstrate that the electoral support of the middle classes for Peronism did not increase with respect to the 1940s and 1950s. On the contrary, these sectors continued to be rather elusive for Peronism, in more and less developed provinces alike.[32] Indeed, when one takes into account that more than half of the electorate did not vote for Peronism in a context in which 54 percent of the country was composed of popular sectors and the working class, both overwhelming inclined toward this party, one can conclude that on March 11 the middle classes mostly chose non-Peronist options.[33] CIMS estimated that 90 percent of "popular" and working-class sectors (which he calls the lower class) supported Peronism in the March 1973 elections, composing at least 72 percent of the Peronist vote.[34] In 1975, when analyzing Peronism's social composition, the historian Félix Luna underlined that, even taking into account its incorporation of youth sectors of the middle class between 1966 and 1973, "Peronism is basically proletarian and its force is rooted in this sector."[35]

Thus, in the electoral innovation of 1973 was the defeated party's recognition of the legitimacy of the elected Peronist government, not the creation (or the expansion) of a middle-class Peronist vote.[36] Perón himself affirmed a year later that his willingness to respect minorities created the conditions for minorities to respect the majority.[37] Thus, Perón renounced authoritarianism; and the main opposition party, whose votes came primarily from the middle classes, renounced conspiracy.[38] The triumph of Peronism in 1973, then, included two novelties: first, that those who did not sympathize with Perón were convinced that without him there could be no solution to the political situation. Second, and as a condition of the first, that a part of the traditionally non-Peronist society believed Perón was not the same as he was in the 1950s.

In this sense, Cámpora's electoral campaign was quite paradoxical.[39] On the one hand, it depended on the activism of the youth sectors of the movement, who were in their majority middle-class—the slogan that dominated the campaign, "Put Cámpora in office, put Perón in power," was a creation of the Peronist youth. But on the other hand, it did not succeed in converting the large nonactivist middle class who viewed this youth approach toward Peronism with a mixture of fear and cynicism. The militant tinge that the youth gave to the campaign also played a role in the rejection of the Peronist formula by the nonactivist middle-class sectors—the slogans of the youth during campaign events, which ranged from "Cámpora for president, freedom for the combatants" to "We have a general, who is a marvel, he fights against capital, and supports the armed struggle," were hardly attractive for nonactivists.[40]

Cámpora's election campaign closed a generational circle in the political history of the middle classes. This circle had been opened in the 1950s and 1960s when part of the middle classes, teaching their children their anti-Peronist views, ended up pushing many of them into Peronism's ranks. In 1973, in contrast, it was the youth who provoked effects that were counterproductive to their designs, as their support for Perón did not manage to alter their parents' non-Peronist convictions.

It is significant that, in September 1973, one month before once again assuming the presidency, Perón reminded the young leaders of the armed organizations that Peronism arose from working-class youth, not from that of the middle class. "You should not forget, my boys," Perón told the leaders of the Montoneros and the Revolutionary Armed Forces (FAR; Fuerzas Amadas Revolucionarias), "the youth made October 17th [1945] but it was the trade union youth. The other youth was against us. They went out every day to throw stones at us in the Labor and Welfare Department; I took a stone here and it was from the middle-class and university youth, who were not with us from the beginning. The trade union youth, however, they were with us, they organized and they were the ones that made October 17th."[41] The majority of the parents of the Peronist activists of the 1970s belonged to this "middle-class and university youth," which was not with Peronism from the beginning.

By 1973, things had changed. University students, the children of anti-Peronists, had joined the working-class children of Peronists. But both youth were not the same. The working-class youth voted for Peronism because they understood that it was the political force that best represented their interests as workers. For their part, the middle-class youth were more worried whether or not they were being interpreted as youth.[42] In other words, the working-class youth defined itself as working-class first and youth second. The university youth that embraced Peronism, in contrast, did so as a means to challenge an entire (academic, police, political, family) order that they felt limited them primarily as youth.

Since his fall in 1955, Perón had turned into "the great elector," ordering his followers to cast blank votes in 1957 and to vote for Frondizi in 1958, from a semiclandestine position that did not diminish the effectiveness of his orders. Wherever his finger fell, the votes followed, and if this was possible in the worst years, it was even more feasible in 1973, in the context of the political opening launched by General Alejandro Lanusse. Cámpora received most of his votes from those who saw him as Perón's delegate, a condition that, together with his unconditional loyalty to the general,[43] he never missed an opportunity to emphasize. Both Cámpora and his running mate, the popular-conservative Solano Lima, tended to warn that their main challenge rested in successfully attracting the vote of the middle classes. Indeed, few people warned more than they did that the orators at their rallies, frequently organized by the Peronist youth, spoke to reaffirm the faithful instead of to attract traditionally apathetic sectors. "There is a significant sector of the middle class," Solano Lima commented to La Opinión, forty days before the March elections, "that is still undecided. We should win them over instead of scaring them away," he declared, opposing the militant slogans of the youth wing.[44] In this sense, the FREJULI vice-presidential candidate agreed with his adversaries in the military government, who months before the elections assessed that "Cámpora scares away the votes of the independent middle class."[45]

Once he was elected president and having seen his low support among the middle classes, Cámpora redoubled his efforts to send a reassuring message to the non-Peronists who increasingly disliked the upsurge in guerrilla activity and viewed his future government with lower expectations.[46] Upon beginning his second campaign in the provinces in which new elections would elect governors in the runoff, this moderation was reflected in two ways.[47] First, there was the conciliatory orientation of Cámpora's messages.[48] Second, the union leadership headed by José Ignacio Rucci and the leaders of the 62 Organizations—emblematic symbols of orthodox anti-Marxist Peronism—was included for the first time on his tours.[49] In this way, Cámpora attempted to counteract the impression that his government would be taken over by the radicalized youth sectors.

In sum, the enthusiasm that Cámpora awoke in the middle classes should not be exaggerated, as, despite his efforts, it did not transcend the boisterous but minority sphere of the activists and some (quantitatively irrelevant) intellectual circles.[50] The access to power that these groups enjoyed was partial and brief. "Their fifteen minutes of fame ended with the fall of Héctor Cámpora," wrote the journalist Heriberto Kahn in 1974, "or perhaps more precisely with Juan D. Perón's return to the country on June 20, 1973."[51]

Perón: Seducing the Middle Classes

The excessive emphasis that is sometimes given to the "Peronization of the middle classes," which, in fact, was a process limited to youth sectors, often ends up underestimating Perón's unprecedented (and inverse) move of trying to approach positions and discourses typical of the middle class. By demonstrating understanding and dialogue with the political forces that had historically represented the middle classes (especially his rapprochement with the leader of the Radical Civic Union, Ricardo Balbín, who almost joined an electoral ticket with him,[52] and his alliance with centrist political groups, such as Arturo Frondizi's Integration and Development Movement [Movimiento de Integración y Desarrollo, MID]),[53] Perón sought to become closer to the middle classes, even and perhaps especially those who had never voted for him. Julián Licastro, a young army lieutenant who was so loyal to Perón that the press called him "Perón's lieutenant,"[54] asserted that in 1973, the objective of the Justicialist leader consisted in "incorporating the non-Peronist middle class in his national, popular, anti-imperialist, and revolutionary front, because beyond superstructural political alliances, this class constitutes the objectively necessary social component for the consolidation of the process of reconstruction obtained and led by the Peronist working class."[55] The blurring of the Peronism/anti-Peronism division as the essential contradiction in Argentina indubitably contributed to Perón's objective. Toward the beginning of the 1970s, many political, union, military, and religious leaders emphasized the opposition between nationalist and liberal currents, or, to a lesser extent, between revolutionary and counterrevolutionary currents, at the expense of the traditional opposition between Peronists and anti-Peronists.[56] In parallel, the generational renovation contributed to a decrease in the intensity of the anti-Peronism of the 1950s. Until Perón's death, the Peronism/anti-Peronism antinomy played a minor role in both political rhetoric and public opinion.

Much of the society saw the fact that there was a sector within Justicialism that proposed alliances with other parties positively. Indeed, in 1972, a survey showed that a considerable percentage of the population predicted that Peronism would come to power not only allied with other parties, but even with a candidate from outside the party.[57] The following year, when it was already known that Cámpora was the Peronist candidate and his victory was taken for granted, another poll directed toward discovering the opinion of the "broad middle class" confirmed that 55 percent of respondents considered an eventual programmatic compromise between Peronism and Radicalism to be positive (only 26 percent opposed it).[58] Even in the hours that followed the March elections, the idea of shared government between a victorious Peronism and the largest minority party had not been dismissed in Radical circles.[59]

Days before the presidential elections in September, a television program on Channel 13, *Dialogue with Perón*, obtained both extremely high ratings among the middle class, and the unanimous judgment among commentators that Perón was speaking directly to this sector.[60] This new Perón, who was conciliatory and friendly with the opposition, managed to get part of the middle classes to come closer than they had in all their history to entertaining the same vision of him that he had already for some time had of himself: that of an "eternal father" capable of embracing all of his children, regardless of the sympathy they had for him.[61] Perón himself mentioned this communion of friends and adversaries when, shortly before his death, he spoke to the population on the state channel. There, he remembered not only the massive support of those who elected him but also "the indulgence of those that did not do so but later showed great understanding and a sense of responsibility."[62] That same day, he reaffirmed his centrist program from the balcony of the Casa Rosada. "We know our goals perfectly well and we will march directly toward them," Perón asserted in what would be his last speech, "without being influenced by either those who pull us from the right, nor those who pull us from the left."[63]

Days before Perón was elected with an overwhelming majority, Félix Luna—perhaps the most influential historian for the less-politicized middle classes—wrote that the Justicialist leader would now enjoy not only "this amount of infinite faith from his own people" but also a new element, independent of the voting: "the sectors that are not Peronist will also support him as long as the government progresses toward the goals set by that nonpartisan statement [referring to *La Hora del Pueblo*]."[64] If in the years of Peronism's rise he was an "impossible candidate" for the middle classes and later "the tyrant" in office, Luna wrote that this third Perón appeared to be someone capable of saving the nation from "unnecessary messes and costly headlong rushes," opposing his calls for restraint to "the urgency of his youth vanguards."[65]

Perón himself promoted this moderate image, eliminating the traditional association between the "people" and the collective of "workers" in his discourse—typical of Peronist rhetoric until 1955.[66] It was not coincidental that in one of his addresses to the General Conferation of Labour (CGT), less than a month after taking charge of the presidency, Perón remembered Napoleon, who after the French Revolution found himself "like the 'ham in the sandwich,' between two forces that were watching him and could depose him at any time." [67] In that context Napoleon, Perón said, "an extraordinary man in all aspects [. . .] called on the bourgeoisie [that] was on the fence looking at everyone from the outside." Napoleon was an allegory for Perón himself. He felt himself to be in this situation in the Argentina of 1973, and he attempted to make a call that, if *aggiornado* to the times and the national context, was fundamentally similar to that made by his admired French politician. [68]

This fact helps us to understand that his attack on the radicalized youth inside and outside his movement had its counterpart in his justification of and support for the essentially bourgeois and domesticating space of the family. In a time when the universities had become revolutionary cauldrons, Perón extolled the education of the home. "Between birth and six years of age," Perón said in 1973,

> children form their subconscience. This is the mother's task, and when I see a boy who is five or six years old go out on the street and make the V for Victory sign at me with his little hands, I think the following: "This is due to his mother's action." Because of this, I wanted to pay tribute to those mothers who have given their children sufficient guidance in their homes. We want nothing more than to raise good men, because we think that in order to give a man cultural weapons, the most important thing is for him to be good. God save us from a wicked man with great intellectual ability to harm his fellow men! This is the first political and social school that Argentines have; first, the household, and second, mothers. [69]

If Perón had encouraged the radicalized youth to secure his return to the country, he needed to discipline them to govern. It was now necessary to appeal to the spaces and sources typical to bourgeois security: he wanted homes instead of universities, he praised mothers instead of intellectuals, he needed "good" men, not revolutionaries. In his speech on May 1, 1974, confronting the Peronist left, he returned to the type of people that the "hour of the motherland" demanded. "We want a healthy people, a satisfied and healthy people, without hatreds, without useless, ineffective, and unimportant divisions," Perón declared as the radicalized youth of his movement finished filing out of the plaza. [70]

After the fall of Cámpora, the September 1973 elections were the occasion to test this widening, not of Peronism itself, but of the conviction that the political conjuncture, which in many aspects resembled a civil war inside this movement, [71] could only be defused if the "father" sat down at the head of the table once again and his words once again had the force of law, especially for his most rebellious children. The 12 percent more that the Perón-Perón ticket received in the September 1973 elections compared to Cámpora–Solano Lima in the March elections,[72] left no doubts about the deep (or perhaps better said, the last) hope that a portion of the traditionally anti-Peronist middle class placed in the leader's bargaining power.[73] Many voters believed that the General himself had promoted this very war only a short while before, and now they judged that he was the only one that could bring the conflict to an end.[74]

The so-called special formations and the youth activist sectors that saw them as their vanguard were perhaps the only ones who, in this context, would have preferred the combative Perón of the 1950s, who would lead one part of the people to attack another part, this time without second thoughts.[75] Instead, Perón preferred the social pact between businessmen and workers and the opening of markets in capitalist Europe economically and "integrated democracy" and accords with the opposition politically;[76] in sum he strove "to go toward the center," as *La Opinión* affirmed days before the September elections,[77] a discouraging direction for the radicalized groups who could only interpret this course as a betrayal.[78]

For part of public opinion, it was not Perón who had betrayed the radicalized youth, but rather youth who had constructed a Perón that had never existed. In the winter of 1974, distinguishing between the different loyalties that the Justicialist leader had received in the elections, a political analyst wrote that "while the workers' support did not arise from illusions, the youth judged that Perón had returned because of and for them, defended by the weapons of their militias."[79] In this vision, the political problem was rooted in the fact that the youth realized too late that they, for some time now, had been working for a centrist leader, a man of order and a defender of the system. "They haven't, by chance, noticed," the analyst continued, "that the Justicialist caudillo returned protected by the armored cars of the army, and that a legion of practical men celebrated the Peronist restoration as the victory of order and good sense politics." In the same vein, Félix Luna laid blame on the youth, and not on Perón, for the misunderstanding between them. "The error was made by those who 'imagined' Perón," wrote Luna, and "created him from an image drawn from their desires."[80] In short, while the young activists, who mostly came from anti-Peronist families, began a class exodus in the late 1960s toward a leader who they dreamed of as being revolutionary and pro-working-class, Perón took the opposite route. Once back in the country, he created a rhetoric that emphasized the meanings associated with the middle classes who had always been hostile to him as he had never done before, seeing in the possibility of attracting them the attainment of a consensus unprecedented in Argentine history, which would relegate the radicalized sectors to the solitary confines of maladjustment and irrationality.[81] In part, Perón's exodus was demonstrated by the state's punishment of the disobedient children of the anti-Peronist middle classes. These youth, paradoxically, fleeing from a middle-class political and cultural sensibility, ended up submitting to the word of a "middle-classized" leader. History's irony: they moved toward Peronism in the very moment that Perón moved away from it, less Peronist than ever.[82]

This final hope that a portion of the middle classes placed in Perón's capacity to resolve the political situation, however, lasted only as long as he remained in the government. His death on June 1, 1974, closed a period that was as brief as it was unique: for the first time, the main opponents of Peronist legitimacy had not been the traditionally anti-Peronist middle classes or the parties that historically represented them but rather internal factions of Peronism itself. Both Perón and the different wings of Peronism had reached the conclusion that, politically, outside the movement there were allies and adversaries, but only inside were there real enemies.[83] As Oscar Landi has indicated in one of the first studies of Peronism in 1973, "the absence of a Justicialist Party and the different objectives—as factors of power—of much of the trade union leadership, the conflict with the radicalized youth, the guerrilla actions, and terrorism, sharply limited his [Perón's] own political options."[84] Paradoxically, then, the Perón who garnered the most citizen support was also the most fragile in terms of his intrinsic political possibilities.[85] When he managed to create a climate where his movement dominated the country, he suffered violent opposition from within.

After Perón's death, the relationship between the Peronist government and the middle classes only got worse. The obvious ineptitude of Isabel, her sinister minister López Rega, government corruption, the unexpected economic adjustment of 1975, and the political violence (which the Alianza Anticomunista Argentina, known as the Triple A, took to levels unseen until that time), created a general situation that reaffirmed the prejudices and revived the worst memories that the middle classes held of historic Peronism. If both prejudices and memories had been put aside in the September 1973 elections, at least for the sector of the middle classes that voted for Perón in hopes of national pacification, conditions then became propitious for their return. Only a year and a half after Perón's death, the Peronist leader of the National Senate, Ítalo Luder, declared that his party should "recover its image among the middle class, because it is there where Justicialism has been the object of challenges."[86] On the same occasion, he added that it was "necessary to recover the confidence of the middle class, which does not move because of economic interests but rather because of its faithfulness to norms of conduct, certain lifestyles, and political styles." One does not need to share this last judgment to accept that Luder was far from wrong when he perceived the middle classes' lack of trust in Peronism. The middle classes and Peronism once again reaffirmed themselves as being on opposite sides of the political debate.

The Other Face of Anti-Peronism

In March 1976, another coup d'état put an end to the government of Isabel Perón and initiated the so-called National Reorganization Process (el Proceso) (1976–1983), led by General Jorge Rafael Videla.[87] This new attempt to restructure society from above, while setting the political economy on a liberal instead of a developmentalist path, differed from previous military initiatives in the form and the scope that its repressive actions took. Later on, there will be an opportunity to analyze how the middle classes lived through this period, which crowned the most violent decade in Argentina's twentieth-century history. Now I will focus on the attitudes that they assumed toward the second Peronist experience in power and the military declaration that brought it to a close.

The massive celebration of the middle classes after Perón was overthrown in 1955 was an evident symptom that the anti-Peronists had not resigned themselves to living in a Peronist country. The initial euphoria that followed its collapse showed to what degree the military victory was also theirs.[88] Nothing of the sort occurred on March 24, 1976; there were no celebrations, rallies, or overflowing plazas. How can this fact be explained, if the military revolution of 1976 also did away with a Peronist government, one that was without a doubt more chaotic than that of 1955?

Two consecutive attitudes seem to be fundamental in understanding the behavior of the anti-Peronist middle classes during the period that stretches from the return of Peronism to power in 1973 up to its decline and fall three years later. In first place is an attitude of resignation, followed by that of desertion. Resigned to the irrefutable fact of a Peronist country, the non-Peronist middle classes deserted: they abandoned the hope of a country that was governed and governable by a force without a Peronist majority. That resignation was a very different attitude from the behavior of the old anti-

Peronism, which had been characterized by a clandestine resistance to the Peronist government (1946–1955). Whereas in 1955, after the regime had fallen, such an attitude had expressed itself in celebration, with masses in the streets commemorating the "hour of freedom," in 1976, after Isabel's government was overthrown, this resignation of the middle classes ended up offering a deserted landscape.[89]

By 1973, the passing of time, the proscription of Peronism, the failure of the Argentine Revolution, and a moderate Perón open to dialogue helped to attenuate what I have called the anti-Peronist sensibility. Although Peronism continued to symbolize in large part much of what these middle sectors opposed, in this new historical juncture the immense majority of the society accepted the return to a full constitutional order willingly, without proscriptions. But this acceptance was accompanied, at least in a part of the non-Peronist middle classes, by the attitudes of resignation and desertion to which I previously referred. In 1973, the Peronists were the majority and could win almost any election comfortably, both at the national level and at the provincial and local levels. Beyond voting and losing, the anti-Peronist middle classes could do nothing. I will now analyze some of the different ways that both attitudes were reflected in daily life. I focus primarily on three: self-absorption, cynicism or irony, and pride in being a minority.

Seeing the images of the battle that occurred between different Peronist factions awaiting Perón's landing in Ezeiza in the documentary, and hearing the speech delivered by the returned leader that night, Jorge Van der Weyden said "I owe Perón a piece of furniture." I interrupted the screening, and we had the following dialogue:

SC: What do you mean, you owe him a piece of furniture?

JORGE: Well, there were so many days off that I made a sofa at home, I had time . . . That was a national shame, one of many . . .

SC: You didn't see any kind of hope in Perón's arrival, any kind of . . .

J: Well, eh . . . I don't know. I try to be impartial, but I realize that I'm very anti-Peronist [laughs]. No, it's true. It might be because I lived in that moment, from the very beginning. [. . .] I was in my house making myself a piece of furniture thanks to Perón.

SC: Because they had given you a day off . . .

J: Three or four days . . . Whether or not the plane lands . . . and so on. I thank him for that.

One of the things that caught my attention in this anecdote was that, several months earlier, Linda Tognetti gave a testimony in Correa that was easy to associate with Jorge's. The dialogue with Linda occurred as follows:

SC: And here in the town, did anything happen when Perón died?

LINDA: They must have held some ceremony, but I didn't participate in any. I painted a sewing machine. I took advantage of those days, I didn't know what to do. There was sacred music on the radio, and on the television was Perón's entire wake. Well, watching it now [referring to what we had just seen in the documentary], like seeing Evita's wake and all of that, is all right, but you see it like a movie. But when you turn on the television and see it, like you are watching soccer for twenty-four hours straight, it kills you. So I sanded and varnished my mother's sewing machine. And I had never varnished before!

Both Perón's return and death were massive, multitudinous events. In these mobilizations, it became evident that Peronism was an irrefutable, majority-supported, and, in a certain sense, omnipresent social fact. These events paralyzed the country. It was practically impossible to keep oneself separate from them if one had any contact with the world, if one turned on the radio or the television or went out on the street. Jorge and Linda closed the blinds on their respective worlds, they became absorbed in themselves. They did not want to hear more about something that was as undeniable as it was unbearable for them. They devoted themselves to work around the house, in an attitude typical of a servile conscience in the Hegelian dialectic: prevented from enjoying the world, they resign themselves to working, as if they were seeking to transfer all their negativity to the sofa in Jorge's case and the sewing machine in Linda's; as if through the work they were trying to free their conscience from the constraints imposed by material reality. It is easy to imagine this attitude multiplied in many other ways. Flavia Amoroso, for example, who was a thirteen-year-old adolescent in 1974, remembers that when Perón died, her father told her: "Get ready, we're going to the country." Flavia remembered she responded to her father, "But how? If today is Monday! [. . .] and school?" Her father answered her, "No, if Perón died there will be four or five days off, I'm sure." Imitating her father's voice, Flavia concluded the anecdote by saying: "He said 'I'm sure there won't be class,' rather disparagingly."

The events that provoked these attitudes were the concrete manifestations that the country was Peronist; in the face of this evidence, the reaction was of withdrawal. Jorge and Linda retreated to doing domestic work, behind closed doors, seeking to at the very least make use of a time that they judged to be lost if they went out in the world. Self-absorbed, they sought to deny the irrefutable fact of a Peronist country in their domestic space. Flavia's family exiled themselves to the country, far from any possibility of receiving or seeing news. All three fled from a reality that they considered to be both intolerable and unchangeable.

A second mode was irony or cynicism. The interviewees remembered a wide repertoire of jokes in response to my questions about how they perceived, in those years, events such as Cámpora's victory, the Ezeiza massacre, or Perón's death. For example, during the 1973 elections in Tucumán, a story circulated about the last Peronist governor of the province (1952–1955), Luis Cruz. "He was a brute, a brute, the biggest brute I've ever seen in my life," María Emilia Palermo remembered, prefacing the joke, and continued: "What was his name? Well . . . his last name is Cruz, I don't remember his first name. He was a Peronist, a railroad worker. What did they say about him, the joke? There was a very nice story: he was in the station, because in those times people traveled by train, and his daughter was already more educated, studying foreign languages, and she tells him: 'Au revoir, au revoir, Papa' [and the governor responds]: 'No, my daughter, I won't steal anything else' [a play on words between 'revoir' and 'robar,' which in Spanish means to steal]." The story that María Emilia remembers condenses the previously mentioned elements: Peronism was uncultured, immoral, and corrupt. In the joke, the Peronist ex-governor not only appears incapable of understanding his daughter's greeting in French, but also confesses, without any prompting, that he had been corrupt.

Even more symptomatic than the jokes through which the anti-Peronist middle classes processed the irrefutable events of their time was their cynical attitude. I analyze only one example of this attitude, although the series of events related to Peronism in 1973 provoked reflections of this type in various interviews.[90] Seeing the scenes of Perón's death in the documentary, Carlos Etcheverría remembered:

> That was a show. We had a lot of fun. A friend called me — in those days, I shared a room with him and he was the secretary of the Radical Party senator León — and so he calls me and tells me: "At two-thirty they will announce Perón's death" [. . .]. Something like that. Because he had already died, but they were going to announce that he had died — they were almost certainly teaching Isabel the lines, to make her repeat them, because she was who announced it on the national station. And well, naturally, of course, I went out to buy things, as it was a habit that

every time we heard a march on the radio, everyone went out to buy pasta, rice, and all these things, because you feared that there wouldn't be anything for three or four days—that was a habit, a custom, in other words: there's a revolution, we're off to buy pasta; that's the funny part. And what the hell were we going to do? I left the bank, I was in my apartment here in Buenos Aires, and I met up with him [the secretary of the Radical senator] and some other friends, who weren't Peronists, of course. "And what should we do?" "Let's drive around with the car!" "But the roads are all blocked!" And then, he [the senator's secretary] says: "Hey, I'll put on the license plate of the Senate and let's go." He put on the Senate plate in the car's windshield, and we went and the people were there, although it was raining, making a line around 9 de Julio Avenue and Corrientes, and we were coming up Corrientes in the car. And [the Peronists who were directing traffic] told us: "Let the comrades of the Senate pass!" They were Peronists, dressed up. Do you know how I distinguish Peronists from Radicals? Because [Peronists] come all dressed up with their little formal ties. In other words, the others are more normal. Not these guys, who are really stuffy. They were Peronists. It was a logic. Don't forget that we had a senator, I think it was in '73, in Santa Fe, who didn't know how to read or write.

Perón's death generated an interminable procession of people waiting to bid him farewell that lasted for days. Carlos and his friends lived this as if it were a spectacle. As Carlos declares, they did not go there driven by compassion or curiosity. "It was a show, we had a lot of fun," he started saying. He later remembered Isabel's ineptitude, the habit of going out to buy supplies before any "revolution," the funny episode where the Peronists directing traffic confused them for "comrades," and finally the "stuffiness" of the Peronist employees of the Senate—a trait that denoted their lack of culture. The scene of a group of young anti-Peronists going around streets crowded with Peronists, however, has a meaning that goes beyond the supposed entertainment. The attitude of Carlos and his friends in the face of Perón's death, much like the jokes that were told about the uncultured governor of Tucumán in 1973 (and various others about Cámpora, Isabel, and other Peronists) were at the same time ways of sublimating a reality that they did not like much and in response to which they could do little more than take refuge in irony or cynicism.

A third mode of displaying these attitudes of resignation and desertion is seen in the satisfaction that many seem to experience in presenting themselves as a social minority condemned to losing elections. The bedrock of this thinking is to be found in the pride of the cultured person, of one who believes that they have on their side the privilege of reason even though (indeed, perhaps precisely because) they are not in a majority. The first two dialogues took place in Tucumán, the first of which I held with Ricardo Montecarlo and the second with Dora Giroux, both born in the 1940s.

SC: In this period, in 1973, did you already know Alfonsín well?

RICARDO: Balbín was the leader in the 1970s. He [Alfonsín] was like on a second tier until he won out. What happens is, there was an electoral moment [1983], when the possibility of beating Peronism at some point in life was crucial. Because I was losing, losing, losing, my entire life. I always voted for the loser. To win once, one even feels . . . a personal satisfaction . . . But well, [Alfonsín] made huge mistakes in the economic part, huge mistakes.

DORA: For me, the great return to democracy occurred with Alfonsín, in '83, which was [like saying]: "finally." And with Perón, it was lighter, with Cámpora it was lighter [referring to the sensation of having returned to democracy]. I don't know why exactly. I don't know if it was known that Perón was going to win, but I didn't agree with that very much, I didn't agree that we should elect Cámpora so that he has Perón come back.

SC: You didn't vote for Cámpora?

D: No, no! I didn't vote for Cámpora, I didn't vote for Perón, thank God. I would cut off my hand first. I didn't vote for Menem [Peronist president 1989–1995 and 1995–1999] or any of them. I tell you, I've never voted for any of those that were in the government, never.

In both accounts, the interviews emphasize that they form part of a minority that is generally destined to lose, as neither was willing to vote for a Peronist candidate. Ricardo justified his vote for Raúl Alfonsín negatively: he did not vote in 1983 for Alfonsín himself or because he felt that he was a Radical—at least that is not what he mentions when he justifies his choice. He voted for him "for the possibility of beating Peronism at some point in life." What is most interesting is that Ricardo presents himself as someone who, until the rise of Alfonsín, had been losing systematically during his entire electoral life. The same thing occurs in Dora's testimony: she did not vote for Cámpora, Perón, or Menem, which is to say, she always voted for candidates that lost their elections ("I didn't vote for any of those that were in the government.") Dora omits remembering that she actually did support someone who won at some point: in 1983, she voted for Alfonsín. Indeed, according to her own account, this was her "great return to democracy." But in the account that she makes of herself, spontaneously, the memory of her vote for the victorious Radicals in 1983 cedes to her impulse to present herself as someone who never voted for a government that had been elected.

I now cite the third excerpt, this time from Linda Tognetti, of Correa, in which this discourse is even more intense:

SC: Do you remember who you voted for in '73?

LINDA: Not for Cámpora.

SC: The Radical ticket was led by Balbín.

L: I must have voted for Balbín.

SC: He passed through Correa in that period, right?

L: I don't remember. I know that Sylvestre Begnis [a developmentalist who was twice governor of the province of Santa Fe, in 1958–1962 and 1973–1976] was here. But I never went; it would have been strange if I would have gone [to the city hall to see Balbín]. I didn't go when Sylvestre [Begnis] was here, nor when Reutemann was here [the Justicialist governor of the province in 1995–1999 and 1999–2003]. Who did I vote for? I voted for Frondizi, I think, I voted for Illia, who continues to be the democrat for me, I voted for Alfonsín. Of those that won, I only [voted] for Alfonsín, don't worry . . .

This dialogue clearly illustrates the "proud minority" attitude of the anti-Peronist and non-Peronist middle class, an attitude that was absent in the times of the first Peronist government and took form only around 1973. Linda remembers, for sure, having not voted for Cámpora. She did not vote for Perón either—something that, beyond being obvious, she says explicitly in another portion of the interview. She remembers having voted for Frondizi, Illia, and Alfonsín but asserts that "of those that won, I only [voted] for Alfonsín." This phrase represents a flagrant contradiction that Linda doesn't perceive. If she voted for Frondizi and Illia, as she says she did, it is not true that she won only with Alfonsín, since both Frondizi and Illia were elected and governed 1958–1962 and 1963–1966 respectively.[91] Why, after finishing her memories of the victorious candidates for whom she voted for, did she omit mentioning Frondizi and Illia? Why should I be concerned if her candidate had won more times, something implicit in her last clarifying imperative: "don't worry"? Why else if not because Linda believes that she was always part of a losing but fundamentally correct social minority?

These testimonies clearly show certain satisfaction in presenting themselves as a minority largely destined to lose. This pleasure, however, is not in the act of losing; indeed, all three had been part of electoral victories.[92] Their satisfaction seems to reside in the fact of knowing that they are part of a social minority that is right but does not have the votes to prove it, that knows but doesn't win, that votes but doesn't govern. Ultimately, the pleasure stems from presenting themselves as non-Peronists, as individuals that "would cut off their hand" before voting for a candidate from this party background.

Between 1973 and 1976, the non-Peronist middle classes adopted two attitudes, manifested themselves in different ways, such as self-absorption, irony, or cynicism, and the fact that these middle classes considered themselves to be an enlightened, but losing, minority. Both resignation and desertion represent the other face of anti-Peronism. This sentiment did not only have a ferocious, vengeful, conspiratorial side, determined to celebrate the fall of any Peronist government. In 1973 it showed another face, which was by no means favorable to Peronism, but was resigned to it. This middle class felt that it lost when Cámpora won but did not feel triumphant when Isabel fell. It abandoned the Argentine political scene by surrendering to the impassive and, by that point lost in a psychic desert, received the news of the 1976 coup with the indifference of the predestined.

Eva Perón or Anti-Peronism by Other Means

Up to this point, my analysis of the anti-Peronist sensibility has omitted references to certain positive aspects of the first Peronist governments (1945–1955) that these middle classes recognize today. While it was uncommon for anyone to find even some virtue in the experience that began with Cámpora and ended with Isabel, the first Peronism is recognized to have instituted social and labor legislation that benefited the workers, promoted a vision that the country should deepen its industrial development, and stimulated the growth of the internal market through the opening of new social sectors to consumption. Some interviewees also mentioned that Perón saved Argentina from communism, protected the workers through the massive unionization of workers, gave the right to vote to women, and, above all in Correa, transformed the land tenure system and created a statute of rights for rural laborers. These recognitions, however, are frequently accompanied by a "but": it is true that Perón put into place positive labor legislation, but these ideas had already been presented by the Socialist Party; it is true that he unionized the workers, but he did it in exchange for them paying homage to him; and so on.

However, Eva Perón, an essential component of Peronist ideology, is emphatically praised by many of my interviewees that came from a non-Peronist tradition. In this section, I argue that the posthumous discovery of Eva Perón by these social sectors is a way to reaffirm their anti-Peronist sensibility.

I will now briefly comment on two testimonies from interviews conducted in Tucumán in order to later concentrate on the case of Correa with greater detail, which is of particular interest. The first testimony belongs to Juana Alberdi, a woman who worked with literature and languages in Tucumán and was born in the 1940s. The second testimony comes from María Emilia Palermo, a nurse from Tucumán who was born in the 1930s. In neither of the two cases was the praise of Eva provoked by a question about her. With Juana, it arose while we were watching images of Isabel Perón in the documentary; with María Emilia, in response to a question about her memories of Perón's return in 1973.

After imitating her "hysterical voice" and stating that Isabel was "a puppet," Juana added:

> Look, of the women that have lived in our country, for me, the only one who is redeemable . . . —apart from the people that everyone knows, if you know your history, like [Juana] Azurduy [Latin American independence heroine]. [. . .] Well, of those that are well-known, the only one that deserves my respect is Eva Perón. First, because she was beautiful. Second, because she was intelligent, because she learned quickly, because in reality she was a remarkable learner, because she wore her clothes like they were meant to be worn. In other words, not like a puppet. Because she was passionate and because I believe that she took up her role as if it was a theater play, she took it up fully and had the decency to die when she was thirty-three years old, in her prime. She was a romantic character! She died in the prime of her passions, with that son of a bitch of a husband who would have done her in himself if she hadn't died. He was capable of killing that woman. Because he realized that that woman had something that he didn't have. [. . .] Because this woman believed. I don't know if she was right or wrong, but she was convinced of what she was doing.

Juana starts her praise of Eva by differentiating her from Isabel. But once she gets there, the emphasis on Eva's virtues begins to be contrasted with Perón's perversity. Unlike Isabel, Eva was pretty, intelligent ("she wasn't a puppet"), and quickly learned to leave behind the signs of her lack of culture ("she wore her clothes like they were meant to be worn.") She also had the virtue of dying young and full of passion. This exemplary, romantic character that Juana sees in Evita empowers the sinister character of Perón, "that son of a bitch of a husband who would have done her in himself if she hadn't died." Perón would have been capable of destroying his wife. Eva, instead, believed in what she was doing. In this game of opposing mirrors, everything that is added to one side is subtracted from the other, and the more romantic Eva's figure was, the more sinister Perón's became.

María Emilia recalled that Perón's return in 1973 had caused her "great annoyance" and, to explain where this attitude came from, clarified:

> I was a loyal follower of my father on this. My father had taught me that this word [Perón] could not be repeated in the house because it was a bad word, he taught me this from when I was young. The day that Eva Perón died, I committed a huge outrage . . . My dad had already died. And, on July 26, at 8:25 in the evening, Eva Perón dies. My mom was with the radio, in the kitchen, and I was doing my homework. I was sitting in the kitchen. My mom was a Peronist and she began to cry. And I said: "Oh, what luck!" — it came from inside of me. And I was a big girl, not a little kid. And she gave me a slap that almost threw me from my seat. I was fifteen years old. Dad died in December of '51 and Eva Perón in July of '52. Then I said: "Oh, what luck!" How could it have occurred to me to say "Oh, what luck!" about a person that just died?! But that was the happiness that people felt . . . poor thing . . . And afterward, with time, I said, "She was a poor woman used by her husband." They used the poor devil, with her cancer, and they took her out in the car, propping her up so that the people would see her.

As in other testimonies, the praise that María Emilia had for Evita came with time. When she was only fifteen years old, she celebrated Eva's death; her cry of joy was an impulse that "came out from within" her. She had inherited that sensibility from her father. The praise that María Emilia has for Eva takes the form of pity. Unlike in Juana's testimony, Eva appears as a "poor devil," a "poor thing." Nevertheless, as in Juana's testimony, this compassionate attitude toward Evita is once again used to condemn Perón ("She was a poor woman used by her husband").

The case of Correa is of particular interest. A town of its size allows us to better appreciate the impact the antinomy that opposed Peronists and anti-Peronists had on daily life, at least until the Liberating Revolution. Until the appearance of Peronism, Correa was a town with a strong Democratic-

Progressive party majority. From that point on, Justicialism won every election for which it fielded candidates until 2009. The vast majority of the middle classes, however, remained Democratic-Progressive or Radical, and from the late 1950s on also developmentalist, but in any case, anti-Peronist.[93]

The 1970s were politically quiet in Correa, but the 1940s and 1950s were not. The local Liberation Alliance (Alianza Libertadora), a group of between twenty and thirty people who "watched over" the interests of the Peronist regime, played an effective role in its task of persecuting the "*contreras*." Those interviewed mentioned everything from the jailing of anti-Peronists to commercial boycotts, as well as public ridicule and bullying against those who resisted the Peronist leaders. On the other side of the antinomy, an episode involving the figure of Eva Perón stood out.

In 1955, after the fall of the Peronist government, a caravan of autos left from a neighboring city near Correa on Route 9, the first of which pulled behind it a bust of Eva attached to its rear bumper by a chain. Upon arriving at Correa, the caravan entered the town and drove around the main plaza, passing by the municipal building, the church, and the social club. Every once in a while, it stopped so that the people could approach it. Even today, Correa residents say that they remember details of this event: people applauding the passage of the caravan from the sidewalks of their homes, the almost unrecognizable bust of Eva (the town was unpaved in 1955), the honking of car horns, the shouts, the noise of the children. No other political event from the town's past was remembered by all of those interviewed. The bust finally ended up in the stream of neighboring Cañada de Gómez. I knew this because Silvia Lagomarconi, the leader of one of the town's *unidades básicas* (Peronist party locals) told me that she went to save it. Amanda Gómez, who was in charge of the other *unidad básica* in Correa, could not accompany Silvia. As she tells it today, the town's police told her that she should "split" the same day that Perón fell. Amanda went into exile for over a year in the countryside, living in the houses of Peronists in rural areas, after digging a hole in the floor of her house and hiding all that she had in her unidad básica. The only thing she took with her was her gun.

This story allows us to perceive both the virulence that the opposition between Peronists and anti-Peronists had in a small town like Correa and the emblematic character of the figure of Eva Perón. Even three years after her death, Eva was the symbol that best condensed the Peronist regime, both for those who supported and those who opposed it. More than half a century after the anti-Peronist middle classes of Correa applauded the passage of that caravan, Eva Perón is praised. The following two passages that I transcribe belong to Correa residents Ema Mateo and Claudio Mastrángelo. Once again, in both cases the praise for Eva Perón did not originate in a conversation about Eva. Ema was responding to a question about Perón's return, and Claudio to a question about what he was reading in the 1970s.

> EMA: Look, Perón came to get his revenge. That's why he put that woman [Isabel] in power. They say that it took them many days to convince him to put his wife [Isabel] in. He didn't want to do it. If he was someone like he should have been, he could never have put that woman in. If she was a useful idiot. If it were Eva, it would have been a different story, because Eva had more fighting spirit. Eva was the one that made Perón. Because, without being a Peronist, I recognize that during Perón's first government, there were many improvements, although we shouldn't be confused and think that they were Perón's ideas. It was a global evolution. [. . .] All of these things such as protecting minors from working, and so on, these were things that changed the face of the world. So, here, Perón did that too. That was good; not everything, but there was much good. [. . .] But in the second [term] Eva died. And Eva was a brake. And from then on, everything fell apart.

> CLAUDIO: I read everything that fell into my hands, but in that period Cortázar was very famous, and it was the snob who read Cortázar, who read Borges, who read *Las venas abiertas de América Latina, El varón domado* by Esther Vilar, *Un árbol lleno de manzanas*, who read *Los Burgueses* by Silvina Bullrich, those were the books of our epoch, we liked reading all the issues of *Sur* magazine a lot, we read Victoria Ocampo's *Sur* magazine a lot, she was ahead of her time, as she wanted to make a union between the Americas and Europe, eh? Just like Eva Perón was, ahead of her time. [. . .] I always say that 75 percent of Perón's government was Evita. It was 75 percent her. Because people saw her works and saw that they were being listened to and taken care of thanks to her, who at five in the morning was already in the Ministry of Labor helping people.

The two testimonies share one element in common. In both cases, the figure of Eva is valued in an inverse proportion to the disparagement of Perón; the game of opposing mirrors is repeated. For Ema, Eva was a battle-hardened woman (she "had more fighting spirit" than Isabel), Perón's *artífice* ("Eva was the one who made Perón."). Additionally, Eva was the "brake" that the regime had so that "everything didn't fall apart." In her story, Perón existed thanks to Eva's presence, and the regime fell apart because of her absence. Eva intensified the best and calmed the worst of Peronism. For Claudio, Eva explained three-fourths of the good that can be attributed to Perón's government. Claudio's response is noteworthy because the context into which the praise of Eva is inscribed had no relation to politics. The only link is that Eva was ahead of her times, like Victoria Ocampo (a woman of letters, culture, and money). Claudio can praise Eva as long as she is stripped of all political purpose.

A final story, also from Correa, synthesizes the way in which praise of Eva Perón reaffirms the anti-Peronist sensibility. This testimony belongs to Beatriz Garrido, to whom I will devote the second excursus. Like many others in the town, Beatriz maintains negative memories of the Peronist years. The majority of these memories refer to subjects already mentioned: lack of freedom, surveillance by the people of the Liberation Alliance (Alianza Libertadora), job discrimination against her Democratic-Progressive father, and so on. One of these subjects, however, stands out from the rest. In two of the three meetings that we held, Beatriz told me the same anecdote, without great variations. Provoked by my question about how the town had lived through the ten years of Peronism, she said about Eva Perón:

> Since I was very young, I [heard] my father telling me many things about where that woman came from. I love her, after reading about her life, I love her. I love her as a woman, I didn't love her before. You know, there was a man that would come to my house, and I would see him every time he came, and he came with a different appearance: with sideburns, with glasses, and so on. And I'm very curious, and well, one day, the man didn't come, and then he didn't come for one month, two months, three months. And I asked, "Papá, why didn't he come?" [What happened was that] this man worked in the variety show with Eva Duarte de Perón. Then he was able to escape, he had gone to Uruguay. He was able to come back after many years, but he was disguised, and afterward, he disappeared. We never found out what happened. He was persecuted by the government so that there wouldn't be any witnesses of her previous life. Logically, there was much killing.

The second time that she narrated this anecdote, several months after the interview cited above, while we were watching images of Cámpora during the electoral campaign in 1973, Beatriz said: "Perón killed . . . You know that Evita went from the lowest of the low of Buenos Aires, despite being a great woman, who always moved me, but all those that were from the can-can—because Evita worked in the nude—Perón killed everyone."

sc: He killed them?

beatriz: He killed everyone so that nobody leaked anything that they knew about her.

Eva Perón's origins have been studied by serious researchers.[94] The accusation that Perón had ordered the murder of those who could bear witness to Eva's past, however, has never even been suggested. The contrast between the two sentiments that Beatriz allows us to glimpse in her testimony—her love for Eva and her hatred for Perón—is interesting. Some anti-Peronists do not recognize Eva's virtues and maintain an entirely negative perspective of everything that has to do with Peronism. However, this is not the most common attitude. In general, these middle classes, once die-hard anti-Peronists, now praise elements of the Peronist experience and especially praise the figure of Eva.

Thus, Eva has been for several decades a bounty fought for by those who needed to negotiate the validity of their own discourses with those of the Peronist orthodoxy. In the 1970s, for example, when the Montoneros began to oppose Perón, they used Eva as a channel to proclaim themselves Peronists and challenge Evita and the Justicialist leader himself. If the Montoneros found the antibourgeois and anticapitalist side of Perón's doctrine in Eva, the nonactivist middle classes found in her an antiperverse, antispeculative, antihypocritical figure that, in other words, was the anti-Perón. Through the current praise that these classes express for Eva as a caring, charitable, transparent, romantic, and compassionate soul with a genuine love for the poor, the middle classes negotiate the validity of their anti-Peronist discourse with their adversaries' accounts. The credibility of their discourse would be challenged if they were blind to certain social advances in the Peronist years that are hard to deny. However, when they recognize them, they insert them within their traditionally anti-Peronist sensibility. The praise for Eva reaffirms this sensibility; it is a contemporary way of continuing anti-Peronism by other means.

Having analyzed the middle classes' political culture, we are now in a better position to examine the complex middle-class response to social, revolutionary, and state violence. This examination begins with a return to a moment before the outbreak of protest, before the escalation of violence, when Perón's return to the country was nothing more than mere speculation—in the relative economic success and political calm of the first years of Argentine Revolution's government.

"In a world that seems everywhere on fire," *Panorama* magazine wrote in February 1969, "Argentina is an island of order."[1] Based on an investigation conducted in the first weeks of that year, the magazine affirmed that peace reigned in the university, the union movement, business sectors, the church, and the army. A month earlier, in an article that synthesized the conflicts that had been resolved without great difficulty during the previous year, the same magazine wrote that 1968 had been a "socially peaceful year."[2] This was not an isolated evaluation. In an article devoted to summarizing the student conflicts in the United States, Italy, Germany, France, Eastern Europe, Japan, and other parts of Latin America, the journalist Heriberto Kahn wrote in April

1968 in *Confirmado* magazine that "Argentina, in these moments appears to be one of the nations of the world where the student body has not convulsed."[3] Also in 1968, when asked to comment about the year's most important news stories, the editors of the main political analysis publications mentioned various violent situations, but all of them referred to international events (the assassinations of Robert Kennedy and Martin Luther King Jr., the invasion of Czechoslovakia, the student revolt in Europe, and violence in the United States).[4] The contrast with the wider world was common for local observers, who never ceased to marvel at the tranquility of the Argentine landscape, "so much more peaceful, ordered and conformist when compared to that of other nations, from France to Uruguay, Mexico, Colombia or Venezuela."[5]

The guerrilla phenomenon, moreover, appeared to occur primarily outside the country's borders in the latter half of the 1960s. Indeed, with the exception of a group of fourteen Peronist militants quickly disbanded in Taco Ralo (Tucumán), news about guerrillas abounded in Argentina, but came primarily from Bolivia, Colombia, Venezuela, Uruguay, and Guatemala.[6] Neither public opinion nor the military authorities took the Tucumán episode seriously. Until the social uprisings in 1969, the subject of violence was absent from public opinion studies in Argentina. Even polls commissioned by the national government did not ask about violence, but about government policies, particularly in the economic sphere, and the public's perception of institutions such as the unions, the universities, and the armed forces.

Some researchers have indicated that the image of "supposed calm" during the period that preceded the 1969 rebellions only disguised protests that occurred in 1968, such as those that occurred on the two-year anniversary of the Argentine Revolution.[7] This makes the fact that much of the contemporary press perceived the social climate to be peaceful even more revealing, up to the point of qualifying the first years of Onganía's government as a "three-year period of constructive peace" or a "*pax revolucionaria.*"[8] In a society like Argentina's, rich in its history of repression and violence, many actors in the 1970s assumed that a certain level of both was a necessary part of national life.

With the series of uprisings that occurred in 1969—in April in Tucumán,[9] and in May in Rosario, crowned by the Cordobazo on May 29–30—the sense of calm vanished. From that time, the only thing that seemed clear about the political future was that it could no longer be the same as the past. President Onganía himself recognized this, stating several days after the events in Córdoba that from that point neither the country nor the government would be the same.[10] "In the history of Argentina," *Panorama* magazine wrote at the end of the year, there were two 1969s, or, more exactly, there were two historical stages divided by May 1969. Until that month, Argentina, "happy" and "confident," considered itself to be distant from many evils: it did not belong to the Third World, it was not an underdeveloped country; the existence of urban guerrillas was impossible in its territory. From May 1969 on, it suddenly became aware of the reality in which its life occurred. The conflicts and the evils that afflicted the world also blow through the air of this reaction by the cities and fields of Argentina.[11]

There was a sense that the onset of violence had been delayed but was also expected and desired by many. As one headline put it: "Violence kept its appointment."[12] The judgment that the appearance of violence should force the Argentine Revolution to revise its course and open a new scenario for the coming years was far from being confined to one social sector. With the exception of a minority that was still aboard the ever more confused and haggard enterprise led by Onganía, a satisfaction with the rupture of the calm could be found among the leaders of the majority of political parties, in the universities, in sectors of the church, in the unions that were not subservient to the government, in not insignificant sectors of the military, and in some groups tied to the establishment. For example, Mariano Grondona, a political analyst who had celebrated Onganía's coup in 1966,[13] when asked a question about the violence unleashed from the events of 1969, responded: "I don't know what has been more surprising, this year's violence or the lack of violence in 1967 and 1968."[14] In brief, the rise of a much-delayed violence put things in their place not only for the participants in the rebellions and for the left wing, but for a wide range of political and social sectors coming from dissimilar ideological backgrounds.

In immediate terms, the Cordobazo provoked changes in the national cabinet, overthrew the authorities of the province of Córdoba, and caused the formation of a War Council. In the long term and seen retrospectively, it began a spiral of violence that did not cease to multiply and acquire new forms until the end of the 1970s. Large sections of the press warned of a change of era. "The Argentine political scene," a journalist wrote a little more than a month after the May 1969 uprisings, "seems to already contain a protagonist which advances at full speed: violence."[15] In its first issue of 1970, *Panorama* predicted not only that the insurgent violence would continue to increase but also that its repression would not lag far behind. "The politics of subversion and the politics of repression," the magazine wrote, "are already ready to confront each other."[16] Three months later, *Análisis* confirmed that "violence as a political factor has entered the daily life of the country."[17]

The beginning of the 1970s showed a different landscape from that portrayed by observers before the events of 1969, now consisting of student and worker protests, uncontrolled police, and military forces on the streets. The greatest novelty, however, was the entrance on the scene of armed left-wing organizations that gained unquestionable notoriety through their spectacular acts. Political crime returned one month after the May revolts, with the assassination of the union leader Augusto Vandor, and reached an even higher expression when the Montoneros organization kidnapped and assassinated ex-president General Pedro Eugenio Aramburu on the first anniversary of the Cordobazo.

As a consequence of this and other acts of political violence, *Panorama* chose "terrorism" as its person of the year in 1970. Its director, Tomás Eloy Martínez, commented to his readers that, having evaluated other possibilities (the newly elected president of Chile, Salvador Allende; the Nobel Prize winner in chemistry, Luis Leloir; or the Brazilian soccer team, the world champions that year), "the daunting list of the terrorist attacks that shook Argentina throughout the year put an end to the debate: the dynamite, the machine gun, the kidnappings, the political robbery were—taken together—not only the dominant character of these twelve months: they have also marked Argentine history with fire."[18]

The most influential newspapers of the interior regions of the country studied here, *La Capital* of Rosario and *La Gaceta* of Tucumán, reached similar conclusions. "We are living through monstrous times of insensibility and violence," editorialized the former a little over a month after Aramburu's kidnapping.[19] "In this 1970 that is coming to a close," affirmed the latter in an editorial, "we have suffered the tremendous impact of violence unleashed in periodic spells and assuming the most varied of forms. The revolt in the streets, organized and dangerous urban warfare—an exclusive product of this second half of the twentieth century—aerial hijackings, political kidnappings, unjust and indiscriminate terrorist activity and insane attacks and crimes have frequently occupied the attention of the man of our times."[20]

In mid-1972, Mariano Grondona, the political analyst who shortly before was shocked at the lack of violence in 1967 and 1968, asserted that the "social sphere is invaded by worries of violence." In 1973, after reminding readers that Argentines had "a tradition of violence that returns today in the form of subversion, using the methods of the guerrillas," he added: "I believe that we cannot underestimate the importance of this phenomenon, and moreover: I believe that this is the most important phenomenon today."[21] In a short time, much of the press and public opinion went from perplexity at the scarcity of violence to astonishment at its abundance.

Social historians as much as sociologists of history have pointed out that ordinary people were at the same time active agents of the historical process, victims, and silent witnesses of it. So we need to uncover the story of "people without history." —Eric Wolf

Two   Social Violence (1969–1974)

Days before the Cordobazo, two students were murdered by the police, one in the city of Corrientes and the other in Rosario.[1] In response to these two events, and the 1970 and 1972 student rebellions in Tucumán, the middle classes of these cities reacted, on the one hand, with an understanding attitude of support for the students, and on the other, with anger toward the police who used repression and fear in the face of uncontrolled violence. In Corrientes, for example, the local government review highlighted both attitudes. "The sudden, unexpected death of the student Cabral," the official report stated, "generated a double impact. In succession: outrage over the event and widespread solidarity with the students; afterward, fear and withdrawal."[2] In Córdoba, where the events were more serious, Carlos Caballero, the governor overthrown by the uprising, asserted in a report sent to the national authorities that, once in the street, the demonstrators enjoyed the support of the population. "Bourgeois neighborhoods collaborated spontaneously and enthusiastically in the action," claimed Caballero, although this support "became more reticent after witnessing certain excesses."[3] The sociologist Juan Carlos Agulla, in one of the first studies dedicated to the Cordobazo, wrote that the population of the area where the confrontations developed "only participated, actively or passively (or tolerantly), between 11:30 A.M. and 4:00 P.M. on May 29th. From this moment on, the entire population [. . .] was terrified and afraid."[4] These descriptions attribute to the population, and in some cases specifically to the middle classes, an attitude of initial support and solidarity followed by one of caution and fear of the violence unleashed during the protests.

Urban middle classes' sympathy for students was not new. Surveys conducted before 1969 established that the middle classes disapproved of Onganía's 1966 intervention in the universities, and considered that student demonstrations expressed demands for legitimate rights. In 1967, a CIMS study showed that a majority of 55 percent of the Buenos Aires middle class was in favor of university autonomy, while 35 percent supported the government intervention. The relationship was reversed in the upper class, where 53 percent approved of the intervention and 47 percent backed autonomy. Among the working class, while those who supported autonomy (41 percent) outnumbered supporters of the intervention (32 percent), a high percentage replied that they did not know or did not respond (27 percent).[5] In the following year, A&C affirmed that 63 percent of the middle class attributed the university conflicts to legitimate student demands, against 32 percent that considered them the work of agitators. In this case, while the upper class once again responded in an opposite way, the lower class equaled the middle class in its support of university student demands (63 percent).[6] The available statistics demonstrate that, toward the end of the 1960s, university students—the majority of whom were middle-class—found their main allies in their own segment of society. Various authors have indicated the sympathy and even complicity that the first social uprisings provoked among the middle classes.[7] However, there has been very little scholarship about the nature of these attitudes, their implications and their limits.

The solidarity with the first social protests tended to wane as the demonstrators radicalized their actions. This did not reverse the discontent of the population toward the government of the "Argentine Revolution." Unlike those who participated in the university world—who knew what went on inside based on their own experiences—those that did not were limited to the information and opinions spread by the media. It should then be noted that, shortly after the spiral of social violence and repression was unleashed, the media consumed by the mass of the middle classes no longer emphasized the spontaneous and authentic elements of the social unrest and began to underline the premeditated and planned nature of the revolts, stressing the role of subversive infiltrators or professional agitators. An analysis of this media discourse provides a necessary context and, at the same time, allows for the exploration of the limits to the thinking of the majority of public opinion. These limits may have been flexible, but this did not make them any less real.

In the case of Tucumán, La Gaceta, the newspaper owned by the García Hamilton family, occupied a privileged space in its capacity to shape public opinion, especially during the period under examination in the present study. Its slogan "Yes, it's true. La Gaceta says so" ("Sí, es verdad. Lo dice La Gaceta") expresses the spirit with which this daily paper presented itself to Tucumán public opinion. Although in those days Tucumán already had a local television station, Channel 10,[8] the newspaper continued to be the media source that set the news agenda for the province. Its local competitors, the evening paper Noticias and the morning paper El Pueblo, never challenged its supremacy.[9]

As soon as the student revolts began, La Gaceta published an editorial titled "The Appropriate Moderation" ("La conveniente moderación"), in which, echoing the interior minister's "call for the pacification of the university youth of Argentina," it urged students to abandon their violent attitudes.[10] The editorials that dealt with the revolts tended to underline the participation of foreign elements that appropriated legitimate demands and converted them into subversive programs. In early July 1969, after denying that the violent acts seen in demonstrations were "entirely the work of Argentines," La Gaceta claimed in its editorial that "at their core, there seems to be the ghost of extremist ideologies, completely foreign to our national sentiment."[11]

The social violence always appeared on the newspaper pages as a phenomenon that did not bear relation to the idiosyncratic particularity of Argentina. After the first "Tucumanazo" in November 1970, La Gaceta wrote that "no well-intentioned citizen of Tucumán" could agree with the expressions of violence, no matter how young their authors were. "Argentina is not a country where violence can exist as an element incorporated in its daily life," the paper declared on this occasion; "on the contrary, as we have demonstrated in the most fateful of circumstances, our people are naturally peaceful and wish to live far from the rancor which divides other nations of the Earth."[12] La Gaceta tended to present the violence as a sickness or social ill that afflicted other, particularly Latin American, countries with less capable people and more intractable problems than those of Argentina. In this view, the infiltration of this sickness into minority sectors, who in no way represented most of society, was directly opposed to Argentine customs and traditions. After the first Tucumanazo and after further unrest in the neighboring province of Catamarca, La Gaceta affirmed "our distinctiveness as a cultured and civilized people cannot be reconciled with wide-eyed insolence or destructive violence."[13]

This antiviolence posture, which its editorials stressed as a distinctive feature of the newspaper since its founding, did not imply a blindness to the legitimacy of the causes that gave rise to the revolts. Demetrio Oliva, the newspaper's humorist—whose pseudonym, Agapito Chancalay, is still remembered by his former readers—tended to combine the rejection of all forms of violence with a concern for social injustices in his columns. With his own distinctive writing style interspersed with colloquial language, he directed a letter to General San Martín, the Liberator—a strategy that he used to show the smallness and triviality of the men and political times in which he lived—in which he said:

tell Manuel Belgrano
of our endless drama;
tell him that it was useless
his immortal sacrifice;
tell Martín de Güemes
that over there, in his native Salta,
the poor masses are hungry,
just like in Tucumán,
in La Pampa and La Rioja
in El Chaco and San Juan
tell all the heroes
of this country like no other,
that we're a'thirsting for justice
that we've got to quench
that or we all drown
or we save ourselves.[14]

Faithful to the editorial line of the paper, this columnist-humorist affirmed that he was a "mortal enemy of violence" and, with similar emphasis, left no room for doubts that he never considered it just, clarifying that he rejected both violence "from above" and "from below," both that which came from the state and that which originated in the worker or student rebellions.[15]

The paper's position regarding social violence included, in some cases, calls for attention targeted equally toward the demonstrators and the political authorities.[16] On the other hand, especially when the victims were students from Tucumán, the paper never stopped expressing deep condolences for the loss of human lives, together with its call for the calming of passions. When the student Villalba was killed during the second Tucumanazo, La Gaceta wrote that "the event has shaken the most intimate fibers of our citizens since, although all human lives are equally valuable, the absurd interruption of a young life is doubly significant, because, by definition, this closes off a project which will never be realized."[17] In a context where death was not yet a fact of daily life, shock was an almost spontaneous response both in the press and in public opinion. From May 1969 until the second Tucumanazo in 1972, La Gaceta demanded that the state watch carefully how, in which circumstances, and with what intensity the law is applied.[18] However, as the violence began increasing and the role of terrorist-style actions overshadowed social struggles, La Gaceta went from calling for moderation in repression to demanding its effective application.

In Buenos Aires, the middle classes were among the last sectors that withdrew their confidence in Onganía's economic team. In any case, because they were in the epicenter of political power, the social unrest in the provinces was a topic of conversation and concern. The conviction that when something happened in the provinces, especially in Córdoba, it would later spread and provoke changes in the national order enjoyed great popularity. Moreover, the Buenos Aires university student population showed periodic signs of a rise in the level of political agitation and mobilization with demonstrations that frequently led to confrontations with the police.

To the extent that social protest began to take increasingly violent forms and occur with greater frequency, some media began to emphasize that its protagonists were minority sectors. The most influential magazines as well as television news programs tended to agree that the majority of the population was not involved in the violent episodes and disapproved of them. Many diagnoses saw the population in general as a "silent majority," trapped between two extremes that were not consistent with its moderation.[19] The weekly paper Análisis read the Rosario disturbances of 1969 as a confrontation between "tiny minorities of agitators and extremists" and a "government without civil support," in the midst of which "the immense majority of the country remains outside the process, while suffering from its effects."[20] A little more than a month after the Cordobazo, the magazine's editor, Fernando Morduchowicz, wrote that "in the moment of truth, no one should be fooled. On one side, there are those that believe in certain cultural, political, and economic values. On the other are the wrathful, who seek to go back to the drawing board, who seek a total rupture."[21] In many cases, the editorials combined this diagnosis with a call to the citizenry to break their silence and make their demand for sanity and nonviolence heard. "The vast majority of Argentines," *Gente* magazine wrote two months after the Cordobazo, "are repelled by the burning of supermarkets, the outrages in Córdoba, the bombs in the banks and neighborhood businesses, the urban guerrillas, the destruction of universities, and so on."[22] After claiming that the average Argentine is characterized "by this condition of the uncommitted observer," the editorial warned of the risks of the nation remaining in its typical "don't get involved" state, the "foundation of the strategy" of the violent.

With the arrival of the first anniversary of the Cordobazo, the resurgence of agitation in Rosario, Córdoba, and Tucumán provoked, according to *Panorama* magazine, "a wave of alarm in the majority," which no longer supported the protests.[23] Six months before, a reader had sent a letter to the magazine praising an article recognizing the existence of social injustices but highlighting the inappropriateness of urban guerrilla actions and personal attacks to resolve them, signaling that "both sides" were wrong. The government was wrong because it went too far in its repression of youth violence, and the youth because they were venting their urges and creating an unjustified disorder. "On the margins of both sides, who are more and more violent and unjust in their attacks and their repression," the reader finished his letter, "there is a country that wants to work in peace."[24]

This diagnosis of one country that wishes to work and study and another that wants disorder and violence was not uncommon in the metropolitan media, especially those directed toward the middle classes.[25] In June 1971, the television program *Camino Crítico* (Channel 7), directed by Pedro Larralde, dedicated one of its installments to debating "what does the silent majority think?" about the national situation. In advertising the show, a commercial rhetorically asked, "To what extent do certain noisy minorities represent the opinions of the majority?"[26] Days earlier, *Panorama* magazine had warned that, if the violence continued to increase, "the silent majority could become *gorillas*," predicting a future demand for greater repression of rebels.[27]

Moreover, the opinions of many of those consulted by the mass media converged into a discourse condemning violence and questioning the groups that exercised or justified it. The Spanish philosopher Julián Marías, frequently interviewed by Argentine media, held a dialogue with "two left-wing youth" in which, in response to the affirmations of the students that violence was the "only possible solution" in the face of social inequality, stated that the solution was "talent, work, and freedom."[28] While the young people in the dialogue situated violence as an element that made history progress, the Spanish philosopher considered it to be a restraint against its advancement.[29] Víctor Massuh—a Tucumán intellectual of national standing judged by *Panorama* (who employed him as a contributor) to be one of the "sharpest Latin American thinkers" —also made public commentary along these lines, in addition to writing a book on the subject.[30] In his television presentations in 1975, Massuh spoke of two sides that were dividing the world, with their corresponding local manifestations, the side of life and the side of death—a diagnosis that anticipated future statements from Admiral Massera.[31]

For its part, *La Capital*, the Rosario-based daily newspaper, which was the paper of record in the city of Correa, went beyond circumstantial calls on politicians to work harder in attacking the roots of the conflicts. Its editorials condemned violent social protests as attacks against the country, against institutions, and against "our way of life," underlining that "violence will not bear any other fruit but violence."[32] An episode of social violence in June 1969, however, received analogous coverage to that of *La Gaceta* on the occasion of the second Tucumanazo. At the same time that it condemned the violence of the demonstrators, who were in this case students, it also asked for restraint among the repressive forces. "We have borne painful witness to a frenzy of violence," *La Capital* opined, but "also to a frenzy of repression." Like *La Gaceta*, the paper reserved its most severe criticisms for the police, whose "barbaric spirit in surrounding and savagely beating anyone who was in front of them" was more reprehensible than the "docile and naïve mass of idealists" at the service of "various extreme ideologies."[33] To the degree that violent demonstrations began repeating and grew in magnitude, the target of media condemnation began to shift.

Of all the media analyzed, *La Capital* condemned violent worker and student demonstrations with the greatest vehemence. When the second Rosariazo caused a convulsion in Rosario's social and political landscape in September 1969, *La Capital* took on the voice of the "immense majority that still has not understood why these movements [conflagrations, attacks, truly warlike confrontation] have attained the scale that they have." It called on the security forces to act with the "speed that the disturbances demand, in the proportion that they grow," without bringing up "any jurisdictional arguments."[34] In other words, before the end of 1969, *La Capital* did not hide its support for an effective repression that matched the intensity of the revolts. A year and a half later, in the editorial published about the 1971 revolt in Córdoba, the paper reiterated and amplified its prior diagnosis. "While the immense majority, practically the entirety of the residents of the city of Córdoba, distanced themselves from the events whose results were expected," editorialized *La Capital*, "a few thousand workers and students formed the indispensable human mass required by the agents of disorder to advance, with mathematical coldness, their program of aggression.[35] Regarding university activism, echoing a report from the Tactical Operations Center of the Command of the Second Army Corps, at the end of 1971 the paper warned of "the anarchization of university life" converted into the "epicenter of violence" for "subversion."[36]

In all three sites studied, the media that had the most influence over the less-politicized middle classes worked to install a common sense in regard to the phenomenon of social violence. Part of the journalistic common denominator was the idea that a fundamentally peaceful society — a society accustomed to resolving its conflicts in a civilized fashion — should confront, from 1969 on, a new and growing phenomenon called "violence." With some nuances, a significant portion of the most influential media sources agreed to condemn violence in public demonstrations and, less frequently, disagreed with indiscriminate repression, especially when the victims were students. Regardless of the level of understanding that the media had of the causes of the social unrest, in general it tended to characterize acts of violence as the responsibility of organized minorities, with more or less subversive objectives, which were foreign to almost the totality of the population, the "silent majority," which generally occupied the space of moderation and rationality.

Tato Bores, the Humor of the Middle Class

One way of approaching middle-class perceptions of politics is to analyze the discourse of emblematic artists of the period, whose art was principally consumed by and deliberately directed toward the middle classes. Among the artists that fit this description, the figure of Tato Bores — a talented humorist who eventually came to be considered by many to be, as he presented himself, the "Comedic Actor of the Nation" — acquires relevance because he also had two other qualities. On the one hand, Bores always maintained a large audience, especially among the middle classes.[37] On the other, and unlike other artists of the period, politics served as the raw material for the humor in his shows.

Tato's humor, present since the 1940s on the radio, and in the theater and on television since 1957, constituted a solid tradition for its audience by the beginning of the 1970s.[38] During this period, his monologues ironically examining the politics of the day had become a ritual for much of the middle classes. His programs consisted of lengthy speeches, sometimes complemented by sketches, in which the comedian spoke at full speed for several minutes, which ensured that the audience paid him the utmost attention.[39]

Both the contemporary press and statements from politicians, military officials, and the comic himself give us a glimpse of Bores's importance in the political scene. In the days before the coup that overthrew Illia's government, the protagonists of the uprising admitted two concerns: first, the opinion of the United States embassy, and second, what Tato would say on his show the following Sunday.[40] What was a concern for politicians and military officials served his audience as a way to be informed and laugh (and think) about what was happening in the halls of power. In 1970, a journalist affirmed that when political events occurred, "everyone wanted to know what Tato Bores says."[41] In the year of the return to democracy another journalist wrote, "as has been happening for more than a decade, it is foreseeable that in 1973 a certain portion of the public will wait for Sunday to find out, laughing, what is happening around it."[42] Even after four years of absence, when he went back on air during el Proceso, "everyone was awaiting the return of Tato, to hear what he was going to say," as a journalist noted, and the show "almost completely monopolized the television audience."[43] Although Bores never stopped claiming the role of actor and rejecting that of the politician, both his supporters and his detractors always considered him a political figure with the capacity to mold public opinion.

The close link between the middle classes and the comic profile of the character embodied by Borenstein — his true last name — was sometimes explicit, as when the comedian declared that his show did not refer to himself, but rather "symbolized the everyday poor sap. On stage, the typical things that happen to our middle class happen to him."[44] Bores spoke as a citizen who was at the same time concerned with and distant from politics. Neither very right-wing nor very left-wing, his humor presented a vision equidistant from all extremes in which an important portion of the middle classes liked to recognize itself. The intense complicity established between the comedian and his audience was used as a selling point for his programs. His 1973 season *Say Yes to Tato* (Channel 13) was advertised with the slogan: "This is the ticket: Tato . . . and his partner." The advertisement showed two faces, one of the comic and another empty one, which symbolized the viewer. The program's successful couple was "TATO-YOU."[45]

Bores spoke to the middle class, and much of this class felt that, somehow, they spoke through him. His monologues were directed toward a public that was informed but not necessarily intellectual, attentive to the politics of the time, and wanted to laugh about the weaknesses, contradictions, or defects of those who ruled over the destiny of the country. His humor was massive but not "popular" or oriented toward the working classes. This is how he was understood by the Peronist government in 1974, after President Perón admonished the humorist in a radio address for his jokes about the government, and decided to pull his series from Channel 13 for being an "elitist program," distant from the "national popular television" that the country needed.[46] Tato Bores was a critic of Argentine politics who succeeded in capturing the middle classes as very few other public figures could. In the years we are concerned with, his humor was not characterized by audacity or excessive transgression. It was probably this quality that, while later earning him some accusations for not sufficiently challenging the powers that be, at the time helped him captivate broad sectors of the middle classes who saw him as a referent. The majority of critics also contributed to highlighting his talent and relevance.[47]

Bores posed ironic complaints that his audience could identify with. His monologues at the beginning of the 1970s took aim against the tax burden the middle class was suffering, the ineffectiveness of the state bureaucracy, the excesses of military uprisings, economic hardships, fuel shortages, and the lack of agreement among politicians. Although he did not declare himself to be for or against any political party, it can be deduced from his scripts that he was not a Peronist. In this section, I analyze Bores's monologues from the period that runs from the end of the government of the "Argentine Revolution" until Isabel Perón's government. I focus my analysis on questions of violence and youth radicalization, as well as the vision of political and social realities.

In 1972, in *Forever Tato* (Channel 11), Bores dedicated a program to emphasizing society's separation from the two-fold process of political radicalization and increasing violence. During the week of Perón's first return to the country after sixteen years of exile and General Lanusse had opened the electoral route, Tato was astonished at those who described an Argentina at war with itself.[48] The monologue parodied the declarations of politicians and military officials in those days: "Let's reconcile! Dialogue! Let's coexist! [. . .] Pacification, agreement, coexistence, concomitance!"[49] As he usually did, in his monologue Bores simulated meetings with politicians and conversations with different people. In this case, all were concerned with the level of confrontation that existed in Argentine society. "Tato, if only the reconciliation were with you," he claimed ex-president Arturo Frondizi told him. Upon arriving at his house—the monologue continued—he received a call from his cousin Zoilo, who lived in the United States, who told him:

Tato, finish up with that program already, lock up the house and come here at once, with Berta [his wife] and the kids, bring everything up to the canary! [. . .] Don't be stupid, you can't risk having your family in a country where even the schoolteachers are going around with bombs, where people are killing each other across from the newspaper boards . . . where the Juancistas [Peronists] go around the streets to the shout of "huija!" with their shotguns mounted and those from the Concentración Cívica on horseback with their swords in the air!

After finishing with his cousin—Tato recounted—he received a similar entreaty from the caretaker of his summer house in Punta del Este, Uruguay: "Tato, come here, come here . . . We already have a house ready for you. How can you live in a country where people go armed, even just to go to the pools of Nuñez? [. . .] You all are on the verge of civil war, and if the Government talks about the need for understanding, it's because you are against the sword." Shortly thereafter, he received a letter from Tel Aviv addressed to his wife. "Dear cousin Berta," the letter said, "I can only imagine the times you must be living in the middle of so much anxiety and living in this climate of tension, lacking in supplies and without even being able to go outside . . ."

The monologue continued relating similar encounters with Radical leader Enrique Vanoli and Lanusse's press secretary, Edgardo Sajón. Tato responded that it was not so to each one of his interlocutors, that they were mistaken, that Argentina was not on the verge of civil war and that he was not at war with anyone. After all these exchanges—Bores said—"I went out on the street to see if I was politically colorblind." There, in the real world, Tato described another Argentina—a retired person sleeping in a plaza, babysitters strolling with babies, a girl playing with a dog, laborers working while others made a barbecue; in other words, the ordinary, peaceful lives of people outside the political confrontations. Upon contrasting both realities, Tato exclaimed: "But I don't see collective rage; the fact that students don't agree with the rector, the workers with the foreman, and the judge with the prisoner, doesn't indicate that the country is about to explode!" The contrast was evident: the country that was at war with itself was not that of the average citizen, but instead that of those who were involved in politics, be they civilians or military. Finally, Tato finished by saying:

You [the politicians] are responsible for the fact that abroad they think that we Argentines are living in a constant battle . . . by the end, even we ourselves are going to believe that we are disunited! For years, we have lived through Juancistas [Peronists] versus Anti-Juancistas [anti-Peronists] without any problems, and now we discover that we have to reconcile, pacify, agree, coexist . . . that should happen among the leaders! [. . .] I returned to the plaza near the corner of my house. I sat down next to the pensioner that slept in the sun [. . .] The pensioner's radio softly said:

—The Armed Forces will guarantee the electoral process . . .

The old man opened an eye and commented:

—In politics everything is moving, the same person that hits you later does you the favor of putting on a cold compress.

He changed the station. The report said:

—The Minister of the Interior insists on the need to approve a minimal agreement.

He changed to another station, and a politician swore:

—I will struggle for the reunion of the Argentine people . . .

The pensioner opened an eye, and I asked him, imploringly:

—Chief, you and I, are we disunited, are we in conflict?

The old veteran replied:

—Also in politics they set fire to the house, to later serve as the firefighter . . .

—Mr. Pensioner, there isn't even a fire here!

The pensioner went back to sleep, but before, he managed to tell me:

—Let them put it out anyway, or in order to be right, they'll set a real fire . . . and then they won't have enough hoses . . .

This monologue of Bores describes the perception of many of those that were not directly involved in the political struggle. The need to pacify oneself is presented as an imposition on society by politicians. Society itself is not portrayed as at war with itself, but rather as watching a struggle it did not generate but must suffer through. The "rage" was not "collective" but rather "between leaders." It was not society, but politicians, that needed reconciliation. Additionally, politicians were responsible for the perception that Argentines lived "in a constant battle." They rushed to put out a fire that did not exist. Society was not disunited. And if society had to allow politicians to put out a nonexistent fire, this was to ensure they didn't set real ones.

In 1973, the electoral year, Bores's television show was called *Say Yes to Tato* (Channel 13).[50] In one of his monologues he reviewed both the political situation that followed Cámpora's election victory and the radicalized youth strengthened by this victory.[51] The monologue opened with a negative reference to the price controls that Peronism implemented. Tato related that, in his habitual visit to his butcher, five ladies blocked his exit, ordered him to verify the prices, and forced him to show them the merchandise that he had purchased. The scene alluded to the price control commissions that the Peronist "base organizations" were organizing to demand that business owners respect the official rules, something that brought back to memory the anti-speculation inspectors set up by the first Peronist government.[52] When Tato warned "*compañera doña María*" not to put her fingers in the meat that he had purchased and the butcher asked the group of "inspectors" who exactly they were, and what they were doing, one of them responded, "We are who we are, and we are helping the community! We are going to report you to the authorities right now." Another of the ladies, "*compañera Filomena*," made absurd objections to the tripe the butcher was selling. Finally, Tato told the audience that he ended up not buying the meat because the inspector had put her fingers in it. The anecdote was finished by the butcher, who told the comedian: "Don Tato, don't get offended, but that is called a return to the past." Thus, the return of Peronism in 1973 appeared to be a regression to an arrogant, authoritarian, and overly vigilant Argentina, to which the majority of the middle classes were not eager to return.

In Tato's discourse, the difference from the earlier Peronist period was rooted in the role of young activists. After leaving the butcher's shop, Tato said, he went to the Municipal Radio for a job interview. Upon wanting to enter, a young man stopped him at the door, announced to him that the director had resigned, that the staff had decided to occupy the radio station, and that "since we were there, we changed its name," so that the radio was no longer called the Municipal Radio, but rather that of the City of Buenos Aires. When Bores explained to the young man that "only the House of Representatives could change that," he responded: "Come on, Tato, we are the People!" and added: "as a representative of the *juancista* (Peronist) movement, we also decided to change the programming," because the previous programming "was not Justicialist, strayed from the party's program, and was elitist." Tato reflected on this and understood that he was living in "special times," in which "the illusions of the youth" gained ground, but he wondered if occupations of this style were acceptable or not. His legal advisor, José Pleitos, one of the imaginary characters who Tato dialogued with, responded: "Tato, in a sense, they are carrying out the work of a popular militia, which is what Galimberti proposed . . ." Thus, the youth activists, one of whose leaders was Rodolfo Galimberti—who had in fact called for the formation of popular militias in April 1973—appeared as the protagonists of the excesses that peaceful members of the society suffered.

Furthermore, the actions of youth activist were presented as the result of caprice and irresponsibility. Tato continued narrating other occupations that ranged from occupations of high schools to that of the City of the Children (La ciudad de los niños). "If this continues, they'll occupy everything up to the sewers," Tato said a politician from Córdoba had confided to him. In obvious disagreement with the series of occupations and seizures, at the end of the monologue the humorist warned of the possibility that those who defended Cámpora's victory through arrogant and illegal means, would end up "throwing sand in the gears by not following the laws." Bores satirized the slogan used in some of these occupations, "what is the People's, returns to the People." In line with what many members of the nonactivist middle class of that age remember they thought, these slogans appeared as being stained with demagoguery and populism in Tato's monologues, often justifying acts of violence.

Form 1971 on, Bores alluded to young activists as "lefties" (*zurdos*) and "bomb throwers," and sometimes as "long-haired" and "bearded." In the monologue that he devoted to the presidential inauguration of Perón in October 1973, Tato made a subtle comment on the question of weapons and youth.[53] At that time, Tato pretended to have a fervent sympathy for Peronism. The day of the inauguration, he told in his monologue, with his "very own drum" and his "banner as an autonomous combatant," he called on the National Congress to "be with the People a little bit." After singing "all of the choruses," he went toward the site where Perón would take his presidential oath. "We arrived right when the general was entering," Tato said, and at that moment,

> A young man stopped me very nicely.
> —Tato, I'm with the volunteers—he told me—I'm going to pat you
>   down for weapons.
> —Alright, but since I'm also a volunteer, I'm going to pat you down
>   for weapons as well.
> —Perfect, comrade, we should demonstrate good will.
> And we began to pat each other down reciprocally . . . A guest wearing
> a turban asked in French:
> —What is this patting-down ceremony?

What was happening in Argentina was presented as an incomprehensible absurdity for a foreign observer, who, incapable of accepting what he saw—that those attending the event were checking each other for weapons, mutually suspicious that the other might be carrying arms—imagines a local cultural ceremony of patting each other down. The activist youth, moreover, appear directly associated with violence in Bores's response to the young man that wanted to pat him down: "alright, but I am going to pat you down as well." Activists, weapons, and an atmosphere of mistrust are imposed over the event; even—or, perhaps, especially—between "comrades" (*compañeros*), your neighbor could be your enemy.

The next year, Tato's season was called *Give Tato Some Credit* (Channel 13).[54] The political situation in many provinces was delicate because the Justicialist formulas that had been triumphant a year ago in the majority of districts combined candidates that came from different segments of Peronism. In May 1974, shortly before Perón's death, Tato referred to the topic in a monologue that emphasized descriptions of the internal conflicts within Peronism, especially those featuring radicalized activists.[55]

Tato commented that the national government had charged him with traveling to the interior provinces to normalize the situation, because only he was capable of "pacifying, verticalizing, and orthodoxizing." His presence took on an air of urgency, the humorist said, because "any [province] that isn't burning, is smoking." In Salta, Tato recounted, "orthodox students" (those sympathizing with the Peronist right) occupying a school had been evicted by "unorthodox students" (sympathizers of the Peronist left) who were now the new occupiers. "I went swiftly to dialogue with the students," the humorist continued, but "they didn't open the gate for me." Through the door's peephole, he was able to have the following dialogue with the students:

—Why did you occupy the school?
—We occupied it because it was occupied and we had to clear it.
—But if you cleared it of its occupiers, why don't you yourselves clear out now?
—Because if we clear out, the others will occupy it again.

The monologue ironically presented a negative dialectic of violent occupations that soon forgot their original motivations, and were sustained so that other sectors would not gain ground. This was how the world of political activism was portrayed. Next to this world, without having much to do with it, ordinary, nonactivist people existed, represented by a woman looking for her son. While Tato was speaking with the students—he continued—an elderly lady approached him and said:

—Please, sir, would you be so kind as to help me to see if my son is around? He passes the whole day going from school to school.
—Your son is a student, madam?

—No, he's an officer of the infantry guard. Do you know what a nice job
   it is? He is getting to know all of the country's universities!

The old lady and her son represented this other world that existed outside
the world of political activism. Foreign to politics, their lives were divided
between familial affection—the mother looking for her son—and the work
of the young officer. Bores presented himself as an impartial observer, but
his conclusions always tended to emphasize, and frequently ridicule, the di-
vorce between the political world and that of the common people, that of
the political activists and that of common workers. Back in his home, drinking an aspirin smoothie, Tato finished his speech thinking: "If Foreign Secretary Vignes has any luck with his politics and we reconquer the Falkland
Islands [Islas Malvinas], I already see myself coming down to Port Stanley to
try to make peace between the governor, the vice governor, the JP, the JUP,
the JVVP, the JNP, the JR of the NP, the CGT and the penguins!" The internal spats within Peronism and the numerous acronyms that divided it appear
here mixed up with others that are nonexistent and distorted, symbolizing
the absurdity that they represented for the population. That, in the face of
an eventual recovery of the Falkland Islands, Tato imagines himself bringing peace to the authorities, the political groups, the workers' union, and
the penguins demonstrated the irrationality and surrealism that politics had
reached, for Tato and a good part of his loyal audience. His program, finally,
was a way to laugh about a reality—and a power—which, taken seriously,
satisfied few and frightened many.

Tato Bores's monologues permit us to examine what in this book I call a
"middle-class sensibility," understanding by this a way of seeing the world
that includes the beliefs, ideas, and feelings of those who remained aloof
from political militancy. With respect to the question of violence and political
activism, this sensibility was characterized by observing political radicalization from a distance and thinking of its own place as equidistant from both
extremes. This sensibility, in part, combined doses of concern and cynicism
to politics, well reflected in Bores's humor. However, there are nuances and
differences within the world of the nonactivist middle classes. The perception of violence and of political activism varied between the university and
nonuniversity worlds.

The sensibility of the middle classes was also formed by other elements that add other tones to the conclusions derived up to this point. At first students found their principal allies in the middle classes. The solidarity with student protests also formed part of this sensibility. Defining the range and content of this solidarity is thus crucial to account for, if not its coherence, at least its compatibility with other already identified elements. This solidarity translated into concrete actions. In the case of Tucumán, where there were two important instances of social unrest—one in 1970 and the other in 1972, both led by students—the middle class protected students fleeing police repression or helped them reinforce their barricades. However, these attitudes had less to do with ideology and support for political projects than an attempt to protect those who suffered the ravages of the police forces and antipathy toward government authorities—especially the police and others charged with repression.

A news story of the events of May 1969 in Rosario, days after a police bullet ended the life of the student Bello, gives an idea of both the closeness and the distance that existed between the mobilized students and the population that was not involved in the political struggle. On one side, the article listed chants of the student groups, such as "Rifles, machetes, what we need / for another October 17" or "Action, action, for liberation." On the other, the article observed that the chants "referred almost exclusively to the police and—eventually—to President Onganía, but with a sense of opposition and direct confrontation rather than an alternative political program." [56] Thus, refrains such as "Mur-der-ers, Mur-der-ers," chanted by a population in solidarity with the student protests and directed toward the police forces, expressed a rejection of repressive actions without regard for political-ideological considerations. The same occurred with the people that threw objects from the balconies of central Rosario so that the students could feed their fires. The shouts that this middle class directed at the men in uniform were highly offensive and did not omit racial epithets—"brutes," "illiterate blacks," and "beasts," as the news story tells it—but, taken on their own, were apolitical. The difference between the politicized university students and the middle classes angry at police abuse and unhappy with the military government did not go unperceived by a student who, called upon to interpret the phenomenon, declared that "it's the center of Rosario, and it's the *gorilla* [conservative] middle class that is turning a political problem into an emotional issue." [57] *La Capital*, the Rosario daily paper, also underlined the emotional component of the original support when it indicated that a month after the events the population no longer sympathized with the revolts. "The sympathy which the movement awoke in its first moments," the paper editorialized, was due to "a feeling of being emotionally impacted by the tragic toll of the repression."[58] The news stories cited place greater weight on the emotional aspect, to the detriment of any political-ideological component. This represents a fundamental difference between the activist and nonactivist sectors of the middle classes: unlike the nonactivists, the activists tended to judge that the introduction of moral arguments about the facts of political life were the product of the hypocrisy of the powerful or the ideological weaknesses of the petty bourgeois.[59] If the activists saw political solutions to all sorts of problems, including those that concerned morality, nonactivists tended to prioritize moral solutions for all problems, including those relating to politics.

Inside the student community, the limits to the initial support and solidarity for the revolts were seen in the way in which activists and nonactivists understood the university and politics. In this section, I analyze the perspective that nonactivist students had of the process of political radicalization that some of their peers experienced. Linda Tognetti, a native of Correa born in 1942, began studying literature at the beginning of the 1960s at the Universidad Nacional de Rosario and in the middle of the decade left the university and enrolled in a training institute for history teachers in the neighboring city of Cañada de Gómez. While at the university, although she did not join the Students' Center—hegemonized by left-wing forces—or the (Catholic) humanists, she sympathized with an independent group where "ideologically, every member could have their own idea." "We fought for the school, to get things for the students," Linda remembers, "but not for an ideology. We didn't drape ourselves in a political banner, we maintained ourselves independent of ideologies." In another meeting, upon remembering this experience, she affirmed that "I participated, when I was at the university, in 'Independent Students,' which was neither black nor white, it was in the middle. And I didn't really 'participate.' In reality, I supported them. They were neither the Catholic humanists nor the Students' Center." Once outside the university, the Cordobazo found her finishing her final year at the teacher training institute. Evoking her reactions once she learned of the events in Córdoba, she stated:

LINDA: I supported the Cordobazo, I believe. Yes.

SC: And what did your support consist of?

L: It's that, as a student, they had killed students. It was a student thing that brought us together. Besides, I had classmates in the teacher training institute who were communists, classmates who were Peronists, classmates who were Radicals, and classmates who were nothing like I was, and so you lived with all of that. More than ideology, it was an opening to "the friendship of . . ." [. . .] I had ex-classmates from the university that had actively participated in the Rosariazo, which was when they set loose lathered-up pigs [so that the police would fall as they tried to corral them].

In Linda's memory, her support for the Cordobazo and the Rosariazo appears to be mediated by a previous, more general predisposition of student solidarity with a generation and a group that she was part of. She did not participate in the events in either Córdoba or Rosario, and probably, had she been able to participate, would not have necessarily done so. However, this did not stop her from feeling that she was a member of a student community. I am interested in stressing that her independent position, her "not being anything" in ideological terms, was compatible with support and solidarity with students repressed. But the claim that Linda makes of her political independence, as well as the emphasis on her political neutrality and her friendship with other students, do not lead her to extend this support to a political-ideological level. The elements upon which this support appears to be based—generation, social group, and friendship—are less political than emotional.

In a passage of *Pretérito perfecto*, Hugo Foguet's novel about Tucumán society, one of the narrators describes the second Tucumanazo,[60] saying: "I could see 25 de Mayo street covered in clouds of gas and above the clouds, the peaks of the Law School, the heads of the students, covering their faces with bandannas, with slingshots: David versus Goliath, imagination against the bulldozer and the armored car, the legions of blue helmets (the shield ready, the club held high) that descended from the cars under the protection of the banners of common sense and the established order, and close ranks."[61]

David against Goliath, slingshots against tear gas and armored tanks, unarmed adolescents against the police power of a regime that governed by autistically confusing silence with approval and youth with delinquency. The middle classes of Tucumán do not doubt which side they should be on. Also in Tucumán, as a journalist wrote referring to Córdoba and Rosario, the student revolts showed that "the middle class was very sensitized to the deaths of young students and because of this eager to get out of a moment in history when it could not ensure the lives of its children."[62]

In 1972, in the year of the second Tucumanazo, Susana Mancuso was studying in her last year of high school. Her family sympathized with the

FIGURE 2.1. Students with slingshots in their hands on the roof of a house during the second Tucumanazo, June 1972. *Source: La Gaceta* archives.

students, opening the doors of their home to them to protect them from the tear gas. Upon remembering the student demonstrations and confrontations with the police, she said:

SUSANA: I live four blocks away from the Rectorate. So, we were blocked in: on one side, by the police, and on the other side, by the students. We helped the students a thousand times, letting them come into my house. There were bonfires, there were injuries, on one side and on the other. At night, the famous state of siege. What I'm telling you about was at the moment of the big revolt.

SC: And this sort of collaboration with the students was common?

S: All of the population was like this. It was generalized.

SC: And why?

S: Because of humanity. My father said: "If the youth don't express their ideas at this age, then when?" That's what it was. So I can't judge that a person who has ideals and is twenty-two or twenty-three years old is a criminal. That was my father's idea. And I grew up like that.

For example, there were the bonfires, and he took all the tires that there were in the house and fed the fires with them. The police would come advancing—because they also threw tear gas left and right, to tell you that we had three, four cases at home, all with their eyes destroyed [by the gas]—and he would open the door to the boys that were escaping.

Later, he would tell them: "Hey, man . . ." And there came the sermon. Of course. "Hey man, be careful, don't throw bombs, don't do that." The "hey, man" came from that side. Ideology of violence, no. It was just to cover up for them.

Unlike the majority of secondary schools in Tucumán, there was a Student Center, and discipline and authority were not important pedagogical criteria in the "university high schools" like the Sarmiento school that Susana attended. Although they were not "leftist," as they were accused of being, these schools were "liberal" in the sense that they based their pedagogy on teaching students to control their freedoms. In 1972, Susana decided to write a diary of her last year of school and jotted down impressions that preserve the perspective and the thoughts of a "liberal" student, who like her father was supportive of the mobilized students, but at the same time was separate from political or ideological projects.

Susana's diary constitutes an atypical source that provides, in addition to her primary concerns—her friends, sexual coming-of-age, her liking of physics or her distaste for French, the preparations for her graduation trip—a glimpse of the political world she experienced in the form of teacher strikes, student assemblies, and violence. What follows is a transcription of what Susana wrote in her journal during the last week of March and on April 13, 1972:

Monday 27: We didn't have class. There was an assembly. From it came out: an active strike to 1) support the teachers' strike (the government owes them since February); 2) against the high cost of living; 3) to repudiate the police repression of a popular demonstration against the high cost of living. These were the three main goals. Until they proposed all of them, Olga and I fooled around with Silvia (she couldn't skip the meeting). We gave her a nickname: "Aunt Thing" (the aunt from "The Addams Family"), because of her hair.

Tuesday 28: We didn't have class either. We were convened to an assembly and after much discussion, they came to the conclusion that we would strike for 36 hours after that moment. Afterward, I went with

Clara to the Technical [high school's] assembly. There, after waiting for a long time, finally it didn't occur, and we went home to have some tea. Wednesday 29: The teachers' strike was lifted but we continue ours. I don't know where we are going to stop. We won't have class all week. What's up? Because Thursday, Friday, Saturday and Sunday are Holy Week.

Thursday, April 13: We didn't have class today either, and today it isn't justified because the government asked for a 6 PM deadline to confirm the classrooms that they had promised in the Universidad Católica and also classrooms will be available within the Commerce school. But we went to point out that the dictatorship, the high cost of living, et cetera, et cetera, et cetera.[63]

These excerpts from Susana's diary combined the student political language of the 1970s ("assembly," "popular demonstration," "the high cost of living") with household chores and rites of friendship, such as drinking some tea after a failed meeting or "fooling around" with a friend during an assembly. On the one hand, this tells us something obvious: politics were not everything for Susana, which is even more evident if one reads the entire diary. But it also allows us to perceive the distance that there was between political acts, such as strikes or demonstrations, and the students who were less involved in politics. The decision to continue the strike after the strike was already lifted was something that Susana commented on with irony ("what's up?"), making it clear that she considered it to be an excess. The same occurs with the expression "point out the dictatorship," an argument that Susana interpreted as being a rhetorical strategy of the strikers to continue not having classes.

In June 1972, the second Tucumanazo broke out. That week, Susana wrote in her diary:

Friday, June 23: When we left school yesterday, I found out that there had been a student revolt downtown. Today when I went to school, they convened an assembly to inform us of what had happened and to take a position. Finally, it was decided not to go to classes and to make a statement to *La Gaceta*. Almost at the end of the assembly, Ms. María Elena Dappe announced that tomorrow we would not have classes, as the school was declaring a day off for safety reasons.

The following days: There were big messes between students and police due to abuse of authority by the police against the university cafeteria. The confrontations between students and police were tragic, as a

DESPREOCUPADO DEL TENSO clima que se vivía en esos momentos, este joven apareció súbitamente en medio de los efectivos policiales que procuraban desalojar la Quinta Agronómica. Las sonrisas que provocó el monociclo que montaba, terminaron al ordenarse su detención.

Por supuesto la nota cómica no podía faltar. Por desgracia, los odiosos soldados, y a pesar de haberse divertido, lo detuvieron. ¡Pero fue ingenioso el tipo! ¡¡Qué ocurrencia!!

El Ejército Exhortó a la Población a Cooperar

EN un comunicado el comandante de la V Brigada de Infantería, general Ernesto F. Della Croce, exhortó el lunes a la población "a cooperar con las fuerzas del orden y evitar verse envuelta en operaciones de represión, ante la actitud de activistas que la usan para encubrirse procurando, por tal medio, su propia impunidad". El documento indicaba asimismo que a partir del lunes a mediodía, "este Comando de Brigada se hizo cargo de la restitución de la tranquilidad y el orden alterada por los sucesos que son del dominio público".

FIGURE 2.2. "Of course the comic note could not be absent. Unfortunately, the hateful soldiers, despite having fun, arrested him. But the guy was ingenious! What an idea!" One of the pages of Susana's diary with clippings from the newspaper *La Gaceta. Source:* Author's archive.

student of the technical night school died (Villalba). As a consequence of all these messes, they ordered a one-week recess, but due to the events it was prolonged further. Thus, we had more than three weeks off (from June 23 to July 16). I will now paste some of the photographs that the newspapers of the last few days put up, to have more or less of an idea of what happened.[64]

The "big messes between students and police" always found Susana on the side of the former, as she was a student herself. However, she did not make any political comments nor did she show any ideological sympathy with the students, whose demands or slogans we cannot identify from Susana's account. What most impacted her was the death of the student Villalba, the confrontations between students and police, the abuse of authority on the part of the police, or, as can be read on her journal page above, the "detestable soldiers" who, despite enjoying the humor of the unicyclist, arrested him anyway. In another journal page referring to the Tucumanazo, Susana pasted a column from La Gaceta's humorist, Agapito Chancalay. The column read:

> Many years ago, I went to the circus. We were in the best part of the event. We had already enjoyed the trapeze artists and the magicians and we had laughed with the clowns. At that moment, a tragedy that we didn't expect occurred: a lion killed a boy who was the trainer's assistant, and all of us were left with our laughs stuck to our faces. Here, the same thing happened: we lived in a circus, with a tightrope walker and everything. We laughed at the skills of the artists that are in the ring. We laughed despite the cost of living, elections and politicians. Our people are like this: when we don't like a government, we laugh. Of course, at the end, the people are left with their laugh and the government with everything else. And when we least expected it, death came and once again we are left with the laugh stuck to our face.

Agapito Chancalay's articles constitute a way to access a certain imaginary of the nonactivist middle classes of Tucumán. They present an ironic view that is rather suspicious of politics, which in the transcribed paragraph appears in the idea that in Tucumán, one lived in "a circus, with a tightrope walker and everything." The citizens were the artists whose skills in the art of survival in the "ring" were amusing. The laughter that elections, politicians, or the cost of living generated hid a disgust with the situation and the government. The death of the student finally made the circus stop and exposed the charade. This, however, did not cause the humorist to rebel against the government, much less an economic system. That some change was necessary did not imply, in this imaginary, revolutions that would overthrow the capitalist order, nor did it justify violent means. Agapito Chancalay's column continued,

> let's not place the blame on anyone: neither on those that command nor those that obey, neither on the students nor on the police. The unjust society in which we live is to blame. We have to change it. But not by force, because force is stupid, whether it comes from above or from below. When we make a mess, the innocents fall: your son, my son, doña Rosa, who is passing by across the street. Also, force is used by those that are not right, and the people are right [. . .] force should be used to defend the homeland, but not for brothers to kill each other.[65]

In 1973, Susana started studying medicine at the Universidad Nacional de Tucumán, at the peak of political agitation in the country, in Tucumán, and in the national universities. Like the majority of university students, she did not come from a Peronist family, but unlike some of her peers, she did not become a Peronist or politically active. Neither was she anti-Peronist, in the sense that her parents' generation would have been. To understand the vision of the university students who did not become politically active, it is necessary to describe both some structural features of the higher education of those times and the discourse of the activist student sectors.

In 1969, the total number of university students enrolled in national universities was 202,921, more than half at the universities in Buenos Aires (82,300), Rosario (15,974) and Tucumán (9,398).[66] In terms of their social composition, only 5 percent were children of the working class, 40 percent of business owners, 8 percent of business managers, with the rest divided between technicians, professionals, and teachers.[67] While the entire middle class did not attend university, the university censuses never failed to confirm that it was almost exclusively this social group that had effective access to the institution.[68] Toward the end of the 1960s, the universities had become places that were not only politicized, but politicizing. While this occurred more in some fields of study than others, many students who had remained aloof from political concerns until that time became active activists soon after entering the university, generally with the left-wing. However, it is often overlooked that, even in these same spaces, some did not become politically active.

A survey conducted in nine of the ten divisions of the Universidad de Buenos Aires in late 1969 indicated that while 23 percent of students wanted student movements to be more revolutionary, 48 percent more democratic, 18 percent more conservative, and 18 percent had no opinion. The poll also conveyed two other important facts. On the one hand, while 33 percent considered that the university's mission was to produce "change," 41 percent thought that the objective should be training professionals and public citizens, 12 percent prioritized research, and 9 percent did not have an opinion. On the other, almost 60 percent believed that university student groups did not accurately represent the student body, but rather political forces outside the university, while only 21 percent held the opposite view, and 17 percent preferred not to respond.[69] Even though these percentages certainly would have varied with the dynamics of political events in the following years, one should not lose sight of the fact that, even with growing radicalization, some students wanted a university less tied to nonuniversity political forces, one that was more democratic or more conservative but in any case less revolutionary, and one that trained professionals and public citizens instead of being the vanguard of social change. The existence of this other sector of the university student body was made palpable when it came time to select student representatives. At the end of 1972, 70 percent of university students in the country did not participate in the elections for their respective student centers.[70]

It is undeniable, however, that the public university in the early 1970s became the space that most clearly expressed the will to overthrow the existing social order. By then, the debate over secularism in education had already passed, and no student group conceded that there was a "university problem," as the authorities and press conceived it.[71] The revolutionary students of the 1970s had broken with the tradition of the University Reform, although they continued to defend the need for autonomy. For these students, the problem was social in nature, and there was no sense in reforming the university without radically transforming society. They thought that persisting in a reformist attitude would isolate the university from society and turn a blind eye to capitalist exploitation, and they refused to resign themselves to building what they ironically called "the happy island."[72] Jacobo Tieffemberg, the president of the Argentine University Federation, made it clear that students had moved beyond the reformist tradition when he affirmed that student leaders were no longer like those in previous years.[73] Beatriz Sarlo has indicated that even groups tied with reformist traditions, such as the Franja Morada, led by the UCR, turned into anticapitalist groups in the early 1970s, joining, at least discursively, in the radicalization of language, which found in Marxist jargon a common ground for activists of different types.[74] Onganía's intervention against the universities in 1966 had become an unbeatable incentive for student politicization several years later. To the extent that the government of the "Argentine Revolution" was weakening in the society, the student left was strengthening in the universities.[75]

In early 1972, in a debate organized by *Panorama* magazine, young activists were invited to discuss the "fundamental conflict" that they were facing as members of their generation, without specifying which.[76] Belonging to different student groups, unable to agree about the figure of Perón, they agreed on one thing. None of them thought the specific problems they discussed, such as that of the family, could be resolved without radically transforming society. "The problem of the family can only be resolved by a single and total change of structures: this change is political and consists of the attainment of a socialism with national characteristics," declared an activist of the Argentine Youth for National Emancipation. In the same sense, a member of the Revolutionary Socialist Student Tendency indicated that "only by changing the foundations of exploitation and misery of the current society will we be able to organize a new society." Furthermore, the proposals for change did not exclude violence. "One doesn't only have to think about change," affirmed a sixteen-year-old girl, "one has to make it by taking power. If it is possible to accomplish this goal peacefully, that's best. But if they use force on us from above, there is no other choice but to resort to violence, and we must act. Without fear." In the discourse of the 1970s revolutionary activist, "there are no intermediate positions," as one of them asserted.

In the days of the Cordobazo, a young man from the Litoral Student Union declared that the struggle had radicalized to the degree that "those who will continue in the struggle will have to concretely embody in their own actions the idea of confronting the regime with the same weapons that it uses, while the others will return to the safety of their homes."[77] In another debate between activists, this time conducted by the *Confirmado* magazine, a student declared, "the struggle is many things. Terrorism also is. But I believe that in the Argentine political tradition, abstention is, for example, much more dangerous that terrorism."[78] The animosity toward all "intermediate positions" that these statements share made anathema any distance from radicalized political commitment. This logic had concrete consequences in the practice of university activists. Furthermore, the students who weren't activists could not escape some of its effects.

Returning again to the testimony of Susana Mancuso, who finished the first part of her studies in medicine in a university climate dominated by discourses such as those just reviewed, can help us contrast the political activist and nonactivist worlds. They were "extreme moments," Susana remembered, where

> you did not have continuity in classes, suddenly someone would come up to you and tell you: "everyone out, everyone out, we aren't going to have any more class because the teacher wants to give us a midterm and we don't want to take a midterm!" I participated in some assemblies, because I told my friends: "they are taking decisions that not everyone agrees on, and so I've got to participate." But for me, that stopped when I saw that they were saying: "alright, we are going to pat down for weapons, so that nobody enters the assemblies with weapons," and suddenly—we were discussing the subject of midterm exam dates—I remember that someone, the image that I have is: in the auditorium, on a counter that must have been, what do I know, twenty meters long, someone climbs up onto the counter, and starts to swing around a chain, trying to keep others away. "How is it possible"—I said—"that he could have entered with this if they had patted everyone down for weapons?" Well, a fight got started, fists, and I said "I'll never go back again." And I never went back. I said, "I'm not going anymore, because they are using us" [. . .] These were also times of threats against teachers, threats because they had some sort of conduct as teachers. They were annoyed if they failed their classes. They went to the Student Center and intimidated the teacher. If he failed you because you didn't go to class, well . . . it was a disorder. They even went so far as to put bombs in a teacher's car, for example, an excellent teacher, because they said that he was "military" ["milico"]—that's what they said. Being "military" wasn't actually being part of the military, but rather because of his ways, because he cut his hair short, because he demanded respect. I loved him. And I was antimilitary because I thought with the standards that my parents had applied, which were ones of freedom, justice, honesty: values. Here, instead, you began to discover: lies, abuse, violence, disorder, not studying . . .

The disorder and the arbitrariness that characterized student activities in the 1970s are also remembered by many ex-activists. It is less common to find in the memory of an activist the perception that the student leaders were taking advantage of their followers. In other testimonies of nonactivists I collected in Tucumán, the characterizations of the university leaders tended to be negative. In addition to what is stated in Susana's story, the most frequently mentioned aspects had to do with their foreignness with respect to the environment ("he wasn't a typical guy from Tucumán"), their lack of commitment to their studies ("he wasn't exactly the best student in the department, the guy that was concerned with that issue"), and the age difference that they had with respect to the majority of students ("they were much older than the rest of the group"). Overall, this perspective supports an important thesis regarding the evaluation that this social group made of the guerrilla organizations. In references to both the politicized student body and armed groups, the memories of those that were not involved in either tended to ascribe to the leadership greater age, less authenticity, and a great manipulative power over their subordinates.

With respect to violence, the activist and nonactivist conceptions of this term in the 1970s fundamentally differed in that, while the latter's conception defined something specific (related to direct force applied voluntarily against other people), the former considered it an equivalent term (applicable to many other situations or facts). For the activists, violence was not only what was commonly understood by the term. A series of other phenomena, such as social injustice, electoral prohibitions, poverty, a deficient health service, corruption, or inequality were also viewed as violence. On this point there was no difference among activists; Catholics and atheists, Peronist and non-Peronist leftists, all agreed.[79] José María Bosch, a pharmacy student at the Universidad de Buenos Aires and a Peronist activist with the National Student Union, participated in a volunteer work camp in the early 1970s in the north of the province of Córdoba. Remembering that experience, in response to my question about his conception of violence, he stated:

> I did not know that "deep Argentina." To see a girl bitten by the *vinchuca* [a beetle that causes the Chagas disease], and to see her cheek swollen the other day, that was violence. That girl had nothing. She didn't have her house. I learned to cut bricks, I spoke to the people, I stepped on mud, and I began to understand common people better, working shoulder to shoulder with them. There were students from Córdoba, from Buenos Aires, and there were seminary students. So, we didn't see violence only as something with bullets. Violence was starting to accept that these children infected by the *vinchuca*, 10 percent of whom would perhaps die before they turned forty, that these were part of the injustices of a regime that did nothing for them. Then, you start to accept that that also formed part of violence. That image serves you more than ten thousand books you can read [. . .] Humble people, hardworking people, to get to know their thinking, that was a really strong experience. You had no doubts any more. For me, that was crucial about justifying what the later violence would be [. . .] And we

knew that Peronism didn't vote, that there was a proscribed majority in this country, a majority that didn't have the right to elect its leaders, that was another form of violence.

The same year that José María traveled to the north of Córdoba, a young Peronist activist, responding to an editorial about violence, sent a virulent letter to the magazine Confirmado. "Here the violent ones are those who favor the great human injustices," he wrote, "illiteracy, infant mortality, large unproductive landholdings, the stealing of corpses (Evita), the psychological violence in educational institutions over the last 15 years; the lack of communication and participation of the people."[80] In the following year, a Panorama reader responded to Lanusse, who had declared that he would "not compromise with violence," affirming that "the family that lives in a luxurious palace is more explosive than a bomb."[81] In this vision, the imposition of force of someone over another person was only one form of violence among many. This logic implied that, if someone honestly declared themselves to be the enemy of violence in all of its forms, exercising it in its conventional sense practically became a moral imperative, legitimate self-defense.

The context in which this vision of violence extended itself was one of a more generalized political culture that transcended the youth. Separated from its specific task by the banning of political parties and relegated to an improbable future by the Onganía and Roberto Levingston governments, much of the political society of those days, from left, center, and liberal positions, endorsed the idea that "violence from above generated violence from below." Groups ranging from the Movement of Priests for the Third World to nonleftist political leaders such as ex-president Arturo Frondizi agreed on this formula.[82]

On the contrary, for the university youth that did not join the militant student movements, violence continued to define something specific. The chain whirled around in the auditorium, the bomb placed in the car of the "army" ("milico") professor, the gun to the head of the professor to pass a class, the repression exercised by the police; in all cases, specific violent acts not broad equivalents were condemned. This definition, and its condemnation, can also be found in the discourse of part of the youth portrayed by the media.

Just as Confirmado, Análisis, or Panorama organized roundtable discussions with activist students, other general interest media sources with a broader audience conducted interviews with youth that were distant from these movements. This was the case in a series of articles that appeared in Gente magazine in 1970. The common denominator among those youth was that they all rejected extremism and all forms of violence, even if they had political opinions. For these youth, violence and politics constituted separate spheres. In response to a journalist's question about what he believed about violence, a middle-class twenty-nine-year-old man who worked for an insurance company asserted that "our country is not violent" and that "the violence is only a product of isolated groups," which proved that "we Argentines do not consider it appropriate to solve our problems." "We know that not everyone thinks as we do," he finished saying, "and that there are groups that prefer violence and chaos to reflection [. . .] but these groups are a minority. The majority of young people think like we do: that the real solution for our country can be found through work and faith." [83] Part of the mass media called attention to this "other" youth that believed in the values of study, effort, or work, keeping a distance from radicalized attitudes and, of course, violence.[84] On television, many television series during the first part of the 1970s were directed to a "healthy" young audience.[85]

The activists recognized the existence of this other youth, criticizing what from their perspective was a "juvenile, innocent, ignorant, spoiled, and insulated order which exists parallel to the one in which adults agitate and fight in struggles for opposing interests." [86] This representation, however, was not entirely fair. A part of this other youth was interested in politics, although it did not become involved in activist movements or in revolutionary projects. Symptomatic of this is the television show about current political affairs in the country led by the journalist Bernardo Neustadt, an influential representative of the status quo. It had a primarily young audience and called on people under twenty-five to come on air to debate current events.[87] There existed not one but many youths. There was not only one politicized youth and another that was not politicized, but rather, among those who were interested in politics, there was a radicalized sector whose goal was social revolution and another sector that kept its distance from this project.

Some films of the period can help to complete the panorama of the youth world of the 1970s. The commercial film industry, for example, addressed the issue of student rebellion, its legitimacy and its limits. In The Hippie Teacher (El profesor hippie) (1969), a movie by Fernando Ayala, starring Soledad Silveyra and Luis Sandrini, in which the latter played the role of a twelfth-grade high school history teacher, students experienced all kinds of conflicts, but in no case were they linked with political issues. Sandrini, a teacher with a jovial, chummy, and clownish demeanor, always appeared to be closer to the youth than to the teachers and administrators, defending the students' rights to have long hair or offering refuge to a student who had problems at home. The moral was made clear in one of the pieces of advice that Sandrini gave to his students, "You can strike, but without violence." [88] The youth were permitted certain "transgressions," their "look," their music, and their right to protest, but not violence. In the following years, two other productions continued to follow the adventures of this teacher (*The Patagonian Teacher* [*El profesor patagónico*] in 1971, and *The Bomb-Throwing Teacher* [*El profesor tirabombas*] in 1972), both featuring Luis Sandrini, maintaining the limits of what was permitted and prohibited to the youth relatively unchanged.[89] Although this cinema went unnoticed by some politicized groups and intellectual circles, its success should not be underestimated, especially in some areas of the interior of the country, where film was the most common, if not the only, means of entertainment available.[90]

This type of film was abundant in comparison to all the available local productions, and the audience that was primarily looking for entertainment found in them an option that, additionally, included popular artists such as the previously mentioned Luis Sandrini or the singers Palito Ortega, Sandro, Sabú, and Donald. In these movies, youth was associated with happiness, with music and dance, with the desire for a better future or dreams related to success, fame, or love, and in all cases these were embodied by characters who never appeared associated with either political activity, or, of course, with violence.[91] In a 1972 movie, youth even appeared to be "crying out for peace."[92] Advertising also often turned to an image of happy and fun-loving youth, sometimes opposing it to people who refused to live life in this fashion. In Levi's ad for the fall-winter season of 1974, for example, four young people who were called "the appeared" were presented as being "possessed by the magical happiness of living," different from and indifferent to "the gray people that think that happiness is not of this world."[93]

The polarity between activist and nonactivist sectors of the student body was expressed by the nonactivists in terms of their right to study. This demand also implied taking a stand with respect to what the university and politics should be. Claudio Mastrángelo, a Correa resident who was studying optics in the Engineering School and history in the School of Philosophy and Letters (both in the Universidad Nacional de Rosario), responded the following when asked about the 1969 student revolt in the city of Rosario:

CLAUDIO: It caught me right downtown, and my dad saved me. Right in downtown Rosario. It was one of God's miracles, my dad saved me.

SC: What memories do you have of that?

CLAUDIO: Look, that day I had to take a test at the university, in the Engineering School, where I studied optics. I had to take a test, I'm living it as if it were today . . . Well, during all the time that I studied there, the school was always very revolutionary, very much full of posters, very subversive, full of everything from the left, but I never got involved because I went to study, I didn't go for those things [. . .] I can assure you that in my group, with whom we studied, nobody participated in those things. We never gave those things any thought.

Bernardo Curuchet, a student from Mendoza who ended up in Tucumán because the murder of Aramburu in 1970 caused his terrified family to decide to take him out of Buenos Aires, was another student who associated his university life primarily with study. He arrived in Tucumán in 1972 and kept away from political activity both during his studies and when he got married and began to work. Coming from a middle-class family, a child of a state power company employee and a housewife, in the scope of a question concerning his relationship with university activists, he remembered:

I went to the university cafeteria, and there I had the opportunity to see where everyone was coming from. And I saw the different groups, each one calling for their turn to speak, they stopped you, invited you to something, to some other thing, to this and that, and well, while one was eating there, you heard all that but once I stopped eating, I returned to my own things, because I had never participated nor been affiliated with any of the political parties. In the university cafeteria, we ate lunch and dinner, and in these lunches and dinners, each group made a demand for something or other [. . .] There were different groups with different politics. Left, right, center, there were some that called themselves Chinese, Maoists. And I remember that I said, "Mao Tse-tung? What does he have to do with anything here?"

sc: Did you get any invitations to join the political groups?

b: There was too much snobbery, I don't know how else you would call it. The guys that would climb up on the cafeteria tables and say "We have to retake . . . the assembly . . . and . . . !" Maybe it was the mailman that annoyed me, because I didn't know what the letter said. That way didn't get to me. Maybe if they had presented it differently and they had told me, "Come here, sit down, let's have a coffee, look, you know that this is like this, this and this, and really the way of getting to this or that is this path, based on such and such," well supported and everything, probably politics would have interested me.

FIGURE 2.3. "Get out! We want to study," signed: "The ones who study." Painted on the Engineering School of the Universidad de Buenos Aires. *Source: El Burgués* no. 12, September 29, 1971.

This excerpt illustrates two elements of how the nonactivists perceived the student politics of the 1970s: On one hand, the separation from some slogans ("Mao Tse-tung? What does he have to do with anything here?"). This separation was also present in the press of the period. "It is obvious that those who argue over the destiny of China or Cuba, more than about the concrete problems of our national reality," affirmed a journalist in an article on the Left, "end up being alien to it."[94] On the other hand, Bernardo confirms the "enlightened" element already analyzed in chapter 1. In the context of radicalization and mobilization of the 1970s, a part of those who did not participate in activism saw the verticalism that characterized this activism as a trait that threatened their autonomous rationality, their independence of judgment, their freedom of thought.

Claudio's and Bernardo's testimonies, however, are not identical. In the former, the traditional argument that the university is a place for study and not for politics criticizes university political struggles. In the latter, however, there is not a critique of the university political activism per se, but rather of the forms that it took in the 1970s. Many young people of that era distanced themselves from that specific form of activity rather than from politics as such. Gustavo Maíño, for example, who started his engineering studies at the Universidad de Buenos Aires in 1970, was interested in political events but he didn't become an activist because "the music [of radicalized activism] seemed out of tune to me." Watching images of the confrontation between Peronist factions in Ezeiza in 1973 in the documentary, he commented: "Well, the sensation of that confrontation that occurred internally, inside the country, was already very strong. It was like the logic of the 'Peronist Homeland' and the 'Socialist Homeland,' which was expressed with all of its force in Ezeiza. It didn't seem surprising to me. I didn't feel it was a surprising thing. It's like they played cards that they already had. In the university we lived that, that is what we lived, the Peronist Homeland, the Socialist Homeland."

SC: And who were with the Peronist Homeland in the university?

GUSTAVO: That's one of the acronyms I don't remember, identified with the unionists, but in my school they weren't strong. The JUP and the JP were stronger, those that were with the Socialist Homeland. And how much confusion there was! I didn't know very well how those that were further to the left were with the Socialist Homeland. It was like they didn't like it either. Because it was like a fallacy. But I did not understand these arguments much, it was like music that sounded out of tune to me. By feeling, I liked those who were with the Socialist Homeland more, but their argument did not seem to be a sustainable argument. There was more enthusiasm than rationality. Because it was like a fictitious rationality. It didn't attract me. They didn't get to me. The initial proposal yes, but it was like it was exhausted immediately. What was perceived, what was done in practice, was like painted cardboard, lots of trite phrases, little things, it was something that was like put together, put together by them, repeating what the books or pamphlets said, in any case. That was the sensation.

The students committed to political activism did not fail to notice the distance that separated them from some of their peers. "There are youth and there are youth," a student activist told *Análisis*, "the guy that is dedicated to going to the university, getting his degree, and getting better and better paid jobs, he has an orderly world to the extent that he is following the little straight path. The little straight path is safe and orderly."[95] Pichi Di Lauro, an activist of the national left in the Architecture School at the Universidad Nacional de Tucumán in the 1970s, remembered how he argued with that part of the student body that followed "the little straight path."

PICHI: There were many people with whom we argued, because they said: "I come here to study," "I want to graduate." Why? Why do you want to graduate? In what country do you want to graduate? In what economy will you work? In other words, what are you preparing for? For a country like Canada or the United States? Who is going to commission you to make houses? What do you want, to make weekend homes, to design chalets? We want to change the university program. We don't need a program directed toward making pretty houses for the rich. We have to make a program devoted to solving the housing problem in Argentina, where there are people that don't have enough money for a shack, that is what we told those that said "I don't come to the university to do politics," because you, with that attitude, you are doing politics.

What the student interviewed by *Análisis* magazine contemptuously called "the straight little path" had its mirror image in what Juana Alberdi, a non-activist student whom I interviewed in Tucumán, called with no less disdain "the little schoolhouse." Juana, born in 1945, in addition to dedicating herself to poetry, studied English teaching as well as psychology at the Philosophy and Letters department at the Universidad Nacional de Tucumán in the 1960s and 1970s. The university was one place in the morning, where she took English classes with a small group of students, and an entirely different place in the afternoon, when she attended other classes. The English teacher training program, Juana states, had a "bad reputation" politically. In a university like hers, she noted that the English program was linked to "Yankee imperialism or whatever else." "After hearing criticisms of this kind," she recalled the following about the student assemblies:

> I said, well, I've got to go and see what it's all about. So I went to an assembly in the auditorium, to see what they talked about in the speeches, what they talked about. They gave speeches and: ah . . . , fervent applause! Soon there was someone who disagreed about something, made his speech, said: "no, because for me it seems to be . . ." Ah, then came the whistles, the catcalls. "Aha," I said, "I know how this is: all applause or nothing. There are no middle terms, there are no criticisms possible." And I lost interest, I didn't go anymore. I wasn't going to lose time in an auditorium full of people that all agreed with each other and applauded themselves. It was like a match that had already been won beforehand. [. . .] I don't like ideologies, I don't like little schoolhouses, I don't like labels. Probably there is a little piece of this that is good, and a little piece of that which is good. You know what I don't like. When they serve you the dish you eat in your house as if it was a program. It is a program. You have to do step 1, step 2, and so on. It's the same thing that happened to me in the United States, when I was twenty years old, when I went to a mass. It was: get up, sit down, a little song, it was the little schoolhouse!

The worlds of the activists and the nonactivists, those of the "little schoolhouse" and of the "little straight path" existed parallel to one another. They were not alien to one another, something impossible in this context. They coexisted in the universities and university high schools, but nobody thought it was essential to establish an understanding between the two. For the activists, the nonactivists did not rise to the level of becoming a problem. For nonactivists, the activists did not represent any solutions. They were worlds that were connected but did not communicate with each other. However, for almost no one in either of the two worlds was the main enemy a student.

An event that put this basic solidarity among students to the test was the "Trelew Massacre" in August 1972. After a failed escape attempt from the jail in Rawson, sixteen young guerrilla fighters were captured and executed by the armed forces. Ricardo Montecarlo, a medical student without political involvement from the Universidad Nacional de Tucumán, upon seeing the image of one of the militants of the People's Revolutionary Army who was murdered in Trelew, said:

> There's Clarisa Leaplace! I knew her personally. She's from Tucumán. I knew her because we used to go to the students' parties. I had friends in the Economic Sciences School and we organized dances, like that, in the house, and I don't know what she studied, if it was economics or what, but she was the girlfriend of one of the guys that studied economics. She died in Trelew. It was in the Lanusse period. And that hurt me a lot. It hurt me a lot because of the way that they killed them. It was a murder. There's Santucho's wife, Clarisa, and there was another girl from Tucumán as well. And some escaped, I don't remember well who they were, I believe they went to Chile in a plane, and they shot those that stayed. Lanusse gave the order. I went to the wake, there was a great sadness, the injustice made you angry, it really did, people were really sad . . . We all went, even not being of her political ideology, because well, it touched us so closely. It makes you sad because, how can I tell you? [He pauses, and gets emotional.] They must have been such sons of bitches to kill a girl!

Susana Mancuso did not write anything in her journal about the executions in Trelew. Judging by this document, the event seemed to have less importance for her in her last year of high school than the student assemblies or the death of the student in the Tucumanazo. Today she remembers the event being discussed when she started university in 1973. In response to being asked if she remembered discussions of the armed struggle, she answered that

> the armed struggle was talked about, but not in my environment. In the assemblies, they used the martyrs of Trelew and such things as examples. All of that always appeared, but more as the story of the indoctrination that the group had prepared politically. In reality, they were emphasized, more than as examples to follow, but as: "how bad the others are," "how bad, look what they have done to these poor people." And one still believes in these things, because you say, "well, of course . . ." And I continue to think so in some ways, in other words, that when those that have power act in the same way as those that don't, well, I think that they are being as savage, because that is the word, as the others.

Gustavo Maíño, reflecting on his perception of political activism, commented:

August 22, 1972 [the date of the massacre], arrived. The generalized feeling was that of indignation. There is a very strong generational register: this feeling that "they're killing us." Even if I wasn't in any activist current, in the university the feeling was shared by everybody. Except for those that had very clear interests to defend, class interests. And that was noted very clearly: they were taking care of Daddy's wallet [. . .] "They're killing this generation," that was my feeling. It wasn't something that was said.

Beyond ideologies, beyond activist circles, it is likely that, within the university spaces that Ricardo and Susana remember in Tucumán or that Gustavo remembers in Buenos Aires, these feelings were not the exception but rather the rule, especially in urban centers. This is something more difficult to sustain, as shall be seen, among members of the middle classes that did not belong to a symbolic space as clearly defined as the university.

The expression "they're killing us" had an undeniably generational and sectorial implication. This "us" were the youth, but not just any youth, since the guerrillas killed in Trelew, as well as most of the leaders of the armed organizations, belonged to the middle classes and in many cases were or had been university students. Only their political activism differentiated them from Ricardo, Susana, or Gustavo. In everything else, they were the same: young, middle-class, university students.[96]

The growing equivalence being drawn by some sectors of public opinion between university students and (potential or actual) guerrillas began to weaken the old solidarity of the middle classes with students. Moreover, this equivalence was fed by military (1969–1973) and Peronist (1973–1976) state discourse and by the university activists who considered the armed organizations to be their vanguard. However, among students, student solidarity continued to prevail.

The World Outside the University

A consideration of the testimonies of the middle classes that did not participate in the university world leads to three general conclusions. The first, which is no less true for being obvious, is related to geographical location. Both in Buenos Aires and in Correa, which did not experience social unrest like Córdoba, Rosario, Mendoza, or Tucumán, the recollections about the uprisings were diffuse. While in Tucumán the unrest that occurred in the city has remained in the memory of the population with clarity, this is not so in the other sites. Thus, it can be said that for the middle classes not directly involved in the political struggle, the memory of social violence appears determined by proximity to the events—something that is interesting to compare with their recollections of guerrilla violence, where the same thing does not occur.

A second conclusion, valid with nuances for all three sites studied, is that both social unrest and political activism tended to inscribe themselves within the context of more general memories and opinions, framed by the memory of both guerrilla and state violence.[97] Many respondents skipped from one topic to another carelessly. In their memories, the armed actions have tended to eclipse the broader and unarmed social struggles; this is particularly evident in the case of Tucumán. Because of this, the testimonies about violence from these sectors—nonactivist and nonstudent—are analyzed in the next chapter. The repressive violence of the state, however, differed clearly from the others. All the respondents, no matter how apolitical they may have been, knew what they were talking about when they spoke of repression. In the case of the guerrilla violence, the opposite frequently occurred; on various occasions, respondents carelessly moved from speaking about the Rosariazo, Tucumanazo, or university activism to speak about "subversion," "terrorism," or the "guerrillas." By contrast those who were in the universities established differences between student activists and guerrillas and associated them only when they had reason to do so and not generically. Perhaps the best example of this difference is a reflection made by one of the people I interviewed in Buenos Aires, who was not in university in the 1970s (he was born in 1926) and who, in response to my attempt to distinguish the university activists from the guerrillas, told me: "well, for us, they were all Montoneros."

A final conclusion is that the responses of those who were not in university tended to be more heterogeneous. If among those who were students, the attitude toward social unrest and political activism oscillated between sympathy and caution, disapproving of activist violence but maintaining generational and sectoral solidarity, in the nonuniversity sectors these attitudes are not prevalent. Especially in Buenos Aires and Correa, many accounts can be characterized by a distancing from social upheaval and a disapproval of radical activists. It is more difficult to find stories of support for the revolts and sympathy toward the activist groups in this segment of the middle class. I will now analyze two testimonies, both from Buenos Aires, that exemplify these attitudes.

Commonalities between the two respondents make the comparison relevant. Both from Buenos Aires, they are approximately of the same age, neither studied in university because they needed to start working, both were employees of similar pay grades (one was a bank employee and one an administrative worker), both came from working-class families (both are first-generation middle class), and both were able to buy their own house and car for the first time in the 1970s. The main difference was their political affiliation. Although neither participated actively, one was Socialist and the other Peronist.

Carlos Etcheverría, born in 1947 in Haedo, twenty minutes by train from the city of Buenos Aires, finished high school and soon moved to the city, where he lived and worked for much of the 1970s. The son of a Peronist worker and a Socialist mother, he identified more with the political ideology of his mother, whose influence was complemented by that of her brothers — Carlos's uncles — who were active Socialists. His political memories of his childhood and adolescence were tinged with a strong anti-Peronism. In 1969, he was an employee of the Banco Francés-Italiano para la América del Sur, one of whose principal clients was the Fiat company. During our first meeting, when he narrated his life history, he confused the 1969 Cordobazo with the 1972 case of Oberdan Sallustro, the CEO of the Fiat Argentina company who was kidnapped and later killed by the ERP. The confusion, however, had some justification. In 1969, the Fiat company unions, SITRAC-SITRAM, had one of the principal roles in the Cordobazo. The "confusion" indicated something other than a mere error, however. As the other two meetings confirmed, for Carlos, the murder of Sallustro — in reality, the whole saga of the kidnapping, the ransom demand, and finally his killing — had a greater impact than the social unrest.

On two occasions, we spoke about his memories of the social unrest. The first time, before I provided him with any visual stimuli, he responded to my question about how he remembered those episodes, saying: "bringing myself back to that moment . . . I, all actions that are extreme, it's like I reject them from the beginning. Because I'm not accustomed to that. Yes, it's a social demand. Theoretically you can see it clearly, or you can elaborate on it. But in reality, I didn't even think of getting mixed up in that, nothing of the sort. Don't forget that I grew up in the 'don't get involved' period, which was very Argentine. At least those of my generation are like this."

This response caught my attention, especially its conclusion. His time was also that of the youth who became political activists and in some cases took up arms. Carlos was twenty-two in 1969; members of his generation and of the ones immediately following it abounded in activist ranks. What was striking was that when I interviewed former activists of the same age, they also attributed their situation to the totality of their generation—each spoke of themselves as if they were speaking for their entire generation.

When we met again three months later, we saw the documentary, which featured images of the Cordobazo. I asked him once again about this event and about his views of political activism:

SC: Do you have any memories of the Cordobazo?

CARLOS: For me, the Cordobazo was just some news, nothing more. Yes, I read about it in the press, and that was it. I wasn't so absorbed in those types of things. Now, don't think that . . . ; I had the same apprehension or the same ignorance of the army as I did of the unions. All the institutions, how can I tell you? I lived from my work, in my work you had to follow the law, you had to carry out all the obligations that you had, and that was enough for me. I didn't have any need to enter any kind of strange situation of any nature. Then, well, the functioning of the institutions, they have to exist, then let them exist, but they don't raise my blood pressure, nor did they [. . .]

SC: And what perception did you have of the most radicalized youth?

C: And . . . how can I tell you? Yes, my position was structured around living and following the law, doing what I was interested in doing, within what I could and the limitations that I had, which, additionally, were not limitations that were only political or on my freedoms, but also cultural and economic limitations. Now, we were also educated in this way, perhaps because of the fact that our parents come from a time in which there were two classes in Argentina, in other words, when the middle class was not as well developed, and so they educated us not to have any interest in being the president or anything of the sort. So, well, you make your life, you do your work, you follow the law, you do your duty with your family. Now, that load is heavy. Maybe it would have been get involved in some political meddling and get a position that way. So, many times the activists, above all the university students, we saw that "well, but how many years have you been in the university?" Ten years. "How many classes did you pass?" Seven. "Shit! Not even one per year!" How can you not pass one class per year? One! But, alright, you know that the political organizations work that way. So, it's like one knows the plot, and well, doesn't believe them too much. Mind you, that doesn't go against the good orientation or intentions they might have. But, it does degrade them. Then, a little bit, what we said was "these guys like to set bombs more than they like to study." Our attitude was a little like that.

The images of the documentary helped Carlos place the Cordobazo in time. While in this interview we once again spoke about the Sallustro case while on the subject of the Cordobazo—which confirmed the sensationalist impact of this event on the politics of the day—he had now claimed, like others, to have received the news of the social unrest with relative indifference. What followed also appeared in other testimonies: the need to clarify that his distance from the revolts did not mean that he sympathized with the military. "Don't get involved" was a position he asserted implicitly, since at the same time it isolated him from the sectors in conflict and reaffirmed his condition as a citizen who follows the laws and does his job and thus does not have the "need to enter into any strange situations of any nature."

Disapproval of university activism reinforced his negative vision of political practices. The individualism that seems to guide his thought in both answers helps us understand what he thinks of those who did commit themselves to political action. In his view, politics appears marked by the possibility of individual advancement, a view that was probably colored by the evolution of Argentine politics, of rich people who enriched themselves while in public positions. Carlos did not get mixed up in "any strange situations" because he followed the law and focused on his job; and as this constituted a "heavy load," he believed that it might have been easier to "get involved in some political meddling and get a position." Politics refers, for Carlos, to an individualistic option for personal salvation. In the stories of the people who defended their indifference toward the political struggles of the 1970s, the association, if not the reduction, of the university activists to the "bomb throwers" was also not uncommon.[98] Carlos additionally remembered the lack of commitment to study that he attributed to them and believed that their excessive radicalization took away their credibility, and "degraded' their demands.

If Carlos's testimony contains two very common attitudes (distance from social unrest and disapproval of radicalized activism), that of Eduardo Álvarez is an example of an attitude of solidarity with the revolts and of support for certain activist demands. Eduardo was born in 1944, the child of Spanish parents who arrived in Argentina in the 1920s, and he lived in a tenement until 1949, when Evita gave his mother a house in the Perón neighborhood of Buenos Aires, now called Saavedra. His memories of the 1950s and 1960s are the opposite of those of Carlos. Particularly noteworthy were a memory of some older anti-Peronist cousins entering the house and (playfully) telling him, "This is what we'll do to all the Peronists: bam-bam-bam-bam-bam," imitating the sound of a machine gun; and the bombardment of the Plaza de Mayo on June 16, 1955, during which his father could have been killed. Upon finishing high school, he didn't enter university because it was "still something unattainable for us," and in 1961 began to work as an administrative employee for the Molinos Río de la Plata business, of the Bunge and Born group.

During our first meeting, he remembered the events in Córdoba in 1969 thus:

SC: Where were you when the Cordobazo occurred?

EDUARDO: I was in Buenos Aires, working.

SC: How did you receive the news?

E: And . . . With a certain happiness, you see? With a certain happiness. It brought to mind the counterrevolution of '55, no? An act of rebellion.

SC: You saw it as revenge for '55?

E: And yes, yes, more or less, yes. In that moment, eh? I lived through it with a certain euphoria. I was already twenty-five years old. I had already worked for Molinos for eight years, and was earning more or less well [. . .] The Cordobazo had a connotation, even if it came from the left, very much from the left, it had a connotation with the Peronism that would later begin to emerge, the Peronism of the left. Isn't that right? Then there was some connection.

Eduardo perceived the Cordobazo as a Peronist event. In another interview, he clarified that this social uprising was tied with combative trade unionism, but this was something he found out later. At first he remembered having registered it within the context of the Peronist resistance, which he secretly felt part of, because of the seven hundred people in the Molinos administration, only he and a supply chief were known to be Peronists. From the Cordobazo on, Eduardo placed his hopes in Perón's return.

From his place in the business, he lived through the rise of the "base unions," a union movement that challenged the complacent policies of the traditional trade unions, which, in the case of Molinos, were represented by the Argentine Mill Workers Union. He explained his own political affiliation as follows:

sc: Were you ever an activist with any political or armed organization?

EDUARDO: No, no. Not at all.

sc: And with the Montoneros, did you belong to some sector of its sympathizers?

E: I identified with that line of Peronism. I never went to the Peronist party local because it didn't last at all. I didn't have an activist group but rather a group of belonging, of being in agreement with a bunch of things that they were proposing, such as the base unions, that were asking for a bunch of things, improvements, from the company. I participated up to that point.

This testimony was atypical. With the exception of Eduardo, I interviewed either activists or nonactivists; he located himself in a middle ground. He was one step away from becoming actively involved. The mention of the "Peronist party local" that "didn't last at all" refers to what almost constituted his point of entry into political activism. This group was started in the Mataderos neighborhood by two Montoneros activists who were Molinos employees and who invited him to participate, but he never did because shortly after the unit opened it was destroyed by a bomb that he attributed to right-wing Peronists. In a personal context marked by the establishment of his family—he got married in 1970 and his first son was born in 1972—this event convinced him to stay on the sidelines as a sympathizer. The activism that Eduardo was familiar with, and which, without participating directly, he supported in principle, was not university but rather trade union activism: Montoneros and ERP youth who were employees of the company and delegates of the "base unions."

Until mid-1973 Eduardo did not "split from" the political and ideological project whose leadership was embodied in the young Montoneros inside and outside the company. However, the process of radicalization translated into actions and demands that he no longer wanted to support. "In 1973, the takeover of the Avellaneda factory occurred," he told,

a very short time after Cámpora took office. And I am the one charged with making a collection, within the union central to pay for food costs and other expenses. Well, the base union begins to ask for things that were logical. "Alright, that's good, let's keep going," I thought. Until they start asking for just anything, and at that point, I said, "No, now they're wrong." They were taking everything toward a path that was too radical, so much so that the Pasquarosa brothers, who were noble and good people, went armed. They participated in the takeover of the Avellaneda factory, humiliating the managers. Moreover, at one point, after the takeover, they inaugurated a bust of Evita in the central courtyard, and then invited and pressured the managers from the central headquarters to come to the ceremony, and they made them sing the Peronist march! Literally. That is to say, there was total anarchy within what was the company. They asked for the head of one guy, who was the chief of staff of the Avellaneda factory. [. . .] There, I was in disagreement with the radicalized groups.

Later, practically, it was like I lost the reason to become related with something ideologically. First, because I had started a family. Second, because I was at risk of losing the source of my job, because it was total anarchy.

SC: When you say "anarchy," are you referring to the situation of the company, or of the country?

EDUARDO: It was total. Total. In the company and in the country in general. In the country, but also the company. We lived through anarchic acts. In other words, so that you have an idea, they were coming up the Panamerican highway—understand that the industrial park was down in General Pacheco—they were coming up, and, imagine, there were petitions for something and the company didn't grant them, and then, they would take one of the owners' sons, and they would hang him from the second floor of a building, hanging there, and if they refused the petition, they would throw him off! For example, you see? No, no, things were really scary. It wasn't Iraq, but the story was out there. [. . .] I didn't want an anarchic business in this way either. When I started and I became involved with the base unions, I did it with the goal of, "Alright, let's search for improvements, some type of social benefit." Up to that point, all good. But when things transcended all that, no.

What Eduardo found impossible to support included actions beyond the company's domain. For example, in the wake of the mass liberation of prisoners from the Villa Devoto jail that occurred in the dawn of the Cámpora government, he thought "here we went too far." Although he would soon repent and become critical of Perón, until 1973 his hopes had been deposited in the return of the leader whom he had always admired. His sympathy toward the Montoneros also rested on this foundation. As the positions began to radicalize, he remembers, "I realized that there was another project which was not that of either Perón or Cámpora."

Eduardo Álvarez and Carlos Etcheverría summarize two of the most significant behaviors of the nonactivist middle classes during the 1970s with respect to the social uprisings and political activism. One could be described as
their transition from empathy and even support to moderation and, when the
political process began to be radicalized, disapproval. The most noteworthy
trait of the other behavior was distance. Disapproval of the process of political radicalization implied the end of indifference. And, it can be said that this
disapproval was shared not only by those who were initially indifferent to the
project, but also by some (like Eduardo) who at first had been enthusiastic
toward the project embodied by the politicized youth and showed solidarity
with the social rebellions.

It would be wrong to conclude that this enthusiasm or solidarity was "not
enough" to excite the middle classes about the political-ideological project
advanced by the activist youth and the combative sectors of the workers'
movement. In fact, it was always something else. In the phase of disenchantment of the majority of the society with the regime of the "Argentine Revolution," social protests tended to be justified by diverse social and political
circles, including military sectors opposed to Onganía. The middle classes
were no exception to this. However, this support encountered concrete limits
when, with the process of radicalization of social protest and the rise of
armed organizations, violence began to take an exclusive role. The emotional
foundations that determined both their solidarity toward the student demonstrations and their opposition to police repression and the government officials responsible for it did not lead to, either before or after the appearance
of social violence, a support for revolutionary politics.

Unlike Buenos Aires and Tucumán, Correa did not face concrete manifestations of political violence in the period that stretched from the Cordobazo
to the Falklands War (1969–1982). There were no political demonstrations or
social unrest, nor were there political disappearances or repression. Unlike
the 1950s, the 1960s and especially the 1970s are remembered as being not
only peaceful but also economically prosperous.

The recollections of social unrest that I collected in Correa tended to co-
incide on one point: the student and worker revolts, even those in nearby
Rosario, did not go beyond being news in the press or on television that did
not reach or affect them. Phrases like "in the towns these things were not experienced as they were amongst those in the upper ranks"; "here there were
no people involved in these things"; and "nothing happened here; the Cordobazo was virtually unnoticed" were the common denominator of the interviews in Correa.

A document from that time serves to qualify or perhaps complete these memories. Father Ignacio Canavera, the town priest, created a biweekly newspaper called *La Voz de Correa* upon his arrival in 1949, in which both the evolution of the town and the issues that moved its population can be followed in detail. All members of the Correa middle class interviewed were readers of the newspaper. In 1969 it had five hundred subscribers, which according to its editor suggested "an average of 2,500 readers, as a very moderate estimate."[99] By the end of 1982, there were almost seven hundred subscribers.[100] Since there were no radio or local television stations, the newspaper was the only medium that reflected what happened in the town. It mainly published births, marriages, and deaths and chronicled the events in the town that stood out, such as the installation of a factory, the paving of new streets, changes in municipal authorities, or the victory of Correa's soccer team. These characteristics make it important that, at a certain moment, the paper began to mention national issues.

The newspaper marked patriotic holidays; every year, as the date approached, it included a brief history of July 9, 1816, and a program of the town's commemorative activities. In 1969, it added an atypical paragraph. "Lamentably, the current circumstances are not very auspicious to awaken the patriotic enthusiasm of those of us who pass our existence in this nation blessed by God," *La Voz de Correa* affirmed. "The recent episodes," the paper continued, "which have shaken the deepest fibers of feeling in the average man—who represents the immense majority of the Argentine people—have left inevitable aftereffects of discouragement and apprehension and leave a cold breeze of doubt and suspicion floating in the air. It would seem that every day ominous clouds are gathering over the clear horizon of our Nation."[101] Social unrest had an impact in the municipality of Correa. The newspaper was part of a rhetoric present in the national and provincial press that situated the "average man" and the "immense majority of the Argentine people" in a place that was alien to the events that "shook the deepest fibers" of their feeling. This affirmation, while confirming the sense of estrangement from the social uprisings, also completes the memories by referring to the effect that they had on the "average man," a category that presumably includes residents of Correa.

La Voz de Correa's worries about the violent course that national events were taking in the 1970s continued to grow. At the end of 1970, in its usual annual issue, it alluded to the "difficult moments that our generation is forced to live through" and the "bleak panorama that our Nation offers."[102] In 1971, it surprised its readership with a reflection about the guerrillas, something unprecedented for the newspaper. At the end of 1972, it published a Christmas message different from those of previous years, which specifically referenced the issue of violence. Speaking of the Christian holiday, the paper affirmed that

> its maximum symbol is the symbol of peace: peace for the mind, peace for the family, and peace for the nations. [. . .] Because of this, it should essentially be a holiday of peace and fellowship between all men, without noisy rejoicing or out-of-tune racket. It should involve deep and collected meditation, sincere and profound prayer that this peace, distant today as never before, finally arrives like the dawn of a new era. Without hatred, without anger, without useless violence that constructs nothing and leads nowhere, in an era of progress and advancement, which due to some painful irony has lagged far behind on the path of peace, cordiality and unity.[103]

No act of violence had occurred in the town. The reflection alluded to the national situation, and in a paradoxical age characterized by both progress and violence, Correa appeared linked to the former, and was alarmed by the latter.[104]

Correa residents were not involved in radicalized political activism.[105] At first glance, the sixty kilometers that separate them from Rosario and the more than three hundred that separate them from both Buenos Aires and Córdoba seem to explain their noninvolvement. However, the geographical distance, not so significant given that Rosario was a politicized urban center, cannot explain this phenomenon. The town was far from isolated; television (Buenos Aires's Channel 7 and Rosario's Channels 3 and 5) and radio were not the only media sources that reached Correa.[106] In addition to the Rosario newspaper La Capital, the national daily papers and the most important magazines could be obtained in the town. Contact with Rosario and with cities surrounding it, such as Cañada de Gómez and Carcarañá — all of which were connected by rail — was a daily event for much of Correa's middle class.

The strong penetration of content produced in the large cities can be observed in local cultural production, an outstanding example of which was the formation, almost as early on as in the metropolis, of a musical group whose audio/visual aesthetics were similar to their contemporaries in the urban centers. The musical group, named Viento en Contra (Against the Wind), was born at the beginning of 1969 and remained active until the end of the 1970s, playing in dances and festivals.[107] Aware of the musical developments of their generation, influenced by the Beatles, Creedence Clearwater Revival, and the national rock bands that these influences generated, Viento en Contra played the popular songs of the time, and its members had the same aspirations of fame and recognition as any other group of its type. Its existence demon-

FIGURE 2.4. Against the Wind (Viento en Contra) on the bridge in Correa on National Route 9, which connects the town with Rosario and Cañada de Gómez. *Source:* Author's archive.

strates the intense rapport that a small town like Correa could have with tendencies, beliefs, and attitudes that originated in foreign and national metropolitan centers.

Political activism, however, was something that the population of Correa kept its distance from. Their political inclinations did not translate to actual political participation in the movements of the time, even among the town youth, because the form that politics acquired in those years did not succeed in attracting them. It is insufficient to postulate that this lack of participation can be explained by the town's degree of isolation from the world or provincialism. Frequently in contact with Rosario, informed of all that appeared in the media, the people of Correa appropriated what caught their interest or provoked their passion. Having been the case for fashion or progressive music, it was not so for political activism or the armed struggle, and this was true of those who frequently traveled to Rosario.

Among the middle classes, the university was the setting for the radicalized form that politics in the 1970s assumed. This explains the fact that in places like Correa, where university students were a small minority, these forms did not take root. Since in Argentina the university was a social fact of undeniably middle class connotations, there has been a frequent tendency to conflate the latter with the former. However, an examination of the broad nonactivist sectors of the middle classes leads to the conclusion that radicalization was only one way of being a university student, particular to a significant part of the minority that went to university.

Almost a year before the social protests of 1969 broke out, *Panorama* magazine made an analogy to the situation in France, affirming that, if rebellion broke out, "Onganía, like de Gaulle, could capitalize on the fearful reactions of the middle class to the prospect of an overflow of violence."[108] The article was mistaken because Onganía presided over a revolution that by that point was no longer in a condition to capitalize on anything. However, the perception that the outbreak of violence would generate fear among the middle class turned out to be prophetic.

When I was young, everyone in the town went armed. My father too, of course.
But nobody ever killed anyone dishonorably, unless they were a coward or a scoundrel. Even
in the old Westerns, we hear the phrase "Turn around so I can kill you" coming from the
mouths of professional gunslingers. Today, they kill by night, without risk, anonymously,
putting bombs in a movie theater where innocent people will die, or cowardly kidnapping
innocent beings. What is the famous moral progress that this implies? — Ernesto Sabato

Three   Armed Violence (1970–1977)

Starting in 1969, armed violence in Argentina went through a process of sustained growth. Juan Carlos Marín counted 8,491 armed acts during the democratic period alone (from May 25, 1973, to March 24, 1976), both from insurgent and repressive forces.[1] Prudencio García estimated that there were a
total of 687 deaths that were caused by left-wing guerrilla organizations and
approximately one thousand murders and forcible disappearances executed
by the Argentine Anticommunist Alliance (Alianza Anticomunista Argentina), known as the Triple A.[2] The armed forces and security apparatus added
hundreds of deaths and disappearances to this total, before the 1976 coup.
In 1975 alone, the forces of order who were fighting the ERP in Tucumán —

where it had launched a rural guerrilla campaign in 1974—killed 253 people.[3] The mass media periodically reported on these acts. In March 1975, *La Opinión* counted two deaths per day from political violence.[4] *Gente* magazine published a list of 850 deaths produced by "the violence in Argentina" at the end of 1975, considering only crimes of the preceding twelve months.[5]

During the seven years that preceded the military dictatorship installed on March 24, 1976, the political dialectic ceded terrain to that of guns and the logic of reprisal that René Girard described in his study on the sacred character of violence; violent acts became the modus operandi of the dominant actors of the period.[6] In this chapter, I analyze the perceptions that the middle classes had of this process. I first consider several public opinion studies ignored until the present day that question the thesis that the guerrillas enjoyed the support of much of society, and especially the middle classes. Second, I study the way in which guerrillas were presented in the media through an analysis of a soap opera that enjoyed enormous popularity in 1972 and 1973. Finally, I analyze the interviews of members of the non-activist middle classes, contrasting, on the one hand, the three sites studied, and on the other, the archival documents and interviewees' testimonies.[7]

The Guerrilla: The Myth of Initial Sympathy

In a study that soon became foundational, Guillermo O'Donnell analyzed the issue of political violence and its relation with civil society. There, he affirmed that, based on survey data taken in 1971 and 1972, the "guerrillas during this period enjoyed the support, or at least the sympathy, of a remarkable proportion of the population," providing an "index of attitudes toward terrorism" that ascribed high levels of citizen support for this phenomenon.[8] Indeed, according to this index, 51 percent of the city of Rosario, 53 percent of the city of Córdoba, 49.5 percent of the population of the country's interior provinces (considered together), and 41.5 percent of greater Buenos Aires (which in the Spanish version of the book is 45.5 percent) approved of the actions of the guerrillas.[9] O'Donnell's verdict ended up installing itself as a cliché within much of academia, as his research introduced hard data regarding a subject then only analyzed through biased impressions and personal testimonies. The fact that O'Donnell himself indicated that he could not certify the reliability of these data, warning the reader that they could have a large margin of error, has been overlooked.[10]

This index was constructed by the American sociologist Frederick Turner who, between February 1971 and November 1972, conducted a project called Opiniómetro together with the IPSA company that aimed to measure the state of public opinion regarding the political situation in Argentina. Turner never published the index in question. Moreover, in one of his articles based on Opiniómetro data, he affirmed that the "sympathetic response" toward "subversive movements" represented less than a third of the population, a number significantly lower than what the index indicates.[11] This disparity is explained by the fact that Turner derived sympathy or hostility toward the guerrillas based on responses that were preestablished by the questionnaire. For example, when asked the question "What do you think about the people who form part of these subversive movements?" the interviewee had three options: "It is the only way to express their protest"; "They are isolated individuals who are motivated by their own need for violence"; and "They are people who don't really know what they want."[12] The first response implied "sympathy," and the other two "hostility."

Still, in the November 1972 Opiniómetro measurement—of the four that constituted the project, the only one currently available at the Roper Center for Public Opinion Research of the University of Connecticut—37.32 percent believed that the people that formed the guerrilla movements did not really know what they wanted, and 15 percent considered that they were motivated by their need for violence; only 23.76 percent opted for the "sympathetic" answer.[13] Unfortunately, the "hole-punch count" of these surveys does not consider distinctions between different social classes. In any case, it is clear that, as an empirical fact, society's sympathy toward the guerrillas was a construction of the researcher and not a concrete response from those interviewed.

Based on the original data collected by Turner, Roberto Pereira Guimarães attempted to identify the reasons for "the support for terrorism" in Argentina, analyzing a question that invited respondents to rank their sympathy for the guerrillas on a scale of 1 to 100. However, he stumbled across a problem that complicated his analysis. Of 737 respondents, 499 gave the armed groups a sympathy level of 0, 123 said they did not know, and 30 did not respond.[14] It would be methodologically erroneous to infer that the 85 respondents remaining sympathized with the guerrillas. As the survey itself explained, all those who mentioned a number under 50 placed themselves closer to hostility than to support. At any rate, Pereira Guimarães's affirmation that prefaces his analysis appears conclusive: "first, and above anything else, it [the analysis of the Argentine case] shows that in 1973 terrorism did not enjoy a high degree of support among the diverse social groups studied by Turner."[15] Reopening this discussion, which had remained practically closed after O'Donnell's investigation, will not only provide a new framework to understand the attitudes of the middle classes toward the guerrillas. It can also help enrich the more general debate about the relationship between political violence and civil society.

As Turner indicated in his article about the study of Argentine politics through survey research, another highly knowledgeable pulse taker in the field of Argentine public opinion was Dr. José Enrique Miguens, whose data were used by both Turner and O'Donnell.[16] Indeed, Miguens and CIMS conducted numerous public opinion studies during the 1960s and the early 1970s. The professionalism of his research was recognized when, during the March 11, 1973, elections, he was the only one of twelve pollsters that correctly predicted the social class composition of the voters that voted for each electoral formula in all districts studied.[17]

The same year that IPSA and Turner launched the Opiniómetro, CIMS devoted one of its studies to looking into the degree of dissatisfaction of the population with the existing sociopolitical situation. The poll included questions referencing the armed organizations. The study is revealing in two fundamental aspects. On the one hand, it demonstrates the level of dissatisfaction at the time (June 1971), high among all social classes although slightly lower among the middle classes. On the other, it indicated a level of support for the guerrillas that is substantially smaller than that accepted to this day.[18] Moreover, this disapproval turned out to be slightly more intense in the middle classes than for the average of the population.

The CIMS study was titled "Public Opinion Study About Degree of Dissatisfaction with and Support for the Functioning of the Existing System,"[19] and questions about the guerrillas were inserted within a wider questioning about the need for major changes in the country. In response to the question "Does it seem to you that the actions of terrorist, Montonero, subversive [or whatever you would like to call them] groups, in general deserve approval or disapproval?" the disapproving response was chosen by 73.5 percent in Capital Federal, by the same percentage in the greater Buenos Aires metropolitan area, by 70.5 percent in Rosario, and by 62.5 percent in Córdoba. Moreover, many who did not respond in such a manner avoided answering or said they did not know. Strictly speaking, those who approved of the actions of these groups represented 9.2 percent in Capital Federal, 14 percent in the greater Buenos Aires metropolitan area, 11.7 percent in Rosario, and 27 percent in Córdoba. In the upper- and lower-middle classes, according to the stratification that the study conducted, the disapproval was higher than the average of the total population, except in Capital Federal, where it was identical (75 percent of the upper-middle class and 72 percent of the lower-middle class, for an average of 73.5 percent). The upper- and lower-middle classes of the other districts chose a disapproving response, respectively, by 91.1 percent and 72.65 percent (81.85 percent average) in the greater Buenos Aires metropolitan area, by 68.8 percent and 73.9 percent (71.35 percent average) in Rosario, and by 71.4 percent and 63.4 percent (67.4 percent average) in Córdoba. If one now considers approval of the guerrilla groups, in three of the districts studied by CIMS, the upper- and lower-middle classes (taken together) responded with 11.9 percent support in Rosario, 10.85 percent in Buenos Aires city, and 9.75 percent in the greater Buenos Aires metropolitan area. Córdoba had an exceptional character, where 24.05 percent of its middle classes, considered together, approved of the guerrilla actions, three percentage points below the average of all the social classes in this city (27 percent). Consequently, the data establish that even at the beginning of guerrilla activity, the social support for the armed groups was restricted to a minority and that this support was less significant among the middle classes than it was on average for the whole population.

A very tough question confirmed this fact. "Although you may not be in favor of the government, nor in favor of the terrorists," the questioner said, "what do you think deserves more support: what the government wants, or what the terrorists want?"[20] Formulated thus, this question allowed for no gray areas; it demanded that respondents declare themselves in favor of a long-discredited government or terrorism. This led many people to not respond or to take refuge in feigning ignorance. Depending on the district, between 28 percent and 40 percent of those interviewed did not respond or said that they didn't know. The positive responses reinforce the thesis of the scant sympathy that armed groups generated in the population. Totals of 50.5 percent in Capital Federal, 60 percent in the greater Buenos Aires metropolitan area, 54.7 percent in Rosario, and 39 percent in Córdoba—the most rebellious district in almost all the surveys—declared themselves to favor the government (which only meant preferring it to the armed groups). Indeed, Córdoba had the largest percentage of respondents who preferred the armed organizations (31 percent). In the other districts, the percentages for this preference were far lower: 10 percent in Capital Federal, 11.7 percent in the greater Buenos Aires metropolitan area, and 13.7 percent in Rosario. If these results are compared with the responses about approval-disapproval of the armed groups, it can be observed that no district had a significant increase in support, even when the respondent did not have any other option than the feeble and discredited military government. Faced with this dilemma (government or terrorists), the middle classes showed percentages of support for the guerrillas' goals that were inferior to the average of the total population, with the exception of Capital Federal. There, 13.1 percent of the upper-middle class and 9.6 percent of the lower-middle class (11.35 percent average) selected the armed groups over the military government.[21] In the greater Buenos Aires metropolitan area, 2.2 percent of the upper-middle class and 12.8 percent of the lower-middle class (7.5 percent average) answered in the same fashion, which was 4.2 percent less than the population as a whole in this district. In Rosario, 13.3 percent of the upper-middle class and 12.6 percent of the lower-middle class (12.95 percent average) did so. Finally, in Córdoba, where the sympathy was greater, 28.5 percent of the upper-middle class selected the armed groups over the government, while 30.2 percent of the lower-middle class did so (29.35 percent average).

The data are consistent with those of another study that CIMS had conducted a year earlier, in April 1970, examining the attitudes of the population regarding "political terrorism."[22] One question inquired whether or not it was appropriate to recognize the right to political asylum for those accused of terrorism. It was clarified to the participant that this right was a tradition in Latin America and that governments were obligated to allow revolutionaries who took refuge in embassies to leave the country. However, they were informed that this treatment did not apply to common criminals. In response to the question of whether this right should be granted to those accused of terrorism or, instead, it was appropriate to treat them as common criminals, the majority were inclined to consider them in the latter category (68.9 percent). Of the remaining percentage, 12.9 percent replied that they didn't know, 5.9 percent refused to answer, and 12.3 percent considered that the right to asylum in these cases should be accepted—a percentage very similar to that of the average of the population that, one year later, declared its approval for the guerrillas.

Regarding how to punish those who committed crimes such as the hijacking of airplanes, 18.9 percent selected the death penalty, 45.6 percent long-term prison sentences, 9.7 percent short-term prison sentences, 3 percent the application of heavy fines, 0.4 percent forced labor; 14.5 percent said they were unsure, and 6 percent preferred not to respond.[23] Only 1.8 percent considered that those who hijacked an airplane should not be punished. Two years later, society seemed to have hardened its position.[24] A survey conducted by IPSA in April 1972 in Capital Federal and the greater Buenos Aires metropolitan area concluded that those who declared themselves to be in favor of either the maximum punishment that the law allowed or the death penalty added up to 31 percent. According to the magazine that published the poll, a comparison of this figure with earlier measurements was evidence of "a notable hardening of public opinion on terrorism."[25] Other authors and studies mentioned, including those of O'Donnell and Turner, agree with this point. In conclusion, the analysis of the data presented is sufficient to question the idea that, at the beginning of their activities, the guerrillas enjoyed high percentages of sympathy among the population and specifically among the middle classes.[26] On the contrary, this support was scant (an average of about 11 percent, excepting Córdoba) and the middle classes were not in its vanguard.

A series of interviews conducted in 1971 by *Panorama*, who named the "average Argentine" as its "person of the year," support these conclusions.[27] At that time, a thirty-one-year-old employee of the state telephone company said that "the kidnappings and the assassinations and all that" angered him and made him see that there was no solution; a thirty-five-year-old employee of a television manufacturing company and technology student declared that he saw the political climate as "dangerous," that "anything can happen to you on the street," and that he didn't agree with violence; and a banker who was almost forty years old said that he didn't agree with either the Gran Acuerdo Nacional[28] or the guerrillas. "It makes me remember that movie, *We Are All Murderers* [*Somos todos asesinos*] that I saw a long time ago," he continued; "I think of my children and I think that I can't give them a climate of violence."

In reality, by 1971 the "Argentine Revolution" had already spent five years disappointing expectations. In March of this year, the doctrine that established that during incidents of unrest, the police should act first, followed by the security forces, and only as a last resort the armed forces, had been replaced by that of preventative action, which authorized them to intervene any time a conflict was foreseen.[29] Regarding the economy, the stabilization of the currency achieved after a huge devaluation of the peso was already a thing of the past. Economy Minister Aldo Ferrer's price controls had proved to be ineffective at curbing the inflationary spiral. In the month of May, A&C determined that 87 percent of the population expressed fear of the rise of prices and wages.[30] This was a major failure for a revolution that had made growth without inflation a primary goal. Devaluations had returned, although by moderate percentages. In October 1971, rates and prices had risen between 45 percent and 50 percent with respect to December 1970, while wage increases did not exceed 30 percent and the issue of housing—which was expensive for the middle classes—had worsened.[31] One of Quino's cartoons masterfully illustrated the sense of impoverishment experienced by the middle classes around 1971. A group of poor people, standing at the bottom of a hillside, yells up to the middle classes not to move down so quickly because it is already too crowded.[32]

It is relevant that the same magazine that named "terrorism" as its "person of the year" for 1970, one year later selected the "average Argentine" as the main protagonist of 1971—"one of the most difficult [years] of the century."[33] The reason for this choice was given once again as violence, as in 1970, but in this case the "person" selected was not one who exercised but rather one who suffered from it. "Member of a violent society—without being violent himself—, witness to and victim of a process that he suffers from but does not direct," Panorama wrote, justifying its choice, "the average Argentine took some beatings that will take him time to digest." Panorama—whose main readership was the middle classes—is a good example of how many of the middle sectors that were not absorbed in the political struggle experienced the early 1970s. From its perspective, "terrorism" was visible, but the "average Argentine" remained hidden. Terrorism had identifiable names, was violent, and the product of a minority. The average Argentine was anonymous, silent, and part of the majority. If Panorama reserved its condemnation for the former, it deposited its hope in the latter. The conclusion that the magazine drew deposited a seed of latent rebellion in the middle class. "Long-suffering and battered," Panorama wrote, "the average Argentine does not resign himself, however, to a country with no destiny, with no happiness, with no peace."

Rolando Rivas, Taxi Driver: Guerrillas and the Moral World

At the end of the 1960s, the issue of the guerrillas began to form part of the social imaginary. In this section, I propose to analyze the way in which, in 1972 and 1973, the guerrilla issue was treated in the successful soap opera Rolando Rivas, taxista (Rolando Rivas, Taxi Driver)—a genre that, as Robert Allen affirms, involves its audience with a degree of depth and breadth that is unprecedented in the history of storytelling.[34]

The soap opera narrated the life of a worker from the lower-middle class, a taxi driver, owner of his vehicle and of a house in the neighborhood of Boedo that was as dignified as it was old. Written by the already acclaimed Alberto Migré, it achieved an unprecedented popularity in 1972 and 1973 and became the most successful soap opera series in the history of Argentine television until that time.[35] The series was broadcast on Tuesdays at 10 PM, and, according to the interviewees, "the whole country stopped to see it." Although the love story between a poor young man and a young lady from high society was not original, this soap opera introduced two innovations.

First, it featured an unprecedented number of references to the political and economic realities of the country.[36] In this section, I deal with those references to political violence and possible solutions to the social crisis of those days, focusing on the political conflict involving the armed organizations. A sign of the program's capacity to shape society's vision of the guerrillas is that the main press organ of the Montoneros, El *Descamisado*, published a furious criticism of the show that was intended to sway the audience away from its "confused and numbing" proposal.[37]

Second, *Rolando Rivas, taxista* brought adult women, who were the traditional consumers of the genre, together with people of all ages and a male audience, perhaps for the first time to such a massive degree. The soap opera had something to say to each generation and each gender. The show's first chapter was preceded by a long appeal by the main character to different types of viewers. The scene was situated outside of the storyline, almost as a prologue. There the author socially identified the audience to which he directed his creation (a housewife, a fashion-conscious twenty-year-old young man, a university student, a merchant, retired grandparents). More than being a show for the whole family, it can be said that *Rolando Rivas, taxista* sought to combine elements that appealed to every member of the typical middle-class family.[38]

Quique Rivas, Guerrillero

Rolando Rivas's family was composed only of siblings; he had neither parents nor children. Nonetheless, the family roles were clear. Noemí (María Elena Sagrera), the oldest sibling, was the sister-mother; a spinster of sorts, she took care of the household tasks and acted like a widow. Juanjo (Pablo Codevilla) studied in high school, did not work, and was the brother–adolescent son. Nené (Miriam Antelo) was the sister–young daughter, who attended elementary school and loved her brother Rolando [Claudio García Satur] like a father and respected her sister Noemí like a mother. The clan was completed by two young but no longer adolescent men: Rolando himself, the brother-father of the family, and Quique (Darwin Sánchez), a brother-brother three years younger than the main character. Of the five siblings, only Quique was married, unhappily, to Matilde (Leonor Benedetto), who in turn was in love with Rolando, in whose house she lived.

Before analyzing Quique's story, it would be appropriate to present Rolando's character, which was in a way the anti-Quique. Rolando was honest, simple, supportive, helpful, willing to sacrifice, and transparent. Furthermore, and above all these things, he was a worker who loved what he did; "he grabb[ed] the steering wheel like Troilo did the bandeneón."[39] After getting to know him, a secondary character in the soap opera defined him as a "man from Buenos Aires, the prototype of the *porteño* that is in danger of becoming extinct."[40] The soap opera tried to sound an alarm about the extinction of not just the character type that Rolando embodied, but of the values that he expressed.

Unlike Rolando, Quique studied at the university. Rolando respected Quique's studies and tended to justify them in arguments with his sister-in-law. Quique was an absent person, who appeared little in the house and communicated least, compared to the rest of the family. The viewer first found out something about this enigmatic character when his wife, Matilde, said that Quique "wasn't studying" but rather "reading Varllosa" or "the other one, Marcós or Marcose," before being immediately corrected by the youngest Rivas: she was referring to Vargas Llosa and Marcuse. Quique was a university student among nonstudents; his wife was as foreign to his world as he was to the world of the family.

The viewer found out more about Quique through other characters than through what the story itself showed of him and his activities. He had practically abandoned his wife, who lived "as if she had no husband," and speaking with him about her unhappy situation was "to lose time." He was a "pretty boy"; he dressed fashionably, paid attention to appearances, and fundamentally lived off the work of others.[41] Although, in fact, the description could have fit the entire family, only Quique was depicted as a "pleasure seeker."[42] Unlike Juanjo and Nené, he was already an adult and old enough to work. Unlike Noemí and Matilde, he did not perform any domestic tasks. In short, Quique was presented as someone unconcerned about his family, concerned about appearances, a reader of "strange" authors, and a parasite living on the work of others. His selfishness contrasted with Rolando's generosity.

To comprehend the outcome of Quique's story, it is necessary to make a brief mention of the soap opera's main plot, the relationship between Rolando and Mónica Helguera Paz (Soledad Silveyra), a high-society girl ten years his junior who was a student at a private religious high school. Daughter of Fernando Helguera Paz, holder of "one of the country's largest fortunes,"[43] Mónica met Rolando by chance when she took his taxi and, after attempting to commit suicide by throwing herself from the vehicle, ended up beginning a relationship with him that would with time become a tangled romance. Before that, however, an event that was unexpected for the audience and certainly atypical for the soap opera genre placed Mónica and Rolando on opposite sides of a political confrontation. Quique Rivas participated in the kidnapping of Mónica's father by the leftist armed organization to which he belonged and was killed when confronted by the police. Mónica's father escaped unscathed—although some time afterward he was killed by Quique's comrades in reprisal for his death.[44]

The viewer learned that the kidnapping was underway when a member of the insurrectional group informed Quique that he had been designated to participate in the operation. The mission was entrusted to him on board a vehicle, in a lugubrious tone that transmitted fear, which was expressed on Quique's own face. The dialogue went as follows:

GUERRILLA: I can't answer you, Rivas.

QUIQUE: Alright.

G: You know how this is [deepening his voice, with a dictatorial tone]: no explanations. The less we speak, the better.

Q: Yes, yes, of course, of course. But I thought that the plan was to kidnap the girl, Mónica Helguera Paz, and not the father.

G: At first yes, but there was a change of plans. It has to be the father. We are going to test how fit you are. And right now. The Army of Revolutionary Demands [Ejército Revolucionario Reivindicador] has great hopes for you. And we're going to see how you behave.

Q: [with a serious, intense expression, he nods without speaking, and remains silent] [45]

Quique was a recent arrival to the revolutionary organization and needed to prove himself to win the confidence of its leaders. Both the images and the speech represent the situation within a guerrilla group as being alienating; Quique was not convinced about what he had been ordered to do, but he would do it without any further explanations. He "knows how it is." He also later accepted the order that his superior gave him to be in charge of the transport of the kidnapped businessman, exposing himself to greater risk than the rest of those involved in the operation.

The contrast between the two Rivas brothers could not be greater. Rolando was a person who was full of life, smiled, made jokes, enjoyed his work, was concerned about others, and loved those close to him. Quique was just the opposite. When he appeared on screen, he looked serious and introverted; he ignored his family and always wore a look of resentment. The night before the kidnapping, upon Quique's return to the house, his brother was waiting for him. The scene occurs in the kitchen, and once again, the contrasts are striking: Quique had some books in his hands and was well dressed; Rolando was wearing house clothes and preparing *mate*. When Rolando put his hand on Quique's shoulder as a sign of affection, Quique reacted by rejecting it. Rolando obligingly offered his brother mate or coffee, but Quique did not ac-

FIGURE 3.1. Quique Rivas and a comrade from the Army of Revolutionary Demands (Ejército Revolucionario Reivindicador) upon learning that he had been assigned to participate in Helguera Paz's kidnapping. Source: Channel 13 and Proartel, 1972, chapter 10

cept. When Quique told him he had arrived late because he had been studying, Rolando asked him not to lie, that he should at least respect and not try to deceive him. None of this, however, occurred due to Quique's political activities, which were unknown to the entire family. Rolando wanted to encourage him to reflect about his relationship with his wife, Matilde, which was at this point nonexistent. However, the conversation turned into an exchange about Quique's plans and social situation. The dialogue was as follows:

ROLANDO: What are you doing, Quique?

QUIQUE: What do you want me to be doing? I'm doing my own stuff.

R: And what is your stuff? Because I don't see you . . .

Q: That's because you have to bust yourself working on the street. When [could you see me]? It's enough to burst, Rolando, to burst. Today a person doesn't even live to eat and dress himself . . .

R: You live, don't you?

Q: Yes, yes. Thanks to you, of course. But unfortunately, you aren't right either.

R: Why?

Q: And . . . because you're pure, you're gentle, you bend over and . . .

R: I like to work.

Q: Yes . . . and be valued and respected, right?

R: Yes, naturally.

Q: But that's going to end, Rolando, it's going to end, remember that. And soon.

R: Yes, the topic is exciting, but . . . let's leave it for another time, eh?

Q: Yes, we'd better go to sleep.

R: No, no, no, wait, I want to have two or three words with you, eh? Anyway, how are your things, your happiness, your studies, in short, everything.

Q: Very well . . .

R: Really well?

Q: Yes, yes, well.

R: With Matilde too?

Q: I'd rather not talk about Matilde . . .

[. . .]

Q: I am going to take a trip.

R: What?

Q: I found out today.

R: Work?

Q: Yes, yes, a little of everything . . . I'll need your car, Rolando . . .

[. . .]

R: If it's important for you . . . if you need it . . . take it . . . Now, it can only be for a couple days, because I need the car [to work]. Listen to me . . . are you going with Matilde?

Q: No.

R: Alone?

Q: You'll find out soon.

R: But why not now, Quique?!

Q: Because it's a surprise, even for me.

R: But, why are you making this so difficult? Why are you so selfish, why don't you communicate, Quique? I don't know, I feel like you're a stranger, I see you as different, different as never before. Listen to me Quique, listen to me brother, talk to me, man, ask things from me, I don't know.

Q: You should ask for things from those that can give them to you, right?

R: Yes.

Q: Well, you'll get to know me and hear in the right moment . . . And maybe it seems bad to you . . . Now, remember that you taught me that you have to do what you like in your life, and commit yourself as well . . . So committing yourself means losing many things. What you like can't always be pleasant. It can also be a sacrifice.

R: But what are you talking about? [disconcerted][46]

This dialogue summarizes how the soap opera presented the conflict between the activist and the nonactivist, between the guerrilla and the "common" person, between political-revolutionary commitment and family-social commitment. Quique was concerned with social injustice, with inequality, and rebelled against the fact that "today, a person doesn't even live to eat and dress himself," although he himself lived comfortably at the expense of his brother. Rolando, instead, was worried about Quique and his sister-in-law and made everything that he had available to help them (money, the car, dialogue). In Rolando's eyes, the subjects that Quique was concerned with were "exciting" but did not cease being abstract digressions. For him, the urgent task, which could not wait, was the family, the need for his brother and his sister-in-law to reconcile. In this dialogue, the hardworking brother criticized the activist brother for the first time: he called him "selfish" and asked him to communicate, to tell him why he was so unrecognizable that he seemed to be a stranger. But Quique could not spend his time on family feuds. If he recognized that he lived thanks to his brother, he disdained his brother's submissive spirit, his gentle disposition to "bend over" and accept exploitation. Rolando defended this manner of sacrificing: "I like to work." Quique, instead, while he was willing to sacrifice himself for the revolutionary cause, did not make any efforts on the domestic level.

That same night, Quique left the house, leaving a note that said, "Don't worry about me, I'm well. I love you. Quique." The next day, the media announced the news of the kidnapping of the businessman Fernando Helguera Paz. In their own homes, Mónica and Rolando despaired; she for her father's kidnapping and he for the mysterious disappearance of his brother, but neither of them suspected the relationship between the two events. Thus, the main characters of the soap opera were united by the same event that, in the end, would place them on opposite sides. "Hey, this is the first time we are united by almost the same problem," Mónica told Rolando when neither of the two knew anything about the whereabouts of their relatives.[47]

Once in a while, the soap opera included a sort of "lay homily" by its protagonist. In this case, responding to the kidnapping of Mónica's father, Rolando devoted one of these sermons to the human condition. The occasion for this was a conversation that he had with his sister Noemí and Mónica in the dining room of his home. After exchanging condolences for both families' situations, the three took part in the following exchange:

MÓNICA: I have so much hope that these people [her father's kidnappers] reconsider . . .

NOEMÍ: Look at the things they're doing! One can't live peacefully . . . Where are we going to stop? I don't understand anything about politics, right, and I don't want to understand . . .

M: In reality, I don't understand much either . . .

ROLANDO: [trying to change the subject, wanting his sister to return to her room] Noemí . . . Let's go . . .

N: No, no, no, no, let me talk . . . Well, I don't even know what I was saying . . .

M: It was about politics . . .

N: Oh, yes, of course, I don't understand anything about that, well . . . the thing could be understood! Oh . . . You hear the politicians talk, you look, and they're all saints. But what happens is that the country hurts itself . . . Yes! But you go out on the street . . . It's enough to go out on the street to see that the "people people," they suffer, just like that.

R: Alright, that's good, but if you don't know, why are you talking, Noemí?

N: You don't think I'm right in what I said?

R: Yes, yes, but even so, go to bed. But before you go, I'm just going to tell you one thing: look, even so, in this country one can still live, breathe, and work, eh? These are not times of plenty. [. . .] And if not, take Nené's book, who is in the third grade, and [you'll realize that] there were always problems, always, there were always difficult times, always. And rich and poor, and the dissatisfied and the conformists and the revolutionaries. Always! You just said that everyone just hurts themselves, right?

N: Yes.

R: And well: yes, that's true. I think so. Yes [while the camera centers on Mónica's infatuated look, who listens admiringly to Rolando]. Human beings tend to hurt themselves, which doesn't mean that politicians aren't bad, of course. This is envy, this is ambition, this is selfishness. Sometimes we can't find a friend, and we want to find a president?

This scene introduces three significant topics. First among these is the relationship of women to politics. Both Mónica (seventeen years old) and Noemí (thirty) presented themselves as "not knowing anything about politics." Noemí expressed a conception that probably represents the feelings of many women of the nonactivist middle class of those years: politics was a dark world, populated by people that spoke like "saints" but acted differently. The "people people," those that did not participate in politics, "suffered, just like that." Second, the scene shows the different relationship of men with politics. Rolando, who recognized that his sister was partially correct but denied her the authority to speak about the subject, did speak about politics, despite not knowing much about it. His vision was more global, historical ("go read Nené's book, there were always problems") and at the same time conscious of economic conditions ("these are not times of plenty"). Moreover, his discourse had a pedagogical tone. In this way, it was made clear that even the men who were not involved in politics were the authorized domestic voice on the subject. Third, the dialogue reflects a vision characteristic of the middle class, which attributes political and social problems to the moral corruption and decadence of the human species, the citizens or their leaders. The real problem was not political but rather moral: the explanation for the fact that someone kidnapped Mónica's father was "envy, ambition, selfishness." If one could not "find a president," this was because of a previous failure on the level of friendship.

Far from the pessimism of his sister and Mónica, who griped about politics, farther still from the violent path taken by Quique ("I do not know how to solve problems by gunshots, I was not born to be an extremist," he said later), what ended up dominating Rolando's moral discourse was his optimistic vision, centered on personal commitment and social peace.[48] Thus, Rolando overcame two extremes; on the one hand, the pessimistic lament of his sister, and, on the other, the (violent) revolutionary optimism of his brother.

However, the soap opera's message about the issue of the guerrilla in its first year (1972) was nuanced. Some chapters associated laudable values, such as social justice and patriotism, with the guerrilla experience. For example, the newspaper that announced the news of Helguera Paz's kidnapping also communicated that the guerrillas were demanding school supplies, three hundred million pesos (AR$300,000,000.00), and the reinstatement of laid-off workers in exchange for the businessman's freedom. Quique, when he had to confront the police patrol that discovered him, reflected out loud: "Yes, I'm afraid, I'm afraid now, but I can't go back. It's for the good of the country."[49] And finally, when Rolando himself learned of his brother's death, he delivered another sermon, this time heavy with sadness, anger, and compassion, which condensed the show's two-fold conclusion about the armed struggle, indulgent and critical at the same time. This took place in the room that Quique had occupied and followed a dialogue held between Rolando and Magoya (Beba Bidart), one of his best friends, when she passed by to offer her condolences. Magoya entered the room and saw her friend stroking a picture of his dead brother. With background music of violins and strings, the scene reached a moment of great drama:

MAGOYA: Rolando.

ROLANDO: [crying, with his brother's portrait in his hands] Leave me . . .

M: But, why is everything like this? [referring to the room, which is in a total mess]

R: The search warrant. They searched the whole house . . .

M: Did they find anything?

R: No.

M: What luck, no?

R: I didn't want . . . I didn't want them to touch anything in his room . . . I didn't want them to put anything in its place, I didn't want . . . I was going to order it myself, when you arrived [referring to Magoya and friends].

M: You're going to hurt yourself . . .

R: More?

M: Let me . . .

[. . .]

R: [Leafing through one of his brother's books] I never . . . I had never touched his books, or his discs, or any of this things . . . Today I realized for the first time that my brother was another country. [. . .] Probably he needed another word of mine, or I should have inserted myself more in his life, in his ideas . . .

M: But if you gave him everything . . .

R: [Crying, screaming] "Everything" couldn't drag him away from this! Four crazies had to come along to put in his head in four days what I couldn't teach him in twenty-four years.[50]

The dialogue reflects three perceptions of the political realities of those days held by nonactivists. First, the existence of disconnected, cut-off worlds, which in some way existed in parallel (see chapter 2). Rolando realized that his brother "was another country"; his books, his discs, his things were all signs of the existence of another reality, foreign to his own. Rolando inhabited a world that was less intellectual, linked to work, which he enjoyed, and to his family, whom he loved. The world of revolutionary political commitment appeared to be "another world," and only his brother's death confronted him with its existence. The second perception, which surprisingly appeared as early as 1972, is seen in the share of responsibility that the main character places on himself for not having been more involved in the life and ideas of his activist brother, for not having taught him in so many years that problems are not solved with guns. From 1976 on, this same idea formed part of the official discourse of el Proceso, which argued that if the mothers of disappearance people had worried about their children before, they would not be bemoaning their disappearance. Third, and linked to the previous perception, there was the idea that the youth who enlisted in insurrectional movements were, as in Quique's case, the prisoners of "four crazies" ("cuatro locos") who "got into their heads."

Rolando Rivas's speech about his brother neither defended nor condemned him. When his friend Magoya suggested that Quique was also to blame, Rolando denied this emphatically and began his final reflection on the topic, the moral that the show offered its audience:

MAGOYA: But understand, Rolo . . . It was his fault too . . .

ROLANDO: No, no, no . . . no, no, no, Magoya . . . No, no. It's the fault of . . . some people, many people, everyone. It has to . . . it has to end! [screaming and crying] It has to end!! Why?! Why?! Why is it so difficult for us to do something beautiful and grand, so difficult that we kill each other?! Look, I hear people all day talking: socialists, conservatives, Radicals, government supporters, what do I know? There isn't one of them that doesn't say the same thing, there isn't one that doesn't have the exact solution to lift up the country: so that inflation stops, so that prices fall, so that wages rise, and, why not, so that torture stops . . . God damn it, Magoya! [holding his head, crying] Why? Why is it so hard to understand each other and move onward? Why? Why? I want someone to tell me why, why! It's not that I want to defend Quique. Quique no . . . I only cry for Quique. But there are almost 20 million, did I say 20 million?, almost the whole world is bleeding like a painful wound, a wound of hunger, injustice and disagreement, and then, what?, then man hasn't advanced a bit, and has gone crazy with pride because he got to the moon, and where he hasn't gotten yet is to walk on Earth! Then, in what have we advanced, Magoya? This is advancing?

M: Calm down . . .

R: I can't, I can't, I can't any more . . . And there are many people that can't take it anymore and must be asking themselves: why is it so hard for us to live in peace, so . . . ? [crying, clutching his brother's portrait].[51]

When thinking about the causes that pushed his brother to his death, the blame extended itself when Rolando attempts to find who was at fault. The guilt was that of "many [people], of everyone." His emotional escalation ended in a shout of impotence and anger: "It has to end!!" The explanation of his brother's tragic death was not political. The problem was that "it's hard for us to understand each other"; ultimately, it was a problem once again tied to the moral decadence of the species, which advanced technologically but regressed in human terms. Rolando felt himself part of an immense majority, of the "many people who can't take it anymore and must be asking themselves: why is it so hard for us to live in peace?"[52] The ideology of the soap opera could be distilled into three elements: incomprehension of political violence, a moral perception of the world, and working hard at one's own task.

The story reviewed condenses elements present in a sensibility that is characteristic of a significant part of the middle classes. At the end of the first year of the series, the soap opera's author confessed to the audience that, for the first time, he wanted the main character of one of his stories to not be just a character but a real person; "you, me, all people, are exposed to a ton of things, of troubles, of smiles, of tears [. . .]. [I wanted] Rolando Rivas to be a real man, from head to toe."[53] Some years later, remembering this success, he declared that "it caught on magnificently in the popular taste and reflected the country and our language and way of being. The more we emphasized this, the more resonance it found among the public."[54] The unprecedented ratings that the story garnered allow us to think that the story succeeded in having its audience identify with its hero. It can be said that the sensibility typical of the middle class flowed through Rolando Rivas's "way of being," in his values linked with the importance of the family and affection for those close to him, in his estrangement from the political world (which he had an opinion about but felt distant from), in his amazement about what he saw as the decadence of the human race, and in his desire to recover a lost world of solidarity and respect.

Natalia Riglos Arana, the Guerrilla Leader's Widow

Quique Rivas remained present in the soap opera until its conclusion, almost like a ghost. Not only Rolando but also Noemí, Mónica, Juanjo, and Matilde allude to his tragic story to extract lessons or make analogies. In 1973, his name reappeared in another character, a five-year-old child who moved across the street from Rolando's house. This new Quique (Marcelo Marcote) was accompanied by a woman whom he called his aunt, a young lady named Natalia Coronel (Nora Cárpena), who was twenty-four years old.

Although Rolando finally married Mónica Helguera Paz in December 1972, their marriage did not prosper. After the series restarted in 1973, Mónica left Rolando. The new love story was between Rolando and Natalia, and in some sense also the child Quique, who captured Rolando's affection much earlier than Natalia did. Natalia's character was mysterious for many chapters, as in the prior year that of Rolando's guerrilla brother had been. The audience gradually discovered the reason for the mystery: Natalia Coronel was actually Natalia Riglos Arana, the daughter of a family of millionaires native to the province of Córdoba. When she was very young, she had fallen in love with Nato Córdoba, whose nickname was "el Coronel," a very famous guerrilla leader with whom she lived clandestinely in the jungle for several years. Natalia and little Quique were not actually aunt and nephew, but rather mother and son. They concealed their family connection to avoid being identified; they were essentially hiding from the comrades of her guerrilla husband, who by that point had disappeared.

The first extensive dialogue about this topic occurred when a guerrilla friend of Nato Córdoba visited her in Buenos Aires. On that occasion, they had the following conversation:

NATALIA: Can I ask you . . .

GUERRILLA: Everything that you want . . .

N: Did you leave that behind?

G: Nothing was the same after the death of our beloved Colonel [Natalia's partner].

N: I understand . . .

G: But deserting is practically impossible, you know?

N: Because of that . . .

G: I escaped. [. . .] And you, nobody has touched you, have they?

N: No, no, luckily not. And I hope that they forget about me forever. I did not belong to the Movement, I never worked for anything related to it.

G: But you were the Colonel's wife . . .

N: We weren't married . . .

G: Everyone knows that you were his great love.

N: [with indignation] His great love was politics, cruel, destructive, and dreadful. The great love was only in me. For much time, it didn't allow me to see clearly. I followed him as if he were a hero. He began to be like a God to me. But he was sick with death and violence. He tried to achieve justice through murder. The last few months by his side, I was horrified. Quique had begun to copy his language, his threats. He wanted guns instead of toys to play with. I think that if they hadn't killed him, I would have done it myself.

G: Don't say that . . .

N: The most serious thing, the worst thing is that death turned him into a hero for many people. While the little boy and I have to hide who we are to live in peace, if you can call what we are doing living.[55]

Natalia was not a guerrilla. She had become involved with the guerrillas because of her love of Nato Córdoba. Very little is revealed about her life with him, but the sole mention of this past transfigured her face into an expression of fear. On various occasions she referred to her past life as a "hell" from which she wanted to save her son Quique. It was a traumatic past that caused her to be on the defensive against people that she met; indeed, when Rolando began to engage in a friendly relationship with her son, she asked him: "Who are you, Rolando Rivas, and what do you want from me? Are you from the Movement?"[56] In the dialogue above, she told one of her husband's comrades that the only thing she wanted was for the guerrillas to forget about her and let her live in peace. She wanted to forget and be forgotten. She wanted to erase not only a painful past but also a mistake. Natalia was sorry for having been involved with a guerrilla leader, whose love had not been for her but for "cruel, destructive, dreadful politics." The characterization of the guerrillas was completely negative: it was affirmed that, sick with death and violence, Natalia's husband sought justice by murder; that separating oneself from the organization was impossible (which implied that the guerrillas killed deserters); that if Nato Córdoba had not been killed, Natalia would have done it herself; and finally, that the worst thing about the death of the guerrilla leader was not that Quique was left without a father, Natalia without a husband, or the guerrilla movement without a leader, but the fact that many others had turned Nato Córdoba into a hero. The dialogue was brief but effective. There were no nuances, as there had been in 1972; the condemnation was absolute. The guerrilla was not "another country," as Rolando had said a year earlier of his brother, but rather a group of people sick with death, violence, destruction, and cruelty.

Another way that the soap opera dealt with the guerrilla issue was through the character of Quique, the son of Natalia and Nato Córdoba. Shortly after arriving in the neighborhood, both the owner of the house that Natalia rented and Rolando and the rest of his neighbors referred to him as a little demon. Different characters called him "Judas's skin," "little snake," "plague," and "cursed doll." Indeed, Quique played in a very violent way: among other things, he punctured the wheels of Rolando's taxi; bound Nené, the youngest of the Rivas siblings, by hand and foot and threatened to burn her; played by pretending that he was in prison or in the jungle; and dug tunnels in his room. Natalia herself, in the dialogue above, lamented that her son had copied the threats, language, and violence from his guerrilla father. Quique was presented as the first victim of his father's guerrilla actions. Only when Quique started to see Rolando as a father figure and himself as his son did his character soften. As tenderness displaced violence, his true identity was able to come to light.

FIGURE 3.2. Quique playing and threatening to burn Nené, tied to the fence of her house. *Source:* Channel 13 and Proartel, 1973, chapter 39

The arrival of Natalia and Quique on the Rivas family's block generated all sorts of comments. In response to one of them, the Rivas brothers (Rolando and Juanjo) had a dialogue that showed a hardening of the main character's perspective about the guerrilla issue.

JUANJO: Tell me, do you know the new tenant living with Don Félix?

ROLANDO: Why?

[. . .]

J: The son of the hardware dealer told me that she's just like . . . I already know that it can't be, I argued him to death about it. Of course, lately all kinds of weird things are happening . . .

R: Tell me already . . . who?

J: To Nato Córdoba's wife.

R: Huh?

J: Do you remember?

R: Who?

J: Nato Córdoba . . . the revolutionary from Córdoba, that one that . . .

R: Ah . . . yes, I know, of course . . . Is he crazy, the son of the hardware dealer?

J: And, you know the devotion that has for those types of leaders, right? He has a huge amount of photos and biographies.

R: And what?

J: He says that the woman is identical.

R: But listen to me, didn't Nato Córdoba die?

J: Well . . . they left him for dead during a guerrilla operation in Bolivia . . . It was . . . more or less two months after what happened with Quique. But the corpse was never found.

R: Listen to me, why don't you tell the hardware dealer's son to stop inventing stupid things?

J: Tell him, why are you bringing it up with me?

R: And end your relationship with that boy, man! He's pretty nuts, right?

J: No, no, no, he's very intelligent . . . He knows a lot of things. For example, he has a movie script written about Nato Córdoba, and you can't imagine how good it is. [. . .] Because the guy's life is a movie and it's also very well written. He put a political part, and I know that you don't like that . . .

R: No, no, no, no . . . It's not that I don't like that . . . You know well how everything that happened still hurts me, right?

J: You don't need to tell me that . . .

R: Yes, I do! Because your brother started off like this!

J: No, no, don't compare . . .

R: Look, don't talk to me like that . . . I catch you in one of these things and poor you . . .

J: Ah . . . no, Rolo, I just read the script! And I was more interested in the human than in the political part. Because you just isolate the love that Nato Córdoba lived with this woman and it makes you tremble . . .

R: Ah . . . And?

J: Seriously . . . because of how everything happened. Look: both of them were from very important families. And they rejected everything to escape together.

R: Aha . . . The hardware dealer's son invented that, and as it had no ending, he moved the protagonist here to the neighborhood, right?

J: Oh, no, Rolo . . . There are biographies of Nato Córdoba, just like there are of Che Guevara. What happened is that Córdoba, toward the end, did a lot of stupid things . . . you see?

R: [Ironically] And since she was left alone, she came to live here across the street . . .

J: Oh . . . why did I even start to talk about this . . . Forget it, forget it. I don't think the woman who is renting from Félix can be who my friend says she is, agreed?

R: No, no, it's not me who you have to agree with, but the hardware dealer's son; [ironically] now you'll go and tell him that since Cortito [Rolando's friend] is taking a long time to come back, I invited Cámpora [FREJULI presidential candidate] over to share the room. Then we're all saved . . . eh?[57]

The different attitudes that Rolando and Juanjo have about the story of Nato Córdoba and the movie script that the son of the hardware dealer wrote about him mark a generational difference. Rolando was twenty-eight years old and Juanjo sixteen; the former was devoted to his work driving his taxi, while the latter, supported by his brother, was finishing high school. Rolando did not show any interest in Nato Córdoba and considered that the hardware dealer's son was "pretty nuts" ["medio chiflado"]. Juanjo, however, expressed curiosity for his script. Rolando feared that Juanjo's enthusiasm might translate into activist involvement and, as the brother-father that he was, on the one hand warned him that if the vendor's son got mixed up "in one of their things [. . .] poor him [because Rolando would kill him himself]," and on the other, reminded him that his brother Quique "started like this." Juanjo, however, calmed him down. He was interested more in the human than the political aspects of the film script, the "made for a movie" love story of the main characters more than the "lots of stupid things" that Nato Córdoba did.

In the series' second year, a dialogue that Rolando had with a passenger in his taxi reaffirmed his moral conception of the world and extended the criticism of the guerrillas to include the activist youth. The conversation is paradigmatic because the passenger was a typical middle-class citizen of Buenos Aires: he wore a suit, carried a suitcase, and took the taxi because he didn't want to risk walking on the street with money. Once in the car, he had the following conversation with Rolando:

PASSENGER: I have to pay some bills . . . and all kinds of things are happening, old man, you want me to tell you? Today, even if it's nine at night you can't feel safe.

ROLANDO: If you're not careful, you can't at nine in the morning either [. . .]

P: It's a streak of kidnappings and assaults the likes of which I've never seen!

R: It's rough, isn't it, eh? I hope that after the 25th [he is referring to May 25, the date Cámpora was (to be) sworn in as the country's president] certain youth will calm down a bit, no?

P: I hope, I hope! [. . .]

R: But I'm not one of those that think that after May 26th everything will be fixed and in order.

P: No, no, no . . . Of course not. Now as never before, we lack the faith and patience to all pull in the same direction and start to see the results.

R: It's very nice what you just said, eh? "Pull in the same direction." [. . .] It's that it is strange to see a country like our own overcome by violence. I might not be the person best placed to comment, but it's like they want to take a blotch of orange paint and replace it with a blotch of red paint. Do you understand what I'm trying to say?

P: Yes, perfectly . . .

R: I already know that everyone is uneasy and impatient. We all have a thousand problems, don't we? But taking justice into your own hands, to go out and burn down a theater, I don't know, taking advantage of a difficult moment to provoke more fear, more confusion, I don't know, for me that is not an advance, that is . . . it's a step backward. And let's not even talk about those that, without eating or drinking, live trembling for a son or daughter, who go out of their house and to see them again have to pay a fortune. You know well, no, and many times they don't even have that much money . . . [to pay the ransom].[58]

This dialogue took place days before Cámpora was inaugurated. Both the middle-class passenger and Rolando agreed on the diagnosis of the situation. People lived with fear, without safety, in the midst of "a streak of kidnappings and assaults the likes of which has never been seen." The expectation created by the elected Peronist government was one of greater tranquility and decrease in violence; it was hoped that "certain youth," referencing the youth activists, would calm down a little. The present was judged negatively: they condemned vigilante justice, the burning of a theater, the kidnappings, and the creation of fear and confusion. Passenger and taxi driver, middle-class and popular wisdom, agreed that the solution was to be found in "pulling in the same direction." The violence did not have a political explanation. It was a mistaken and reprehensible way of reacting to life's difficulties.

When at the end of 1973, the love story between Natalia Riglos Arana and Rolando Rivas reached its conclusion, when after many vicissitudes and conflicts typical of melodramas the couple managed to come together and marry formally in Uruguay, the issue of the guerrilla was also closed, "overcome" by the existence of a new "Quique Rivas," Natalia's son to whom Rolando gave his last name — given that he had not been formally registered by his biological father. Thus, the guerrilla Quique Rivas with the look of fear and resentment that the soap opera showed in 1972, at the end of 1973 was replaced by a new Quique Rivas, a six-year-old boy saved from violence and paternal abandonment by Rolando's love. The phrase that Natalia told her son in the last chapter of the soap opera, "you're going to have a family, a home that until now Mamá couldn't give you," concluded the stories connected with the armed struggle.[59] The guerrilla ended up taking a brother from Rolando, but giving him a son. Quique Rivas died as a guerrilla in 1972, but a love story gave birth to another Quique Rivas in 1973, saved by Rolando from the emotional vacuum that the guerrilla had left him. Love defeated politics, affection won over weapons, and Rolando's moral world triumphed over the decadence of human beings dragged into violence.

Memories of the Armed Violence: Pretty, Clean, and Naïve

The memories of armed violence, in the three places studied, were far clearer than those of social violence. Furthermore, in the majority of cases, they were accompanied by value judgments — something less frequent in the memories of the social uprisings. Even people who defined themselves as being foreign to politics tended to recall guerrilla attacks or other cases of armed violence with more specific characteristics than other political events.

The memories of the violent acts that these sectors have are determined by two factors. The first is proximity. In Correa, for example, the majority of those interviewed remembered attacks that occurred in Rosario, such as the case of General Juan Carlos Sánchez, commander of the Second Army Corps, who was assassinated in 1972 in Rosario in an attack that was attributed to the People's Revolutionary Army and the Revolutionary Armed Forces, in which a civilian who worked in a kiosk also died. The second is that the memory of the violent acts is determined by their spectacular characteristics; the more gruesome or cruel the act, the more sharply it remained in the memories of the interviewees. Indeed, in some cases the respondents do not remember (or confuse) the name of the person who suffered the violent act or the armed group who committed it but recall the bloody details — "Who did they find buried in a well with lime?" asked one of the interviewees.

In this section, I analyze testimonies together with archival material, cultural products, and public opinion studies, which allow us to understand to what degree elements present in the testimonies were already present in the public discourse of the 1970s. I focus my attention only on subjects I consider crucial, such as the vision that these middle classes remember having had of the armed conflicts, their judgments of the guerrilla experience, representations of fear, and the way in which they retrospectively explain the insurgent groups' emergence.

Regardless of what their political and partisan positions were, a majority of interviewees emphasized the fact that the struggle in the 1970s was between the guerrillas and the military, although in various accounts the role played by the Triple A is mentioned with confusion. The armed conflict is alluded to frequently through the terms of "war," "dirty war," or even "civil war."[60] However, nobody seemed to claim that the citizens as a whole, let alone themselves, formed part of one of the two sides in conflict. There is therefore a strong agreement on society's distance and separation from the armed struggle.

Carlos Etcheverría, a twenty-three-year-old man in 1970, upon seeing a guerrilla attack on a police detachment in the first part of the documentary, said:

> I wasn't afraid of the guerrillas. What was like a taboo of mine regarding the guerrillas, was that I did not like the possibility of violence, as I have always avoided it, as violence is ugly. But I did recognize that there things happened because people didn't have any other way to defend themselves. In countries where you have a certain level of well-being, work, education, everything, there is like a structure that you say, "No, I won't allow them to attack this." Then, it's the people who are defending against the guerrillas. Here, no, here there were the guerrillas and the military, and the people remained indifferent.

Jorge Van der Weyden, a laboratory employee who was already forty-two years old in 1970, responded thus to my question about how he perceived the armed confrontations:

I thought that this was a mess between them, without knowing exactly who "they" were, but it was always something that was foreign to me. One kept on walking and kept on living. And it was really something that remained within a political group that was involved with this. Nobody cared; I didn't see anyone worrying about these types of things. At least, in the environment where I developed, in the work environment, in the environment of normal people, let's say, we all saw them as groups of crazy people that could do anything.

Sergio and Ángela Caballero, a Tucumán couple of a generation younger than Jorge's, made similar statements. In response to a question about how they decoded what was happening in Tucumán at the time, Ángela mentioned that those who confronted each other "were two well-defined sectors," a thought that her husband completed, clarifying: "the lefties [zurdos] and the military [milicos]. Those were more or less our definitions: the lefties and the military." Diego Puerta, who in the mid-1970s was a young man from Tucumán finishing high school, declared that "it was really a war, on one side and the other, with us in the middle. The civilians in the middle." Some months later, after seeing the second documentary (1975–1982), he reaffirmed this same diagnosis, saying: "It was never divided. Tucumán was never divided. Tucumán was united . . . Tucumán stayed away, let's say, the rest of the people stayed away. It was a fight that was very well defined between the Marxists, between the guerrillas and the military. You got it?"

In a town like Correa, these confrontations, in addition to being foreign, were also physically distant: they were merely episodes that occurred in the big cities, news on the television and in the newspapers, and to be commented on in the club. However, in terms of how they remember their conceptions of the armed struggle, Correa residents differed little from their counterparts in Buenos Aires and Tucumán.

After seeing the first part of the documentary (1969–1974) with Correa resident Ema Mateo, a question about what she thought about armed violence in those years generated the following dialogue:

EMA: And, for me, it was a civil war. What we had here in Argentina was like an underground civil war. I don't doubt it. For me it was like an underground civil war. The guerrillas were armed and the military was armed, and there was a civil war here.

[. . .]

SC: But who were the two sides in this civil war?

E: And, the military versus the Triple A and the Montoneros . . .

SC: And the Triple A and the Montoneros were on the same side?

E: They didn't get along well. The Montoneros and the Triple A didn't get along well. Perón knew both of them perfectly.

It is interesting to note the similarities that can be established between these memories and the diagnoses that part of the written press and especially television expressed in those years.[61] When Aramburu was kidnapped, which is to say, at the foundational act of the armed guerrillas, *Panorama* magazine started its long article on the subject by declaring: "if Aramburu's disappearance is connected with the agitation, the Republic is facing a scenario of civil war: two minorities — the terrorists and the military — will struggle to impose their views on society."[62]

When the People's Revolutionary Army kidnapped the businessman Oberdan Sallustro, the same magazine once again situated the majority of the population on the margins of this violence.[63] "This silent majority besieged by the crisis," wrote the magazine's editor, "perhaps does not ask if it is good to vote or not, if Juan Perón will stay in Madrid or return to Buenos Aires, if Alejandro Lanusse will be a candidate or announce his 'patriotic resignation'; it only asks, in a tacit repudiation of violence, when it will be able to live in peace, without the threat of misery."[64]

Even in the context of a much-delayed political opening, one year before the return to democracy, for *Panorama* what concerned the "silent majority" were still the economic situation and the impossibility of living in peace. For the magazine, the hopes of this majority were not deposited in either the military or the guerrillas: "The people reject dishonest and incompetent officials, deplore the rise in the cost of living, the growing inflation, the disorder, and political deception. The guerrilla-repressor equation allows us to decipher a single truth: the people will be neutral because they despise violence and don't understand this sort of confrontation."[65]

During the same week that the previous paragraph was published, another political analyst affirmed in *Gente* that "among the popular masses there is a certain outrage about violence because it is, strictly, a thing of minorities. [. . .] In moments of violence, the flags of order triumph because the majority correctly fears the return to universal war, to the law of the jungle."[66]

It would be erroneous to attribute this vision to mere sectoral interests. In the previous chapter, we saw how, in Tato Bores's humor, society was portrayed as a spectator of political conflicts — especially the violent ones — rather than an actor interested in those conflicts. The memories referenced above unanimously recall the battle that the guerrillas unleashed against their political or state enemies in a way that is at the very least compatible with both this portrayal and that vision.

In summary, on the plane of memory, the separation or distance maintained from armed violence is much more marked than that observed in the previous chapter with respect to social violence. Whereas social violence, whether or not it awoke sympathies, allowed for indifference, acts of armed violence pushed these sectors of the middle class to make value judgments. In other words, distance from armed conflict did not imply indifference to violent acts.

Although some respondents related armed insurgence to social injustice, today almost nobody remembers having celebrated or supported guerrilla violence. However, especially among those who were Peronists in the 1970s, a majority distinguish the "Aramburu case," justifying and/or remembering having justified the assassination of the ex-president de facto. It is thus necessary to begin the analysis of the judgments of the armed violence with a testimony that helps us to understand the specificity of the "Aramburu case."

Eduardo Álvarez, the employee of the Molinos company who was already mentioned in the previous chapter, had a Peronist fervor like the activists, although he was not an activist himself. In our first interview, he differentiated the Aramburu case from the rest of the assassinations carried out by the guerrillas:

> EDUARDO: I forgot to tell you about a very special situation that I lived
>   through, and lived through badly, because when the kidnapping
>   of the Born brothers occurred [he is referring to the brothers Juan
>   Carlos and Jorge Born, the manager and the director of Molinos Río
>   de la Plata, respectively], I was there, they had the engineer Picota,
>   his office there, you see? And I felt that I was being watched. They
>   killed the driver there—they said that he was his guard, it was a lie,
>   he was just a poor guy, he was a driver—and they killed the general
>   manager who at that time was Mr. Bosch, a great guy, a great, very
>   humble guy, from a traditional family and everything, but a humble
>   guy, who would come out to the field to play soccer with us. And they
>   kidnapped Jorge Born [. . .]

> SC: And how did you see these acts? If you want, we can talk about the
>   most emblematic, the beginning, which was the kidnapping and
>   assassination of Aramburu . . .

E: No, those are two different things. With the Aramburu case, I would tell you that I identified with it. Not with the rest, with the case of Sallustro, for example, and others, no. Moreover, I wanted Rojas more [he is referring to Admiral Isaac Rojas, an icon of anti-Peronism], who was a sinister guy if there ever was one, than Aramburu. But what happened to the Born brothers was different, because I really didn't have any apprehensions about them, I didn't hate either the business or these men. [. . .] All right, they represented the economic powers within the country. [. . .] but in any case, I lived it differently.

On the second occasion in which he remembered his satisfaction upon hearing the news of Aramburu's kidnapping ("I won't deny that I sympathized," he said), he added that this had been an "isolated act." The taste for revenge that Aramburu's assassination awoke in Peronists, including for those who were not activists, can be perceived in his later clarification: "[the Aramburu affair] was an isolated act, and was in response for the dead of the Plaza de Mayo on June 16, 1955, which could have killed my father, because he was there, there were dead bodies everywhere and nobody thought of seeing how many dead there were."

In 1970, the year of Aramburu's assassination, Eduardo Álvarez was a Peronist who had never seen his leader and awaited him for fifteen years. And for a "simple Peronist" like him, at least until the events in Ezeiza, everything that had to do with Peronism was defensible. When I asked him about the death of the union leader Vandor, assassinated by a leftist Peronist group in 1969, for example, he told me that he considered it "like an attack against Peronism." In 1969, "from the mistaken conception that I had," Eduardo remembered, "more than as an internal problem, I saw it as 'Hey, they are still killing our people!'" Vandor was for Eduardo another casualty of the repression of Peronism. The death of Aramburu, however, meant that, for the first time in many years, the dead were on the anti-Peronist side.

Among Peronists, the conception that Eduardo had was not exceptional.[67] And in this conception, Aramburu's death was not related to a revolutionary war for socialism but with a historical revenge for a persecuted and prohibited Peronism. His expression "I wanted Rojas more" and the clear distinction that he established between this assassination and the Borns' kidnapping, also show that his approval of the Aramburu affair did not imply his support for these methods. The Aramburu case simply symbolized the payment of an outstanding debt for many Peronists.

Although within this social sector, testimonies of people who remember having supported other specific assassinations or guerrilla actions could be found, it is probable, and consistent with the statistics shown at the beginning of this chapter, that these attitudes, uncommon among the nonactivists interviewed here, were not held by the majority.

This certainly was the case in places such as Correa. Alberto Monti, who was for various years the main Peronist leader in the Unión county to which Correa belonged, was a young secretary for the district in 1973, was elected mayor three times after the return of democracy, and is today a provincial senator for the province of Santa Fe. About the armed actions of the guerrillas, he commented that

> here, this was not accepted. Here, in the towns like Correa, it was not accepted. For example, what happened to Vandor and Alonso [he is referring to José Alanso, another union leader assassinated by the guerrilla], despite the fact that the Peronists in Correa understood very well that they were going for a neo-Peronism, because they were talking about a Peronism without Perón, what was not accepted were the murders, you see? I think that here, in that sense, we have a vision of politics that is much more advanced than in many other places. In other words, under no circumstances is killing, or assassination, or aggression for an idea justified. I believe that a democratic feeling is well rooted here, that ideas are defended with words and with reason and not with gunshots.

Without a doubt, this vision is excessively romantic. However, neither the testimonies about the 1970s that I collected in the town nor La Voz de Correa offer reasons to suspect that the guerrillas enjoyed any sympathy. In the testimonies, nobody supported the guerrillas nor remembered that someone had done so in the past (with the exception of the Aramburu case). Those most critical of how the state repressed guerrilla actions mentioned that they had very little information about the guerrillas' objectives, thought that the guerrillas were "people who wanted to destroy the country." But even so, they continued to disapprove of, if not condemn, their violent actions. Indeed, La Voz de Correa emphatically condemned "subversion" on the anniversary of independence in 1971. The dates were no coincidence. The armed insurrection appeared to be an attack on the homeland and its people. "For us, the times in which we live do not seem to be conducive for dignified patriotic remembrances," La Voz de Correa wrote in 1971, "since evils that are present can darken the image of our homeland and project onto her what is the product of today's men. Disunion and discord are becoming more and more prevalent among the children of this earth, where the diabolic seed of subversion has already began to germinate. The sun on the Flag has been blurred, and the bright, happy gleaming of other times when Argentines felt united under the warm shadow of Belgrano's blue and white teachings no longer shines." [68]

The following year, on May 25, the newspaper made a similar diagnosis. Subversion and political violence appeared as events that originated outside and attacked the nation, "blurring the sun of the Flag," troubling "today the sky of the Homeland." [69] "Dark clouds" darkened "the bright, happy gleaming of other times when Argentines felt united." The past was depicted as being harmonious, a time of "unity" and "good sense," and the Argentine people, not only those from Correa, were described as being "gentle and united." As the image of this country—the newspaper said—made Argentines proud across the world, the newspaper's hope and bet was that the storm would pass and the "sun would shine again with its usual splendor." The guerrillas and violence were, for La Voz de Correa, completely foreign to Argentine history and did not originate in social conflicts or pursue political causes.

Tucumán, meanwhile, was a special case. In none of the sites considered in this research were the memories of armed violence more intense, both that of the guerrillas and that of the state and paramilitary forces. If any part of the country had concrete and almost daily grounds to justify the discourse of war that both the guerrillas and the military authorities sustained, it was without a doubt Tucumán. Operation Independence (Operativo Independencie), decreed in February 1975 by Isabel Perón's government with the objective of "annihilating the actions of the subversive elements" that acted in Tucumán, drastically changed the urban landscape and that of its surroundings due to the presence of military troops—first under the command of General Adel Vilas and later General Antonio Bussi. The ERP's attempt to establish an armed uprising in the Tucumán mountains emulating the Cuban experience soon became a nightmare, not only for the few combatants who were camped out in the mountains and the different groups of political activists, and student and union leaders—whose persecution increased—but also for the population of Tucumán, which had to learn to live with fear long before the military took power at the national level. Although these rural guerrillas never went beyond being a geographically limited, failed experiment of a small minority, the bombings, assassinations, kidnappings, and forcible disappearances that occurred in the city, combined with the growing myth that in the mountains the guerrillas controlled considerable amounts of territory, contributed to the propagation of the idea among the population that an "unconventional" war was being unleashed.

Without a doubt, much of the armed violence in Tucumán was caused by the Triple A organization and the military and police forces. The guerrilla organizations, meanwhile, made a double contribution: on the one hand, they carried out various bombings and assassinations that had enormous impact on provincial public opinion and ended up being infamous events, such as the incident with Captain Humberto Viola in December 1974, which cost not only his life but that of his three-year-old daughter as well; on the other, with their insistence on armed actions, they helped to create perfect conditions for much of the society and the most influential regional mass media to see the police and military presence and actions as justified. Even today, many interviewees continue attributing to the rural guerrillas a firepower that they never had, including the possession and use of Soviet missiles and miniature helicopters that could be disassembled and fit into a backpack.

All this imbued the Tucumán case with specific characteristics. The sensation of separation from the conflict between "guerrillas and the military" was accompanied by a fear that those who were involved in the fighting would suspect that this separation was not sufficient. Lucía Di Iorio, who was a twenty-five-year-old Tucumán woman in the mid-1970s who did not participate in political activism or attend university, remembered the following after seeing the first part of the documentary (1969–1974): "You didn't know if they were going to shoot you, because everyone went armed all the time. You didn't know if they were going to touch you, or if when they were shooting at someone else they would shoot you. You didn't know. That was the fear. It was a war! It was like war. Exactly the same! Exactly like a war."

SC: You felt like you were in a war?

LUCÍA: I did. And everyone in my house did too. I felt that we were at war.

SC: And this was a war between whom?

L: And well, between whom? Between the guerrillas and the military. But suddenly it would touch you, or you had nothing to do with it and they would take you away because someone had told them that you did have something to do with it. I don't know if you understand me.

The fear of being randomly caught in the growing armed violence is another ingredient that distinguished Tucumán from the other two sites considered. The gratuitousness and everyday nature of the armed violence appears at some moment in all of the narratives from Tucumán. For example, Lucía Di Iorio in an earlier conversation affirmed that by 1975, "you couldn't go out on the street anymore, because there could be a bomb anywhere. The bombs during the night, you slept frozen with fear because the bombs would go off everywhere, around the corner from your house, on the intersection over there. And Tucumán is small, and so therefore you heard everything, and everyone said: 'Where is it? Where is it? Who did it hit now?'"

Ángela and Sergio Caballero, a Tucumán couple that already had three children by the mid-1970s, remembered: "but there were bombs on the street. You could come walking on the sidewalk if they had put a bomb in the car that was parked there, you would be blown to pieces at the moment that the bomb exploded."

Rubén Rodó and Harry García Hamilton, the former a journalist and the latter a deputy editor of La Gaceta in the 1970s, made similar remarks that were consonant with the testimonies of the middle classes analyzed: "every night, five bombs exploded, anywhere, and one didn't sleep until the fifth bomb exploded, and if it wasn't for you, only then could you sleep. All of us lived very connected to all this violence."

Similar memories are frequently found among all the interviewees of this city, whether or not they had been activists, whether or not they had been involved in political conflicts, and regardless of their partisan political sympathies. Tucumán residents also remember their nearly unanimous rejection of guerrilla violence more intensely than their counterparts in Correa or Buenos Aires—once again with the exception of Aramburu's assassination, which was justified by those sympathetic to Peronism.[70] This was not so much because the guerrillas terrified the population—although this also played a role—but rather because of the fear of being a victim of military or police power associated with the possibility of being confused for a guerrilla. The fear of being reported to the authorities, by anyone for any reason, was not as widespread in Buenos Aires or in Correa as it was in San Miguel de Tucumán.

The city's main newspaper indicated Tucumán's rejection of the guerrillas long before the army's arrival in the province. In April 1973, La Gaceta devoted an editorial to indicating that, in a context in which both political and military sectors had given signs of a tolerant attitude open to dialogue between the different social actors of the time,

> there is a worsening of extremism and violence, which revives the climate of terror that our people want to forget. One cannot but think that the objective of these acts is to hinder this rapprochement by preventing the assumption of power by the new constitutional authorities and creating exactly the climate of confrontation that the Argentine people had rejected at the polls. [. . .] It is not necessary to argue too much for it to be clear, then, how negative this escalation of terrorism is,

which not only goes against the country's interests, but also against the wishes of the vast majority of Argentines, expressed freely and explicitly in their votes. The violence should end: in this sense the citizenry has declared itself massively in favor of a government of peace, order, tranquility, and work.[71]

Agapito Chancalay, La Gaceta's humorist, began to discredit and question the guerrilla actions with increasing severity from very early on. In 1971, for example, he wrote in his column,

> Man, don't they realize where they are taking this country with their violence? They're pretty big now to keep on fooling around. Let's see: what do they think they will get with violence? Undoubtedly nothing. With violence, the only thing you get is an increase in the number of rich people, because the owners of funeral cars and manufacturers of cloth for mourning [will profit]. What's more, violence is a disloyal practice, because it leaves doctors and pharmacists out of the business, who also have a right to live. We've turned the country into a great big cowboy movie, with the difference that here we don't know who's the actor and who's the thief.[72]

This paragraph summarizes two of the subjects referred to in the remembrances of the Tucumán interviewees. On the one hand, the sensation that the violence was getting out of control, even in 1971, when it was far from being as intense and regular as it would be several years later. On the other hand, the society's confusion about this violence: "here we don't know who's the actor and who's the thief." However, in 1971 both the humorist in his columns and La Gaceta in its editorials still included demands for the authorities to take care of the social injustices that were the cause of the violence. "We've got to end the violence," wrote Chancalay at the end of the column quoted, "with both violences, that of the bomb and the attack and that of the closed factory and the shantytown."[73]

Only a year later, La Gaceta hardened its judgments of the guerrillas, closing ranks with the discourse of the "Argentine Revolution." Chancalay bid farewell to 1972 thus:

> What a shame that it's going!
> It was a fun year
> there was everything this time:
> dramas, comedies and gunshots.
> There were kidnappings and killings

enough to fill a book;
and a general fell too
fruit of a sickly hatred.[74]

To the "sickly hatred" of the guerrillas at the end of this year, he added a paragraph praising Lanusse's government, which was challenged for the executions of August 22, 1972. After mentioning, ironically, that the year had passed calmly, he wrote:

Well, not that calmly,
Because there was a mess in Trelew
And I don't know how many died
Of a heart attack.
This and that, it is said,
Caramba! What was said!
Just because they say
That a little bird told them.
But nobody has seen anything,
and I haven't seen anything either.
Because of that, I take the government's [position]
And call it trustworthy.

Thus, La Gaceta's humorist no longer emphasized the violence of social injustice and appeared to call the official version that denied the executions and attributed the guerrillas' deaths to an escape attempt "trustworthy."

Meanwhile, the guerrillas, apart from some Robin Hood–style actions, which had favorable repercussions on some members of the nonactivist middle classes, did little to gain these classes' approval. In addition to armed actions, some of which were unforgettably cruel for their contemporaries, other actions reinforced the disapproval of the large sector that did not view the guerrillas as their vanguard. The occupation of the Historical House of Tucumán by the Montoneros stood out among these actions; in its main room—where the country's independence was signed in 1816—they spray painted slogans alluding to their organizations. It is no exaggeration to claim that La Gaceta's editorial, which affirmed that the "extremist episode" had "aroused the unanimous repulsion of the citizenry,"[75] represented at the very least Tucumán's middle classes.[76] These types of actions of the armed groups provoked, at least for the less politicized sector of the middle classes, more confusion about their political objectives.

Indeed, the relationship between the guerrillas and society seemed to be defined by a lack of communication. The available sociological data from the

FIGURE 3.3. Montonero spray painting in the Historical House of Tucumán, February 1971, with the following: "Long Live Perón (VP)," "Montoneros," "Peronist Party Local Evita Combatant." *Source*: Historical House of Tucumán archives.

period tell us about public opinion in the 1970s and allow us to establish that this difficulty was not an a posteriori construction. In 1972, an IPSA survey of more than two thousand participants across the country included a question about the goals of the guerrillas.[77] The question was "Which of these problems, goals or objectives do you think the guerrilla groups are pursuing?" The survey administrator handed the respondent a card with six pre-established options and an open category ("others"). The options proposed were, in the following order, "implant the socialist revolution in the country," "establish a Fascist or extreme rightist government," "destroy all the power structure without any other final goal (anarchy)," "achieve the return of Perón and the triumph of Peronism," "destroy the present government to achieve a more profound revolution," and "carry the country to the brink of chaos to facilitate the penetration of foreign ideologies (of any kind)." If one excludes the significant 35 percent who responded that they didn't know what these groups proposed, no more than 18 percent selected the same option.[78] Only three options received more than 10 percent of responses: 18 percent responded that the armed groups wanted to "carry the country to the brink of chaos to facilitate the penetration of foreign ideologies"; 14 percent said they sought to "achieve the return of Perón and the triumph of Peronism"; and 12 percent responded that they wanted to "destroy the present government to achieve a more profound revolution." The rest of the options were chosen by between 2 percent and 9 percent of the respondents: 8 percent said that the guerrillas wanted to "implant the socialist revolution in the country," 6 percent that they wanted to "destroy all the power structure without any other final goal (anarchy)," and 2 percent that they sought to "establish a Fascist or extreme rightist government."[79]

Although public opinion could have later begun to identify what the guerrilla groups wanted more clearly, in 1972 opinions varied dramatically, and many did not know what these groups sought. The same year that this measurement was taken, shortly after the ERP kidnapped Oberdan Sallustro, a political analyst wrote, "the guerrillas say they fight for the people, but [. . .] the people don't know who they are and what they propose."[80]

If these social sectors did not clearly understand what guerrillas were demanding, they did seem, however, to have a much less diffuse idea about the type of people that formed these groups. For many people, the youth who turned to the armed struggle and, by extension, the radicalized activists that sympathized with them, originated from the middle or upper-middle classes, with parents or families that were linked traditionally, culturally, or economically more with powerful than with disadvantaged social sectors. While occasionally recognizing the noble deals behind the decision to take up arms, there is a certain consensus within this nonactivist social sector that it was "guerrillas [who had their stomachs] full and not empty," that it was an "upper class revolution," and a movement of "well-off kids" and not of the lower classes.

The idea that the guerrilla movement was an adventure for young people of good or very good economic means, enjoying both material and cultural resources, was a common characterization by the mass media of those days.[81] Landrú, a widely read humorist of the 1970s, wrote a "packaged guerrilla handbook" in 1972, in which he advised that

> to be a good guerrilla it's enough to let your beard grow, belong to the middle class and hide out on the farm of your best friend's father that they use for week-end trips. The guerrilla must wear a really cute shirt with epaulets, ideal for use in the countryside and sold for $80 pesos by a well-known store with an English name on Lavalle street. [. . .] In the library there will be an assorted collection of books from Mao-Tse Tung, Cho En Lai and Fu-Man Chu; as well as Che Marrone's pamphlets, "Capital" by Groucho Marx and "Memories of a Russian Comrade." [. . .] The guerrillas can be far-left or far-right, which is the same

thing. But in both cases they must sign their name with at least two last names [a sign of belonging to the upper class], neither of which can be Italian, of course.[82]

The magazine El Burgués devoted one of its sections to ironic commentary on this subject. In one of its first issues, for example, a young student announces some "big news" to a group of workers, namely that exploitation had ended because he had burned the factory down. The workers reacted by giving him a beating, and in the last frame of the comic, the young "daddy's guerrilla" exclaimed, lying on the floor, that "these people will never understand Marxism."[83]

The journalists who took guerrilla actions seriously and editorialized about their causes and consequences did not stray from the stereotype represented in humor when they characterized their protagonists. "The young fans of Ernesto Guevara," Jorge Lozano wrote in 1974, "resist because of their 'class' from working the earth and using drills, and prefer to use their parents' cars, spend long weeks on vacation, and buy shirts in Paris."[84] The Buenos Aires Herald, which condemned the guerrillas with the same intensity as it did illegal repression, sometimes referred to them in benevolent terms using expressions such as "the snipers of Barrio Norte."[85] Over a year after the coup d'état of March 24, 1976, occurred, another influential journalist, Bernardo Neustadt, made a similar characterization, affirming that the guerrillas "are not exactly children of workers. Nor are they adolescents who 'live badly' economically. Nor those who get up at six in the morning to go to a factory or a job. No. They are the 'children of comfort.'"[86]

The literature that enjoyed the greatest success among the nonradicalized middle classes alluded to the guerrillas with similar portrayals. Silvina Bullrich, who was probably the most-read writer by this social class,[87] devoted one of her successful novels to portraying the guerrilla experience, its causes and the people involved in it. Mal Don, first published in 1973, was an immediate success. At the end of the year, a survey published by La Opinión confirmed that the public considered it the best book of the year, even above Felix Luna's highly publicized De Perón a Lanusse.[88] In it, young holidaygoers from affluent families are portrayed as "modern kids, unprejudiced, violently inclined to the left, toward the guerrillas, the men dreaming of being Che and the women with the nostalgia of never having known him, of never having trembled in his arms."[89]

One of the novel's main characters, who comes from a humble background and belongs to a family who works serving the vacationers, at one point comments on the absurdity of wanting to hide his social origin from these "children of powerful parents," while they "were playing at being the champions of the proletariat [. . .] without depriving themselves of their motorcycles, their cars, the pocket money that their parents gave them, and from time to time, forgetting their positions of rebellion, declining the illustrious last names of their ancestors."[90]

In Bullrich's novel guerrilla and bourgeoisie appear as terms that are more complementary than antagonistic. *Mal Don*, furthermore, tells the story of a child from a humble background who, without any supernatural gifts, ends up advancing professionally until becoming the manager of an important bank, challenging any project of radical social change through violence.[91]

The concrete possibility of becoming a victim of armed violence was, as we have seen, far greater in Tucumán, and to a less intense degree, also in Buenos Aires.[92] However, it is striking that in a town like Correa—where there were no guerrillas, no radicalized political activists, and no forcible disappearances—the memories about the guerrillas allude to the personal fear of being victims of their violence. Analyzing this fear helps us to understand the perception that these middle classes held of the Left's armed actions.

Aldo Círcolo, a Correa resident born in 1945, remembered a bombing that affected him very deeply because it happened in the city of Rosario several hours before he, together with his daughter, passed by the scene of the crime:

ALDO: These people [the guerrillas], they had to stop them, because these people . . . We were there, we got on a bus, Sebastián, and they would put a bomb on it and boom! You go straight to hell. It's not that I'm angry and I shoot you, no. They killed innocent people! And what has stayed in my mind, in the mid-seventies, in the rural exposition in Rosario, they had put like twenty-eight bombs. They say that they defused them, I don't know if there was an anonymous phone call. If not, you know? The rural exposition is done there on the grounds of the Rural Society [Sociedad Rural] that is on 27 de Febrero and Oroño Boulevard, some huge grounds, and the number of people that went was impressive. And these guys had put bombs everywhere! Then, they evacuated all the people, nothing happened because I-don't-know-who let them know. If not, do you know what would have happened? I always went to the exposition, but luckily I didn't go that year.

SC: So the bombs weren't something that you only heard about on television or read about in the paper, but you were also scared of being affected by some attack . . .

A: And because when I went to Rosario . . . I remember one time, my daughter, I think I told you this last time, she was young, I took her to the doctor one Monday, and the day before [Rosario] Central had played a game, against I don't know which team. And there was a bus that came full of people, and they put a bomb on it and sent everyone flying! I remember the newspaper headlines, and the people saying: "Eh . . . these guys are animals." Of course, at any moment we could all have exploded, because you didn't know when, at any moment, they would put a bomb, in a station or something.

SC: They had put a bomb on a bus with soccer fans?

A: No, no, on a bus with normal people. It must have been in '76, around then it went around the news, everyone died, I don't believe anyone stayed alive.

SC: Was there some military official on the bus?

A: That I don't remember [. . .] I remember that everyone had the shivers, of course, I remember the newspaper boy, the guy who had the newspaper and magazine stand in the station, saying "these guys are all crazy, at any moment we could all explode." Of course, probably some guy could just come by, leave a package and boom! Everyone was scared.

The bombing remembered by Aldo occurred on September 12, 1976, and was perpetrated by the Montoneros. In fact, it was carried out against a police vehicle, and in it, nine police officers and two civilians—a couple that was passing by—were killed, and various other police officers and civilians were wounded.[93] In Aldo's memory, however, there were no police but rather "a bus with normal people." Probably he would have been equally horrified if he remembered that the victims had been police officers. But it is noteworthy that, in his memory of both this act and that of the defused bombs in the Rural Society (Sociedad Rural), the targets of the terrorist attacks were not military, police, or political targets—as the bombing against the Rural Society could have been interpreted—but rather common citizens, "normal people." It is thus significant that he mentioned targeted assassinations, whose logic he seemed to understand, if not approve of. By distinguishing between the assassination of a specific person ("I'm angry at you and I shoot you") from a terrorist bombing, Aldo established a difference between the rational and the irrational, between a violence whose motivation could be understood and another that was considered absurd. The motivation that Aldo imagined as understandable, "anger," situated violence in an apolitical realm. Further-more, his fear of being affected by guerrilla violence is clear: "we would get on a bus, they would put a bomb there, and boom!"; the guerrillas "killed innocent people"; "everyone had the shivers"; and the phrase attributed to a newspaper vendor, "at any moment we could all explode." The guerrillas, in Aldo's memories, attacked the society as a whole.[94]

This fear is key to understanding the support of part of these middle classes for the "antisubversive" war that intensified after March 1976, as it does not seem to be the result of an ex post facto construction. Before the end of 1970, a *Panorama* reader from a town in the province of Buenos Aires sent a letter to the magazine in which he asked the government for instructions to defend himself against potential terrorist attacks. "The title *Anarchy or Democracy* and the content of *Panorama*'s 172nd issue," the reader wrote,

> reveal a terrible sight: that of terrorism. I believe that the police and the Armed Forces, despite the fact that they've multiplied in number, can-not cover all of the country's towns or all the sections of Buenos Aires. I think that the terrorists have declared a total war on us and I suggest that the national government instruct us to resist, to face the war. How can one distinguish a false police officer from a real one? How can one prevent their escape? How does one report [terrorist actions], and to whom? In Capital Federal there is no problem, it's enough to call 101, but in the smaller towns, who does one call?[95]

There are four primary explanations given for the guerrillas' motivations. One refers to the objective conditions that gave rise to these movements' appearance. Especially in Tucumán, interviewees mentioned poverty, unem-ployment, or social injustices as the "breeding ground" for these groups. The other three explanations, however, emphasized the subjective characteristics of the groups' members, mentioning snobbery, the rebelliousness of youth, and a generational conflict that these youth had with their parents.

Referring to the university students who were part of the armed groups and who he had met in the Universidad Nacional de Rosario, Claudio Mas-trángelo remembered:

> I believe that these people didn't know what they were doing very well. It was like snobbery. Keep in mind that we came from a very traditional period, very much of the family, very much of mommy and daddy, very much of repressed sex, very much of repressed everything, very tradi-tional. And suddenly, a panorama of "peace and love," hair clips, long hair, and all that opens before us. You were here [Correa], in your little

suit and tie, and then you come out with Oxford jeans, long hair, a hair clip, "peace and love," a joint, and everything else. And you were in the middle and you would say: what am I doing? Many people got involved in these types of things because of snobbery, not conviction.

Here, activism appears as one of the many novelties that the new times offered, together with Oxford jeans, hair clips, and long hair, as if being a revolutionary activist or participating in an armed organization was just one other option of the fashions of the time.[96]

Another motive is that of the inherently rebellious nature of young people. Speaking of Perón's return to Argentina in 1973, Linda Tognetti, one of the interviewees from Correa who was most thoughtful about the guerrilla youth, declared that "I was always afraid of Perón's return, because the youth was very, very angry. And afterward, Ezeiza and all of that, it made me very scared. And even more when he threw them out of the Plaza de Mayo, because anything you do against an adolescent makes him worse."

Dolores Mateo, the sister of the already mentioned Ema, lived in Córdoba until 1976, when she returned to Correa. Speaking with her sister about some activist nephews, she explained:

> DOLORES: You know what happens, Ema? There were many kids out-
> side the house, students. The students in Córdoba weren't all from
> Córdoba. They were from every which place. So, it was a little bit
> like they were just "following someone," following without knowing
> what they were following. Let's say the truth, you see how kids are.
> Lots of ignorance. They were alone, and so these kids didn't have,
> how can I say it, a brake. If Mom and Dad had been there . . . Why
> all these messes? Where were these revolutions thought of? Where?
> Where were mommy and daddy? No. Where? In Córdoba. In Rosario,
> not as much. These kids were sort of like cannon fodder, eh? Igno-
> rance has no limits. Even if they were students . . .

> EMA: Well, they were more fanatical. Don't forget that students are
> always idealists, normally.

In both testimonies adolescence and the rebellious traits associated with it are indicated as the source of the radicalization. Guerrilla warfare, thus, tends to be thought of as a juvenile and immature reaction where politics does not play a fundamental role. It is interesting that in those years, in a prologue to a conversation in *Confirmado* with university activists, the journalist Rodolfo Pandolfi compared terrorism to car racing. "Among upper-class youth that do not belong to the political left," Pandolfi wrote, "the famous car races replace terrorism, in their own way."[97] Guerrilla violence was situated as one of many options that bourgeois youth had to live a bold, dangerous, and risky existence.

This idea is key because it is the condition of possibility for the vision that, as mentioned in the previous chapter, emphasizes the manipulation that many guerrilla youth would have been victims of, guided by a leadership that would have been responsible for the deaths of thousands of activists (who were frequently alluded to as "parsleys," or nobodies). Norma Gontán, who was a housewife and a mother of eight children, remembered having been a furious opponent of the "kids of extremism." In our interviews she mentioned having been "happy when Monte Chingolo happened because they hunted them down well and they burst them well."[98] Today she claims to think very differently. "What the army did was badly done, very badly done, and should be judged," Norma commented, and continued: "But I also say that the Madres de Plaza de Mayo, who should they seize? Those who seduced their children. Because it's an age, fifteen, eighteen years old, that a young person wants to save the world, and if it's with arms, better. They brainwash you. So, those who are responsible for what happened to these kids are the extremists. They are the Montoneros, the Tupamaros on the other side [in Uruguay], and not the army. Afterward, the army acted badly. Judge them. But judge those [guerrillas] who are walking free now."

In this and in other testimonies, coming from those who were adults in the 1970s — Norma was forty-four years old in 1970 — the leaders of the armed organizations tend to be blamed partially or totally while those who made up the lower ranks of the guerrillas are treated more mercifully, frequently depicted as idealistic "kids" who wanted to "save the world," and let themselves get deceived by the leaders because of their naïveté and immaturity. But this conception does not appear as clearly in the media from the period.[99] Instead, the Monte Chingolo incident mentioned by Norma, for example, provoked a reflection from the Catholic magazine *Criterio* that mentioned a certain social desire that the number of young guerrillas who lost their lives in the failed attack be the highest possible.[100] Norma was careful to differentiate in her testimony what she thinks today from what she thought at the moment. Her happiness when they "hunted down" and "burst" the guerrilla group that attempted to take over the military regiment of Monte Chingolo is incompatible with her current idea that there were leaders and "parsleys." It is likely that the vision that distinguishes between leaders (who were perverse) and "parsleys" (who were naïve), today common sense for Norma's generation, was an a posteriori construction, perhaps promoted upon the return to democracy and paired with the reading of the years of violence made official by the Alfonsín government—known as "the theory of the two demons."[101]

The last factor believed to explain the appearance of guerrillas in Argentina is a generational conflict, sometimes rooted in the center of hidden family conflicts that were represented as social conflicts. Gustavo Maíño, who during his time at the Engineering School of the Universidad de Buenos Aires socialized with members of the Montoneros group without ever participating actively with them, commented that

> some guys seemed pretty stupid, they lived on Callao and Libertador and they imagined themselves in a movie that didn't have anything to do with their lives, because never in their damn lives, even though I knew them being backpackers, did they have an idea of what it meant to have just one shirt to use during an entire year. They didn't have a damn idea about that. They lived in another reality. So, they spoke of things that sounded to me like: "Don't come to me with these things . . ." I couldn't believe them. [. . .] I wasn't that gullible. It was like: "And this guy, what the hell is he talking to me about?" Or, for example, Ricardo's [a university friend] sister, Alicia, she too [would say] "We have to kill them all!" She could flee [and escape the repression] because her father was who he was; if not, she would be buried underground a long time ago, cut into twenty pieces. Also, the sensation that all gave me was that their problems were with something else, not with that. Because it was necessary to take concrete actions and produce a transformation of that controlling elite that would later end up taking power. But from these chats with concrete individuals, I found that what I heard was a background of resentment that didn't mesh with the political argument, because their lives didn't have anything to do with what they were talking about, they had other problems! Then, how am I going to believe what you are telling me! You are talking to me about a social problem, when you have a problem with your mom, a problem with your dad! And you are talking to me about this problem that the workers have? But you weren't a worker, sister! Do you understand what I'm saying?

In Gustavo's explanation, the generational conflict between parents and children appears to play an important role in the radicalized attitudes of his classmates that joined the guerrillas. These youth, on the one hand, are characterized as being exaggeratedly violent ("we have to kill them all"), and, on the other, mobilized by a resentment that was more personal than political. Their rebellion and their choice of violence are explained by a certain impossibility of resolving on the family level the duality of belonging to the establishment inside the home and hoping for its destruction outside of the home.

In a later interview, after mentioning both his "enthusiasm for the effervescence of youth" of the 1970s, and his disagreement with some guerrillas' "vindictive and resentful slant," Gustavo said,

> all these kids, with the education that they had—the access to the instruments and levers of power of the establishment of that time—had they had a nonviolent vision, they could have taken advantage of the time in a totally, absolutely different way. They could have started building something that didn't expose them in the way that it exposed them and so many others. Because particularly they [referring to the Montoneros youth from the upper class that he knew], the majority of them survived. The others, they were purged. But they had places to turn to. [. . .] To clarify a little: at the end, everything went badly, but when they were about to grab them by the hair, Daddy put them somewhere else because he knew what was going on [. . .]

In Gustavo's story, a distinction within the guerillas and the radicalized youth in general appears once again. However, in this case the division is not made, as in the testimonies of older generations, between sinister leaders and "parsleys." Here, it is a class distinction that matters: those who belonged to the upper class and those who came from families with contacts that allowed them to leave the country successfully had a greater chance of saving their lives.

A compatible explanation was provided at the beginning of the 1970s by the sociologist Carlos Floria. Shortly after the beginning of the guerrilla phenomenon in Argentina, Floria was consulted on the subject of violence and affirmed that "the social origin of those who practice subversion, for example, calls my attention, the number of cases in which personal or family frustration seems to be a fundamental factor in the choice of terrorism as a course of action."[102]

In mid-1972, IPSA asked Argentines what the "social issues" that had drawn their attention most during that time were. Of the respondents, 75 percent mentioned assassinations, attacks, and guerrilla actions, while only 12 percent referenced problems that are typically considered social, such as housing and the university.[103] According to another survey from that year, the subject that concerned Argentines the most was the cost of living, followed by sports and national politics.[104] One year later, in 1973, the cost of living moved to second place, with the return of Perón going to the top of the list, and a third subject appeared: kidnappings and violence. By 1974, political violence and Peronism's internal problems led national concerns.

Together with the rise of violence to the top of the list of the population's concerns, surveys registered a progressive hardening of public opinion toward the guerrillas. A few days after the overthrow of the Peronist government, a poll conducted in Capital Federal and the greater Buenos Aires metropolitan area showed growing support for repression.[105] Approximately half of those consulted declared themselves in favor of combating the violence through compulsive or intimidating repression, while only 35 percent opted for persuasion or repression through legal means.[106] Referring not only to the insurgent movements but to all who broke the law in the fallen government, eight out of every ten respondents declared that they wanted the new military authorities to proceed with a "firm hand." The dictatorship did not have to make great efforts to convince a majority of these middle classes that the guerrillas, with whom they never sympathized, deserved state reprisal.

*The organic metaphors with which our entire present discussion of these
matters, especially of the riots, is permeated — the notion of a "sick society,"
of which riots are symptoms, as fever is a symptom of disease —
can only promote violence in the end.* — Hannah Arendt

Four   State Violence (1974–1982)

From a certain moment in the process of political radicalization, state repression became terrorist in nature. An early description of this phenomenon read:

> Another notable evolution is found in the political affiliation of the vic-
> tims; evidently, in the first few months those most affected by the re-
> pression were the members, activists, sympathizers or representatives
> of the Peronist Youth and its member organizations; more sporadically,
> those killed or threatened, imprisoned and tortured belong to sectors
> of the non-Peronist left; in a third instance — forming part of a per-

manent repressive system—it became known that unionists were victims of the police or thugs that responded to the politics of the union bureaucracies; and fourth, coinciding with the attacks against the universities, defense attorneys and other left-wing intellectuals, whether they be Peronist or not, characterized by the following traits: having acted publicly in defense of political prisoners and against the repressive system; [. . .] and finally, the privileged targets for the repression are the members of the guerrilla groups, Montoneros and, especially, the ERP. [. . .] In this grim account, the reader can also learn something about the "methods" or systems employed by the repression: raids, immediate detentions, and finally the "finding of subversive material" all constitute a "formal" circuit, which appears to follow legal procedures, but, of course, everything is invariably done without the basic legal requirement, which is a judge's order; then there is another circuit, that of detention and torture which culminate with being "placed at the disposition of the Executive Power" [puesta a disposición del Poder Ejecutivo]; in a third variant, the formalism disappears and the raid is replaced with a kidnapping that results in torture and subsequent detention in the best of cases and murder in the worst [. . .] the disappearance occurs smoothly and plainly, with the corpse perhaps appearing or perhaps not at some moment; in regard to this, some corpses have never appeared, others have been found burned, others mutilated, others buried, others drowned, others simply abandoned with no declaration. [. . .] There have been corpses with more than one hundred bullets in the body; also powerful bombs; blows are frequent in the administration of torture in addition to the traditional system of the electric cattle prod; from survivors' stories, one also hears of sexual molestation and, in general, humiliation and attempted physical and moral breakdown.[1]

The previous paragraph was written in 1975 and referred to the period from June 20, 1973, the day of Perón's definitive return to the country, to December 31, 1974. The initial date of the report, in its authors' judgment, marked the beginning of an unprecedented phase of state repression that they did not hesitate in labeling as terrorist. The report was commissioned by the Latin American Studies Association, which, in its 1974 sessions in San Francisco, judged that it was "urgent" to conduct an investigation about the situation in Argentina because of the "intense repressive system" exercised by the Peronist government. To carry this out, LASA established an ad hoc Sub-Committee on the Argentine Situation, which was charged with documenting the state of respect for personal freedoms and human rights in the country, convinced that "the process of violence in Argentina couldn't be classified as just another conflict or crisis affecting contemporary societies."[2]

This document highlights the early appearance, within a democratic institutional context, of a terrorist state guided by similar aims and using similar methods to those that the military authorities implemented from March 1976 on. The state terror promoted by the Peronist government is judged by the authors of the document to be "no less serious" than that in Pinochet's Chile, according to the report. Toward the end of 1974, Argentina was experiencing "the most serious direct and indirect repression that the country has suffered from in its history."[3] The description of the tortures and the testimonies from those tortured anticipated those that were collected many years later by the National Commission on the Disappearance of Persons (Comisión Nacional sobre la Desaparición de Personas) (CONADEP).[4] The report additionally denounced the complicity of the union bureaucracy, security forces, and the state with repression, the elimination of journalists through bombings and assassinations, the silencing of information related to the guerrillas, censorship and self-censorship in the media, the hardening of repressive legislation, the persecution of Chilean exiles, the destruction of the university through the firing of hundreds of professors and criminal acts against student leaders, the militarization of the police forces, and determined repression against shantytown (villa miseria) residents.[5] Therefore, the article that discussed this report concluded that, at the very latest from January 1974 on, "terroristic repression became a system of rule in Argentina," and "repressive policies put into effect in Argentina in the 1973–1976 period went beyond the defensive reaction of a particular power group bent on preserving its privileges. It appears to be more a coherent program or project of power and raises the suspicion that repression and semi-official violence might be the first stage in a process leading to the establishment of a system that is at once as harsh as and more complex than the authoritarian regimes of neighboring countries."[6]

From the 1976 coup on, death was industrialized. In less than two years, the state killed, kidnapped, or forcibly disappeared at least seventy-five hundred people across the country.[7] The military dictatorship created numerous clandestine permanent detention centers and introduced macabre procedures to dispose of the corpses.[8] However, many of the elements that composed this industry of death—assassination, kidnapping, "placement at the disposition of the Executive Power," systematic torture, and even the forced disappearance of people—had already been present in the preceding period.

In this chapter, I analyze the middle classes' behavior in the face of state violence. I first describe the elements of continuity that can be established between the periods before and after the coup d'état. Afterward, I discuss the most widespread explanations regarding the attitudes of middle-class social sectors during the dictatorship, following the tracks that underpinned their vision of state violence in the collected testimonies. I then question the subject of responsibility in history based on the different registers of speech they employ. I attempt to approach the testimonies about a tragic social past from those people that were not the protagonists of this tragedy, neither as victims nor as victimizers. Finally, I devote the last section to analyzing the issue of state violence through its presence in symbolic space, exploring the content and meanings deposited in the idea of "subversion."

State Terrorisms

In the years before the March 24, 1976, coup, society began to live with the news of kidnappings, assassinations, and even forced disappearances attributed to state or para-state forces.[9] Moreover, torture had been present as a subject in public opinion well before 1976. The revolutionary youth called Lanusse's government (1971–1973) the "torturing dictatorship."[10] Catholic sectors that had very little to do with liberation theology, such as those that were centered around *Criterio* magazine, in 1972 denounced its "increasingly widespread use in our country, a practice [that of torture] which is becoming an institution of our political system."[11] Political activist sectors, for their part, considered torture to be "inherent to the domination of a system and a social class," which made the struggle against it irrelevant unless one also fought to tear down capitalism.[12] Beyond the news and the reports, torture, assassination, and forcible disappearance formed part of the social landscape to such a point that they could be found represented in the arts.[13]

After the rise of Peronism to power and the quick hegemonization of the government by the movement's most reactionary sectors, state repression made a qualitative leap, as the LASA report testifies, and was reinforced by the paramilitary violence organized by the state (the Triple A)[14] through the Ministry of Social Welfare. *Militancia* magazine, the press organ of the Peronist youth, expressed on various occasions that the state itself was persecuting activists. Days before Perón took charge of the presidency, it denounced "the existence of lists of leaders who will be attacked in the coming days, created by political, union and student sectors of the Right, in an operation of retaliation and 'cleansing' that has been growing since Ezeiza."[15] About the identity of the repressors, the *Militancia* editorial added that "nobody ignores the existence of real gangs, armed by the governing structure, whose members are paid with funds from the national budget."[16]

At the beginning of 1974, the same magazine denounced police raids in shantytowns and working-class neighborhoods intended to capture well-known leaders, indiscriminate detentions, searches of private homes, the arrest of union leaders, attacks against Peronist party locals (*unidades básicas*) and activists in Buenos Aires, Córdoba, and Tucumán, the actions of vigilante groups and even the existence of a "death squad and a MAP [Military Assistant Program] ready to exercise repression."[17] Some days before, it had described the reform of penal legislation led by the Peronist government as directed against "the people as a whole and not, as they attempt to make us think, selectively against the armed organizations."[18]

The response of the Peronist government to these accusations was to flip the burden of proof, something that would become a cliché after the installation of the dictatorship: those who denounced the existence of a terrorism of the right, protected by or executed from the state, were in reality members or defenders of the terrorist groups of the extreme left. In February 1974, when a journalist from El Mundo mentioned the existence of extreme right-wing paramilitary groups, President Perón avoided responding, accusing the newspaper's board of being "ultra-left provocateurs" and ordering the immediate indictment of the journalist who asked the question.[19] By that time, the Peronist government had already abandoned any hope of controlling youth radicalization and was concentrated on repressing it.[20]

This clandestine repression—which combined terrorist practices, such as the placement of explosives, with activities particular to state terror, such as kidnapping and forcible disappearances of people—enjoyed the executive's support. In a speech pronounced at the General Confederation of Labour (CGT) before the end of 1973, Perón attacked the radicalized youth in his movement in terms that anticipated the decrees that his wife and her ministers would sign in 1975 with the objective of annihilating the guerrilla movements. Perón said before the trade unionists:

> In the Argentine Congress, there is a painting called "the Sower" which was a gift of Chile's Chamber of Deputies to Argentina's Chamber of Deputies. It is a farmer who goes along, tossing seeds in the ditch; behind him there is another guy who comes and blows them away. That is the image of life. There are always sowers and there are always blowers of seeds that follow them. In this, we have to use our sensibility *to eliminate or neutralize all these blowers of seeds*, who are always people of bad faith. To the man of good faith, a hug; to he of bad faith, *I won't say what.*[21]

The men of bad faith, who were blowing the seeds away, were alluded to in the speech through the figure of the "infiltration." As the military officials would say shortly thereafter about the nation, Perón believed that his movement was suffering an attack from within by agents foreign to it, who, supported from the outside, had infiltrated its ranks. After Perón's death, this conception became dominant in all relevant positions of the government.

Some press sectors left evidence of a perception of reality that was doubly serious. On the one hand, the time in which they lived was violent without precedent. Wrote Heriberto Kahn near the end of the year, "1974 has been one of the most violent years registered in Argentine history."[22] "The number of those dead and wounded for political reasons," he continued, "has reached levels that are unprecedented since the time when the nation was organized." On the other hand, and more important for the purpose of this chapter, nobody was doing anything to calm tensions. A few days after the death of President Perón, Jorge Lozano wrote:

> The proof of violence is the purest. Subject the government and the system to a catharsis, after which both can demonstrate if they can survive. An escalation of terror creates a wind of tragedy in the society, deeper than the mere acts of bloodshed that occur. Suddenly, it is as if the intangible mechanisms which sustained the organized community break loose, each one is left to its own fate. This is, in short, the immediate objective of the violence: demonstrate to each man and woman in Argentina that they are alone. At this exact point, the State should act. Not to serve particular interests, and not to stop the combatants' maneuvers. It has to do with something simpler: to restore the idea that the government exists.[23]

Almost a year after this paragraph was written, an editorial from the same magazine affirmed: "The big issue in Argentina is fear. [. . .] It is something more, much more than a simple physical fear. It crosses, for example, through political parties and press organs. The great argument is that Argentina today is living through one of the largest waves of fear in all of its history. That is for sure, but there is something else: the violence—the bombs and the murders—can be a great argument to not do anything, to not take any risk, to be able to vegetate happily."[24]

Diagnoses like these could be found by the dozens in the press in 1974 and 1975. The state appeared to be primarily responsible for the terror, sometimes by action, as when it organized the Triple A and other related organizations, and sometimes by omission, as when it showed its ineptitude in reclaiming the monopoly of legitimate force.[25] They were "Hobbesian times," wrote Carlos Floria toward the end of 1974, in an expression that was both timely and prophetic.[26] No year of Argentine history was closer to the state of nature than 1975, and no other years would resemble Leviathan more than the first two years of the National Reorganization Process (el Proceso).

Unlike the argument that emphasizes the horror that the arrival of the 1976–1983 dictatorship meant by contrasting it with the "soft dictatorship" ("dictablanda") of the 1966–1973 "Argentine Revolution" government, what I have argued serves to establish connections, not so much between different dictatorships but between different state terrorisms. In this sense, the military officials of el Proceso were more closely related to the Peronist government that preceded them (1973–1976), especially from 1974 on, than in the military government led by Onganía, Levingston, and Lanusse (1966–1973). State terrorism was not contrary to democracy, nor were military regimes necessarily terrorist. State terrorism showed itself to be compatible with both an illegal government and with one elected by the people, with both military and civilian authorities, with both a de facto state and a de jure state.

This should be kept in mind in order to understand the attitudes of the middle classes not involved in the political struggle, who did not lament the fall of Isabel Perón, whose fate they had been indifferent to for some time, and who received the arrival of the military in 1976 with relief.[27] Furthermore, it should be remembered that, based on past experience, these sectors did not register military interventions as inherently terrorist, but rather as regimes that, while authoritarian, represented greater order and less violence than those guaranteed by Isabel's government.[28] These middle classes processed the arrival of the military to power through what social psychology defines as "anchoring mechanisms," the insertion of a new event into a framework of preexisting, already well known and familiar references, that offset the impact of the situation created by a new event.[29] March 24, 1976, could "anchor" itself within social representations drawn from relatively recent history (the overthrow of Levingston on March 22, 1971, and Onganía on June 18, 1970), and others that were relatively similar (the overthrow of Illia on June 28, 1966, and Perón on September 16, 1955).[30]

The overthrow of Isabel, additionally, occurred in a context in which the values associated with democracy and dictatorship, for politicians and military officials, were not opposed to each other as good versus bad, but rather were presented with many more nuances. After Perón's death, the Peronist government increasingly could not combat the feeling of a large part of the middle classes that the growing violence—guerrilla, paramilitary, and repressive—was anarchic and uncontrolled, without a governing logic, however cruel or bloody it might be. The state terror that preceded the dictatorship was perceived as indiscriminate and arbitrary on the pages of La Opinión, the newspaper of the progressive, "enlightened" middle classes. In an article that compared the methods used by Nazism to spread terror during the first period of the Warsaw ghetto to the tactics used by the Triple A and other similar organizations in 1974 and 1975 in Argentina, *La Opinión* wrote, almost three months before the coup, that "the most effective tactic to impose terror is arbitrariness. The more people are exposed to indiscriminate threats, the greater the effects of the terror will be, and, consequently, the greater the possibility of imposing a particular structure on a group, sector or population."[31]

All of this led to an environment in early 1976 that could hardly be more propitious for much of the society—which, as the LASA report mentioned, had not experienced anything similar in terms of magnitude and brutality until that moment—to imagine that the fall of Isabel Perón and the rise of the armed forces to power would bring order to the political, social, and economic realms that, independent of its content, would represent above anything else stability. By the time the coup happened, the military was already able to rely on a fundamental social fact, without which any understanding of the attitude of civil society toward the new military government is destined to fail: violence, as a threat and as a fact, structurally already formed part of their perception of the Argentine political reality.[32] The analysis of the transition from Peronism to the dictatorship should not omit the existence of this inertial structure—one that pushed society, especially its sectors not directly affected by state violence, to look for the novelties introduced by el Proceso anywhere but on the terrain of the exercise of violence.[33]

This fact does not explain the ferocity of the military repression. It does, however, allow us to think about the bases of legitimacy that el Proceso believed it had when it turned the armed forces and the security apparatus into one big Triple A.[34] The new military authorities presented themselves to society as those who came to reestablish an order that did not inspire terror, persecuting the terrorism of the Left and jailing deposed authorities who were corrupt or had links with armed groups.[35] The terror of the military state sought legitimation by emphasizing the terror (and the corruption, disorder, immorality, and ineptitude) of the Peronist state. This was not a difficult task. Much of society, especially its middle classes, shared this damning judgment of the fallen government.[36] The month of the coup, the writer Ernesto Sabato—who, together with Borges and Cortázar, was the most prestigious and famous intellectual of the Argentina of those days—characterized the members of the deposed government as "improvising, politicking and impatient thieves, led by a man [López Rega] who became a symbol of this vast mockery."[37] Nothing showed this fact better than the discourse of memory that reigned in the media and in various sectors of civil and political society.

The call for Argentines to not forget the terrorists' acts, and to remember as a civic and moral duty the ineptitude and corruption of the Peronist government, occupied a prominent place in the press and public opinion.

During el Proceso, the *raison d'état* literally organized, amplified, and, as far as they were able to, concealed death. The state monopolized not only violence but soon terror as well.[38] Clandestine detention centers operated throughout the entire country, in some cases on property located in residential areas. Perhaps precisely because they were located in plain sight, few imagined at the moment that they were sites for the systematic application of torture and the annihilation of human beings. The magnitude of what state terrorism meant was discovered, at least for the vast majority of the population, only with the arrival of democracy and in a relatively gradual form, as the information available and the social disposition to find out what occurred increased. However, multiple cracks in this repressive structure leaked signs of this industry of death, more visible in cities such as Buenos Aires and Tucumán than in small localities like Correa. Moreover, the media and the military authorities themselves, while trying to hide the acts of repression, frequently admitted indirectly what they were attempting to hide.

From March 1976 on, censorship and self-censorship in the mass media became the conditions of possibility for journalism. "The media became part of the network of state," affirmed the *Cuestionario* monthly, directed by Rodolfo Terragno, shortly after the coup.[39] Without a doubt, this claim was exaggerated, but it had a basis as far as the repression was concerned. News about guerrilla actions and state repression made the media look a lot like official bulletins. A reading of the newspapers and magazines that were published in the first years of the dictatorship leave the sensation that much of the press, and with it at least a portion of its readers, rooted their vision of reality in Benjamin's famous aphorism that any document of civilization is at the same time one of barbarism, except that they inverted the phrase.[40] Each document of barbarism was reported as a document of civilization. Praise for the efficiency with which the military government eliminated armed subversion and reordered the chaos that they inherited was abundant.[41] This fact makes it necessary to prioritize the memories of the interviewees over the journalistic documents.[42]

The State Is Supposed to Know

The sociopolitical situation, in addition to an economic crisis that had especially hurt the middle classes from the time of the Rodrigazo on,[43] was sufficiently serious that the sensation of anarchy and state absence was not unreasonable. The terror supported or executed by the Peronist government itself was not conducted in the name of the state. For the citizenry that was not directly involved in the political struggle, the image was not that of a state that was to be feared. On the contrary, what existed was a fear originating in the state's abandonment of its role as the monopolizer of violence. In this context, the rise of the armed forces to power was received by wide segments of the population, and by almost all of the press, as a certain promise of the restoration of order and the monopoly on violence.

The behavior of Argentine society in general, and of the middle classes in particular, during the years of the last military dictatorship has tended to be summarized in the exculpatory maxims "he must have done something" and "it must be because of something," often read as indicators of a complicit attitude toward repressive practices or as a predisposition to ignore what was happening. In this section, I propose to return to this subject, in part because these phrases remain in the discourse of those who were adults in those years, and in part because their permanence indicates that the prevailing interpretation is insufficient. Thirty-five years later, in a social context of widespread disapproval of the methods used in the repression and broad knowledge about everything that happened, these maxims and other arguments that are similarly oriented cannot continue to be explained as mere complicity or ignorance. I propose, instead, to consider them as symptoms of the existence of a civil superstition: the belief in something for which there is no proof, or there is even proof to the contrary, but its raison d'être is not dependent on its truth (although truth does often have a part in the matter). This belief is not constituted as a merely subjective, interior element. "Belief, far from being a purely mental, 'intimate' state," writes Slavoj Žižek, "always materializes in our effective social activity: belief sustains the fantasy that regulates social reality."[44] Every society is based on some sort of belief. In this section, I analyze the content of the civil superstition that hegemonized public opinion during the first years of el Proceso.

Michael Taussig has called our attention to what he denominates as "State fetishism," a sacred and erotic attraction, a combination of fascination and disgust that the State provokes in its subjects.[45] The State appears to the citizens not only as the incarnation of reason, in the Hegelian register, but also as if it were an organic unit, coherently interrelated, a monad that is much more than the sum of its parts. In reality, what exists in the phenomenological world, Taussig indicated, following A. R. Radcliffe-Brown, is the power of individuals: kings, prime ministers, magistrates, police, party leaders, and voters. The notion of the State as a fetish is much closer to a Foucauldian than a Weberian conception of power. But one thing is what power is, and another thing, often different, is how it is perceived. Upon seeing a police officer, one always "sees" more than a police officer (one sees the officer as one link of a chain, as the representation of something that is not there but that empowers the officer and, in that sense, is indeed there). If one saw in the officer only what he really was—a person dressed in a uniform, armed with instruments to exercise violence—the notion that a powerful and supra-individual entity takes care of or watches over us crumbles.

For Taussig, the State is a fiction that conditions practices. Its character as a fetish is rooted in its being a mask; it prevents us from seeing what we actually see (some men in uniform, a tax collector, a person stamping a passport, and so on) and allows and obligates one to act as if it existed. When one pulls away the veil there is nothing to see, but Taussig puts the emphasis on the existence and reality of the political power of this fiction. Even if the State is a fetish, if it doesn't exist with a capital "S" but rather in small doses, in concrete people who are only ideally in harmony with the rest of the agents of the State, the subjects need to believe in its real existence as the only way of not feeling themselves abandoned.

Based on the memories of a Tierra del Fuego sheep herder who participated in a group of the Ona tribe and discovered that all of the power of this primitive State resided in a false belief, in whose creation all the members of the society participated, Taussig concludes that State fetishism depends less on the truths of those who represent the State (judges, police officers, et cetera) than on "the fantasies of the marginalized concerning the secret of the center."[46] The official secret, the true secret of the State, is its nonexistence. The State does not exist as it is imagined by its citizens. But a society could scarcely guarantee its sociability if it was conscious of this nonexistence. The fundamental aspect of Taussig's idea lies in the fact that State subjects act as if it (and with it the reason for its force, for its violence, for its always justified actions) existed. The fetishist character of the State is rooted in this: it is presented as the substrate that gives meaning and rationality to the actions of its agents over individuals. It appears to be a mask that hides an ultimate reason, but it is the reverse; its representatives are the mask behind which it hides, not a rational organism, but simply "a hollow core, a meticulously shielded emptiness."[47]

Viewed from this conceptual framework, the maxims "it must be because of something" or "he must have done something" can be read as something more or even different than mere complicity or ignorance. These were the phrases of a society that clung to the belief that the state had returned and attributed an ultimate, unknown, and even unattainable rationality to the representatives of a power that at the same time was imposed on them, but

FIGURE 4.1. Military authorities, chaired by General Jorge Rafael Videla, at the Monument to the Flag in the city of Rosario, June 20, 1979. *Source: La Capital archives.*

at least ideally sheltered them from a greater chaos. Even when all violence, at least on the discursive level, can be objectionable for the middle classes, that which had its origin in the state had a rationale that, above all else, was a rationale. If one did not know this rationale, one simply supposed its existence. The state does what it does because its violence must have a reason. This is precisely Taussig's central point about the fetishism of the State:

> This necessary institutional interpenetration of reason by violence not only diminishes the claims of reason, casting it into ideology, mask, and effect of power, but also . . . *it is precisely the coming together of reason-and-violence in the State that creates, in a secular and modern world, the bigness of the big S*—not merely its apparent unity and the fictions of will and mind thus inspired, but the auratic and quasi-sacred quality of that very inspiration, a quality we quite willingly impute to the ancient States of China, Egypt, and Peru, for example, or to European Absolutism, but not to the rational-legal State that now stands as ground to our being as citizens of the world.[48]

The previously mentioned maxims tend to be interpreted in reference to the people who suffered from the repression. If one instead observes the other pole of repressive action, the state agent who exercises it, the questions that these maxims open are not related with the presumed criminal, terrorist, or "subversive" activities of those repressed, but rather with the knowledge of the agent that represses: *it is supposed that the State knows.*[49] This civil superstition refers primarily to the activities of state agents and only then, and almost by extension, to the people who suffered from their activities. In other words, more than positioning itself against the victims, the civil superstition rested on the grounds of state necessity. Inquiring into this characteristic of the state, about its supposed knowledge, helps us not only to explain the behaviors of the middle classes of those years, but also to interpret their current memories.

Elsa and Santiago Camporreali, a couple from Correa who in 1976 were thirty-five and thirty-one years old, respectively, appealed to this civil superstition that always supposes the state's knowledge several times. During our last meeting, while listening to one of Massera's speeches, seeing images of him and of the military checkpoints on the roads, I asked them about the memory they had of Massera and the military junta.[50] Elsa responded, and her husband agreed: "Massera was rough. We weren't, nothing happened to us. Probably, other people, who had some weird things going on . . . But I think that, if there were forcible disappearances, there were things. These people must have been doing something, right? Why did they take them? Why did they go inside a house and take away the parents of little children? Why? What was happening?"

SC: And what was your hypothesis? What was happening?

ELSA: I don't know. What I remember is that, it was said, the people here, in the towns, would say: "and how is it that here in the town they didn't come to take anyone away? Why did they only take people away in the big cities?

Aldo Círcolo, a Correa resident of the same age as Elsa, also implicated the supposed knowledge of the state in several comments. During our first interview, in the context of a conversation about daily life in Correa during the military period, he remembered:

All of this [referring to the repression] was seen as something that didn't exist here. Here nothing happened, not in Correa. In Rosario yes, there were various disappearances, but not here. No raids, no green Falcons [Ford cars] here, as far as I remember. In fact, I even went to Rosario every ten days, and nobody ever bothered me or asked me for documents. I always brought my enrollment booklet and they never stopped me. Yes, there were soldiers everywhere but I was an anonymous citizen, a common citizen. They never stopped me, I never had problems, absolutely, never, nobody. But that it existed . . . it existed. We can't deny that.

Four months later, seeing images from the documentary, he completed the same idea:

I started to travel to Rosario to learn to play the guitar, from 1975 to 1980. And I, when the military came in, still had the famous huge enrollment book, I still have it. And they never asked me for it! The trains would take you to Rosario Central, which was seven blocks away from downtown, from Córdoba and Corrientes streets, and the music school was nearby. And afterward, well, I would go on a bus too, and they never asked me for documents. Well, they must know the people.

In both testimonies, this civil superstition can be seen. Also in both cases the belief that the state knows—or should know—why it does what it does is based on an irrefutable truth related to their personal experiences. In Elsa's case, this was the fact that there were no forcible disappearances in the town, where there were no members that belonged to armed organizations. In Aldo's case, this was the fact that he traveled to Rosario, a city in which he knows there were "various disappearances," but where he "never had any problems." These subjective truths, however, would not be sufficient in themselves to understand the interviewees' thinking if they were not completed with a supposition about the state's knowledge. "They must know the people," Aldo affirmed to explain the fact that repression occurred, what "we can't deny," that he, "a common, anonymous citizen," "was never stopped," and "never asked for documents." Elsa implies something analogous: if the state did not know why it was doing what it was doing, if it did not have some rationale to act in the way that it did, "how is it that here in the town they didn't come to take anyone away?"

Susana Mancuso, in Tucumán, also implied in her recollection that she lived as if the state knew what it was doing. The case of Tucumán, however, is more complex than that of Correa because it was not enough to be outside the activities or ideologies that the state was targeting to consider oneself safe. The fear of being betrayed by someone who for whatever reason had intentions to harm you was an important ingredient, absent in the stories of those from Buenos Aires and Correa. However, responding to a question about how the university had changed with the coup—Susana was a medical student at the Universidad Nacional de Tucumán—she said: "In the span of a couple months, [some students] began to disappear, and we knew that some of them were 'disappeared' and others weren't, that is, they had gone, left somewhere else. Their parents themselves had sent their children abroad. Right? Then, that happened. And after that, nothing. Because of that, I tell you, it was like one went on with life and nothing was going happen to you if you weren't involved in that." [51]

"Nothing was going to happen to you if you weren't involved in that" because it was supposed that the state knew who was "involved" and who wasn't. Carlos Etcheverría described the situation in Buenos Aires in the same sense. "Things happen for some reason, they don't fall from the sky," he said referring to the disappeared. It would be erroneous to confuse these testimonies with support for the military repression. In the majority of cases, this, as we today know, was rejected categorically. Additionally, in Susana's case, like the others interviewed from her generation—youth between twenty and twenty-five years old in 1976—the negative memories that the police and the military generated are clear. "The assault vehicles, the police, everything that was theoretically security, was danger for me," Susana said in another interview.[52] But, upon remembering what she thought when the disappearances of her peers began, the "supposed knowledge of the State" appears, the supposition, in that time perceived as real, that the state was not going to hurt her, since it knew "if one was involved in that."

In Susana's testimony, the affirmation that the state knew who "was involved" corresponds to how she remembered she thought in those years. In other testimonies, however, this is asserted as a historical truth. However, the same people who maintain that the repression affected those who "deserved" to be repressed (basically, the guerrillas), at other points affirm that the repression also touched those who had nothing to do with the insurrectional movements.

Claudio Mastrángelo, in the 1970s a young student at the School of Humanities in the Universidad Nacional de Rosario, insisted during our three meetings that the repression affected those who were implicated in terrorism. During out first meeting, speaking of his time in the university, he said: "Look, I'm sorry, I'm going to be a little bad—and if you want to ruin my life with this, go ahead, ruin it, I don't care. I can assure you that I know who they touched. I was the same age and they never bothered me. Do you understand? They never bothered me. I studied, I was in Rosario, I went on the bus, I went on the train, never, never, never did the military touch me. And I was in the crosshairs, in Humanities, eh?"

However, when commenting on the second part of the documentary (1975–1982), the same idea appeared accompanied by another that contradicted it. To cite two examples: "They [the military] knew who they were. Who they bothered, and who they went to look for. They didn't just touch anybody, not just anybody. What I don't agree with, is that they didn't give the young men and women the possibility to be judged, and if it [the decision] was for freedom, then freedom, and if it was for jail, then jail. All of the aberrations they did, I don't agree with them. As a human being I can't agree with them."

SC: And did you already call them "the disappeared"?

CLAUDIO: No. They were "sucked away" [*chupados*]. That's what we said in that period: "they sucked him," "they sucked Mengano away," "if you have some book of his, burn it." And the smoke that would come billowing up from the terraces of the buildings, the terraces or the incinerators! How many books were burned just because they had somebody's signature or address in it! You had to go through everything, everything, because probably: "they sucked away so-and-so," and you had a book that said "so-and-so" and: "what connection do you have with so-and-so?" Do you understand what I'm saying? Yes, that was messed up. But, what do I know, compared to how we lived before [1976], it was nothing. It was nothing in comparison. I'll repeat it again, I'm probably a heretic, and you'll probably go out and say I'm a monster, but they didn't touch someone just to touch them, they knew who they were touching, eh?

Although in these excerpts Claudio reiterated the idea that the military "knew who they were," that they "didn't touch someone just to touch them," he also mentioned, indirectly in the first excerpt and directly in the second, that the repression also fell over those "who weren't." The desire that those accused have a possibility of being judged and "if [the decision] was for freedom, then freedom" implies a recognition that not everyone was "guilty." The mention that someone could be "sucked away" ("*chupado*") for having a text that belonged to or had the name of someone that had already been arrested, the recognition that "that was messed up [*jodido*]," all indicated that Claudio knows that the repression went beyond the realm of the combatants.

Alfonso and Delia Aparicio, an adult couple in the 1970s who had young children in those years, also combined the same contradiction in their discourse. Alfonso affirmed on two occasions that the military "killed who they had to kill." His wife, Delia, questioned the morality of the repressive methods and affirmed, less confidently, "I have my doubts about whether or not all those that were affected were guilty." Both of them mentioned some cases of disappearances that they knew of from neighboring cities and in Rosario in which those kidnapped were "extremists" or "were in the mess." However, in response to my question if they were afraid for one of their sons, who entered the university in 1976, they responded:

> DELIA: I was always scared, because I was always easily scared. I was always scared, because I didn't know, what did I know, in what he could get involved . . .

> ALFONSO: No, I'll tell you why she was scared. I was scared too. Because Daniel [their university student son] has a strong character.

> D: He says what he has to tell you.

> A: Once I was really afraid, when we were across from the Italian hospital—there was a cafeteria there in that period where you could eat well—and Daniel started to rant against the military . . . And there were two guys at a table, and I said: "These guys are military"—because of their haircuts, their posture, when they walked, you saw it right away. And Daniel was speaking badly [of the military] . . . And in those days, those that spoke badly of the military disappeared. I swear to you I felt scared for a month! I was very scared because he studied at the university in Rosario, and I said "they're going to liquidate him." It was an obsession that I had. He escaped. They didn't do anything to him.

Two opposite convictions are combined in the same testimony. On the one hand, the idea that the military "killed who they had to kill," on the other, that in that period "speaking badly of the military" could make one disappear.

Diego Puerta, who in 1976 was in his last year in the Gimnasio (an elite Tucumán high school that was politicized in that period), in the context of a conversation about daily life during el Proceso, said:

> But they [the police and the military] didn't bother you too much, because they knew who they were. At least they never bothered me, or my family, or my relatives, or nobody. But, I did know of people that were related to something, and they were bothered. In the middle of the night, they would come into your house, break down the door, "inside." Bye. They put the hood on you and you're done. [. . .] They knew very well who they were, they did. It was a very good system of intelligence. They knew who they were.

However, only a couple minutes earlier, he had evoked memories that contradicted this judgment. The dialogue proceeded as follows:

SC: For a young man as you were in '76, did the nightlife change after the coup?

DIEGO: No. No. What happens is—you've got to admit it—I tell you, they knew full well, who they were and who they weren't. They went to the key points. So that didn't change much because of that. Of course, you couldn't have long hair or a beard.

[. . .]

SC: Did you also live in fear?

D: Yes, the fear was constant.

SC: What were you afraid of?

D: The excesses. They were brutal. You knew that if you were a pain in the ass, you were done for. You couldn't be a pain in the ass, they didn't exist in that period. Well, they existed, and they would pick them up. Many of them were picked up without being guerrillas, extremists, or anything of the sort. We lived with a lot of fear. Fear instilled by them. No more than three people in the street, it was like a state of siege. You could live peacefully, you could do what you wanted to, the whole story, but you made a mistake and . . .

Watching the documentary (1975–1982), provoked by images of military roadside checkpoints, he mentioned that "this fear [of the military checkpoints] was terrible," that "you saw a police officer, or an army soldier, and you said to yourself 'Oh . . . What did I do?'" Both in these statements as in the previous excerpts, Diego contradicted his idea that the repression was limited to combatants. If various people "were picked up without being guerrillas, extremists, or anything of the sort," if "you saw a police officer or a soldier and thought 'Oh . . . What did I do?'" this is because the repression reached beyond the people involved in the armed insurrection.

How can we explain that the same testimony combines these contradictory ideas? Aren't they mutually exclusive? How can the civil superstition of the supposed knowledge of the state be sustained, and still persevere in some people's memories once evidence that contradicts or nullifies it is known? How can someone at the same time affirm that the state knew who was involved in the armed insurrection and recognize that the repression greatly exceeded the sphere of the combatants?

The dialectic between the law (the institutions and the people that embody it) and the society, especially when the state primarily assumes its police function, is not governed by truth. As in Kafka's account of the law, the guardian, and the stranger, what is important to guarantee a disciplinary order is not that the subjects know the content of the law, but simply that they fear it. And for this to occur, as the priest explains to Josef K. at the end of *The Trial*, it is not necessary that the order of things be accepted as being true, but rather only as necessary. In other words, the society does not believe in the law because it considers it to be true, but rather because it judges it to be indispensable; its necessity is not deduced from its truth, its truth is deduced from its necessity. It is not important that the law's guardians (state agents, police officers, military officials) "convince" society of the truth behind their actions. What is truly important is that the citizens recognize that it is necessary for the law to do what it judges pertinent.

Thus, the knowledge regime that regulates a civil superstition depends on necessity. Because of this, the superstition (in this case, the supposed knowledge of a repressive state) could (and can) be maintained even if the facts contradict it. The sectors analyzed here did not suppose that the state "knew" because they had sufficient evidence. As in Kafka, civil superstitions are based on accepting that what they faced was something from the realm of necessity, not of proof.

Watching the documentary when images of the military junta appeared, Aldo Círcolo commented: "It was a rough period, and I don't know if the military did good or did evil." When we finished watching the film, I returned to this comment and asked him in what sense he had said it, to which he responded:

> Yes, I don't know, because, as I told you, I don't understand much about politics, but maybe they had to do it. Like in Rosas's time, my cousin from San Nicolás, who passed away—a historian who knew a lot about San Martín—[told me that] the guy probably committed excesses, but he had to do it, he said. Well, I don't know. And he always told me: "look son, if they resuscitated Rosas or San Martín, the people leading the country now would be beheaded or in front of the firing squad within ten minutes. Of course, that period was total barbarism. [. . .] What the military of el Proceso did I saw as—there was an extremist group that needed to be stopped. I don't know what would happen afterward, but they had to stop those people . . .

In Tucumán, the disapproving judgment regarding the brutality and cruelty of the military coexists in many testimonies with the judgment that military action was necessary. Referring to one of Videla's speeches that we heard in the documentary (where he mentions the antisubversive war), Ángela Caballero (thirty-six years old in 1976), commented: "I never thought of it as a war. It was like a repression that was necessary. Because you saw these crimes, these attacks, and you said, 'Well, it's like they [the military] are protecting us.'"

Another woman from Tucumán, single and professional, María Emilia Palermo (forty-one years old in 1976), also mentioned the necessity of repressing the guerrillas. After seeing the second part of the documentary (1975–1982), taking advantage of the fact that she admitted having modified her way of thinking over the years, I asked her if she had also changed her judgments of the guerrillas and the military. María Emilia answered: "I continue to have the same posture and think in the same way about the guerrillas, except that I now think that there were excesses committed by the military, just like there were excesses on the other side. But I think that that was the moment and that they needed, it was necessary to do it."

The experience of state terrorism in Argentina shows that the force of a civil superstition in each historical situation is directly related to the intensity of the need for it. The more a society judges it needs it, the less truth a civil superstition requires. In other words, the greater the need for that which the civil superstition demands—a state that monopolizes violence and re-establishes order—the less important the register of truth becomes, which passes to a secondary plane as a mere complement, an inert impulse before the force of necessity.

The recollections of state terrorism of those who were neither involved in the political struggle nor suffered its consequences directly tended to contain paradoxical elements. The civil superstition that presupposed the state's knowledge allows us to explain some of these contradictory elements. Large sectors of the middle classes did not demand "truth" from the state during the years of terror. They believed, instead, in the need for a state whose ruthlessness, especially in its first years, was not enough to seriously question the "supposed knowledge" attributed to its actions.

Memories of One's Own Role in the Horror: The Impersonal Register

In many testimonies, the memories evoked and the responses provoked by my questions and the documentaries underwent a change in discursive register when the topic was state terrorism. I refer to the step from the personal to the impersonal register, from "I" to "one" or to "it was thought/it was said/it was wanted." It is different to affirm that "*one* didn't know what was happening" instead of "I didn't know what was happening" or "*one* supported the dictatorship" instead of "I supported the dictatorship." The analysis of this change in narrative register, from a personal to an impersonal mode, opens a path to explore meanings that appear not in the content of the discourses but in their form. The change in register did not occur when discussing any other subject, only state terrorism. It was not so, for example, when the interviews discussed subjects such as sex, customs, fashion, childhood memories, or even personal political identity. Unlike these topics, in which the testimonies maintained the personal register, questions referring to state terrorism and the disappeared provoked this change in register in many of the interviewees.

The contrast between the personal and the impersonal register is not insignificant.[53] The personal register identifies the subject that narrates at the center of what he/she remembers having thought or done. When a discourse shifts toward the impersonal register, the story rests on an undefined subject—which only includes the "I" generically, in a way that it is clearly not the "I" who speaks. In the middle of the two registers, between the "I" and the "one," allusions are often made to an undefined "we," when the interviewee is speaking in the name of a social group or assumes the voice of society as a whole, impersonalizing their speech. It is relevant to include some of these uses of the plural within what I call the impersonal register.

The coup d'état of 1976, which many interviewees remember as being not only foretold,[54] but also, in a certain sense, desired, tends to appear in the testimonies as something that "the people," "the society," or "everyone" asked for or accepted, but never as a personal demand rooted in the "I." "I can assure you that people were asking for it," Claudio Mastrángelo said referring to the coup. "I remember that there were people that viewed the coup with great sympathy," remembered Luis Martino. Later, he added: "when the dictatorship emerged, it seemed to us that it was going to be something that would save us," alluding in this "us" to an undefined subject. "Everyone was happy at the beginning because Isabelita fell. That was, as people used to say: 'Ay, God bless the military,' " said Ema Mateo in the same sense. A former activist from Tucumán, employee of the Peronist provincial government from 1973 to 1975, told me that "there was a certain moment that you were saying, let this end! Let this end! When the military coup occurred, they say that many people supported it. They supported it because they were scared witless, and what we wanted was for it to end, for the bombs every day to end." In all the cases, what is repeated in the narrative form is the absence of the "I" and the use of a diffuse plural, a "we" into which the "I" dissolves.

Another habitual form that this impersonal register assumes in the testimonies about the dictatorship was the "one." After hearing an official speech in which Videla affirms that Argentina was waging a war against Marxist subversion and thus, as a consequence, there were disappearances, Ángela

Caballero, a seventy-year-old Tucumán woman, told me: "this speech, and also, with all that we knew about Cuba and everything else, one believed it." Also turning to an impersonal register, Ricardo Montecarlo—one of the interviewees from Tucumán who most clearly repudiated the actions of the military government—remembering dead guerrillas "heaped up like bags" in a Salta hospital in which he worked as a resident, told me: "These are very ugly memories for me. They're very ugly. One had to keep quiet many times. I don't know if now you feel like a coward, I don't know, but one has seen many things, many guerrillas that they took to the hospital emergency rooms, tortured, and all those things, and you had to keep quiet. What are you to do?" In Ricardo's case, the impersonal register appears in the second person singular ("I don't know if you feel like a coward;" "you had to keep quiet"). But in all of them the personal register, the "I," disappears.

In the testimony of Linda Tognetti, a Correa resident, the switch from the personal to the impersonal register can be observed clearly every time that my questions or her own story alluded to state terrorism. The excerpts correspond to the three interviews between 2008 and 2010 in her home. During the three meetings, Linda responded to my questions and narrated her memories primarily in the first person, speaking about herself and not in the name of her family or the social groups to which she belonged. When she referred to what her parents, her brother, or her husband thought or did, she included the corresponding subject. The change from a personal to an impersonal register occurred during all the times when we spoke of her thoughts or actions in the years of state terrorism. Unlike the other interviewees in the town, Linda has a globally critical vision of what the last military dictatorship meant. Without recognizing herself as a Radical, her electoral preferences always inclined toward this party. Although she never participated in politics, she considers that if she had studied in La Plata or Rosario at the end of the 1960s, her political commitment would have been greater.[55]

In our first interview, in response to a question about how she remembered experiencing the climate of political violence in the early 1970s in the town, she responded:

No, not here. Nothing happened here. There were no disappearances. If those of us who were . . . , the few teachers that were from here, the university students of the period, were investigated or not, I don't have the slightest idea. I wasn't afraid. My mother was afraid for me. When I traveled around five in the morning, she would stop at the door, watching me until I got to the road. And I used to say: "How stupid! What am I doing here and she over there?" But I wasn't afraid. I didn't commit myself either, I was never in any politics, perhaps I didn't risk enough. And afterward, in the period of el Proceso, one was already working and one didn't get involved. And I think that many people that tell you they didn't, actually applauded the military's arrival. And they're going to lie to you and I'm going to argue hard with them.

Several months later, during our last meeting, as we watched the second part of the documentary, I asked her about the 1976 coup and the following dialogue developed:

SC: Do you remember where you were when the 1976 coup happened?

LINDA: Here, in my house.

SC: Did it surprise you?

L: No. With Isabel, it was like *Chronicle of a Death Foretold*. In addition, it happened at a time that people were already disgusted with Isabel's government, or her lack of government, as I say. There López Rega ran everything, or the unions did. But there was a lack of control. So, that was something that I think was asked for. People really were knocking on the doors of the barracks. It was never thought that [the military government] would go as far as they did. But they asked, they asked. [. . .] In addition to that, I think that people were like, it was like they never found out [what was happening], but, in a way, that's what they had desired. Like it or not, in reality, although people will deny it later. But, in the moment, people wanted a little more order, but I don't know what type of order, if the military order meant . . . , but we were . . . I think that we were tired of this, and the guerrillas were acting already, the Triple A was a disaster, and the Montos were too, because Perón threw them out of the Plaza de Mayo.

Let's see the different registers in the discourse. Linda speaks at first in the name of a specific collective group that includes her, "the few teachers that were from here," and comments that she has no idea "if we were investigated." Unlike other uses of the plural, here there is a defined "we" which included the "I" that narrated. Linda doesn't know if the police were watching her and other teachers from the town; the register of this affirmation is personal, the "we" is a defined, concrete, nameable group. The latter reference to fear is also made in the personal register: "I didn't have any fear," and later, "I didn't commit myself either, I was never in any politics . . ." The change toward an undefined register, the transition from "I" to "one," only occurs in the last phrase, when her account reaches state terrorism: "In the period of el Proceso, *one* was already working and *one* didn't get involved." The final phrase ("I believe that many people tell you that no, they applauded the arrival of the military") once again alludes to an impersonal register, this time to a "them," to a "many people," a collective from which the subject that is narrating excludes herself.

In the second excerpt, the personal register disappears almost completely and different forms of the impersonal mode take charge of the narration. "*People* were already disgusted" with Isabel, the coup was something that "was asked for," the barracks doors "were pounded on," "*people* wanted a little more order," although they didn't recognize that they also wanted military intervention. In the last part, Linda includes a new voice, a "we" that includes her, generically, in a less defined way than when she refers to the "few teachers" of Correa. When she says "*we* were tired of this," she includes herself in the universe formed by those who no longer tolerated the Peronist government. However, the subject on which this weariness rests is not the "I" but rather an impersonal subject, an undefined plural, potentially formed by the whole society into which the "I" dissolves.

Independently of what Linda says in the transcribed text, what interests me now is to show for which type of affirmations or memories her narration uses the "I" form and for which type it turns to non-"I" forms. In response to my question about what happened in Correa when, following the military intervention at the national level, the local authorities changed, the following dialogue occurred:

> LINDA: I think that nothing much happened. Because things changed, and your friend Juan wasn't in there anymore, but now it was your neighbor Pedro, or the doctor or the lawyer. They were people from the town. Afterward, probably, I think that after '84 they analyzed many things. "Oh, this guy collaborated with el Proceso," but why not, if he was a good guy who occupied a position. But I'll tell you this: who didn't collaborate with el Proceso, directly or indirectly? Because the people that were committed, on one side and on the other, for or against, lived it in another way. Here we didn't live through it. Later, you found that, probably, in a neighboring locality, some kid disappeared, kidnapped, was living in that locality, hiding out in a relative's home. But you, until that moment, just knew that "someone's son" was in "someone's house." You would find out later. Or somebody that worked with you and later you found out that they were "sucked away" and tortured. And one what? Was one

ignorant? Did one not want to see? Did one live comfortably? I don't know. This experience of living in the city, with these fears, I don't know if we lived it so much here. I don't know. I don't know what the other people you interviewed told you . . .

SC: That wasn't your experience, you didn't live through it like that . . .

L: No. I didn't live through it so much. Later, one began to put two and two together. I did, when they analyzed my degree, in that episode I told you about [she is referring to when, after asking for a certificate of good conduct from a police station to do some paperwork, a police officer suspected that she might have something to with socialism because she was a social science teacher], and with the people that were disappearing, then I burned a lot of material. Which was idiocy, because *Transformations* [a history publication] wasn't meant to be burned . . .

SC: But how did you find out about this?

L: From my classmate who they killed, [he was] a relative [a distant relative]. Then one started to open [one's eyes] and say, "man, all of these guys that seemed so great, that came in to save us when Isabel fell . . ." —because it was a horrible government [Isabel's government]. Then, when you got to '84, '85, '86, you said "and well . . . ;" with the freedom of expression, when one started to see more, when it had already happened . . . There were people who probably didn't do this, but I know people that buried books, people who were probably being investigated. I didn't bury, I burned. In the face of doubt and terror, I burned them. Was I wrong? Am I a coward? I am. I burned. I didn't get involved either. My brother was in the military service at the time, he was born in '50, no, he was in the service in '70. By then, there were people that they had taken inside, who were imprisoned by the military. But it seemed to you that they [those that were imprisoned] were the bad guys and the others [the military] the saviors. I don't know. I don't know what it seemed to you. I think that one reacted when one saw how close to you the things happened.

The first part of the conversation revolves around a recurring idea in her discourse: in Linda's point of view, all those who were not politically immersed in the struggles of the 1970s collaborated, "directly or indirectly," with el Proceso. What is striking is that in none of these reflections does the "I" appear.

In its place, the "one" carried the weight of the implications of what was narrated: "And *one* what? Was one ignorant? Did one not want to see? Did one live comfortably? I don't know," "*one* began to put two and two together," "then *one* started to open [one's eyes] and say . . . ," "when *one* started to see more," "*one* reacted when one saw how close to you the things happened." The use of the second person singular should also be added to this impersonal register, given that it did not refer to anyone in particular but rather to any "you": "*you*, until that moment," "*you* found out later," and so on.

The personal mode is also present, affirming things that are quite different. While the "I" is absent when the discourse discusses a certain connivance of the society with the dictatorship, it reappears to takes charge over the narration when the implication distances her from this meaning: "I didn't bury, I burned. In the face of doubt and terror, [I] burned . . ." Linda mentioned this memory of the burning of magazines and books, always spontaneously and in the context of different conversations, in all three interviews that we held. I will now transcribe another of these interviews and then the memory of a different anecdote that also corresponds to the years of el Proceso. In both cases, the narration does not rest on some impersonal mode, and the "I" takes responsibility for the events remembered.

> I burned books. There were people who asked me: "Why didn't you hide them?" I burned them. The magazines that I bought—after Perón returned, *Transformations*, from the Centro Editor de América Latina had appeared. Very, very interesting. I had the entire collection. And I used it to teach class. And afterward, when I took it out and had it there, one day my mom told me: "That makes me scared, you leave and I'm all alone." I put them there in a box and I threw them out. I told my brother: "take this," and he went to the mud oven. The truth? A lie? Fear? Because it said "Uncle Sam," the stereotypical American. And I burned all that. I don't know how I hid *The Underdeveloped Countries* by Ives Lacoste. I used it a lot, it was from the Fondo [de Cultura Económica] or the Centro Editor [de América Latina]. I don't know what happened to that book. If I burned it or I lent it to someone, or someone took it for me . . . *Transformations* was really good.

> In the middle of el Proceso, I went to the United States and Mexico on vacation. It was during those years. And I needed a passport. And, well, the police over here [in Correa] gave me a note to take to the Federal Police in Rosario. So, I went, I presented the note, and when I sit down at the officer's desk, he takes out a big gun. "Why are you doing that?" I asked him. "Put it away, guns make me terrified." "Stop that

now," he says. "Ah . . . no," I said, "if you are going to ask me . . ." — that's why I tell you, what lack of consciousness, look at what I told them! They imposed their presence like that, with the revolver. Look at what I got myself into! "Who are you? What are you like? What do you do? Do you work? Do you not work? What do you study? What did you do?" "But you got yourself into the lion's den!" they told me. And I went, just because I needed a passport. I didn't think about it as much.

Both excerpts refer to anecdotes that correspond to the years of the last military dictatorship, but they are not related to personal attitudes about state terrorism. In both paragraphs the "I" is the protagonist of the actions evoked. Unconsciously, Linda's narration during all the interviews rested on all that which was shameful or dishonorable, or that which would be politically incorrect or morally reprehensible to support today on the "one" form, and used the "I" for memories of attitudes or thoughts that could be associated with a certain bravery or, at least, a firm moral conviction of her will. "I" burned books, but "one" supported the coup. "I" challenged the armed police officer when she went to arrange her passport documents, but "one" did not want to see what was happening. "I" did not size up the danger of her actions, "one" collaborated with el Proceso.

At the end of one of our meetings, when already saying good-bye, Linda gave me a sort of advice or warning about people in general, although clearly referring to her fellow townspeople. Before bidding me farewell, she told me: "I think people are really chameleons. They don't admit that they supported [the dictatorship]. I'm not afraid of anything." From my conversations with her, however, the existence of a fear can be deduced from the repetition of the pattern observed regarding the subject used in the narration, as evidenced by the change in narrative register. The "I" fears the "one," or, rather, the "I" deposits in the "one" all that it fears could otherwise be used by someone, perhaps the listener or the speaker herself in some verbal slip, to judge it.

When Heidegger in *Being and Time* investigates the problem of being, he devotes some pages to developing the concept of the "domain of the others," which alludes to the importance that the impersonal figure of the "one" acquires in daily life. The meaning and the implications of using the impersonal register analyzed in this section can be explored deeply if we remind ourselves of the characteristics that Heidegger gives to this domain. It is not any situation but a specific, although daily one, in which every person realizes whether he/she is subjected to a sort of impersonal despotism. This is an existential state, a way of being in the world in which "the others" take away the self. These "others," who take control of the being of a specific man or women, are not determinate subjects with proper names. They are not a political dictatorship or a personal tyrant, nor a political party nor a king. These "others" can represent anyone else, any "other." In a certain sense, everyone belongs to these "others" — and from this comes the power of this impersonal collective, the domain of the others, that through this potential belonging consolidates its domination. I am interested in highlighting that the fundamental part of this conception is that, in Heidegger's words, "the 'who' [of these others] is not this one and not that one, not oneself and not some and not the sum of them all. The 'who' is the neuter, *the they* [*das Man*]."[56] Thus, in the most immediate and spontaneous order in which we live, in our daily lives, every day the "one" displays its power, its true "dictatorship." Indeed, Heidegger writes, "we enjoy ourselves and have fun the way *they* enjoy themselves. We read, see, and judge literature and art the way *they* see and judge. But we also withdraw from the "great mass" the way *they* withdraw, we find 'shocking' what *they* find shocking. The one, which is nothing definite and which all are, though not as sum, prescribes the kind of being of everydayness."[57]

The being of the "one" is "averageness." This is a way of being and speaking in which nothing that we are or say is "bad," nothing is outside what is allowed. The average is always a lack of originality, which does not add, nor risk, nor subtract, nor go out of tune. Because of this, Heidegger calls it "the *leveling down* of all possibilities of being." With respect to the issue that I am interested in, the most important aspect of the Heideggerian concept of the "one" and its "averageness" is that "because the they presents every judgment and decision as its own, it takes the responsibility of Da-sein [of every concrete person] away from it."[58]

In this sense, narration like Linda's can be placed within this conception, giving away its voice to the "one," elevating it to the category of a subject capable of judging and deciding, thinking and acting, so the narration ends up diluting the responsibility of the "I" into an anonymous being, which is no one in particular. Unlike the "one," the "I" voice takes responsibility for what it says or remembers. "I burned books," "I needed the passport," "I told the police officer," and so on, are affirmations that take ownership of what they state. The impersonal register, the "one," instead propels the very idea of individual responsibility far from itself. Thus we can constantly refer to it without being wounded, because although we are speaking, it is the "one" that responds, because although we are remembering or stating something, "one" is not somebody that has to deal with anybody. When we say "one," for example in the expression "one doesn't know up to what point one was complicit," we are not saying that "I" was complicit. It was "one," which is everyone and no one at the same time. It was "one," which would only be "I" insofar as it could be anyone but, and this is fundamental, it is no one insofar as it is "I."

Finally, it is important to note that Heidegger does not describe this operation as a conscious strategy of the Da-sein to hide behind the "one." On the contrary, according to the philosopher, the dominion of the "one" over everyone can be seen in this act: "Everyone is the other, and no one is himself. The one, which supplies the answer to the who of everyday Da-sein, is the nobody to whom every Da-sein has always already surrendered itself, in its being-among-one-another."[59]

It is thus important that the "I," in the sense of the person "himself" or "herself," is lost in the others, in the impersonal "one," in this sort of community without individuals or great individual without a face. Heidegger insists that this fact should not be overlooked. That the "one" is not anybody in particular does not mean that it is nothing. He even comes to state that it is "the most real subject of everydayness."[60] It should be clear that it is not a ruse used by some people to evade the "I"; although it varies historically, the "one" is inherent to the constitution of men and women insofar as they are always with others, are in the eyes of others, and in a certain sense are also these others, although not as an "I." Heidegger thinks that the sole fact of being thrown into existence, which is in turn a coexistence, an existing with other, turns the "one" into a mode of being that is almost spontaneous, immediate, and natural to the everyday.

In what concerns the subject of this chapter, it is important to understand up to what point people can take charge of what has been said and done, acted and omitted, in a past whose evocation is generally problematic, up to what point the individual memory can reach with the "I" and when, spontaneously and without deliberation, it needs to turn to the "one" or to the different impersonal registers that dilute the responsibility of what is being narrated. In the testimony analyzed in this section—the same exercise could have been conducted with other interviewees, and similar conclusions obtained—what concerned personal responsibility for what was done or not done by the subject with respect to state terror tended to be narrated impersonally, with the use of the "one" and not the "I." We must take care not to interpret this inauthenticity of the existence governed by the dictatorship of the "one" as lying. Linda did not lie when she attributed the desire for the military coup to the "one," or when she discussed the possibility that "one" did not want to see what was happening (the disappearances, kidnappings, and so on). The "I" simply could not tolerate taking responsibility for its part in this. The "I" was submerged in the inauthenticity of the "one" because this register always offers the possibility of saying something true, while subtracting personal truth or the place of the person in the truth. That the memories of state terrorism push the narrations from the personal to the impersonal register, from the "I" to the "one," raises questions that are impossible to answer, but not impossible to formulate in this chapter. From what point did the "I" desert? Was there a moment from which the "one" displaced the "I," or were impersonal forms used from the very beginning of the memories of state terrorism? Up to what point does the impossibility of the "I" to take responsibility for history in first person hide a guilty conscience? Up to what point is it not, simply, the result of the fact that the official hegemonic narrative about the past impugns any first person justification of state repression?

"The DGI's Little Tank": The Discreet Charm of Fear

Through the March 24, 1976, coup, the state reclaimed for itself the monopoly over violence and exercised it without restrictions, according to the explicit and implicit norms that the new military government established for itself. Through the decree 1,329/76, the military junta declared that on August 1, 1976, all the licenses that authorized the possession and/or carrying of firearms, regardless of their caliber, would expire and gave citizens until August 20 to deliver these permits to the National Registry of Weapons (Registro Nacional de Armas) (RENAR), setting a penalty of up to ten years in prison for those who carried arms without authorization or an expired license.[61] Several days after the decree, due to "multiple queries submitted to RENAR," as the press reported, the Ministry of Defense clarified that, in accordance with current legislation, weapons for civilian use included carbines, hunting rifles, shotguns, manual and semiautomatic pistols, revolvers, hunting pistols, and so on.[62]

This act had its correlation in the symbolic space. Although they also existed before, news articles alluding to "weapons stockpiles" belonging to "subversive cells" or "extremists" decommissioned by the "forces of the law" multiplied and were joined by others of the same character that involved members of the Justicialist government, such as López Rega, and unions strongly identified with his actions, such as the Metal Workers Union (Unión de Obreros Metalúrgicos [UOM]); of course, the news stories and images also showed the weapons "in their right place," that is, in the hands of the military, the police, or the gendarmes. Various companies that used revolvers or shotguns in their advertisements, such as Cosak, Levi's, or Sorpasso, ceased doing so, and the industries that manufactured or marketed guns de-

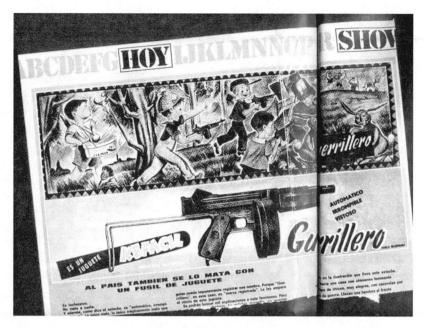

FIGURE 4.2. "The gun 'Guerrilla': the country it also kills with a rifle toy."
Source: Gente, no. 561, April 22, 1976.

creased or notably modified the advertising of their products, especially in terms of the exhibition of firearms.[63]

In a perfect parallel to what was happening on the crudely material plane of reality, the symbols of violence became the monopoly of the state, which did not hesitate to exhibit them and promote itself as a Leviathan willing and able to monopolize all the violence possible and exercise it whenever it judged necessary. The violent metaphors used to market goods or services (which, as shall be seen in chapter 5, were commonly employed in previous years) dwindled until disappearing. Days after the coup d'état, the Musiplast company, responsible for the production of the "Guerrillero" toy machine gun, published notes in Clarín and La Razón directed to wholesalers, distributors, and toy retailers, announcing that it would stop producing it and asking for it to be retired from sale.[64] Julio Pisarewcz, the owner of the toy company, publicly apologized for having launched this product.[65]

Among the advertising campaigns conducted by the state during the dictatorship to explain and/or justify its policies — fundamentally on two fronts, the economic and repressive — the one conducted by the state tax collection agency, the General Revenue Directorate (Dirección General Impositiva)

(DGI), synthesized the change that occurred in the symbolic sphere with respect to the legitimacy of the exercise of violence in an exemplary fashion, while combining, better than any other advertising campaign, the two main struggles that the military government claimed it embodied: against corruption and against subversion, with limits between the two that were not always clear.[66] The campaign was launched in movie theaters and on television between June and October 1977 and later appeared in print media. The idea was attributed to the treasury secretary, Juan Álemann, and its primary objective was to combat tax evasion. The ads' main character was a military tank, which would soon be popularly called "the DGI's little tank," and its reception in movie theaters was judged to be very favorable by agency psychologists.[67] *Gente* magazine considered the little tank to be "the person of the year for 1977."[68] *Carta Política* wrote: "You see it once, you see it another time, and you keep laughing. On television or in the theaters, the troubled little tank continues to suffer the pitfalls of an existence that is not in accordance with what the law prescribes."[69] Other media sources, such as *Confirmado* and *Somos*, devoted lighthearted, approving articles to the campaign.[70]

The advertising series effectively combined sympathy and terror.[71] The cartoons were similar to the affable protagonist of the cartoon show *The Inspector*, widely watched in Argentine homes. Both the text and some of the images are intimidating and, seen retrospectively, not lacking in transparency about state's clandestine actions. The official discourse about tax evaders was analogous to that utilized toward subversion. The tax evader appeared portrayed as an "ill-fated character" of the country's social reality, who was "ever more alone, more marginalized, more compromised." If he didn't reconsider and change his ways, the state warned that he would be "the only one responsible for the price he will have to pay."[72]

Some of these advertisements asked honest citizens to turn in those who evaded taxes. Riding on the little tank, a (white) doll who represented the good contributor, pointed at another (dark) doll, the tax evader. "Identify the evader," the text ended by saying.[73] Another advertisement was titled "Point out the guilty."[74] The most eloquent ad to this end showed two grocers (one white and the other dark), one across from the other and the DGI's little tank between the two. The white doll—the honest business owner—pointed at his neighbor—the corrupt grocer—as the little tank looked on menacingly. The text implored those who were honest to denounce those who were corrupt, something that the state also expected of the honest citizens toward the "subversives."[75] Although turning each citizen into a potential informer was not something new in the Argentine political environment, it was during el Proceso that this achieved its greatest extent.[76]

The discourses referring to the corrupt and to subversives were analogous. For both taxes and subversion, it was emphasized that those who had nothing to hide had nothing to fear. One ad underlined that only those who were breaking the law should be worried. It recognized that at times the honest citizen was "mortified" but promised that this would change once the tax evaders were found. Thus, we "must discover the tax evader, and quickly," said the advertisement.[77] The tax offender was presented as analogous to the enemy *par excellence* of the country, the subversive. Both were compared to villains, opposed to those "who risk themselves every day for their neighbors: the firefighter, the policeman, the soldier," giving "their effort and even their lives for others." On the contrary, the evader was presented as a "selfish and antisocial marginal."[78] In another advertisement, the evader appeared as the enemy of the Argentine family, symbolized by two good (white) dolls seated at the table who see the (dark) evader arrive with his napkin tied around his neck ready to join them at the meal. In this case, the ad said that the evader "did not deserve to be [seated] at the common table."[79] The tax evader, like the subversive, was not just the government's enemy; he was everyone's enemy. For this reason, the DGI was committed to searching until it found him, although he "remained hidden." The state would find him, it promised in its advertising, since "the tax evader attacks both the present and the future. He is everyone's enemy."[80] The equivalence drawn between the tax evader and the terrorist, implicit in various drawings or texts of the advertising series, became explicit in the installment titled "Sabotage," where the tax evader appeared exploding dynamite inserted in a pot that symbolized the country.[81]

The certainty of pursuit was accompanied by the promise of punishment. In one of the ads the little tank was putting up a "wanted" poster with an image of the tax-evading doll, while the text read that when he would be discovered, he would be "punished ruthlessly, as befits a criminal."[82] Another declared that "the tax evader lives in permanent risk," compromising both "his security and that of his household."[83] A third advertisement warned that "the evader can choose" to turn himself in or "continue hidden." If he selects the latter option, "the DGI will continue searching for him."[84] In the advertisements, the state appeared omnipotent in its capacity to find criminals, and it was made clear that it had resources that the criminals could not even imagine to carry out this task. One of the advertisements affirmed that the tax evader was neither "the first nor the only one" to consider himself invulnerable. The criminals "believe that they haven't left anything to chance and that all the traces have been perfectly erased," read the advertisement. However, although "they are convinced that they will never be caught [. . .] they ignore that there is always a trace that remains" and that "this clue, sooner or later, will be discovered and will mark the beginning of the end."[85] Nicely, with cartoons of dolls and tanks, the state warned civil society, in the movie theaters, on the television, and in printed media, that it saw almost everything, that it could find what it didn't see, and when it caught those they were looking for, it would not hesitate to punish them. In an advertisement called "Checkmate," it was declared that the tax evader "was now appealing to all kinds of combinations and prolonging the game in a futile attempt," a senseless attitude since "the agents are on their way, they are looking for him, and they will find him." Threatening, the ad warned: "The next move is the DGI's."[86]

The advertising series also refers to the changes since March 1976 in the state's capacity to carry out its policing functions. In an advertisement in which the tax evader appeared with a net, about to take over the country—once again, the analogy with subversion was perfect—the little tank, this time with furious eyes, followed him with an even larger net. The text affirmed that in the past, criminals were cleverer than the laws were, but that now, thanks to the modification of the corresponding legislation (Law 11,683 of the Procedural Code), the law had been turned into a "perfected weapon to fight against tax evasion. A weapon that will destroy the infrastructure of tax crime. A weapon intended to put the tax evader in his place. That is, behind bars."[87] In another ad, the tax evader appeared grasping the bars of a prison cell.[88]

In some advertisements, the violence was explicit. In "In Self Defense," the honest doll hit the criminal doll in the head with a stick. The tax evader appeared on the ground, with crosses for eyes, holding his head. The criminal was not only committing crimes against the country, in abstract terms, but also against every good citizen. "You who pay taxes, the tax evader is robbing you. Turning him in will be an act of self-defense."[89] In this case, the criminal was being hit not by the state but by an honest, tax-paying citizen. Even more aggressively, the ads titled "With His Hours Numbered" and "Your Husband in Danger" revealed the illegal repression. In the former, the tax evader had his body tied down and appeared wide-eyed, sitting over dynamite, as a DGI inspector lit the fuse that would make him explode. In the second, the tax evader clung to his wife when he saw the state agent. The text appealed to the wives of the criminals. "Your household is in danger. When your husband is discovered, the indexing of his fiscal debt could affect your property. And you will be left without a house. Or without a car. Or with your husband in jail."[90] In another ad, the tax evader's son appeared playing, with a pacifier in his mouth, looking at his father through the jail bars. "When the tax evader's son finds out that his father ended up in prison for refusing to contribute," the advertisement read, "he will want to know the reasons. And the tax evader will not be able to answer him easily."[91] The phrase "refusing to contribute" was the tax law translation of the "refusing to cooperate" used for those who did not confess what was asked of them under torture.

The subversion-corruption binomial functioned as an effective device to apportion blame during the first years of el Proceso. Almost to the same extent that the former ceased to represent a real threat, the government began to emphasize the importance of its war against the latter. Like other components of the official discourse, this relationship between subversion and corruption was also shared by sectors of the press. The Catholic magazine *Criterio*, for example, in an article that was not sympathetic to the military government, wrote in their editorial "No Argentine of good faith is willing to compromise with subversion and corruption."[92] The equivalence drawn between these "social evils" had a double effect. It threatened tax evaders, offering them punishment disproportionate to their crimes at the same time that it made banal the barbarous repression that the state was exercising against those it considered subversives.

On May 29, 1977, in an event commemorating the creation of the Argentine Army in 1810, President Videla made a speech in which he distinguished the just from the sinners. After establishing that "subversion and corruption are intimately linked" and promising the population that "subversion on all of its fronts" would be defeated—when in military terms, they had already vanquished the guerrilla—Videla announced that in the near future, the government would work together with civilians, who "will be the descendants of this process of national reorganization so that it can be transcendent throughout time."[93] This future, however, was not for everybody. "As soon as we open the necessary channels," Videla continued, "a broader and more generous dialogue will deepen, *with the sole exception of the corrupt and the subversives*.[94] These—the corrupt and the subversives—have particular names: therefore, it is not just to adopt a simplistic solution of identifying them with a specific activity, social category, religious belief, or political affiliation."

Three months later, the education minister of the military government, Juan José Catalán, implored the citizens of the province of La Rioja to get rid of any teacher who attacked the armed forces' policies in any way or form.[95] With the disappearance of the guerrilla threat, the concept of "subversion" or of the "subversive" survived as a ghostly being that the military government invoked to classify any difference it considered not easily integrated to the nation. A part of the press also accompanied this effacement of the limits that separated what was "subversive" from what was not. *Para Ti* magazine, in the context of its campaign to counter the accusations of human rights violations that the military government was receiving, while triumphantly announc-

FIGURE 4.3. "With His Hours Numbered." *Source: Gente, no. 669, May 18, 1978*

FIGURE 4.4. "Sabotage." *Source: Gente, no. 679, July 27, 1978*

FIGURE 4.5. "Your household is in danger." *Source: Gente,* no. 684, August 31, 1978

FIGURE 4.6. "The rules of the game." *Source: Gente,* no. 685, September 7, 1978

ing that in 1978 "peace [was] a special guest that has already moved into the living room" of the Argentine people, affirmed that "now it needed to do so in the entire house."[96] Thus, the geography of the home was used to express the military's idea that subversion had multiple faces, not only the armed face (the living room) but also the psychological (the rest of the house). Official and press declarations to these ends can be cited at length. El Proceso divided the population into angels and devils. Culturally and politically, as Oscar Landi has indicated, it attempted to retrace the borders between good and bad and between normal and abnormal, guided by one principal foundation: the recovery and reaffirmation of original essential values that existed at some time and that the political conflict of the period prior to 1976 had forgotten or distorted: order, hard work, hierarchy, and responsibility.[97]

In this sense, especially from the time that the armed groups no longer represented a real threat, "subversion" functioned by embodying a fundamental impossibility, making possible the ideological fantasy of a harmonious lost society, whose recovery constituted a moral imperative for all those who considered themselves honest and patriotic. If the origin was characterized by harmony, the healthy republic, class integration, and so on, the contemporary chaos and corruption could be explained by the arrival of an external element, "subversion," which at the same time homogenized the society, hiding the heterogeneity of its constituents. The DGI's advertising campaign, with its combination of humor and fear, expressed this conception clearly. If laughter was the vehicle to affirm the fraternal bond that imaginarily linked honest Argentines, fear constituted the threat that this ideal society, peaceful and without contradictions, would be unveiled as that which had existed until the present moment: a complex web of interests and projects of improbable compatibility. Once the "subversive" had disappeared from the military scene, he embodied the impossibility of the Argentine society. He was the ghost that allowed much of the society to dream that their origin and their destiny were the healthy integration of different social sectors; but at some point this good society corrupted by subversion, a foreign element whose annihilation would put the country back on the path of harmony and prosperity.

Forty days after the 1983 election of President Alfonsín, La Semana magazine—"Closed by the military government. Reopened by justice," according to its slogan—published a national survey that asked about the expectations aroused by the new government.[98] Sixty-four percent of respondents wanted, above anything else, "order and peace."[99] The demand for peace, little more than a year after the country signed its surrender of the Falkland Islands to Great Britain, had less relation to the "antisubversive war" than to the war in the South Atlantic islands. The demand for order, however, referred more to the internal situation, to the desire to not return to the years that immediately preceded the military government.

Those years were long associated with violence and chaos in the memory of the middle classes. This had a favorable impact on Alfonsín's triumph in 1983. A poll conducted by IPSA in the country's most important urban centers in May 1983 indicated that, while 42 percent of the middle classes approved of the first (1946–1955) Peronist government, only 9 percent viewed the second one (1973–1976) favorably.[100] The disapproval for this government, while achieving majorities among all social classes, was more overwhelming among the middle (74 percent) and upper (82 percent) classes than the "low-formal" and "low-informal/marginal" classes.[101]

In the beginning of the 1980s, political violence had left a mark that was difficult to erase, and the reading that a big portion of the middle classes had of it did not differ essentially from that offered by military discourse. Before the end of 1981 *Gente* magazine conducted a poll that evaluated the government of the armed forces according to the opinions of its readers, the majority of whom belonged to the middle classes.[102] Although the magazine topped the list of the media that supported the dictatorship, the results seem credible since the responses were damning for the military administration in the majority of areas. From a scale of 1 to 10, almost 70 percent classified the performance of the justice system between 1 and 3, and in the areas of education and social welfare, more than 60 percent gave ratings that were lower than 6. The terrain on which the government received the highest ratings was that of "internal peace": 74 percent of readers judged the government's performance on this issue between 8 and 10, and only 8 percent rated it with a score under 4. In the area of human rights, 20 percent gave the government a low rating (1 to 3 points), 15 percent an average rating (4 or 5 points), 20 percent a good rating (6 to 7 points), and 43 percent a very good rating (8 to 10 points). Although this would slowly begin to change when, in the democratic period,[103] the details of the repression and the atrocities committed became irrefutable, it is also true that toward the end of el Proceso, much of the middle classes judged that the peace achieved was an invaluable good.[104]

Excursus II   A Model Kit

All testimonies contain internal contradictions. Moreover, when the circumstances remembered relate to difficult years whose recollection is filtered
through decades of silences and voices, through judgments about oneself
and others, the tensions and incongruities multiply. Although it may be true
that this description applies to all the testimonies, there was one in which the
tensions or incongruities threatened the very intelligibility of the discourse.
While atypical today, this narrative could have been part of a more general
sensibility in the past.

   Beatriz Garrido was born in Correa in 1942. The descendent of Italians
who arrived in Argentina and the town in 1902, daughter of a baker who later

opened a general store, she finished high school in the Colegio Nacional Florentino Ameguino in the city of Cañada de Gómez, an achievement that was relatively uncommon for women of her generation in Correa. Single, she worked as an administrative employee of the area's most important furniture factory for almost forty years. Her economic situation, as she remembers, did not change greatly during her life. "I was able to support myself through my work; I was never without a job. When I was fifteen years old, I was already working in an office. In the factory, I started at the lowest and ended up in the top position of the administration." Beatriz's self-perception, like that of many people of her generation, is organized around work ethic and effort.

I came to her because several people in the town had advised me to interview her. "If you are doing a history project, you have to see Beatriz," a neighbor told me. When we first met, she situated my visit within a certain spirit of an age. "Now, we are all in the wave [fashion] of the past," she said. Politically, Beatriz was raised in the anti-Peronist tradition and sympathized with developmentalistism from her youth. The lack of freedom that non-Peronists experienced in Correa, the surveillance exercised by about thirty people in the Liberation Alliance (Alianza Libertadora), and the memory of Peronism as an oppressive regime forged a solidly anti-Peronist feeling in Beatriz. Her sympathy for developmentalist ideas and, especially for ex-president Frondizi — for whom she claimed to have had a "Platonic love" — and Sylvestre Begnis, the twice-elected developmentalist governor of Santa Fe (in 1958–1962 and 1973–1976), contributed to this feeling.

Her support for these figures was accompanied by a more general nostalgic vision, and a yearning for a better and now definitely lost world that was not limited to politics. In this world, values were the axis of sociability: young people's amusement "didn't come through drugs or alcohol," "women respected men, first of all, with their mouths," and even the brothels of the past were more decent than those of the present day, since "the women that worked had a health certificate [libreta sanitaria] and received doctors' visits every morning. Now, they just work for sex." In many aspects, this nostalgic vision does not exclude the years covered in this book. For Beatriz, the past is a lost paradise, an irrecoverable world that is better than the present in any comparison.

Although she is interested in politics, she never participated in political activism and did not want to occupy positions in the municipality of Correa. This reticence has a relation with her conviction that "power is what kills men," that "it's like fame, when you don't have anymore, you're nobody." Somewhat paradoxically, Beatriz's discourse combines a vindication of politics, an interest in following political events, and a generalized suspicion toward the concrete exercise of politics and about the people that exercise this power at all levels.

The first political mention that she made was in response to my question about her memories of the fall of Peronism in 1955.

> We lived through the "Liberating Revolution" very calmly. The only thing that I remember happened when I was at the National High School in Cañada de Gómez, in my first or second year. The principal comes and says: "those from the outside [who were not from Cañada de Gómez, like Beatriz], put your books in your desks and run to catch the train." That I'll never forget. And when we were going to the train, the businesses were all closing their shutters. When we arrived, the train didn't come. I swear to you, it was terrifying until I got to my house. Afterward, because I was a very curious girl, I went to see the trains with the tanks and everything else coming in, and I have it stuck in my head as something terrible. Because of this I tell you that we, our people, have no memory. The Argentine people have no memory, not at all. Today we're over here, tomorrow over there.

Reinforcing what she wanted to say, she mentioned an article that she had read after the end of the Falklands War, written by a French sociologist whose name she did not remember, in which he said that Argentina was a "totally cyclothymic country." After this, she concluded: "this is why I tell you, we are like chameleons, we change colors to suit the occasion," with which she reinforced her idea that "today we're here, tomorrow we're over there." This idea reappeared later linked to other political memories. Both the lack of memory and this manic or chameleon-like attitude were inscribed in a more general vision of the social and, above all, moral decadence of contemporary life.

After affirming that "our people don't have any memory," in response to my question about the 1955 coup, the following dialogue developed:

SC: Why do you think that our people have no memory?

BEATRIZ: I think that there was a lot of intelligence in that part [of society]. Because, those who were taken out should be governing us today. That would be the intelligent part, that they did away with. Because they exterminated the intelligent part of the people that were in politics. Not anyone can be in politics, Sebastián, no matter what degree they have. The people that left us, left us because of the intelligence they had.

sc: Who are you talking about?

b: I'm talking about, you know, the genocide.

sc: The forcible disappearance of people?

b: Of the disappearance of the intelligent people, who were fighting with their heart, they were fighting with that. Then they made them disappear. And today, I can assure you that Argentina is a country of fighters, but now they are using another weapon: drugs. That's how the intellects disappear now.

This response was not related to her memories of the 1955 coup, but rather with the phrase that my follow-up question had generated. It added an example of the Argentine people's lack of memory. In the context of the 1955 coup, it was not clear what should have been remembered but was not. Instead, in this new response, the forgotten past was that of the last dictatorship. This was the first time that Beatriz mentioned the ideas of "genocide" and that "those that were taken out should be governing us today." These comments did not draw my attention. The idea of "genocide," although atypical in her generation, can be inscribed within the "Holocaustization" of the experience of the last dictatorship, something that received official support in 2003 with the rise of the Kirchner family to power. The mention that today "those who were taken out should be governing us today," however, differs from the Kirchners' discourse, which tends to identify themselves as the survivors or the heirs of the disappeared, while Beatriz only marked the absence of those who should be in the government.

The conversation that immediately followed was diverted toward her concern about the problem of drug addiction, which was recurrent and genuine. Only when I finished the three interviews with her and went back to listen to them did I understand that this association between drugs in the present day and the genocide in the past was united in her discourse by the same political logic. In this first interview, in an attempt to return to these issues, I asked about her memory of the military governments, to which Beatriz responded:

I'll tell you, for me, someone who didn't know what went on in the inside of all of this, but for me, it was my happiest period when I could travel where I traveled without any problems, with my education. And I'll tell you, simply to tell you something: I had my father [who] was sick, my father had a pacemaker—a catheter cut, his pacemaker was bipolar—and a change in pacemaker. Because he lived with a pacemaker for eleven years. Well, during the military period, I went to ask for the pacemaker at 10:30 in the morning and at 12:45 the pacemaker was in my hands.

SC: In what year was this?

BEATRIZ: That was in . . . '76, I think. And for the last one, I had to wait two months. Do you see the decay? Do you see the total decay that we have in our health system? I traveled to Rosario every weekend, with no problems. I traveled, because we took five little vacations each year, which I can't do now because I have a 92 year-old mother. And I never had a problem. Not with work, nothing, nothing, nothing. Now, we can't travel to Rosario. Because I'm scared, I travel by taxi. Because it's a disaster. So, you know what? I thought that during my life we were going to be moving to something better, not to something like what we have now. [. . .] You know what's happening? It's that, for a long time now, we are living through money. We don't take care of the heart. We don't take care of our feelings of solidarity, and so this is turning into an absolutist country. [. . .] And they're killing the hen that lays the golden eggs of youth, through drugs. It's a macabre, macabre plan, what they're doing. There's a very, very big problem that's developing among the youth. What are the next generations going to do, these kids? So you see, those in the government aren't stupid, they're cruel. When AIDS appeared, even we here in Correa had a Women's Work roundtable discussion, we brought in some specialists. There were 650 kids here in the club to listen about AIDS. Tell me what kind of campaigns there are against AIDS? They erase everything that could be useful! See what great business they're doing with us!

This response was more complex than the one that preceded it. My question had been political in nature, directed toward a specific political actor (the military) and referring to a circumscribed historical time period (their governments). What Beatriz responded only partially answered my question. Now I knew that under the dictatorship, she lived through her "happiest period," she traveled without problems, she did not have any problems at work, she lived safely, and the public administration still functioned—this was the purpose of her example about her father's pacemaker. However, the same response added other elements that, upon my listening to the interview, clarified things. Her idea of a "macabre plan" aimed at destroying the youth, the mention of the stupidity and the cruelty of "those of the government," and the conspiratorial vision ("they erase everything that could be useful") helped me to better understand the comment she had made earlier about the social problems caused by drugs. For Beatriz, drug addiction among youth was part of a deliberate and perverse plan carried out by a diffuse "they," who, if not concretely defined, "those of the government" were complicit with.

In any case, her references to the current political situation interested me only insofar as they were in some way related with the period studied. After our first interview, my conclusion about Beatriz's memories of the last dictatorship was that, for her, the generation that today should be governing Argentina disappeared in a genocide (whose perpetrators she did not name). The atypical aspect of her narrative was that this vision coexisted with the evocation of the military period as a time of personal happiness, security, and administrative efficiency, something that was present in other testimonies, but which only Beatriz's testimony blended with the topic of the genocide.

In our second interview, four months later, we saw the first part of the documentary prepared for this investigation (1969–1974). Viewing images of the kidnapping and the death of Aramburu, in response to my question if she remembered that this act had some sort of impact on the town and on her, Beatriz responded that "yes, it was a very important event, because it was the beginning of the big kidnappings for ransom." She added,

> that was the general commentary everywhere, something that doesn't happen today. The youth are less interested. Before yes, totally, everyone asked. Here we've stopped thinking about politics, here nothing is important. We are, you see, I'll give you an example of the things that are happening. Seba, here we had an early election in order to be able to disrupt a country in a few months [she is referring to the 2009 legislative elections that the Kirchner government sped up]. And you see that before, at least, the people came out onto the street banging pots and pans [she is referring to 2001 protests against the Alianza government], with this and that. Today there's nothing. It's like the [people] are defeated, exhausted, because nobody talks about anything anymore. They took everything, the culture, everything. The most serious thing about the genocide is that it took all the men who should be governing us today, who had culture, who had ideals—they did a very good job to destroy all of that. Tell me, who knows what they are voting for? People aren't conscious about anything!

As on other occasions, in response to a question of a political nature about a concrete event from the past—the assassination of Aramburu—Beatriz answered by quickly resolving the specific topic and moved on to the present day, marking the contrast between a decadent present of social indifference and a better past once again (associated with the idea of the genocide and the missing generation). The dialogue just transcribed evolved in the following fashion:

> SC: At one point, you said that the generation that should be governing us was the one that they killed.

> BEATRIZ: They risked their lives for an ideal, Seba, these people risked their lives! They [those who killed them] knew very well who were the ones that could rule our country. They knew full well. They didn't kill everybody. I'll tell you something: nobody came to talk to me. Because I always traveled, I went to Rosario every Saturday, and nobody ever bothered me, because they knew that I wasn't involved in politics. They were very sharp. They had to take out that part [of society] that had the intellect and they killed it. Maybe, if they had remained, they wouldn't have done anything. But I believe that they would have, they would have done a lot. And afterward, I tell you, Argentina I believe that as never before—until the 1960s, there were those that risked their lives for an ideal—but today, the politicians are those who sell themselves to the highest bidder. And I'll tell you more, all that we have today is "idiotizing" the country.

This response generated two questions about my initial interpretation of her discourse about the last dictatorship. The main question originated in the fact that the genocide was named without a subject, without definition, without specific names. "They" knew very well who to kill, "they" knew who was involved in politics and could govern the country, "they" didn't kill everyone, "they" were very sharp, "they" tried to take out the intelligent part of the society. Who were "they"? It went without saying that they were the military officials, but were they "the military" for Beatriz? A second question was related to those killed. Who was she referring to concretely? Her account omitted references to political or armed organizations. The mention of those that "risked their life for an ideal" seems to imply that she was referring to revolutionary organizations. Those who vindicate those who "risked their lives for their ideals" in the 1970s refer to these activists or to a broader social group that does not exclude them. Both questions were not resolved until our third and last meeting.

We continued to view the documentary and, in response to a news clip about an ERP action, I asked her about the impact that this type of news linked to the guerrillas had on her and on the town. Her response once again jumped from the past to the present. This typical trait of the memory, the desire to *also* say something about the present, was quite evident in these interviews:

> BEATRIZ: It was seen with fear. Fear was what we felt. The same fear, although not as strong, that we feel today with the lack of public safety.

> SC: These feelings were not as strong as they are today?

> B: Yes, it's that before the fear was about what we couldn't see, about not knowing what was going on. Not today. Today we are scared to go out on the street. For me, what's going on today is more of a genocide than what happened years ago. Because now it affects all of us. Before they wanted to kill the intelligent class, because if these dead youth were governing the country, do you know how the country would be? First, it would be nationalist, because they were the first nationalists. But today, it's more genocide! Because you have the faces of the spoiled, drugged, drunk youth, and you're scared to go outside because they don't look at class, they don't look at color, they don't look at anything, they just kill you for the sake of killing. Then, the others had some idea of who they wanted to kill. They wanted to kill the class that was to govern us, the country's intelligent class. How can we recover them now? Now, these guys are killing us. They are killing everyone with drugs and alcohol. Within ten years, what minds are we going to have to govern? What mind? It makes me despair.

Her discourse was becoming clearer and vaguer at the same time. My question had been answered succinctly, without much detail. The news of the guerrillas "was seen with fear." In her jump to the present, however, it was made explicit that for Beatriz there were at least two "genocides" and two of "them," equally perverse, who were responsible for each case. Both the past and the present were explained through a binary logic of good and evil, of perverse minds against noble people, of "them" against "the intelligent part," in the case of the past, and of "them" against "us," in the case of the present.

Four months after the second interview and eight months after the first, we met for a third time, with the second part of the documentary (1975–1982) and my questions on the agenda. Watching scenes of the coup d'état of 1976 — newspaper headlines from the days before, images of the fall of Isabel Perón, the military communiqué that announced the coup to the population, troops on the street, and finally a message from Videla, where he expressed the reasons for the coup—Beatriz remembered that she heard this news on the radio, that she was at home, and that it wasn't a surprise for anyone, that it was expected. Immediately, she added:

> I tell you, at this time, I don't agree with the genocide, but I tell you that if the military were in the street today, it would be different. Well, they're talking about a new military service, have you heard? I believe that the youth, starting off at eighteen years old and staying in until twenty, within a place that is like a reformatory, I think that this would stop the drug abuse, and not only for men but for women too. When they eliminated military service, I can assure you that it touched me, internally, it seemed very bad to me because I said, "this will end in disaster." [. . .] I, my interior cries out for the military. And I'm not just telling you this now, I've been saying this my entire life. [. . .] I tell you, having done what they had done, an unguarded country isn't a country at all.

Upon rereading the interview, I realized that only here, provoked by images of the coup, did Beatriz mention the military together with the idea of the genocide. The paragraph, however, was not altogether illuminating because the reference to the military was far from negative. She clarified that she did not agree with the genocide but added that if there were more soldiers on the street and active military service, the social problems linked to drugs and alcohol would be moderated, in addition to confessing that, inside, she "cried out for the military."

At this point in my interview, however, I had fewer doubts about her thought about political violence and repression in the 1970s. The "they" of the genocide now had a name, the military officials, but her condemnation did not extend to the institution, which for her should continue playing an important role in the society. However, it was still necessary to discover more about her thoughts about the generation that "should be governing us," to which she had always referred to in generic terms. In this case, she had also avoided mentioning a concrete subject up to this moment.

In this interview, she confided to me that, in the years prior to the 1976 coup, she had a relationship with an activist from the Universidad Nacional de Córdoba. I asked her why, having such positive impressions of this activist movement and having been the partner of an activist, she did not join the movement herself. She responded that it was a "role that required commitment" that she couldn't fulfill because she had responsibilities within the home, helping her sick father who needed her. "If I had been presented with a situation that was different from what my house was, from what my life was, I would have gone to the death with them," she told me. Referring to her sympathy for these youth, the following conversation took place:

SC: Your sympathy with these youth . . .

BEATRIZ: It was for their intelligence. I love intelligence. I think that these people's patriotism was so beautiful, so beautiful, Sebastián, so beautiful.

SC: What are you referring to?

B: I'm referring to the young people that struggled for this . . . you see? What they were killed for. They killed them because [the activist youth] would have destroyed them. When they [the activist youth] talked to you, they spoke in such a way, that I believe that, well, in it lay the birth of a new country. Well, and they [the activist youth] had very good advisors: he who fell, fell. And they didn't care. Because you see them, they did it with total confidence in themselves. So, they were really deeply a part of what the country was, more than just politics. They felt the country's nationalism, what they wanted to make the country. Not like these guys [today's politicians], who are all rotten!

Although she now added that the youth fought with "patriotism," with "total confidence in themselves," and identified more with "the country's nationalism" than with politics, Beatriz's discourse was once again imprecise in terms of why they were struggling and who these youths concretely were. Was it a specific group, or was she speaking about all radicalized groups? Did she include those who had taken the path of armed struggle among this youth? When she returned to the subject, I asked her explicitly if she included the guerrilla groups in her definition. The dialogue developed as follows:

BEATRIZ: What I felt is that these people gave their body, soul, intelligence, they went for an ideal.

SC: But do you include the guerrillas, the Montoneros, the ERP as part of these people?

B: No, no. Not those people. Those people were murderers. They were murderers. And what we have today above us [referring to the national government]. Look, today they don't murder us with the revolver, but they murder us in fifty thousand other ways. Don't we have two Montoneros running the country? [referring to the current president, Cristina Fernández, and her husband, former president Néstor Kirchner] Have people forgotten about all this? [. . .] That's why I tell you that they killed those who should be running the country. Those people were well prepared, I don't know if they would have been able to do it, because in the middle of all this, they were swept away. You think that thirty thousand people died in the genocide? No! There were many more!

sc: Many more?

b: Many more, it's logical. Many more. This didn't come out of Buenos Aires. No. It came out of the most long-suffering provinces. The provinces suffered much more. What happened is that Buenos Aires always lived because it had everything. It never suffered with the country like we who are in the interior provinces did. You know that Buenos Aires ends at General Paz [referring to the avenue that divides the city of Buenos Aires from the province of Buenos Aires].

As the conversation took a different course at this point, I returned to the topic several minutes later. I asked her how she saw what she now evaluated as a genocide of over thirty thousand people at the time that it was occurring. Beatriz responded: "What happened is that I couldn't see the two sides [referring to the military and the youth]. I could never penetrate it. Something was always lacking for me from both sides."

sc: What was lacking?

BEATRIZ: I never ended up understanding the thinking of the one side and the thinking of the other. Why were they confronting each other?

sc: You never clearly understood why they were confronting each other?

b: I'm pretty terrible with my mind; when I don't want to pay attention to something, I don't.

Beatriz would have preferred to stay on an abstract level about the concrete social actors of the 1970s. On one side, there was a "genocide" perpetrated by a "them" vaguely associated with "the military" and on the other intelligent, brave, patriotic, and nationalistic youth that were willing to put their body and soul on the line for an ideal, but were not identified with specific names. My questions were forcing her to define actors. In this last testimony, Beatriz introduced some new elements, for example that the genocide had killed many more than thirty thousand people and that she never ended up understanding why the youth and the military confronted each other. By this point, it was so difficult to integrate her account into a body of coherent thoughts (for me), that I did not ask for further clarifications about what she said. My sensation was that, even though I felt that I had forced some definitions on her part, I had obtained the necessary responses to understand her account and not to relegate it to the waste bin of incomprehensible discourses.

An unexpected reflection, however, forced me to rethink everything yet again. At a certain point of the documentary (1975–1982) Videla appears at a conference, responding to accusations of human rights violations. There, Videla says:

> because it was precisely to defend freedom and the dignity of man that Argentina had to confront this tremendous problem of a war whose price [the country] paid in blood. A war that we did not want, that we did not declare, that was imposed upon us. And Argentina, and I repeat, Argentines have nothing to hide and nothing to be ashamed of in this regard because this occurred precisely in the defense of the human rights of the Argentine people which were gravely threatened by the aggression of a subversive terrorism that sought to change our way of life. And to avoid their taking that away from us, we fought and we paid for it in blood, for the same human rights that the Pope demands.

Before we finished listening to this statement together, Beatriz exclaimed: "I tell you, sincerely, that I continue to like that guy." I asked her for an explanation of what she said, and Beatriz answered: "He had people around him that brought him to do what he did. I consider that this guy was very, very patriotic. Very patriotic. And I would bet that no matter how he was involved in everything, he was surpassed by the people he had around him."

SC: Are you referring to Massera?

BEATRIZ: Exactly. With Menéndez and all his followers. I don't know what happens with human beings. It's something very typical of human beings, that power makes us animals. I always said that I would have liked to talk about this with a psychologist, or something like that, which I never did, what part of the human being, which it is, how can I tell you—which part of it changes them. Because you know someone, you see them every day, and when they start to get into power, you see that they get more and more egotistical; but in the majority of cases, they were people that you saw at your side! Power, what does it do to the brain? Because they don't reason anymore, "This is what I think, and just what I think. You can even see this right here in town [referring to Correa]. Does power annihilate the human mind so much?

sc: But in Videla's case . . . ?

b: In Videla's case, I think that they got the guy involved like that . . . But in all the political rallies, of all the times that I've heard Videla, of everything that I've lived through, with my security through him and everything else, he was a guy that was really of the country [. . .]

sc: Now, when you say that Videla was a "guy of the country," and you say that the young people you met, who were university students, intelligent, etc., were also "nationalists." How do you explain that these young people were killed by Videla? What happened?

b: Look. These young people were killed. But it wasn't Videla. I think that some of the same things happened to Videla as happened to Yrigoyen, when they gave him the newspaper that they wanted him to read. Do you understand me? And when you're here, sitting by yourself, and you have everyone around you here, you don't know what the truth is. I think that probably, Videla, in his heart, was on the side of all these young people. I bet my head on it. I bet my head that he was on the side of all those kids. Because he was very pure in his ideals, and very pure for the Argentine people. But they went around him, he was surpassed by these perverse minds.

The interview continued, and we spoke about different nonpolitical subjects present in the documentary. I finished the interview thinking that I was not going to be able to work with her testimony. How could the new comments introduced in the final excerpt be integrated within Beatriz's account of the "genocide"? How can her support for the disappeared youth be made compatible with her support for Videla? Given that this support was revealed in our last meeting and in response to hearing the voice and seeing the image of Videla, not as a response to a question on the subject, what meaning should be given to this late confession?

A possible interpretation arises from framing her account within the value-system particular to these middle classes, where ideology and politics are not fundamental elements in establishing judgments about reality. For Beatriz, Videla and the youth were "of the country"; both were patriotic, in the most literal sense of the term; they put their homeland above any other motivation. The youth were "much deeper in what the country was than in politics, they felt the country's nationalism, what they wanted to make of the country." Videla "was a really patriotic guy," "was someone clearly of the country." However, Massera and the guerrillas were not. In her discourse, both of them appear to be murderers, situated in the opposite extreme of the spectrum from that occupied by Videla and the intelligent youth. The fundamental categories with which power is judged are not political but rather moral. Beatriz does not globally justify the military government, in the sense that discourses that are more homogeneously promilitary do. Neither does she completely condemn the government without nuances, similar to the way that, for example, the Argentine left does. There is instead a sort of negotiation between the political and the moral in which the latter takes priority. Massera and the guerrillas are on the side of the murderers. Videla and the intelligent youth are on the side of the patriots, where "homeland" has a meaning that is less political than emotional. The history of the 1970s appears here to be crossed by moral judgments in which Videla is "a man of the country," "very pure in his ideals and very pure for the Argentine people"; "in his heart he was on the side of all these young people," who also had ideals, were pure and men of the country, and patriots and nationalists. Indeed, Beatriz never understood the thoughts of either the youth or the military officials and never understood why they confronted one another. The dispute that Beatriz describes avoids identifying the two political sides and presents itself as a confrontation between good people and bad people, between people "of the country" (Videla and the intelligent youth that were disappeared) and murderers (Massera, "his whole entourage," and the guerrilla organizations).

The thesis that there were hawks and doves among the military leaders of el Proceso was very widespread during the early years of the regime. Among the hawks, bloodthirsty, and savage, were Suárez Mason and Menéndez; among the doves, softer and more reasonable, Videla and Viola. With the passing of time, this distinction faded and both in the press and in some research, the generic reference to "the military officials" or "the military dictatorship" homogenized military power. In this regard, it is interesting that twenty-five years after the coup, James Neilson, journalist for the Buenos Aires Herald, declared that, for him, Videla, like Eichmann, was someone "who, in more benign circumstances, would not have ordered the torture or murder of anyone" and that "despite everything that has been revealed and said until now, I have not changed my opinion too much."[1]

Beatriz Garrido hasn't changed her opinion either. She has incorporated much of the information discovered since, often just as it was discovered. Her thinking about the 1970s, however, is atypical because she has been able to conduct this incorporation without altering a sort of hard core in her thought in which the men "of the country" continue to be so despite the role that they have played in history, or better said, despite the role that History, as if it were fate, had reserved for each one.

The characterization of the military repression as a "genocide" together with support for Videla, the repudiation of the guerrillas as murderers together with the idealization and yearning for the disappeared generation — these typically incompatible elements coexist in Beatriz's account in a manner that calls for at least two considerations. The first consideration deals with the limits of hegemonic discourses. Beatriz's testimony proves that their subjective incorporation is never linear: these discourses must negotiate their validity with the memories and habitus of their intended recipients. The narrative that characterized the state repression exercised by the last dictatorship as "genocide" was not decoded by Beatriz in the same way it was issued. The tendency to view the world through moral categories first, with political considerations coming in at a distant second, was only strengthened by the incorporation of the concept of the genocide, which in and of itself contributes little to thinking about state repression in political terms. Phenomena of very different natures, such as drug addiction and state terror, can be conceived under its aegis.

The second consideration is related to the necessity of inserting the "contradictions" in Beatriz's narrative in the context of her political memories. Her mention of the cyclothymic character of Argentines in our first interview, her insistence in pointing out, during all three meetings that we had, the "lack of memory" of the Argentine people every time we touched on political subjects — doesn't this indicate a dissatisfaction with the way that the years of terror are remembered? The "incoherence" of her account, then, could perhaps be interpreted as the memory of that which, for her, "the Argentines with no memory" don't want to remember: that at some point, the coup d'état and the purity of ideals, Videla and the intentions that were "clearly of the country," were compatible.

The unsettling views of Beatriz, with her emphasis on the similarities between opposing actors, suggest that there may be other points of hidden or unappreciated convergence. As the concluding chapter will show, it was not only the case that the guerrillas and the military conceived of violence as a legitimate means to impose their views. Beneath the level of conscious strategy, in a pre-ideological realm, violence was also an effective social mode that occupied a privileged space in the symbolic realm.

If a society's culture were defined by the circulation of symbols
that takes place in it, our culture would appear to be as homogeneous
and well-rooted as a small ethnographic society. — Roland Barthes

Five   Desire and Violence (1969–1975)

The survey mentioned in chapter 3, which established that in 1971 a majority of the middle classes rejected the guerrillas, also inquired about how the social crisis should be solved. In all four districts—Capital Federal, greater Buenos Aires, Rosario, and Córdoba—large proportions of the middle classes selected "start from scratch and change everything from the root."[1] In Capital Federal, 47.3 percent of the upper-middle class and 55.4 percent of the lower-middle class selected this option, while the figures were 42.2 percent and 47.5 percent in the greater Buenos Aires metropolitan area, 55.5 percent and 61.5 percent in Rosario, and 42.8 percent and 44.5 percent in Córdoba. Interpreting these results, CIMS concluded that society had a "basic predisposition to receive sympathetically any attempt to introduce fundamental changes in the existing [social] order." CIMS also confirmed a marked social skepticism about the "capacity of the current order to find a solution to the crisis." Another measurement, conducted by IPSA/Turner in November 1972 (after the military had called for elections), also showed that large groups of the population inclined toward drastic solutions.[2]

Read together, the statistical information portrays a society with contradictory traits. For the most part, the middle classes did not approve of the actions of the guerrilla organizations. In great proportion, and increasingly from 1968 on, they did not support the "Argentine Revolution" military government either. Dissatisfied with the reigning social order, the majority of the middle classes rejected gradual transformations and advocated for a radical, total, and immediate change.

Based on an analysis of representations of violence, in this chapter I will explore this social mood by incorporating a perspective that helps to understand the behavior of large social sectors, fundamentally but not exclusively from the moment when the state monopolized violence in March 1976. This understanding demands that the analysis stretch back to the long half-decade (1969–1975) that preceded el Proceso.[3] The material considered comes from magazines intended for mass consumption, both those focusing on political analysis and those devoted to sports, fashion, or general interest, from some of the main daily newspapers read in the three sites studied, and, to a lesser degree, from television and cinema. The nature of the cultural products analyzed enhances their meaning. The great majority combined brief speech (slogans, phrases, or headlines) with striking or shocking images. Although I reprint only a few of these, one should not lose sight of the intrinsic force that they condensed, inherent to the field of visual representations.[4]

Edgar Morin wrote that the cultural industry constituted a second industrialization, one that was no longer dedicated to producing objects but rather to producing images and dreams.[5] This "industrialization of the spirit," in line with Theodor Adorno and Max Horkheimer's critical conception of the cultural industry, was conceived by Morin in terms of the alienation of the subject. However, from the 1960s in the United States and Europe, and some time after in Argentina, the critique of the mass media mutated into a reappraisal of audiences' capacity to infuse media messages with new meanings.[6] This debate, however, is not relevant for the analysis I propose here. Instead of highlighting the dialectic between emission and reception—and therefore, focusing on how much reproduction and how much resistance there was among social actors—I emphasize the raw material of the discourse, the "clay" from which some of these messages were molded and the forms that they assumed, seeing in them less the cause than the result of a community of shared beliefs, ideas, and values.

Nevertheless, some of the ideas pioneered by the critique of the cultural industry are helpful for my analysis. Morin's idea that there is a double contamination of the real and the imaginary in the relation between the society and the media, as well as his argument that the cultural industry is directed at the "average man," an imaginary figure whose stereotype is confirmed by the most salient characteristics of the middle classes, are of particular interest for my purposes.[7] The cultural products that I analyze in this chapter were primarily aimed at (and were largely consumed by) this "average Argentine man."[8]

Among these products, I focus on those that come from the advertising world for four reasons. First, because few commodities are so accessible that they will be consumed by everyone, even if nobody promotes them, as advertisements do. In a way, these advertisements are commodities twice over. They aspire to seduce the consumer, inducing him to buy what is being advertised at the same time that they are immediately consumed by those who see, read, or hear them. People see advertisements in a variety of formats whether they want to or not, and this was already a well-established fact in the 1970s. In 1976, for example, a cultural and linguistic critic indicated that everything in contemporary publicity was designed to create a "mood" in the advertisement's receiver that was apt to provoke, stimulate, convince, and persuade him/her to act in a concrete and determinate sense: to consume.[9] What I investigate in this chapter is related less to consumption than to the forms that advertising took to stimulate this "consumerist mood."

Second, beginning in the 1970s and as a consequence of the development of foreign capital, advertising investment began playing an unprecedented role in Argentine society.[10] Every individual, and especially those of the middle class, became a potential consumer for advertising agencies.[11] Between 1960 and 1972, ad spending rose from 79,000,000 to 1,840,000,000 pesos ley.[12] In 1971, Advertising Age magazine demonstrated that Argentina had spent a higher proportion of its GDP on advertising than France, England, and Canada.[13] This expansion was at the same time a symptom and a cause of the consolidation of a massive and modern system of communications media.[14] In 1976, Argentina exhibited the greatest degree of media development in the hemisphere, behind only the United States and Canada, based on the number of newspapers and magazines sold per thousand residents, movie theater attendance levels, and the number of radio and television receivers.[15] In addition, as Anibal Ford and Jorge B. Rivera have indicated, qualitative changes occurred in the magazine publishing market during the 1970s. On the one hand, the development of general interest magazines such as *Gente* (from the Atlántida publishing house) began, and this publication would come to lead sales statistics during the 1970s along with *Siete Días* (from the Abril publishing house). On the other, weekly political analysis magazines such as *Primera Plana, Confirmado, Panorama,* and *Análisis* were launched, and would come to be influential in both public opinion and political society.[16] This expansion was accompanied by, if not made possible by, a similar boom in their advertising spaces. Their consumption was concentrated in the middle classes, even in the case of the popular magazines such as *Gente,* which one activist publication called the "*Radiolandia* of the Barrio Norte."[17]

Third, I prioritize advertising because, by its very nature, it needs to speak the language of those it seeks to attract better than anything else. "One of the mechanisms of modern advertising," wrote *Primera Plana* in an article with a damning tone in 1972, "is based on the principle of the identification of the *character* with the scene. This is to say, the more we are the *character,* the more we will look for and desire the product that this character consumes."[18] A historian of Argentine advertising wrote in 1974 that "the good advertiser foresees the tendencies of the public [and] detects the tastes of the consumer."[19] "Good" advertising—in terms of efficacy—is that which tries to understand every gesture of the public, that which speaks to them as if it knew their secrets. Therefore, the art of advertising works in the intersections between custom and desire, which it grasps and represents in images and stories. It was not coincidental that during the 1970s the advertising industry incorporated the contributions of semiology, communications theory, and structural psychoanalysis, using teams composed of filmmakers, psychologists, sociologists, semiologists, and messaging specialists.

Finally, analyzing advertising is pertinent because at the end of the 1960s and with growing force in the early 1970s, violence became part of the discourse of marketing itself in Argentina.[20] Indeed, it was around 1968 that the "lamentable tendency" toward emphasizing "negative characteristics of the human personality" took on a larger dimension.[21] This caused broadcasters, advertisers, and ad agencies to draft a binding "Code of Ethics for Television Commercials."[22] In 1970, the Argentine Chamber of Advertisers released a document warning: "The customs of our people throughout its entire history lead us to be fully convinced that our people are not prone to violence nor to contempt for their traditions. The idiosyncratic particularity of Argentines shows us their marked inclination toward pleasing images and for all that which functionally represents the honest and peaceful man, a staunch advocate for his family, devoted to healthy and constructive amusement."[23]

If this idiosyncrasy ever existed, little or nothing was left of it by the early

1970s. The same entity, while aspiring to restore this image, indirectly acknowledged its disappearance. Four years later, the president of a leading advertising agency called for new norms, given that "the people [. . .] feel attacked daily, at their jobs, in the newspaper headlines, through threats and uncertainty."[24]

My analysis rests on two basic suppositions. First, in regard to both advertising and other forms of consumption, I assume that nobody deliberately communicates something in a manner or format that is foreign to the message's recipient. Inducing consumption—or laughter, in the case of humor—implies discursive efficacy, capturing the attention of the intended recipient (and not just anyone) in the terms that are effective (and not in any other way). Second, I do not think that the unique characteristics that advertising took on in those years can be explained by the advertising agencies or their clients. Instead, I understand advertising products (ads, commercials, and slogans) to be vehicles of values and beliefs that went beyond those of business leaders;[25] like gears in the machine that mediatized social desire, they both directed their products toward desire and fed off it.[26]

Guns

During the late 1960s and increasingly during the early 1970s, guns began to occupy an atypical space within journalistic and advertising discourse. They sometimes accentuated manliness, security, ambition, or the readiness to embrace drastic solutions. In other cases, they connoted values such as friendship or the will to lead an exciting or adventurous lifestyle. Finally, both in fashion and in other consumer goods directed toward women, weapons served as metaphors of sensuality and seduction.

Carlos Monzón, the world champion of boxing from 1970 and an indisputable idol of Argentine society, posed with guns in various press articles.[27] In 1972, *Gente*, the magazine with the largest readership within the general interest world, photographed him gazing toward the horizon of a country landscape, alone, hugging his gun, armed with a belt of ammunition. The image took up a whole page and was titled "Monzón trains to live" (see figure 5.1)[28] One year before, *El Gráfico*, the best-selling and most prestigious magazine of its type within the sports market, had shown him aiming a shotgun at a poster of one of his rivals, the Italian Nino Benvenuti, whom he promised to "kill" and "give it to him from the beginning without pity" at their next fight (see figure 5.2).[29]

It is true that violence is spontaneously associable with Monzón's sport. Presenting him posing with guns could have been merely a metaphoric juxta-

FIGURE 5.1. (top) "Monzón trains to live." *Source: Gente,* no. 375, September 28, 1972

FIGURE 5.2. (below) Carlos Monzón aiming a shotgun at a poster of Nino Benvenuti. *Source: El Gráfico,* no. 2658, March 23, 1971

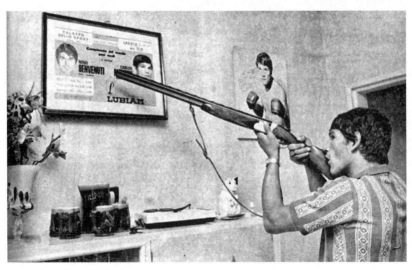

position between the power of fists and shotguns, the lethality of one and the other. However, similar articles were devoted to stars in other sports. In another issue of El Gráfico, "el Beto" Alonso—star of the Club Atlético River Plate soccer team—swore revenge against those who criticized him as he posed for a photo that occupied much of the article's two main pages. In the photo, he appeared with a gun in his hand, ready to shoot, with his eyes squinted like someone who is aiming at a target with precision (see figure 5.3).[30]

The naturalness with which popular stars such as Monzón and Alonso promised violence with guns in hand in mass media with a huge readership is striking. It would be erroneous to conclude that this was solely related to the characteristics of these ads' protagonists or to the fact that they were athletes. Neither Monzón nor Alonso posed with weapons *because* they were violent. Independent of how violent they were, the presence of rifles and shotguns in these images and this choice as a manner of presenting them before public opinion are indicators of a positive connotation that guns had.

This can be confirmed when we direct our attention outside the sporting world—which always lends itself to relations between rivals and enemies, opponents and fighters. The following examples come from the world of show business. In one case they feature a young couple of models; and in the other, an acclaimed soap opera actor. Marta Cerain and Horacio Bustos, a successful pair of models at the moment, told *Gente* about their lives and their desires, which represented them as an ideal couple: successful, hardworking, ambitious, beautiful, and in love with one another. In the article, Cerain and Bustos declared that they wanted to be actors and have two children, at the same time claiming that they studied and worked more than fourteen hours a day. He said that he admired her simplicity and sweetness, and she, his strong personality and unique charm. The main photo that illustrated the story, which was not coincidentally titled "A beautiful couple," showed them elegantly dressed, looking into each other's eyes. He was pointing a shotgun at her and she a revolver (see figure 5.4).[31] Arnaldo André, an emblematic soap opera leading man, appeared in a 1974 story in the same magazine where he expressed his desire to begin a more reflective chapter in his life. The story's main photo also showed him firing a shotgun (see figure 5.5).[32]

In the 1970s, hunting was an activity associated with a variety of positive values. Not only do magazine stories, such as the ones devoted to entertainment figures, corroborate this, an abundant list of products destined for the wealthier portions of the middle classes testify to the notable sign of distinction—in a Bourdieuian sense—that this sport constituted.[33] Jeans, shoes, pants, shirts, sports jackets, cigarettes, shaving creams, colognes, and automobiles were among some of the products that were sold in association

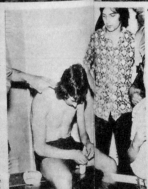

with the activity of hunting, always displaying guns in their advertisements. The art of handling weapons was associated with a series of values, such as friendship, status, masculinity, and a lifestyle full of excitement, adventure, and danger.

"Enjoy the season of friendship and live in Levi's," read one of the slogans of this jeans brand, among the most popular in the 1970s. The image showed two young men, one with a beard and a beret and the other with a moustache and long hair, the latter with a rifle. The Shelton cigarette brand—one of whose slogans, "for those in the know," denoted an elitism that was not so

BETO ALONSO

"A MI ME LEVANTARON DE GOLPE, ME ENDIOSARON, ME USARON Y AHORA ME TIRARON A UN COSTADO. HACE SEIS MESES ERA UN FENOMENO PARA TODO EL MUNDO. HASTA ME LLEGARON A LLAMAR EL PELE BLANCO. AHORA NO SOLO NO SIRVO, SINO QUE INCLUSO ME INVENTARON TODA CLASE DE CONDUCTAS VERGONZOSAS DE MI PARTE. RECIEN TENGO 20 AÑOS, PERO YA HE APRENDIDO BASTANTE DE LA VIDA. ESTO ME HA VENIDO BIEN PARA MI FUTURO. SE DONDE ESTOY, SIGO CREYENDO EN ALGUNA GENTE, ME HACE BIEN CREER, PERO TAMBIEN COMPRENDI QUE HAY QUE ESTAR EN GUARDIA. Y PARA TODOS AQUELLOS QUE ME HICIERON MAL LES TENGO RESERVADA MI VENGANZA..."

"Crei mucho en Sivori. Me defraudó totalmente. Lo de la diabetes fue una buena excusa para borrar me. El tiene experiencia como para saber cuánto duele eso... En River me trataron especialistas y se vio que era mentira. Igual no me llamó ni me dio explicaciones... Me mató... De él me desquitaré mostrándole como se equivocó de proceder..."

"En este Nacional volverán a ver al Alonso ganador. Y volverán a aplaudirlo. Quisiera que me vendieran a Europa para ganar plata, pero me gustaría jugar este último torneo para River. Allí me vengare de todos los que quisieron destrozarme en forma malsana. Mi gran venganza estará en la cancha. Ya lo verán todos... todos..."

FIGURE 5.3. "The revenge of Beto Alonso." *Source:* El Gráfico, no. 2815, September 18, 1973

much economic as aristocratic, in the literal sense of the term—promoted its packs through an image of a select group of people in friendly conversation, smoking and holding guns. The words of the advertisement completed the image, affirming that its subjects "could spend hours talking. They know the subject well. They understand guns. And cigarettes too."[34] A later ad for the same brand incorporated technical details into the wording and included an enlarged photograph of the gun displayed that was more prominent than the actual product being promoted.[35]

That virility was associated with guns to promote products for men or boys

FIGURE 5.4. (top) "A beautiful
couple." *Source: Gente,* no. 181,
January 9, 1969

FIGURE 5.5. (right) Arnaldo André,
emblematic leading actor of soap
operas of that time. "No . . . you don't
understand. I am in something else."
Source: Gente, no. 482, October 17, 1974

can be verified in a variety of advertisements. For example, Sorpasso, a brand of shoes, promoted one of its products displaying a pair of gloves, a shoe, and the body of a shotgun. Austere, the message read: "Masculine and unique."[36] Fittipaldi, a men's cologne, made an analogous association between men and guns. Four men, all armed, surrounded a dead animal. "It's a man thing," the slogan read. The weapons company Pasper promoted two of its products, the Robin Hood rifle and pistol, with images of the guns and a cartoon of the archetypal hero. "Introduce your son to the manly sport of target shooting," the advertisement finished.[37]

Most of the clothing brands that associated their products with guns instead emphasized the status assigned to those who used them. "Finister is the shirt, the man is you," this men's clothing brand's slogan affirmed. A series of close-up images of the model showed the neckline, the back, and the sleeve of the garment. A final image showed the subject in full for the first time, in a living room next to a log cabin. Next to the shirt, all of the images displayed, in part or in full, a gun.[38] Cashmilon, a brand of sports jackets for "people who have cash," advertised its products with two elegantly dressed men, wearing plaid sports jackets and carefully examining a shotgun.[39] Cosak, a brand of men's dress pants, decided not to even show the product it was advertising. The advertisement showed a man's hand on the barrel of a shotgun, a cigar between his fingers, and an elk's head mounted on the wall. "He definitely wears Cosak," read the slogan (see figure 5.6). Different automobile brands also sought to associate their products with guns. Ford Fairlane and Dodge 1500 advertisements both had basically the same four elements: the car owner, a woman by his side, the vehicle being promoted, and a shotgun.[40]

Other companies preferred to associate their products with guns for what they assumed they implied in terms of an exciting and adventurous lifestyle — characteristics compatible with socially ascendant values such as dangerousness. The L&M cigarette brand tended to show upper-middle class people in a wild context with cigarettes in their mouths and weapons in their hands (see figure 5.7).[41] Lord Cheseline, the well-known shaving cream brand, also featured guns prominently. "Between us . . . I recommend a new instant emotion," said the ad's text, whose image showed a man, with a steady, strong gaze and his face covered in shaving cream, holding a canister of Lord Cheseline in his right hand and a handgun in his left (see figure 5.8).[42] In another version of the same advertising campaign, the protagonist was not a sailor but rather a hunter, but the elements combined were the same, with the only change being that instead of a handgun, a shotgun was featured.[43]

In addition to the advertisements that sought to associate their products

with guns, the guns themselves were commonly advertised as products in the mass media. The General Office of Military Manufactures (Dirección General de Fabricaciones Militares) advertised its weapons, such as the FM "S1" 20 caliber shotgun, not only in newspapers and magazines that were oriented toward sports and hunting, but also those focused on general interest topics and political analysis.[44] The information about where to purchase them was accompanied in the ads with images of pistols, revolvers, or shotguns, both for hunting and self-defense, and by headlines like "This news is a gunshot" or slogans like "A gun for every occasion."[45] It was at the very least paradoxical that some of the same magazines had both gun advertisements and editorials against violence in the same issue. This was the case for the Auto Club magazine, which was distributed free to more than half a million members of the Argentine Automobile Club—the vast majority of whom were middle class. In the issue that followed the murders of General Juan Carlos Sánchez and the general manager of Fiat Concord Argentina, Oberdan Sallustro, Auto Club combined obituaries for each one and an editorial against violence with sponsorship of an arms factory and two gun-sales businesses.[46]

Some national and provincial newspapers included information, instruc-

FIGURE 5.6. (opposite left) "He definitely wears Cosak." *Source: Auto Club,* no. 54, September–October 1970

FIGURE 5.7. (opposite right) "Shelton: For those in the know." *Source: El Gráfico,* no. 2583, April 9, 1969

FIGURE 5.8. (left) "Between us . . . I recommend a new instant emotion. Lord Cheseline shaving foam. Instantly softens the beard!" *Source: El Gráfico,* no. 2588, May 13, 1969

tions, and advice for the use of guns, not only related to hunting, but also for nonsporting ends.[47] The Tucumán evening-paper *Noticias,* for example, compared in detail the advantages and disadvantages that a revolver and a pistol had for personal use. The article's writer concluded by noting that "he who hits first hits twice, and a modern high-caliber semiautomatic pistol can hit more than twice."[48] In the same newspaper, Canigo, a Tucumán business, advertised the sale of a German 22 revolver similar to the "Colt Frontier," suggesting that the consumer should "invest their Christmas bonus well."[49] In the Rosario daily *La Capital,* under the headline "Your pocket revolver," the arms factory Italo GRA advertised a 22 caliber revolver and invited the customer to ask for it at the store that they trusted.[50] In metropolitan political analysis magazines, articles about technological advances connected to weapons could also be found. The weekly magazine *Análisis,* for instance, dedicated an article to the arrival of the *Singlepoint* scope to Argentina, which started by affirming that "from now on, attacks will be channeled with greater precision."[51]

The vast majority of advertisements in which guns were displayed were directed toward the consumption of the middle and upper classes. Hunting, as a sport or merely as a leisure activity, target practice, and the taste for guns itself were without a doubt "classing," in the sense that Bourdieu meant it.[52] Associating a product with hunting or target practice was a widespread and probably successful marketing strategy. But there were also guns associated with products in contexts that had no relation to hunting. This is the case of a test published in the automobile magazine *Corsa*, which evaluated the technical characteristics of the Peugeot 504 E—the motor, the clutch, the gear box, the steering, the suspension, the brakes, and so on. The story included a photo of the vehicle in motion with two people in a get-away scene; one of them, stretching his arm out the window, sported a revolver. Nothing in the article explained the relationship between the only photograph and the evaluation of the automobile (see figure 5.9).[53] The Citroën Argentina company attracted its clients through a full-page notice that invited them to become members of the Ami 8 Club, participating "in what people like you have." The vehicle occupied a small part of the advertisement. The main image was of a collection of four pistols from the eighteenth century. The advertisement did not provide any more information, beyond stating that the Ami 8 Club was a "subtle result of the Citroën philosophy" (see figure 5.10).[54]

Guns were not exclusively associated with products directed toward male consumers. In a curious ad promoting one of the last issues of 1969, the women's magazine *Para Ti* displayed an image of a gun accompanied by a caption that said "Extra oxygen for you." In finer print, the ad justified this by announcing that the next issue would include a preview of the premiere of *Marseille 1930*, a movie starring Alain Delon and Jean Paul Belmondo (see figure 5.11).[55] Two years later, in 1971, the same magazine devoted an article to educating women about their rights within a civil marriage. The article was titled "Down with Violence! Long Live Marriage!"; and its main illustrations featured first two men with their hands behind their backs, as if they had been arrested, and then a sole man in the same position being pointed at by a shotgun wielded by a woman (see figure 5.12).[56]

During the first half of the 1970s, both *Para Ti* and *Claudia*, another publication directed at a female audience, illustrated some of their extensive articles about suede garments, tricot fabric, and practical designs for winter vacations with shotguns, revolvers, and phrases extracted from violent rhetoric. One of these was structured as a story of criminal gangs confronting each other, pursued by the forces of order. Another, conducted on the grounds of the Argentine Federal Shooting Range (Tiro Federal Argentino), was headlined, "Shoot the tricot . . ." (see figures 5.13 and 5.14).[57]

Under the title "For Turbulent Times," the entertainment section of *Gente* magazine showed the image of a young woman showing off a new purse as

FIGURE 5.9. (top) Photo illustrating a technical test of the Peugeot 504 E. *Source: Corsa*, August 22–28, 1972

FIGURE 5.10. (left) "Become a member of the Ami 8 Club." *Source: Claudia*, no. 190, March, 1973

FIGURE 5.11. "Extra oxygen for you." *Source:* Para Ti, no. 228, December 4, 1969

FIGURE 5.12. Educating women about their rights within a civil marriage. *Source: Para Ti,* no. 2539, March 8, 1971

DISPAREN SOBRE EL TRICOT

Producción:
SUSANA C. de GUZMÁN
Asistente: ANNY SCHOL
Fotografías:
JUAN C. FRANCESCHINI
Maquillaje:
CRISTINA GONZÁLEZ
EVELYN BERGER

...porque es cálido y suave, porque es práctico, y envolvente, porque es "moda" para todos los días

Dos abrigos supersport. A la izquierda,
cardigan en lana jaspeada, con amplio cuello solapa,
lazo anudado en la cadera y bolsillos plaqué
($ 3.000) Ars. A la derecha,
minigordo en lana melange con cartera abotonada
y amplias mangas ($ 2.600) Ars.

Un cancherísimo dúo. El primero,
verde botella y un clásico sacón con cuello
y mangas tejidas Antolina.
El segundo, cardigan beige
con parches en los codos y bolsillos plaqué
La Azotea.

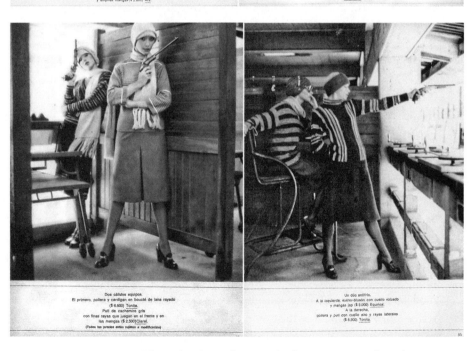

Dos cálidos equipos.
El primero, pollera y cardigan en bouclé de lana rayado
($ 6.500) Tonita.
Pull de cachemire gris
con finas rayas que juegan en el frente y en
las mangas ($ 2.900) Clarel.
(Todos los precios están sujetos a modificación)

Un dúo antifrío.
A la izquierda, suéter-blusón con cuello volcado
y mangas jap ($ 3.000) Equinox.
A la derecha,
pollera y pull con cuello alto y rayas laterales
($ 6.500) Tonita.

FIGURES 5.13–5.14. "Shoot the tricot . . ." Source: *Claudia*, no. 225, March 1976

FIGURE 5.15.

TV program: ". . . and a lace ribbon marking the high waist. Thank you, Alexandra.
  We'll now see Monique on the runway, very in style, showing off a . . ."
Mafalda: "machine gun?"
TV Program: "a white muslin skirt . . ."
Mafalda: "then she's not that in style."
Source: Quino, *Todo Mafalda* (Buenos Aires: De la Flor, 1997)

she was beating a man up. The man, curled up on the floor in a fetal position, covered his head with his arms, asking for mercy. The woman, standing next to him, had one foot on the floor and the other on the man's body. The purse was shaped like a machine gun, with bullet shells hanging out of one of its pockets.[58] In summer 1970, the "Dolce Far West" fashion was one of the new fads. In essence, this was a line of jeans for women, and its advertising also featured guns.[59]

Perhaps nothing better illustrates this association between fashion and guns than a comic strip featuring Mafalda, Quino's emblematic character, who was already very famous in the 1970s and printed in both high-circulation weeklies such as *Siete Días* and newspapers such as Tucumán's *Noticias*.

In the strip, Mafalda's mother was watching a fashion show on television. Upon passing, Mafalda heard that the person conducting the program said: ". . . and a lace ribbon marking the high waist. Thank you, Alexandra. We'll now see Monique on the runway, very in style, showing off a . . ." and the little girl asked "machine gun?" When she heard that she was mistaken—the model was wearing a "white muslin skirt . . ."—Mafalda left the room muttering "then she's not that in style" (see figure 5.15).[60]

In August 1973, now in a democratic context, the executive branch modified the national law regarding guns and explosives by decree, justifying this decision by the need to restrict their existence, as it was believed that the presence of weapons was interfering with the pacification process under-

FIGURE 5.16. "A look from the inside of the window." *Source: Gente*, no. 513, May 22, 1975

taken by the Peronist government.[61] Two years later, however, *Gente* magazine published a story that sought to call its readers' attention to the rise of guns. In its style, the main text of the article read:

> Any downtown street. A shop window. It's not a fashion boutique, and it's not a "Prode" agency [a lottery game involving soccer]. There are no lottery tickets offered for sale there, nor are there stereos, radios, or recorders. There, simply, guns are exhibited. It's the shop window of a gun store. If you haven't noticed, we'll tell you: the most popular shop windows, today, are those of the gun shops. Think about that. Look from this side of the window. See those curious faces. And think about why people are looking for a revolver, a pistol, or a shotgun, these clear symbols of violence (see figure 5.16).[62]

Although incomplete, the selection of advertisements serves to corroborate the positive connotation that the knowledge of, use, or mere presence of guns brought with them. Associated with activities that denoted status and social prestige, such as hunting or target practice, and used to assert ideas such as friendship, or to indicate an adventurous and risky lifestyle, guns flooded the symbolic space, accompanying goods and celebrities.

Their presence combined with the ascent of new values. In regard to women, different advertisements stressed the values of aggressiveness and of daring to live dangerously, the latter of these imported from the heritage of Mussolini's maxims.[63] Leila, a women's underwear manufacturer, promoted one of its garments with the slogan "Bold, aggressive, dare yourself!"; Floo-Crem, a women's beauty products company, headlined its ads with the titles "Now! To look aggressively . . . feminine"; the Festival toothpaste presented itself as "the young toothpaste with an aggressive flavor!"; and the Miss Ylang company, which produced makeup and hair removal products, tempted its clientele through the concepts of "70s Woman . . . aggressively feminine" and "living dangerously."[64] A 1970 soap opera titled *Woman*, broadcast by Channel 7 across the entire country, also promoted itself alluding to this idea: "Woman, aggressive, almost ferocious, but always . . . a Woman."[65] The celebration of feminine aggressiveness can also be found in advertisements aimed at men, such as those of the Juvencia company, which made products to avoid hair loss. Its advertisement read: "Guys who have lost a little hair: If their [women's] summer aggressiveness has you at bay, come to Juvencia."[66]

If living dangerously and aggressiveness were feminine values, boldness, mercilessness, and the search for power were those of the masculine world. In July 1969, before the Argentine guerrilla organizations acquired notoriety, that is to say, when the world "guerrilla" still recalled the romanticism that part of public opinion associated with Che Guevara, killed in 1967, the menswear brand Sportline launched an advertisement in which it assured that "only if you combine the boldness of the guerrilla and the solvency of a playboy are you fit to wear Sportline."[67] After the guerrilla started to be a local phenomenon as well, the marketing strategy changed, but not the values connoted with it. Accompanied by a sensual and provocative female gaze, another of its advertisements read: "If a look like this makes you quiver (and you're also worried about the gas bill), then you're not fit to wear Sportline."[68] Boldness, here, was opposed to hesitation, to those who let themselves be intimidated by others' glances, and for those who think about the little things, the ordinary, the "gas bill." Doubt, indecision, and intermediate positions were clearly viewed negatively. Even mercy was presented as a weakness. The clothing brand Modart, for example, celebrated that its clothing was for "men that dress without compassion."[69] Other advertisements, such as those of the Fiat company in 1973, turned to large letters to publish sentences such as "No forgiveness" or "Unforgivable."[70] In 1975, the Lutz Ferrando company used an allusion to the biblical phrase that sanctifies revenge. "An Eye for an eye . . . a client for a client," read a curious advertisement with two young women wearing glasses.[71] Even when the text accompanying these advertisements gave the messages different meanings—for example, in the last case, the company clarified in fine print that it served every client according to their needs and their "look"—it is still significant that the imaginary to which their slogans and images alluded was related to violence, revenge, or mercilessness.

Danger was also valued for men. Modart's garments, for example, were presented as "the weapons designed by Modart for dangerous men."[72] Vitess hairspray promoted all of its products declaring that these were for "high-voltage men."[73] The value that was outstanding, however, among a wide range of products primarily aimed at a male audience, was the pursuit of power. For example, a brand of automotive lubricants, whose products in any case could give more strength to a vehicle, were advertised by alluding to the idea of power. "Bardahl is power!" exclaimed its advertisement in 1972.[74] The Sunbeam razor was "the power machine," which a text in much smaller font clarified as being "the power to decide. The power to deal with truly transcendent things. The power of having very little time to shave at any moment."[75] This whole set of actions, which had little relation to what is understood by the concept of "power," was presented in this advertisement as its "aura." In 1970, Ford advertised its Fairlane vehicle alluding again to this idea: "More power," the ad read. It then showed an image of the vehicle, and below it, completed the message with the caption "Fairlane gives you more [power]." Three years later, Ombú, the line of work clothes from the Grafa company, marketed its products with the slogan "the power of resistance."[76] Even a collection of scientific information, the Science Book, distributed its booklets with the exclamations "Enjoy the power!" and "More power for you!"[77] Toward the middle of the decade, Perfecta Lew, a clothing brand, advertised its garments alluding to the idea of domination, with boxing champion Carlos Monzón and the actress and model Susana Giménez, the most famous Argentine couple of the times, as the models for its campaign, whose slogan was "the dominant personality."[78] Monzón and Giménez embodied the parable of the marriage between strength and beauty.[79]

Both the notable presence of guns in the symbolic space constituted by the media and the vindication of aggressiveness, living dangerously, mercilessness, or the pursuit of power constitute a way to access the world of values and the system of ideas that predominated in the 1970s. Affirming that there was a positive valorization of guns in the symbolic space opens questions about what exactly they represented. In this sense, it cannot be overlooked that a gun is, in itself, a symbol of a drastic, final, irreversible action. Its use is linked to a radical, total, and instant closure, which at the same time is a promise of an entirely original beginning, cut off entirely from the past. Guns call for solutions of a magical character. The new world starts after the pull of a trigger. A shot, a bullet—these are signals of both closure and inauguration. At odds with the ideas of patience, tolerance, and moderation, guns are perfect metaphors for urgency, intolerance, and the extreme. Aggression, danger, and mercilessness; in short, all the values that the advertisements extolled, were merely the temperamental dispositions that those who shared the imaginary implicated in guns should show.

It is clear that it isn't important how far or how close guns were to the members of the middle classes. The point was not to establish a linear relationship between them and the guns, or between them and aggression or mercilessness. It is not relevant, for example, if they enjoyed target practice or not. The question really lies in how society must have been and how the middle classes analyzed here must have been, so that guns and these values constituted effective strategies of attraction within the symbolic space of advertising.

Guns were, in the early 1970s, archetypal symbols of a series of beliefs, values, and desires shared by a large portion of the middle sectors of the society. "A clean slate," "changing everything at the root," "starting from scratch"; the attachment of much of the middle classes to what these expressions and other similar ones symbolized, together with the rejection expressed for gradualist solutions, incremental changes, and a phased strategy for social change, are attitudes compatible with what guns represent on the symbolic plane. Solutions must be immediate, things must change radically, changes were deemed effective only if they were similar to shocks — and these views were totally independent from being in favor or against the guerrilla organizations or the military government, or of being closer to the left or the right. The 1970s, to a greater degree than the decades that succeeded it, combined a cult of ruthlessness of action with a shared need to produce or desire the production of irreversible facts, from which no return is possible. As a young sociology student affirmed during the dawn of the decade of the 1970s: "I think that we need to take the example of some adventurers. We have to be like Cortés: burn the boats, so that there is no return. The only way to commit oneself is with irreversible acts." [80] This idea not only reflected a desire held by activists; much broader, it was probably shared by many social sectors. Whether they were close or far from the struggles of those days, activists and nonactivists of the middle classes tended to agree with some military leaders and the guerrilla groups on a belief founded on the rejection of gradual processes and a faith in extraordinary, almost magical actions that would split history in two like a lightning bolt.

The positive valorization of guns joined together the threads of these aspirations rather neatly. Roland Barthes has indicated that not only written discourse but also photography, cinema, journalism, sports, entertainment, and advertising can all serve as a support for mythical speech.[81] For the reasons indicated at the beginning of this chapter, advertising businesses can then be studied as pillars of the mythical speech of a historical period. The characteristic of a myth, Barthes wrote, is to transform meaning into a form; to steal a signifying language and naturalize, through this, a form. Mythology is the study of ideas as forms. In this sense, it is meaningful that the form that guns are referred to can be expressed with the same words that the survey cited at the beginning of this chapter: "clean slate," "starting from scratch," and "changing everything from the root."

The mission that the different political projects attributed to themselves, at least from 1966 on, obeyed the same logic, regardless of their military or civilian nature and of the specific political project that they embodied. The nation had to die and be reborn: Onganía sought to "revolutionize it," Peronism sought to "reconstruct it," and the dictatorship sought to "reorganize it." The syllable "re" in each case testifies to the intention to "wipe the slate clean" and the vocation to "change everything from the root," always judged to be necessary. In other words: the myth of a radical closure as a necessary condition of another myth, a foundational myth, which presumes that history does not have its own history, but rather starts from zero after making a "corpse" of the present it aspires to abolish. Nothing expresses both myths better than guns. Their positive valorization in the first half of the 1970s and their notable presence in the symbolic space are consonant with desire for a total and instantaneous change, which starts anew from a clean slate.

Violence as Metaphor

If many advertisements of the early 1970s alluded positively to guns, an even more significant number turned to metaphors of violence, with or without guns. On May 29, 1970, the Montoneros kidnapped and later killed former de facto president Aramburu. In July, some days after his corpse was discovered, the famous menswear store Modart advertised discounts in its products, publishing an advertisement that it had not previously used. It read: "This is what it means to liquidate!"[82] The pun on "liquidation" (of product stock) and "to liquidate" (a person) was also used by other clothing stores in Buenos Aires, Rosario, and Tucumán. Rosario-based firm Piacenza Magliera announced reduced prices in 1972 through an advertisement that showed a woman armed with a gun—in addition to a revolver next to the store's name—and a caption that read "A liquidation that is a shot" (see figure 5.17).[83] In Tucumán, the La Mundial store advertised its sales assuring that "in the winter, La Mundial liquidates upon arrival," with the largest font reserved for the word "liquidates."[84] A Rosario store turned directly to the idea of murder to promote its sale. "We kill . . . prices," read the caption, with the word "kill" standing out in size; at its side was a well-dressed man with machine gun in hand.[85]

The metaphor of kidnapping also began to be used often after the first abductions conducted by the guerrilla organizations. In a manual for the "jet set" (*gente paqueta*), the humorist Landrú included suggestions that the man wear "a multicolored bathing suit" to the beach, "so that his wife can distinguish him rapidly from the crowd in the case that someone tries to kidnap him."[86] In 1971, LT8, one of the most important radio stations serving Rosario and its surroundings, including Correa, advertised its broadcast of the soccer finals of the Copa Libertadores de América with newspaper ads that announced, in huge font: "This night . . . we will kidnap the audience!"[87] That same year, the Néstor Paternostro movie *Paula contra la mitad más uno*, starring Federico Luppi, Juan Carlos Gené, and Dimma Zecchin, featured a gang that planned the kidnapping of Boca Juniors soccer players and asked for a multimillion-dollar ransom. The advertising for the movie showed part of the Boca soccer team in the crosshairs of a riflescope, and the main headline read: "Luppi and Gené kidnap the Boca Juniors team."[88]

The use of riflescopes and circular targets were also successful advertising strategies. These could be found everywhere from magazine covers to advertisements for industrial bearings, in political ads for elections and in their satires. *Panorama* entitled its issue on the ambush of the C-10 regiment of the Armored Cavalry from the city of Azul by the ERP in the province of Buenos Aires, "Córdoba in the Sights."[89] This act irreversibly angered Perón, and rumors deepened of a hardening of the executive branch with respect to the sectors that were least amenable to its designs, such as the government of Ricardo Obregón Cano and Atilio López in Córdoba. The cover showed the lens of a riflescope aiming at the province of Córdoba (colored in red; see figure 5.18). The advertisement for SNR industrial bearings put a man in the scope's sights under the caption "I accuse you" (see figure 5.19).[90] The advertisement for the Nueva Fuerza (New Force) Party, whose dominant figure was Álvaro Alsogaray and whose presidential candidate in 1973 was Julio Chamizo, consisted of a poster with a drawing of a target, in which the electoral act of voting was compared to shooting at the target (see figure 5.20).[91] Satiricón magazine satirized this on their cover, with a drawing in which Alsogaray and Chamizo were featured naked over the target, fighting off arrows, eggs, and knives being thrown at them, with red stains visible around the circumference of the target (see figure 5.21).[92]

The idea of the gunshot (*balazo*) or something similar (such as the shot [*tiro*], the cannon shot [*cañonazo*], or the bomb) were used in various adver-

FIGURE 5.17. "A liquidation that is a shot." *Source: La Capital*, February 10, 1972

FIGURE 5.18. "Córdoba in the sights." *Source: Panorama*, no. 349, May 24–30, 1974

tisements, connoting efficacy. "It's a gunshot for your thirst!" read a beverage slogan in 1969 (see figure 5.22).[93] The ad was enigmatic not only because it did not show the face of its protagonist, but also because beyond a smoking revolver in his right hand, it did not offer any other information. Four days later, the same newspaper published a second ad where "Defend your *Talca*" could be read and added below, "It's a gunshot for your thirst. Take off your hats! . . . Talca has arrived . . . For your thirst. Fresh . . . Refresh! Take aim with Talca . . . the bold flavor!" In this second advertisement, a woman drank the promoted beverage while leaning on the back of the protagonist while he took aim at the reader with a revolver in each hand.[94]

If Talca was a gunshot for one's thirst, Slim, an "exclusive" brand of jeans and jackets, was a gunshot in clothing. Its slogan simply read: "It's a gunshot!!" (see figure 5.23).[95] And the digestive medicine Carqueja Trop was "a gunshot" to normalize digestion; its "thirty drops" were compared in its advertisement to "thirty shots."[96] Lear, a brand of shorts for men and boys, advertised its garments with a revolver from whose barrel the slogan "It's like

FIGURE 5.19. "I accuse you." *Source: Auto Club,* no. 62, January–February 1972

FIGURE 5.20. "New Force Party." *Source: Para Ti,* no. 2587, February 7, 1972

a shot on the beach" came out.[97] Rosario's Channel 3 attracted new sponsors through the exclamation "Shoot at the market!!!"[98] A fuel oil from the Shell company, the "Supershell Sprint" gasoline, was also inspired by the metaphor of shooting. "It's a shot!" affirmed the advertisements that in some cases included a model firing at the reader with a fuel supply gun.[99] In 1974, *Billiken* magazine, from the Atlántida publishing house, widely read by school-age boys, advertised one of its issues with the slogan: "A *Billiken* that is a cannonball," alluding to the fact that the next issue would include a gift of a gun that shot "harmless plastic projectiles," which was called the "*Billicañonazo*" (figure 5.24).[100] Two years earlier, another gift that accompanied the magazine was a pistol that shot spinning tops. The issue's advertising read "Aim . . . Play!" *Billiken* magazine provided a gift "so that [boys] can fire the most harmless and the most fun gun."[101] A car dealership between Rosario and Correa, Guerrero Automotores, several times made use of armed metaphors. In one of them, for example, the caption "the bomb is at Guerrero," written over the image of a lit explosive, invited the customer to buy an automobile

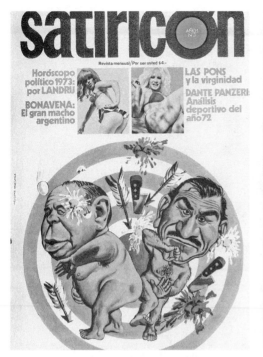

FIGURE 5.21. Front page of *Satiricón* magazine. *Source: Satiricón*, no. 3, January 1973

FIGURE 5.22. "It's a gunshot for your thirst!" *Source: La Capital*, November 5, 1969

without fees and in interest-free installments, so that he/she "explodes from happiness" (see figure 5.25).[102] A humor magazine promoted itself by declaring that it "explode[ed] the first Tuesday of every month."[103]

The national commercial mass cinema, meanwhile, also presented scenes referring to attacks and bombs. In *El verano de los Campanelli*—a 1971 film that emerged from the success of the television series *Los Campanelli*—the opening of a soda water factory turns into a scene of collective desperation, originating in a misunderstood rumor.[104] "I have a bombshell" (*"Tengo una noticia bomba"*), the origin of the misunderstanding, is interpreted as meaning that there was a bomb in the place; so as one of the characters shouts "there's a bomb," everyone runs out of the establishment. The movie, like almost all those of its style, is inconsequential on an aesthetic or cinematographic level. However, it is still significant that national films directed at a wide audience had already introduced by the beginning of the decade a parody of a potential attack on a place full of common civilians.

"Gun" was a common word in the metaphorical universe in which jour-

FIGURE 5.23. (right)
"Slim is a gunshot!"
Source: El Gráfico, no.
2648, July 7, 1970

FIGURE 5.24.
(below) "A Billiken
that is a cannonball."
Source: Gente, no. 479,
September 26, 1974

FIGURE 5.25. "The bomb is at guerrero." *Source: La Capital,* December 15, 1969

nalism and advertising operated. The insurance department of the Popular Savings Bank of Tucumán (*Caja Popular de Ahorros de Tucumán*) advertised its vehicle insurance services by asking the reader: "If something happens to you, are you armed?" Underneath the question, next to a destroyed, burned car, the ad explained that "if your car is insured by our insurance department, you are armed" (see figure 5.26).[105] In late 1972, four months from the elections, an official notice—a sign of the times—read "if you are less than 25 years old, we present you with a weapon you don't know yet," and below this caption a voting booth was shown.[106] "Use it for the solution," it finished saying, after emphasizing that the importance of the act of voting lay in that young people who voted for the first time would be "rejecting violence" and "choosing the peaceful and clean determinations of the voting booths."

That same year, the Braun company released an electric lighter whose advertisement remarked that its grip was black "like a gun's," and that "its trigger responds. Always"; the main caption read: "Mach 2. The firearm" (see figure 5.27).[107] In 1973 Modart added to its men's clothing advertisement the slogan "the Weapons to take them [women] over."[108] In 1974, the company

FIGURE 5.26. "If something happens to you, are you armed?" *Source: Noticias,* August 1, 1969

FIGURE 5.27. "Mach 2. The firearm." *Source: La Capital,* June 12, 1973

FIGURE 5.28. "Arm yourself with humor." *Source: Panorama*, no. 356, March 21–27, 1974

Charrúa y Cía., a manufacturer of raw materials for making clothing, sought to attract the public that visited them in the International Clothing Fair with an ad titled "Our weapons."[109] The same year, the humor magazine *Lucky Luke* advertised its issues through the slogan "Arm yourself with humor" (see figure 5.28).[110]

The footwear industry, in this context, had the metaphor all cut out for it. To "go around wearing shoes" (*andar calzado*) in popular slang meant to "go armed," carrying firearms. In 1975, both Grimoldi, one of the most popular shoemakers, and La Provincial, a Tucumán-area clothing store, turned to this allegory. For the Day of the Child, Grimoldi came out with the slogan "a well-armed life for the entire family."[111] For Father's Day, La Provincial advertised its prices with the slogan "For well-armed dads."[112]

It would be wrong to establish a causal relationship between the abundant presence of guns and metaphors for violence in the symbolic space and the political violence that characterized the first half of the decade. The analysis that I propose instead argues that, beyond the concrete manifestations of violence and of individuals or groups that instigated it, these years unfolded over a background of an increasing violence subconsciously shared by broad sectors of the society, a sort of pre-ideological second nature. It is significant, however, that a magazine noted the relationship mentioned above. In

CUANDO LA PROPAGANDA LEVANTA ESTA BANDERA...
(Rafi para una publicidad de cigarrillos).

...LAS MAESTRAS JARDINERAS SE HACEN GUERRILLERAS.
(En la foto: Norma Arrostito, implicada en el asesinato del teniente general Pedro Eugenio Aramburu).

FIGURE 5.29. "When advertising raises this banner . . ." and ". . . the kindergarten teachers will become guerrillas." *Source:* El Burgués, no. 16, November 24, 1971

November 1971, the magazine El Burgués, which was characterized by its high-quality full-page photographs, showed a draft for a cigarette advertisement in which the model, looking menacing, held a revolver in one of her hands. On the next page, the magazine showed Norma Arrostito, a member of the Montoneros armed organization, walking and smiling. "When advertising raises this banner," the text under the model read, even "the kindergarten teachers will become guerrillas," concluded the magazine under the photo of Arrostito (see figure 5.29).

Even more significant is that the same magazine that made this connection did not refrain from using references, often on its covers, to guns, grenades, and bombs which, while utilized to criticize the actions of the guerrillas, also contributed to the proliferation of violent metaphors and symbols that the same magazine questioned.[113] The critique of violence resorted to using the symbols of violence (see figures 5.30–5.33).

Advertising did not shy away from ideas related to the armed political struggle and its ideological dimension. "We are trying to prolong the war," declared the Banco Popular Argentino in an advertisement, referring to their claim that they offered better and more services, in a context where some

¡OJO A LA BOMBA!

FIGURE 5.30. (left) "Take care with the bomb." *Source: El Burgués,* no. 35, August 16, 1972

FIGURE 5.31. (below) "Refrain Trotskyist-Peronist: Arm one another." *Source: El Burgués,* no. 40, October 25, 1972

FIGURE 5.32. "Best Wishes: Montoneros." Source: El Burgués, no. 19, January 5, 1972

FIGURE 5.33. "Argentina unarmed." Source: El Burgués, no. 30, July 7, 1972

Latin American guerrilla groups had proclaimed the slogan of "prolonged people's war."[114] The aviation company Austral, in a full-page advertisement, promoted its service through the headline "Not with the Left" and an image of an executive in a suit and hat. The ad's text indicated that the airline's flight attendants were "young ladies that know what they are doing," and thus, when they serve the reader on a flight, although they might "hold the tray with their left hand"—something that the ad deemed to be "tolerable"—"they will serve you with their right." The humorous conclusion was: "if at some point they serve you with their left hand, let us know. That means we've been infiltrated by a leftist [zurda]" (see figure 5.34).[115] The newspaper El Cronista Comercial advertised itself declaring that if Fidel Castro, whose image the ad displayed, would have read their paper, "he would know how to better organize subversion" (see figure 5.35).[116] The ad for an aftershave proclaimed that "if the ends are justified . . . Vitess is the means."[117] The advertising language of the first half of the 1970s is full of these types of lighthearted allusions to the metaphors of violence. It constitutes an unequivocal record of the surprising naturalness with which the ideas of killing and dying, of war and subversion, or revenge and firearms, and even of infiltrators and informers, were alluded to.

It was also in the early 1970s when the verb "to kill" became a positive superlative expression, especially for young people, synonymous with something great or spectacular, so that something that "killed" surpassed the expectations that one could have about something or someone.[118] This expression displaced another which gradually fell into disuse: "a kilo." What was "a kilo" in the 1950s "killed" in the 1970s. In a dictionary published by Gente in which the words used by youth of 1975 appeared, the expression "killed a thousand" was defined as "something sensational, that attracts attention, that causes surprise. Example: The girl put on some new jeans and killed a thousand."[119]

The term entered the entertainment and show business press as well as advertising and cinema. Hundreds of examples in which the allusion to "killing" had a positive connotation can be found in articles, headlines, advertisements, and commercial movies. In 1972, the Valet Gillette company came out with an advertisement showing the bottom portion of a man and a woman's body lying on the floor, as if they had been shot. "This cologne . . . kills!" said the slogan.[120] It was written that Andrés Percivale, a successful TV host, had a "TV program that 'kills.' "[121] It was said that the poet Kahlil Gibran, rediscovered by some youth in the mid-1970s, "killed a thousand."[122] In 1974, Para Ti magazine advertised its next issue in newspapers with a photo of Paul Newman and the caption "If it kills like this . . . imagine it in full color,"

FIGURE 5.34. "Not with the Left." *Source: Corsa*, no. 227, August 25–31, 1970

FIGURE 5.35. "If this gentleman read El Cronista Comercial, he would know how to better organize subversion." *Source: Confirmado*, no. 478, October 14–20, 1970

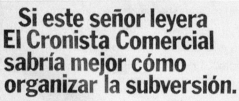

alluding to the fact that that issue would include a color poster of the American actor.[123] After the March 1973 elections, the famous television character from the series Controversy in the Cafe (Polémica en el Bar), Minguito Tinguitella, played by actor Juan Carlos Altavista, asked his friends in the café about the Peronist victory "And? Did we kill or didn't we kill?"[124] That same year, an interview with a group of Argentine soccer players who won in Europe had the headline "With the Argentines who 'killed' in Monaco."[125] Los Pumas, the national rugby team, earned a similar headline upon triumphing in the eighth South American tournament in Paraguay. "Los Pumas killed in Asunción," headlined El Gráfico in 1975.[126] A year before, this same magazine had celebrated the latest victory of Argentine boxing champion Carlos Monzón over José "Mantequilla" Nápoles with the headline "He left like he came: killing!"[127] Moreover, "I'm going to kill you," "come here so I can kill you," and other similar expressions, the majority of times with sexual connotations, became commonplace in the picaresque films of the 1970s, especially in those films starring Alberto Olmedo and Jorge Porcel.

Political language—and to a great degree, journalistic language as well—also experienced a growing radicalization in its expressions and metaphors. In 1972 a foreign journalist noted that "the majority of metaphors employed in political debate have military undertones" and that these are applied to "normally peaceful political or commercial relationships," making them a significant feature of the Argentine panorama.[128] The commonplace analogies to the world of war present in the coverage of political events—through the use of words such as "war," "battle," and "weapons"—also extended to domains that were not political during the first half of the 1970s. For example, a story about the news programs Teleshow, En vivo y en directo, and a new series whose name was unknown, directed respectively by the journalists Hugo Guerrero Marthineitz, Andrés Percivale, and Lucho Avilés, had "the evening in arms" as its headline. In addition to qualifying the competition in terms of war—the television hosts were called "combatants"—the article affirmed that "all battles produce corpses" and that "the first is already lying on the battlefield," referring to a soap opera that would no longer be broadcast.[129]

Perhaps the most paradigmatic cultural artifact that embodies the spirit of the times was a television commercial from the Bonafide company, released in 1970. The commercial was successful and, according to Héctor Solanas, president of Grant Publicidad, the agency that created it, "emptied Bonafide's shelves."[130] The scene showed a highly sought after actor of the period, Antonio Grimau, dressed in a suit, neatly groomed, sitting placidly at his desk, enjoying some of the company's candies. The camera angle was short, focusing almost entirely on the actor's face and shoulders, so as not to give away what was happening in the rest of the scene. An off-camera voice asked: "Excuse me, you're eating candy, right?"; to which Grimau, who doesn't speak at any moment of the commercial, responded affirmatively, nodding his head. "And as far as I see, they are the extra fine candies from Bonafide," continued the speaker. Grimau responded that they were, once again with gestures. "Yes, I know, those ones that are chocolate covered; they must be delicious, right?" asked the speaker, and the actor's response continued to be affirmative. When the off-camera voice asked that Grimau give him one, the actor took out a revolver and killed his interlocutor. The sequence was the following: "Will you give me one?" asked the speaker, and the actor shook his head. "Come on, don't be like that, just one. Come on, I'll take one, eh?" were the speaker's final words, before receiving a bullet from a silent and satisfied Grimau.[131]

"Extra fine Bonafide candies. For the selfish," the commercial concluded (see figure 5.36).[132] Although this advertisement can be analyzed referencing its underlying values, such as individualism or greed, what also deserves attention is the form rather than the content of the television commercial. The art of advertising tends to push the idea that a product is so delicious or so fabulous that those who possess it would do anything not to share it. In this sense, there is nothing surprising in Bonafide's ad. What is nothing short of amazing forty years later—something that probably did not cause surprise in 1970 as the thesis that I propose in this chapter suggests—is that a commercial strategy would include the staging of a murder in its promotion of product, in a message conceived to attract an audience.[133] In 1972, the authorities ordered the removal of another commercial, this one of a pastry called "the Little Black Angel" (*Angelito Negro*) aimed at an audience of children, whose conclusion consisted of the execution by a guardian angel of a boy disguised as a black angel.[134]

I would like to advance two conclusions, one aesthetic and the other ethical. First, it seems clear that the representation of violence in the early 1970s turned into an art form. And this occurred not only in commercial art but also in art that presented itself as being "[politically] committed" and circulated in more restricted environments. "Ferocity will make us free" was the proclamation that a leftist artist attached to his work *Project for a Monument to the Disappeared Political Prisoner*, which called for art to "liberate our colonized culture, opposing against it a counterculture of violence."[135] Between the end of the 1960s and the middle of the 1970s, in tandem with the increasingly

FIGURE 5.36. Photos of a TV commercial for candy. *Source*: Bonafide Company, www.veoh.com, COMA 13: *Del Cordobazo a Malvinas, Trece anos de historia en imágenes*, part 1.

more technical and sophisticated exercise of what could be called the art of violence in the political field, the symbolic field was developing its representation: violence in art.

In reference to ethics, it can be said that in the 1970s, violence became a social bond, although this may seem paradoxical. In part, this happened because, to the extent that violent practices multiplied and became commonplace, they began to be taken for granted in a very similar manner to that noted by Hannah Arendt in her book *On Violence*. In other words, they became part of what everyone considered obvious, natural, and, up to a certain point, indisputable.[136] The fact that violence played a large role in the cultural consumption oriented toward the middle classes does not make these classes more or less violent. It instead indicates to what degree a community had incorporated violence into its habitus, as a curious form of sociability.[137] Pierre Bourdieu called *doxa* the set of ideas, existing in all societies, that are assumed prereflexively, also defined as that community of values and beliefs prior to any deliberation that translate into an immediate adherence to what is evident.[138] Social and mental structures overlap in the experience of the social world of the doxa. A particular historical order of relationships appears to be naturalized both in reality as well as in thought.

If killing a person on camera to sell candy was an act that a company was not afraid of being associated with, this is not because it wanted to appear linked with the idea of death, but rather because murder was an act that was socially trivialized, because violence had become banal.[139] If we examine the concrete exercise of violence and the naturalness with which its promise and realization were contemplated in 1970s Argentina, the idea of the banalization of violence can help us to think about that doxa, that background of tacit social acceptance of violence as an implicitly admissible method to resolve conflicts or disagreement, and even of relating to one another. "Nobody examines or questions what is obvious for everyone," Arendt wrote of violence.[140] The analysis conducted here shows to what degree violence in 1970s Argentina was there, was something obvious, was an unwritten rule. It formed part of everyday reality and its most convincing expressions came from radicalized social actors involved in the political struggle and from the state institutions charged with their repression. But it also made up a symbolic order that went beyond the particular political actors involved, and it is in this order where the social fantasies that served as a support to the behavior of broad sectors of the society can be traced.

Violence as Fantasy

During the first half of the 1970s, images, metaphors, and plays on words referring to violence were often used in advertisements that emphasized women's sensuality and their seductive power.[141] The use of sensual and seductive women in advertising was—and continues to be—a typical tactic of the advertising business. The change that was introduced in 1969 was the combination of this tactic with guns and slogans that denoted violence or death.[142] Different from those advertisements that included sporting or hunting firearms, the ads that combined sensuality and violence made use of revolvers or pistols, which implies more specifically violence against humans.

In the advertisements analyzed in this section, women that are either ready to use their weapons or have just done so appear in positions of domination or control of the situations that the ads represent. Although what these images depicted does not belong to the political realm, the combination of danger and determination that they connote did not fail to have a correspondence with the form that the Argentine political struggle was taking. In 1970, in a context in which the press was speaking of "a wave of attacks," the police used the gender of the suspects to deduce if the attacks were conducted by common criminals or "subversives."[143] If there were signs of female participation and the use of guns or explosives, they deduced that it was the latter. In reality, the "guns-women" association was a political indicator.

In advertising, however, this translated into the language of consumption, cultural transformations, and social fantasies. In the early 1970s, a motorcycle released by Gilera Argentina "created for today's people" achieved some popularity. The advertisement that promoted it displayed the motorcycle in the foreground, and in the background, a woman holding a revolver pointing straight ahead. The caption that accompanied the ad indicated that the SP 70 motorcycle was "the only one with a license to fire . . ." and in parentheses added "and how!" (see figure 5.37).[144] "Please remember that I am made of wool . . . and have pity: Don't rinse me!" a sweater with its arms raised exclaimed in an advertisement for Wash Lan Oro, a cleaning product for wool fabrics. The scene was completed with a stylishly dressed and groomed woman who held a lit cigarette in one hand and a revolver pointing at the heart of the sweater in the other (see figure 5.38).[145] Carqueja Trop, a digestive medicine, was advertised with the image of a woman blowing the smoke of her recently fired revolver to indicate to consumers that the product "eliminates discomfort" (see figure 5.39).[146]

The advertisements of women with guns in hand are, on the one hand, a symptom of the questioning that had been going on since the 1960s about traditional feminine gender roles both politically and above all culturally. Even in the ad where the woman appeared doing household tasks, such as washing clothing, both the cigarette she held in one hand and the gun that she gripped in the other betray a feminine ideal different from the typical figure of the housewife.[147] On the other hand, the combination of women and guns shows that this ideal, this new position that the woman began to occupy in society, ran parallel to a transformation of the values of that society. In line with the ascendant values mentioned in the previous section, the woman celebrated in these advertisements (moreover, not just any woman, but always a young, middle-class woman) was one that had taken the bull by the horns. She went from being solely in the gaze of others to being, without ceasing to be looked at (desired), the person who imposed the conditions under which desire was channeled. Thus, the appearance of armed women in the symbolic space is a sign of the process of mutation of the old gender role, at the same time that it revealed a masculine universe threatened by women's willingness to assume values that were traditionally at odds with what supposedly corresponded to their nature.

In his research about the world of images and symbols of the members

FIGURE 5.37. (right) "sp 70 Motorcycle: The only one with a license to fire . . . and how!" *Source: El Gráfico*, no. 2617, December 2, 1969

FIGURE 5.38. (below) "Please remember that I am made of wool . . . and have pity: Don't rinse me!" *Source: Para Ti*, no. 2436, March 17, 1969

FIGURE 5.39. "Carqueja Trop: It eliminates discomfort." *Source: La Capital*, June 14, 1971

of the Freikorps—the volunteer armies that fought against the revolutionary German working class between the end of World War I and the rise of Nazism—Klaus Theweleit analyzed the role played by the riflewomen (*Flintenweiber*) in the symbolic imaginary of these German soldiers.[148] The threat that the riflewomen presented for these men was not vaginal but rather phallic. Both fantasized about and feared, these women appeared as the bearers of symbolic penises (rifles) that represented, in the masculine fantasy, the threat of castration. Thus, Theweleit concludes that, for the Freikorps, armed women were more dangerous than armed men, because they symbolically condensed a terrifying sexual power that threatened them doubly, both on the real political-military level and on the symbolic level of virility and manliness.

On the contrary, in the Argentine advertising that I analyze, the symbolic union between women and violence did not involve only male fantasies but also fantasies that were shared by the entire society. If in Theweleit's proletarian communist women the fantasies associated with armed women were terrifying, in this case the images carried a greater ambiguity. Sensuality and violence in these advertisements had a connotation of both seduction and death. Guns strengthened the seductive character of the women just as women's beauty sweetened the guns' cruelty. In line with the rest of the examples considered in this chapter, desire and violence appeared as a pair that was not only compatible but also complementary. The violence of beauty was at the same time the beauty of violence.

But on the other hand, death was alluded to doubly: literally in the images and the text that accompanied them, and also as a trope that included both metaphor and metonymy, in the sexual nature of desire involved. Sex and death, desire for love and desire for destruction, Eros and Thanatos, combined in a unique and unprecedented way. In 1970, a Paris company advertised one of its products, the "Mediaslip," with a set of advertisements whose slogan was "When it's time to kill." In the ads, a young woman in a dark room sensually sits on a chair or lies on a table, wearing only a vest, a hat, and the product promoted. In one of the ads she holds a revolver pointing upward; in the other, the gun points straight ahead at the reader.[149] The image immediately catches the eye: the sensuality of the model and her seminudity, combined with the word "kill" and with the gun, obviously combine sex and violence. Sexual conquest is associated here with subjugation by arms. The fantasy that the guns imply is doubly present. From the perspective of women, represented by the model, it implies that to achieve a goal, one must be ready to kill. From men's perspective, whose fantasies the ad deals with, it implies that to attain what one desires, one must be ready to die. Furthermore, in both cases, both the killing and dying are presented as events that are not exceptional but rather commonplace and ordinary, as natural as the use of the pantyhose (see figure 5.40).[150]

Something even more suggestive occurs in an advertisement for Tymsa, a *soutiens* (brassiere) brand. From a wooden wall, which could belong to a cantina or other semipublic place, the presence of a fugitive woman is announced through the exclamation "Wanted!" The image posted on the wall shows a young, attractive woman wearing a bra and a fur hat, after having fired a revolver whose smoke she is blowing. Below the model, "for killing in intimacy" is written.[151] The ad, at the same time that it claims to search for the woman who has "killed in intimacy," plays with the masculine fantasy of wanting to "kill" (possess) a model like the wanted one. The phallic shape of the revolver—an evident connotation when guns and women are combined, as Theweleit indicated—is reinforced by the barrel's proximity to the model's mouth (see figure 5.41).

FIGURE 5.40. (above) "When it's time to kill."
Source: Claudia, no. 157, June 1970

FIGURE 5.41. (left) "Wanted! For killing in intimacy." *Source: Para Ti, no. 2675, October 15, 1973*

The meaning connoted in this case adds another element, absent in the Paris advertisements: the weapon has already been used, the woman has already "killed." She has killed someone in an intimate situation and is enjoying the murder, sensually blowing the smoke from her recently fired gun. If the smoke symbolized the ejaculation that was already produced, the image reflects less the sexual act itself, although it refers to it, than the postcoital moment. It is the moment after the orgasm, a moment of relaxation and serene enjoyment that follows the sexual pleasure itself. Consequently, killing was the orgasm, the climax alluded to by the image. Death itself appears as something to enjoy. The murdered victim is no longer in the scene; what is important is that he dropped dead under the firepower and seductive power of the model. In this advertisement, the eroticism implied is very intense and murder acquires the characteristics of orgasm.

If it is granted that at the origin of the cultural goods' subjective construction process, social desire carried out the objective moment, or in other words, if it is accepted that the foundation upon which these symbolic elements rest is desire (the real substrate of human action), then the enormous presence of allusions to violence in the symbolic space could be defined, in Lacanian terms, as an "insistence." Upon finding itself "beyond the field of consciousness,"[152] closer to, or to say it improperly, "before" existence, desire insists. Desire insists on existing. The conceptualization, the conscious expression of any impulse or original force comes after desire in the discursive order; it feeds off desire while also domesticating it through symbolization. Thus, what is left to analyze, once the (existing) symbol is exhausted, is this insistence.

"Sex and its significations," Jacques Lacan affirms at the end of his eleventh seminar, "are always capable of making present the presence of death."[153] Sex is linked with an archaic element, an original impulse that precedes consciousness, that speaks from the base of the culture. It does not have the quality of presentifying just any death, but rather that which results from a struggle, from a fight "to the death" (as Hegel affirms in the Master-Slave dialectic, where Lacan gets this idea), in which desire has the objective of dominating the other and, at the limits, destroying the other. "Born from Desire," wrote Alexandre Kojève (whose lectures on Hegel were instrumental for Lacanian formulations), "the action tends to satisfy it, and can only do so by 'negation,' the destruction or at least the transformation of the desired object."[154] In a strict sense, this philosophical tradition (Hegel-Kojève) understands desire as the struggle to annihilate the other, as the confrontation in which the subject searches for recognition through the subjugation and death of the other. What Lacan adds to this conception is, on the one hand, the Freudian notion that desire is unconscious desire, and, on the other, that the real object of desire is a lack of being, the *objet petit a*.[155]

A psychoanalytic analysis of these artifacts can take us beyond them; it allows us to interrogate that which escapes the artifacts analyzed but is nevertheless still there. What lies beyond the most evident fantasies connoted by these advertisements? This is not about what is symbolized in these documents but rather what is *not* symbolizable within them, with what is present in them without being present explicitly. In other words, it has to do with the substrate or the base of the representations of sex and violence that the ads express.

On this level, the analysis leads to the realm of the "drive."[156] The fact that the images and slogans of the previously presented advertisements subject their appearance to the pleasure principle seems rather obvious. At the same time that they assure the woman who uses the advertised garments an unbeatable position on the terrain of seduction, they promise men the satisfaction of a fantasy, namely, that of feeling themselves at the whim of an overwhelming sensuality. The (men's) pleasure of desiring and the (women's) pleasure of feeling desired are present in a tangible way. But beyond this pleasure principle, on a more primal level, what this principle domesticates through its symbolization is an elemental drive, the death drive.

These advertisements condense much of the symbolic world of the early 1970s because they allow us to see until what point the death drive, always surreptitiously present, was explicitly manifested in the social imaginary, as if the inhibitory cultural mechanisms that favor social order were broken or became impotent. Violence and the eagerness for death appear eroticized in them. This is a phenomenon whose conditions of possibility and appearance should be traced beyond their most evident determinations, to a destructive drive in which sexuality plays a double role: that of Eros, insofar as it seduces and excites passions, but also that of Thanatos, as it empowers the metonymy that situates death in the place of love ("when it's time to kill" in place of "when it's time to love").[157] In these images, sex and violence have the capacity of "presentifying" each other. Through guns and slogans, sexual desire presentifies death. Through the positions, clothing, and attitudes of the models, violence presentifies sex. These advertisements have left an uneven record of their times, one in which love and death were confused to the point of explosion.

Focusing primarily on the case of the Montoneros, Hugo Vezzetti has called attention to the impact that the combination of "politics, erotic drives, and religion" had on violent revolutionary practices.[158] This section allows us to see until what point, regardless of political content and without referring to the concrete struggles of those times, the erotic dimension of violence was present in the symbolic order that included the middle class. The death drive was a common ground. Politics was, without a doubt, the stage upon which it erupted with the most force. However, we would remain far from understanding this phenomenon if we ignore the unusual form in which sensuality and aggressiveness, love and death, desire and violence, were combined in the 1970s.

Violence as Satire

Just as violent metaphors sold products or promoted artists or athletes, print humor made society laugh by reflecting the violent state that politics had taken. Once again, it should not be inferred that those who made these cultural goods, in this case, humorists, legitimized violent acts. Instead, the fact that political violence had been, in many cases with great wit, a cause for laughter, is symptomatic of the way in which society in general, and particularly the middle classes, conceived of the nature of politics—and also, of violence. Political humor did not create conventions or social behaviors; instead, these found a channel of expression in humor.

Unlike the late 1960s, where the humor dealing with violence focused on the international situation,[159] in the early 1970s domestic political violence became a frequent subject of vernacular humor. Caloi and Quino were two of the most famous Argentine humorists, who published their work in very popular magazines and newspapers. What Jorge B. Rivera wrote about one (Quino) could easily be said about both of them; they "condense[d] the 'ideology' of their middle class readers in an exemplary fashion."[160]

In a 1970s cartoon titled "The rules of the game," Caloi depicted the situation within the Metal Workers Union (Unión Obrera Metalúrgica [UOM]) through a drawing of a saloon in the western United States in which the union leaders, presented as Wild West cowboys, fought with one another.[161] The drawing depicted a fight within the union that, in the days before, had ended with two deaths and several wounded at the metalworkers' union hall (see figure 5.42). Several months later, a meeting between members of the government and the general secretary of the CGT, José Ignacio Rucci, was depicted in another joke entitled "Modus vivendi." Government and union representatives shook their right hands while hiding their left hands behind them, in which they carried sticks, a knife, and an axe (see figure 5.43).[162] The negotiations between unionists and businessmen in March 1971 were portrayed by Caloi in a drawing in which the two parties sat face-to-face at different tables, each one of them with a bomb under the table (see figure 5.44).[163]

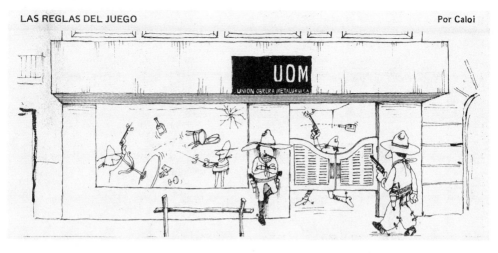

FIGURE 5.42. UOM (Metal Workers Union [Unión Obrera Metalúrgica]).
Source: Análisis, no. 464, February 2–9, 1970

Thus, violence was depicted, as two of the cartoon titles suggest, as the given state of affairs, as the tacit rules of political life, as a naturalized way of living.

The previous cartoons were situated in the political context of the ill-fated "Argentine Revolution" that by 1970 and 1971 had enjoyed scant and decreasing sympathy. Two years later, in a different context—on March 11, 1973, the elections that declared the Peronists victorious were held—the humor continued to reflect the strong climate of violence. A month before the inauguration of the new authorities, Quino described the political climate conjugating the verb "to love" with the six personal pronouns: I love, you love, he/she loves, and so on. In each of the scenes, the characters appeared stealing a heart, always with larger and larger guns in hand (see figure 5.45).[164] Loving and killing were combined in the same people. Less than a month after the new government assumed power, Quino returned to this idea, drawing a person dressed in a suit writing a letter that he started with the salutation: "From my most appreciated esteem." He had a revolver near his chest and guns and ammunition clips on his desk (see figure 5.46).[165] Once again, although now referring to politics, love and murder appeared linked, with one being the counterpart of the other. The violence in these cartoons allows us to see this widespread mode of thinking, surprising today, but naturalized and a cause for laughter yesterday, as beloved causes were asserted by means of arms. Probably, the intention of the humorist was to underline the absurdity of proclaiming rhetorically that one loves while in the real world causing deaths. If Quino represented a humor typical of a specific middle class—educated but

MODUS VIVENDI   Por CALOI

FIGURE 5.43. "Modus vivendi." *Source: Análisis*, no. 509, February 15–21, 1970

PARITARIAS   Por CALOI

FIGURE 5.44. Negotiations between unionists and businessmen. *Source: Análisis*, no. 521, March 9–15, 1971

FIGURE 5.45. "I love; you love; he/she loves; we love; all of you love; they love." *Source: Panorama*, no. 312, April 19–25, 1973

FIGURE 5.46. "From my most appreciated esteem . . ." *Source: Panorama*, no. 319, June 7–13, 1973

not politically committed—these drawings express a vision plausibly shared by much of this social sector around 1973. On the one hand, the characters' violence and readiness to kill lets us glimpse the disbelief toward those who took up arms "for love." On the other, since violence and death threats were caricatured in a jocular manner, we can also see up to what point this disbelief was translated into irony, much more so than indignation.

Alfredo Grondona White, *Satiricón*'s cartoonist,[166] caricatured a scene on the eve of the 1973 elections in which two young men, of a worryingly hippie "look," walked around the city, with one saying to the other "Don't get angry! [*No te hagas mala sangre!*] After the eleventh of March, everything will be alright." Behind them were tanks, soldiers, protestors, a jail, a factory, a helicopter, explosions, some people fleeing, others dead, and two men leaning out of the windows of their cars firing machine guns (see figure 5.47).[167]

The same magazine published other drawings, jokes, and texts that made reference to the reigning political violence that year. Two examples: days before the elections, and in advance of the "winter wave of 1973," the magazine joked that soon Buenos Aires would have "the best women's footwear for its elegance and durability (even after the cease-fire)." This was the "tank look," pairs of armored shoes with guns at their tips (see figure 5.48).[168] Shortly before the assassination of union leader José Rucci by the Montoneros, *Satiricón* invented a table wine with his name, whose bottle's mouth had the shape of his face—satirizing a well-known table wine that actually existed on the market, the Crespi Seco. The ad read: "Rucci Seco. Guarded by experts," and the ad depicted caricatures of three bodyguards—people regularly associated with the union leader. The shadow of Rucci's head reflected at the bottom of the drawing had the shape of a revolver (see figure 5.49).[169]

Another talented humorist, Roberto Fontanarrosa, also devoted some of his cartoons to the political violence of the 1970s. In one of these, for example, three men informed a blindfolded, but smiling foreigner—whom they referred to as "signore Ferrantelli"—of three things: "First, we are no longer at Patikindoulous's party. Second, we aren't playing blind man's bluff anymore. Third, we've just kidnapped you . . ."[170] Also in the early 1970s, Fontanarrosa drew a television reporter announcing the news of the kidnapping and murder of a big business man. The cartoon was that the same journalist that reported the news was getting ready to kill him (see figure 5.50).[171]

Humor did not ignore torture, which, as has been seen, was not a new method in Argentina but was increasingly implemented as a repressive practice. The famous Mafalda, which included various references to violence in its comic strip, upon passing by a street under construction where three men were working with a sledgehammer, drill, and shovel to bore into the con-

FIGURE 5.47. "Don't get angry! After March 11 everything will be all right."
Source: Satiricón, no. 5, March 5, 1973

FIGURE 5.48.
"Tank look: American
Shoe." *Source: Satiricón,*
no. 6, April 3, 1973

FIGURE 5.49.
"Rucci Seco. Guarded
by experts." *Source:*
Satiricón, no. 5,
March 5, 1973

FIGURE 5.50. "And now Channel 25, 'First in the news,' with exclusive coverage of the kidnapping and murder of strong entrepreneur . . ." *Source: Panorama*, no. 385, November 19–25, 1974

crete, asked: "What are they trying to get this poor street to confess?" (see figure 5.51).[172] In 1973, now in the democratic period, Fontanarrosa drew a torturer and his victim. Shackled to the torture table stark naked, facing his tormentor—who had his face partially covered and a cattle prod to torture him in hand—the victim asked the torturer: "So tell me . . . Do you tell all this to your analyst?" (see figure 5.52).[173] The following year, the same humorist returned to the theme. The cartoon this time portrayed a queen—Isabel, with her royal name, was already governing—whose subject respectfully asked her: "and due to new leaks of humidity and the presence of rodents, I wanted to ask you for better sanitary conditions in the name of all the boys who work in the Torture Chamber" (see figure 5.53).[174] In March 1974, the cultural criticism magazine *Crisis* drew two priests speaking. "They've told me, young man," said the older one of the two, "that you are rather severe in the confessional!" to which the young priest responded: "Come on, come on, I just put a little voltage in the cattle prod!" (see figure 5.54).[175] Two years earlier, in his instruction manual for the jet set, Landrú suggested that those arrested for smuggling should testify before the judge or commissioner: "Come on,

FIGURE 5.51. Mafalda: "What are they trying to get this poor street to confess?"
Source: Quino, *Todo Mafalda* (Buenos Aires: de la Flor, 1997), 250

Judge. Will you let me go free if I give you the two hundred cattle prods that I brought from the other side of the Iron Curtain?"[176]

The democratic opening in 1973 did not decrease but rather accentuated this process of the naturalization of violence. With respect to political violence, there did not seem to have been change but rather continuity between the democratic and dictatorial periods. The journalist and cartoonist Vides Almonacid, for example, in his comic strip Goyito—published in the Tucumán daily *El Pueblo*, positioned to the left of its provincial competitors *La Gaceta* and *Noticias*—made various references to the climate of violence that Tucumán faced during the return to democracy. Its main character, Goyito, a shoeshine boy, in one of the strips read the newspaper during a storm, when the first drops of the approaching rain began to fall. Surprised by the absence of violent news, he exclaimed: "Eh! And the sport in vogue? No bombings or assassinations today . . ." After it began to rain harder and harder, Goyito concluded: "Aha! . . . They must have suspended it because of bad weather . . ." (see figure 5.55).[177] In another episode, Goyito explained to a friend that "if we all work for National Reconstruction [the Peronist slogan in 1973], we will be a free, just, and well-respected country . . ." The explanation was then interrupted by the explosion of a bomb and people running away, something that led Goyito, facing his friend's angry expression, to change the topic to a classic children's story.[178]

In various periods of the country's history, political humor has been a tool in Argentina to say what would be difficult to say in any other way. The common reading of this type of humor tends to value this quality of presenting a raw chronicle of reality, sometimes also committed to the denunciation of corrupt or immoral acts. The jokes connected to torture could be an example. However, it is also true that both the humorists' audiences and the humor-

FIGURE 5.52.
"So tell me . . .
Do you tell all this
to your analyst?"
Source: Panorama,
no. 331, September
20–26, 1973

FIGURE 5.53.
". . . and due to new
leaks of humidity
and the presence of
rodents, I wanted
to ask you for better
sanitary conditions
in the name of all the
boys who work in the
Torture Chamber."
Source: Panorama,
no. 389, December
17–23, 1974

FIGURE 5.54.

"They've told me, young man,
that you are rather severe in
the confessional!"

"Come on, come on, I just put
a little voltage in the cattle
prod!"

Source: Crisis, no. 11, March 1974

ists themselves do not let themselves laugh about just any subject. It would not be very likely, for example, that some cartoonist today would craft a joke about the appropriation of children born in the detention centers during the last dictatorship, nor would such a cartoon be published; moreover, neither the cartoonist nor his editor would be able to imagine an audience who would find such humor funny. What a society laughs about teaches us what is within the limits of the acceptable, the naturalized, that which is converted into "the rules of the game," as Caloi titled his excellent drawing, and what remains outside of those rules.

The banalization of violence went to surprising extremes. On the night of May 4, 1976, less than two months after the beginning of el Proceso, Alberto Olmedo, one of Argentina's most famous television and film comedians, staged his own disappearance. Upon starting the series El *Chupete*, the announcer, Jorge Nicolao, announced with a serious air the "unfortunate circumstance" of Olmedo's "disappearance." He did not say "death," but "disappearance."[179] Disappearance, even when the practice of "disappearing" people was occurring at the highest levels as an official policy, could be taken in jest. In the following year, in one of the film comedies in which he starred with Jorge Porcel, the same actor acted out a jocular allusion to torture. Showing a Buenos Aires hotel to a contingent of foreign women that believed they

FIGURE 5.55.
"Eh! And the sport in vogue? No bombings or assassinations today . . ."
"Aha! . . . They must have suspended it because of bad weather . . ."
Source: Vides Almonacid's Archive

were touring a castle, he explained the moans of pain that were coming from one of the rooms by telling them "that is the torture chamber."[180]

When trying to understand how it was possible, when in 1976 state violence surpassed all predictions, that a society was willing to accept the certainty that hundreds of people were not in their homes and nobody knew anything about them, the banalization of violence that occurred in the long first half of the decade (1969–1976) is an element that must not be ignored. An inevitable process of mimesis in the social sectors that were not involved in the political struggle, which both the cultural products of the period and the actions and discourse of the key figures of political life testify to, had already accustomed a good part of the society to the fact that torture, assassination, murder, execution, bombing, terrorism, war, and even disappearances and kidnappings were not words or acts that were unheard of. During the first half of the decade, a unique social link was constructed in the portions of civil society least involved in politics, based on the idea that violence was intrinsic to it, and this idea, as has been seen, transcended the limits of politics. Violence was naturalized and when it seemed to reach its end with the decision of the military to overthrow a government, which many judged to be anarchic, it only increased. From a misrule, which Arendt characterized not as "a Government of Nobody" but rather as "a tyranny without a tyrant," the society moved to Leviathan, a tyranny with a tyrant.[181]

During the first half of the 1970s, violence exercised an attraction that was all but irresistible. If advertising incorporated guns and metaphors for violence into its language, this was less because it was imposing a habit on consumers, than because, on the contrary, it incorporated a social form into its art. There are many records of this in the newspapers and magazines of the period. Various testimonies of those times collected on the street and in letters to the editor confirm that aggressiveness and violence were a sort of common ground of sociability.[182] In 1972, Landrú specifically related aggressiveness to the young jet set, belonging to the upper-middle and upper classes.[183] The same year, Alfredo Alcón, the most successful Argentine film actor, promoted his last film by declaring that, in the present day "there is such a need for violence, that the audience desires to see itself expressed through a type of violent action that is similar to the emerging fantasies of this need."[184] Even in regard to Correa, a town that remained immune to all forms of political violence in the 1970s, one can find news in the press of an unusual degree of aggressiveness.[185]

In politics, violence was the distinctive sign. However, the excessive emphasis that researchers have placed on either justifying it ideologically or condemning it morally most of the time has come to overshadow the connection that existed between political violence and this aggressive and authoritarian cultural background that was both its foundation and stimulus. Bruno Filliol, ex-activist of the Peronist left in Tucumán, responded, during our last meeting, with the following to one of my questions about the issue of violence: "I think there are many attitudes that are censored today and you see them as negative, or as excessive, that were quite the opposite in those days. It was natural. It was as it should have been. Thus, I was violent and all of society was violent. Moreover, if you weren't violent, you were a queer. That concept was around too. And I remember, so to speak, that you had to make a girl who was acting up pay, for real."

In the 1970s, violence and desire met and intertwined on a terrain that had been constituted for many years by different cultural traditions that found their roots in ideologies that were quite heterogeneous, although these were not unrelated to each other, such as male chauvinism, nationalism, or militarism. Not being ready or prone to acting violently was a sign of weakness, of inauthenticity, of a lack of manliness in men or a lack of courage in women. "We have reached the point," a journalist wrote in 1974, "that any appeal to peace seems to be melancholy moralizing, a cheesy sentimentalism of weak spirits."[186] Guns in advertising were, from a symbolic point of view, the phalluses of a society that evaluated its members based on how far one was willing to go, individually or collectively. Being willing to kill and die was the ultimate expression of bravery, and this aspiration brought with it prestige and honor. Not only the guerrilla organizations, but activism and political involvement as a whole were some of the clearest expressions of this.[187] But additionally, violence, in a general sense and not necessarily linked to weapons or political in nature, was incorporated as a form of being macho and not effeminate men, brave and not cowardly women. The 1970s were characterized by abhorrence for all gray areas, for the middle ground, and for intermediate positions and viewpoints. The world that was coming, no matter what it might look like, did not seem to be for the indecisive or the hesitant but for those who were ready to conceive of it in black and white, as all or nothing. In this sense, guns condensed what was associated with being healthy and full of life on the symbolic level: a glorious triumph or professional success, a romantic conquest or a political victory. The violence of desire was also the desire for violence.

This analysis of the social imaginary of violence completes the reading advanced in the previous chapters. On the one hand, it seems probable that some of the sympathy that the guerrillas awoke among the middle classes not involved in the political struggle—which, although less than what is accepted, is a phenomenon that must be acknowledged—can be explained more by this desire for drastic solutions than by ideological agreement with the armed groups, whose political projects were never widely known by the average person. On the other, the initial support for el Proceso and the later acceptance of its repressive discourse can also be partially explained by this desire.

During the 1970s, death was not thought of as a problem but rather as a solution. The most outstanding aspects of the symbolic space predominant during almost the entire decade, at least from its beginning through the first three years of the dictatorship, can be seen as different intonations of the same metaphor, modulations of the same myth. More than indicating a class consciousness, these intonations formed part of what Bourdieu called "class unconsciousness," schemes of thought and action inscribed in class habitus.[188]

During the brief and unstable democracy that began in 1973, Rodolfo Puiggrós, an intellectual with much influence within activist circles of the Left who was named rector of the Universidad de Buenos Aires under Peronism, declared that the academic appointments that he had made were "positions in the struggle." Unlike what some of the "men of '55" thought—that Peronism was a cancer that needed to be eradicated—"it has already been demonstrated," Puiggrós said, "that the Republic's health is in the Justicialist movement," that "the cancer to be eradicated is on the other side of the street," and that "we cannot be tolerant with those who conspire against the country, openly or secretly."[189] A short time thereafter, appealing to identical surgical metaphors and conspiracy theories not substantially different from those of Puiggrós, a commitment to extermination that was far deeper—but by no means new, as the myth was the same—was embodied by the state and unleashed itself with unparalleled fury toward the end of the Peronist government and the dark first years of el Proceso.[190]

Politics is not made up of power relationships; it is made up of relationships between worlds. —Jacques Rancière

It is the middle class that proposes the framework and values that predominate within a particular society. —Wilhelm Reich

Conclusions

Disapproving and critical judgments tend to fall on the Argentine middle classes. There is a tendency, which originated in the 1950s but which is still prevalent today, to judge them by comparing them to what they ought ideally to be. They should have been less fervently anti-Peronist in the 1950s, massively revolutionary in the 1960s and 1970s, decidedly opposed to the military dictatorship in 1976, less indulgent with Alfonsín's concessions to military and economic powers in the 1980s, anti-Menem in the 1990s, and once again more revolutionary, although differently, during the economic and political crisis of 2001. Paradoxically, then, at the same time that they labeled CEPAL's (Comisión Económica para América Latina y el Caribe) diagnosis that the modernization and democratization of the entire society rested in the potential of the middle class as illusory, these judgments frequently seemed to be based on a similar or even bolder diagnosis, only to condemn the middle class for not rising to the occasion. However, the middle classes are what they are and not what they should be. In this study, I have tried to understand their behavior during the most violent period of recent Argentine history, fundamentally seeking to explain how and why they acted as they did and to analyze the memories that have been erected about their actions and omissions.

Despite the turmoil of the times, the middle classes' political identity remained largely consistent during the period studied in this book. Although they changed their opinions of particular political actors, a majority of the middle class maintained centrist and center-right positions. Unhappy with Onganía from 1968 on, they later participated in the return to democracy in 1973 voting primarily for parties of the center (like the Radical Civic Union [UCR]) or the center-right (like the Popular Federalist Alliance [*Alianza Popular Federalista*]),[1] remained within the heterogeneous terrain made up of non-Peronist and non-leftist forces. The anti-Peronist sensibility of the middle class, forged in personal or inherited memories of historical Peronism (1946–1955), determined how the political events from 1973–1976 were read and interpreted.

Therefore, the triumph of Peronism in March 1973 found the middle classes resigned. After almost twenty years of attempted de-Peronization, the country continued to be Peronist. The democracy of the 1973–1976 period, which was imperfect and anomalous in many ways, added to its deficiencies the desertion of the middle classes, a corollary of this resignation. This explains why the rise of the military dictatorship, while bringing tranquility to much of these middle classes, was not celebrated. For them, the 1976 coup was the natural and unsurprising outcome of a political process that alternated between two ungovernable situations, the situation provoked by Peronism's absence and that by its omnipresence.

Politics and violence were united during the 1970s as never before. The popular rebellions, especially those led by students, enjoyed the approval of part of the middle classes, principally in the cities where the events took place. However, the primacy of the emotional element prevents us from translating this approval into an ideological conviction. Instead of demonstrating what these social sectors wanted, rebellions like the Tucumanazo expressed what they did not want anymore. The "Argentine Revolution" had promised them a modern and prosperous society that was slow in coming and demanded the indefinite postponement of the political debate for its achievement, bringing instead an unjustified and excessive authoritarianism.

The middle classes shared the rebels' disgust for this government, but not their most radical aspirations.

This distance was clearly manifested in middle-class attitudes toward the guerrillas, even when they first appeared. The immense majority of the middle classes did not sympathize with the insurgent groups. This sympathy or support was concentrated in the activist sectors, mostly youth and university students. These sectors were fundamental actors during the years studied but were in no way representative of their social class as a whole. Politically and ideologically distant from the aspirations of a majority of the middle classes studied, the guerrillas were challenged on moral grounds, both in today's memories and in the past.

It seems paradoxical that this moral opposition to guerrilla violence did not express itself more virulently against state violence. This paradox is resolved if one considers the civil superstition on which el Proceso was founded. The perception of its violence (at least what was visible of it, as its most gruesome manifestations remained secret) was linked to the feeling that the State, in Taussig's sense, had returned. Thus, Leviathan occupied the space of a "supposed knowledge"; the citizens attributed to it a knowledge that was not required to correspond to reality because the superstition was based not on the truth but on the need to believe. "It must be for some reason" was, above all, a way of saying that "the state must know why it is doing what it is doing."

But the state could not have used and abused violence, at least in the way and with the intensity that it did so, if its actions had not been preceded by long years in which violence occupied an unprecedented space in both the political and social realms. It would be a mistake to conclude that the middle classes were either proviolence or pacifist. In reality, they combined contradictory elements, which made compatible the disapproval of armed actions with the conviction that the solutions for the country must be immediate, radical, and possibly violent. The violent images and metaphors that populated the social imaginary are testament to an aggressive and authoritarian social substrate defined less by ideology than by a latent, almost unconscious, fascination for the irreversible.

The return of democracy in 1983 only served to confirm that the middle classes continued leaning toward non-Peronist options, this time coming together en masse for the Radical Civic Union (UCR).[1] If in 1973 the middle classes had divided their vote between the UCR and other centrist and center-right political forces, ten years later they tended to concentrate their votes in their traditional party, which they saw triumph in an election with no proscriptions for the first time.[2] A small percentage of the middle classes voted for the Left, which obtained a total of 4 percent of votes,[3] and another minority voted for the Peronist candidate. The bulk of these middle classes constituted, without a doubt, the majority of the 50 percent (52 percent if blank votes are not counted) that Alfonsín obtained.[4] In June 1982, an electoral poll conducted by IPSA established that Peronism had greatest support in the lower social sectors, and Radicalism in the middle and high social sectors. A year later, the same company stated that UCR support continued to come from middle and high social sectors, and Peronist adherents from the "lower" social sectors.[5] Another study in 1983 and 1984 established that, both in Capital Federal and in La Matanza county in the province of Buenos Aires, the further one rose on the social ladder, the greater the vote was for the UCR and the less it was for Peronism.[6] In both districts, a significant proportion of unskilled workers had voted for Peronism, and a large majority of professionals for Radicalism.[7]

In summary, the middle classes confirmed their non-Peronist electoral preference in 1983, deepening their position with respect to the one they had held ten years before. In terms of the ideological orientation of Alfonsín voters, the majority came from the traditional supporters of Radicalism and those that had supported center-right options ten years before.[8] With Alfonsín the middle class came to power ideologically faithful to itself, without essential changes with respect to where they had stood a decade earlier.

Alfonsín's government quickly proved to be to the left of its own electoral base, something that added to its mismanagement of the economic situation and thus caused much of its voters to punish it at the polls only four years later.

The years after the 1970s were not lacking in conflicts but were undoubtedly less violent. It is then around the issue of political violence that the principal transformation emerged as a corollary of the 1970s, probably not only for the middle classes but rather for society in general. This was the deepest transformation and will likely be the most enduring as well. As soon as the last dictatorship had ended, the Argentine people were convinced that transformations were not desirable if they did not occur gradually. In May 1983, IPSA conducted an investigation that concluded that 37 percent of the population preferred "social changes without an alteration of their current lifestyle," 31 percent "gradual social changes," 16 percent "accelerated social changes," and only 6 percent "revolutionary social changes."[9] In the two decades that followed, this tendency only deepened.[10] The decade of the 1970s spilled enough blood for an enormous majority of the society to end up rejecting radical alterations in the social order.

These data leave the impression of a lesson learned at very great and painful cost. The new generations have not been tempted to take up arms, except for an isolated attempt by a handful in 1989, even with levels of social injustice, unemployment, and poverty that are worse than in the 1970s. If violence no longer represented a program of action for any social sector from 1983 to today, breaks in the institutional order also met this fate, especially after several military uprisings between 1987 and 1990. Society as a whole, not without voicing strong criticisms toward the political leadership, seems to have agreed that the worst political leadership was preferable to the best military coup.

This consensus "toward the future," however, should not be confused with a consensus about the past. Even if nobody approved of the methods implemented by el Proceso in their persecution against those that they considered to be their enemies, the vision of the 1970s of the middle classes tended to oppose two forms of violence of opposite signs, both unjustifiable and reprehensible, where the existence of one explains and even makes the other necessary. This is not a majority opinion at the present time, not so much because society has changed but rather because it has been renewed. Today's middle classes are mostly composed of generations that did not live through the 1970s as youth or adults and whose way of perceiving the years studied has been influenced by a variety of factors including education, the work of human rights organizations, and the revalorization of democracy as the least imperfect of all forms of government, as well as the greater level of knowledge of the crimes committed during the military dictatorship.

Nothing proves this fact better than the different types of demonstrations and events that occurred after the return of democracy to repudiate the 1976 coup. Their audience always was (and continues to be) fundamentally young, born in the 1970s or later, and those who were adults in the 1970s and attend these events largely have an activist past or belong to intellectual or university minorities. The bulk of the society that lived through the 1970s as youth or adults did not and do not participate in these demonstrations. The trial of General Bussi, for example, conducted in San Miguel de Tucumán in 2008, was attended by only several hundred people, the vast majority of them young, among which activists of small left-wing parties in the city of Buenos Aires that mobilized their members to come to Tucumán stood out.

However, although the political violence and the coups d'état have been left behind, the 1970s are still with us. In March 2008, the Peronist government of Cristina Fernández de Kirchner announced a new system of export taxes on grains that generated a major conflict. In only a few months, Argentine society became divided as had not occurred in a long time. Protesting against the government measures, agricultural entities carried out long strikes in favor of the commercialization of their products and blocked roads across the country. The government upped the ante, mobilizing its supporters and increasingly hardening their discourse against the strikers. The past suddenly turned into a discursive toolbox, which different actors turned to in order to construct both their place in the conflict and that of their adversaries. The leaders of the agricultural sector turned to the "Grito de Alcorta," a famous rebellion of small and medium-sized farmers in 1912 against large landowners. In their vision, they were the heirs to that civil uprising. On their part, the government turned to the "people versus oligarchy" antinomy, so effectively used by Perón during his first government, and accused those who did not support them of defending or being tied to the interests of the latter.

In the face of this situation, the middle classes were divided. A minority, which was a mobilized and convinced sector composed mainly of youth, supported the official position and organized actively in its defense. On the other side, a majority, composed primarily of people without prior political activist commitments—who were not even indirectly affected by the government's measures—supported the demands of the rural interests (see figure EPI.1). The conflict began to worsen, involving harsh verbal confrontations, large demonstrations in various cities, and finally, a legislative vote that divided the National Senate.

The years analyzed in this book, the ferocious and violent confrontation

FIGURE EPI.1. A demonstration of over 200,000 people in favor of rural interests in the Palermo neighborhood of Buenos Aires, June 2008. *Source: Clarín's* Archive.

between different political groups, the disposition to die and kill held by various principal actors of those times, all this formed part of the past and had no place in the year 2008. However, the prism through which that new reality was read was strongly tinged by this past. The episode confirmed that we can never claim that part of the past has been buried forever. When we believe it to be dead, it is only sleeping. The conflict between the rural interests and the government awoke the past analyzed in this book and put it at the disposition of the present, as a general store of metaphors and categories to conceive of situations that were structurally different but symbolically comparable.

In those days, I found myself around Rosario, alternating between interview work in the town of Correa and work in *La Capital*'s archives. Shortly before, one of the largest demonstrations in favor of the agriculturalists' position had occurred at the Monument to the Flag in Rosario. A multitude composed of the middle classes of the city and its surroundings praised the leadership of the agricultural entities, sang the national anthem, and chanted against the government.

Nothing attracted my attention, however, more than some street graffiti I saw in a central street of the city, painted on the entrance gate to a parking

FIGURE EPI.2. "Peronist Youth 'Descamisados': 4 × 4 or 5 × 1." Graffiti in Rosario city center, taken in December 2009. *Source*: Author's archive.

lot. The graffiti was signed "JP Descamisados" and it read: "4 × 4 or 5 × 1." Short and effective, the slogan combined the present and the past in a witty and ingenious fashion. The present was alluded to in the "4 × 4" side of the implied equation, which referred to the landowners' four-wheel-drive vehicles, "the 4 × 4 trucks." One of the arguments of the government position consisted in inferring that those who possessed these types of goods were wealthy in their agricultural pursuits ("if they have 4 × 4 trucks, they can't be doing so poorly") (see figure EPI.2).

The second part of the graffiti equation, the "5 × 1," alluded to the past and had its origin in Perón. In 1955, shortly before being overthrown and in the face of harassment by opposition forces, Perón said that Peronists would answer their enemies' violence with a greater violence, and that "when one of ours falls, five of theirs will fall."[11] The slogan took on new life when 1970s activists made it their own ("Five for one, no one will be left" ["*Cinco por uno, no va a quedar ninguno*"]).

In the context of 2008, unlike in the 1970s, "5 × 1" cannot be confused with a program of political action. What sense did it have to bring back this slogan, in a conflict that bore little resemblance to that which confronted the right-wing and left-wing factions within Peronism three decades earlier, or that which confronted the military with Peronists toward the end of the Argentine Revolution's government? What sense did it have to bring up a violent slogan in a context in which conflicts are channeled institutionally or sometimes extra-institutionally, but in no case by threatening to physically eliminate opponents? However, the graffiti in Rosario, ironic but not false, fed the emotional consumption of the activists, both the old 1970s activists and the smaller contemporary politicized youth movement. But in addition to this, it once again raised the political realities of the old school. The reality had changed, but the lens through which it was interpreted hadn't.

The past analyzed continues operating on the present. It provides ways of seeing, interpretative frameworks, and schema of understanding, impregnated with a certainty that reality has only refuted but that on the symbolic level always finds points of support and ground to expand on: the belief that history is cyclical, circular, repetitive. The 1970s will not be repeated exactly as they were. However, they will remain there, in the trunk of the past, tempting different actors to use them to facilitate or hinder the understanding of the present.

Socioeconomic statistics allow us to separate the country's regions in the 1970s into three areas. First comes the area that contains the metropolitan (the city of Buenos Aires and the greater Buenos Aires metropolitan area) and Patagonian (Chubut, Santa Cruz, and Tierra del Fuego) regions. Second is the area that groups together the Pampa (Buenos Aires province, Santa Fe, and Entre Ríos), Comahue (Río Negro, La Pampa, and Neuquén), Cuyo (Mendoza and San Juan), and central (Córdoba, San Luis, and La Rioja) regions. Finally, the third area is formed by the regions of the Northwest (Tucumán, Salta, Santiago del Estero, Jujuy, and Catamarca) and Northeast (Chaco, Corrientes, Misiones, and Formosa).[1] Between 1946 and 1968, the growth of the first area was above the national average, the second similar to it, and the third below it. For this reason, I selected a location from each one of these areas.

To better reflect the heterogeneity of the middle classes, I added the variable of population density to the geographical criteria. In 1970, 8,353,000 people lived in cities with more than one million inhabitants, 8,464,000 people in cities that had between ten thousand and one million inhabitants, and the rest (6,549,000) in cities with fewer than ten thousand inhabitants. The three locations selected corresponded to a different one of the three types of population categories in 1970. On average for the entire period, the city of Buenos Aires, the city of San Miguel de Tucumán, and the town of Correa had three million, 350,000, and 5,000 inhabitants, respectively.[2]

Thus, geographic and demographic considerations are two of the four criteria used to establish similarities and differences in this study. Unlike these criteria—which were selected a priori—the other two, generation and institutional belonging, arose after the results were obtained. The institutional distinction refers to whether or not the interviewees belonged to the university world in the 1970s. Additionally, the generational variable proved to be fundamental when considering the issues of violence and Peronism.

In 1970, 70.6 percent of the population was fifteen years old or older (all of my interviewees, with one exception, were over fifteen in 1970). In the 2010 census, the same population (which is now fifty-five or older), represented only 19 percent. The universe of memories with which I work, thus, does not correspond to the vision of the current middle classes (mostly formed by generations that did not live through the years studied as youth or adults). Instead, it focuses on those who formed the majority of the population in the 1970s.

This study has been crafted from many sources. Apart from the censuses, the electoral results, public opinion polls, the interviews conducted by media sources, and some documents of a personal nature, such as private diaries or correspondence, two other types of materials inform the analysis that I conduct in this study: interviews and cultural goods. See the introduction regarding the former. Regarding the latter, I considered those directed to (and consumed by) middle-class sectors. I focused on those that had the largest audience and had the greatest impact on public opinion. In terms of political information, I worked primarily with the daily *La Capital* for Correa, *La Gaceta* for Tucumán, and political analysis magazines from the metropolitan area (*Panorama, Análisis, Confirmado, Primera Plana, Extra, El Burgués, Carta Política,* and *Cuestionario*) also consumed in the rest of the country.[1] I also consulted other sources, such as the dailies *Noticias* and *El Pueblo* in Tucumán; the newspapers *Clarín, La Nación,*[2] *La Razón, La Opinión,*[3] and *La Prensa* in Buenos Aires; two Correa publications, *La Voz de Correa* and *El Sentir del Pueblo,* and one from Cañada de Gómez, *La Estrella.* I placed great importance on general interest magazines that combined information about the entertainment world with political articles.[4] *Gente* stands out among this type of magazine, as it had widespread readership and a national scope.[5] With regard to magazines directed toward a male readership: I analyzed the sports magazines *El Gráfico* and *Corsa,* and *Autoclub*—a magazine published by the Argentine Automobile Club (Automóvil Club Argentino).[6] Of those oriented toward women, I worked with *Para Ti,* the oldest of this genre, and *Claudia,* targeted toward upper-middle-class women.[7] Of the humor magazines, I considered *Satiricón, Tío Landrú,* and *Humor,* as well as the books of the most important humorists of this period.[8]

Less exhaustively, I reviewed *Criterio* (directed toward a Catholic public), *Nuevo Hombre*, *Redacción*, *Atlántida* (all three of a political character), the *Polémica* collection (with articles of a historical nature), *Crisis* (of a cultural character), *Revista Chacra* (for the agricultural sector), *Nocturno* (for a female audience), and *Tal Cual*, *Siete Días*, *La Semana*, and *Selecciones del Reader's Digest* (all four general interest). For the viewpoints of the activists, I consulted *El Descamisado*, *Militancia*, and *La Causa Peronista*, as well as documents from the political groupings and the armed groups.

Introduction

1. David Viñas, "Talesnik: Denuncia y compasión de la clase media," preface to Ricardo Talesnik, *Cien veces no debo* (Buenos Aires: Talía, 1983), 6. The play depicts a middle-class family, the Siri, who must face the situation of their daughter's pregnancy. It had its debut in August 1970, in the Margarita Xirgú Theater in Buenos Aires, and two decades later reached the film world. In 1976, Juan José Jusid released *No toquen a la nena*, a movie with similar themes. In 1973, another film, *Repita con nosotros este ejercicio*, directed by Edgardo Kleinman, dealt with the issue of the middle classes' political and sexual repression.

2. Tomás Eloy Martínez, "Los del medio, mayoría domesticada y consumidora, enemiga de todo cambio," *La Opinión*, November 1, 1972, 8.

3. Martínez, "Una tabla de valores dictada por la necesidad de aparentar y ser aceptado," *La Opinión*, November 2, 1972, 8.

4. Martínez, "El psicoanalizado burgués nacional puede convertirse en un marginal," *La Opinión*, November 4, 1972, 8.

5. Néstor Tirri, "Las armas de la clase media," *Panorama*, no. 328 (August 20–September 5, 1973): 47. Other film reviews can be consulted in Carlos Morelli, "Pepe Soriano matando llega y se va"; "Las venganzas de Beto Sánchez," *La Prensa*, August 24, 1973; and "Pepe Soriano en una excelente actuación," *La Nación*, August 24, 1973.

6. The play was presented in the Payró Theater in Buenos Aires and in 1971 and 1972 was performed in other cities.

7. Monti defined himself as a Marxist, and although his theater would later abandon these political pretensions, both this play and *Una noche con el Sr. Magnus e hijos* (in this play released in 1970, the children of a middle-class family murder their father, in an allegory for what radicalized youth were doing with their elders' generation) express how political commitment and criticism of the middle class were combined in the early 1970s rather well. Works with similar themes were Guillermo Gentile's *Amorfo '70* (1970), Alberto Adellach's *Chau papá* (1971); Walter Operto's

Ceremonia al pie del obelisco (1971); Patricio Esteve's *La gran histeria nacional* (1972); and Carlos Anton's *¿Hasta cuándo?* (1972). In the 1960s, José de Triana's *La noche de los asesinos* was an important predecessor to *Una noche con el Sr. Magnus e hijos*. An analysis of Monti's theater can be seen in Osvaldo Pellettieri's preliminary study, "El teatro de Ricardo Monti," *Teatro (Tomo II)*, 9–79.

8. Kive Staiff, "Una obra imagina la historia política argentina de este siglo como un circo poblado de payasos locos," *La Opinión*, October 28, 1971.

9. An account of this scene can be seen in Ernesto Schoo, "El gran teatro del mundo," *Panorama*, no. 236 (November 2–8, 1971): 47. In an interview with the author, Ricardo Monti commented that after its release, he and the director, Jaime Kogan, decided to eliminate this ending because it lent itself to misinterpretations. According to Monti, they had introduced this character to problematize the question of violence, but the audience thought that it was an exaltation of violence, and, more explicitly, the guerrillas.

10. Luis Alberto Romero. "La violencia en la historia argentina reciente: Un estado de la cuestión," in *Historizar el pasado vivo en América Latina*, ed. Pérotin-Dumon (Santiago: Universidad Alberto Hurtado, Centro de Ética, 2007), 103. The reader interested in further exploring the state of the field presented above in regard to the issue of violence has an exhaustive inventory in this work.

11. Walter Benjamin's notion of developing a practice of historical analysis derived from the visual/film notion of montage is synthesized in the Arcades Project where he says, "Method of this work: literary montage. I have nothing to say, only to show." In that sense, the idea of the documentary is to let the file footage speak for itself and thus try out Benjamin's idea of eliminating all overt commentary so as to allow meaning to emerge solely through my interviewees' experience of the shocking montage. See Theodor Adorno, "A Portrait of Walter Benjamin," in Adorno, *Prisms* (Cambridge, MA: MIT Press, 1997), 239. See also Susan Buck-Morss, *The Dialectics of Seeing: Walter Benjamin and the Arcade Project* (Cambridge, MA: MIT Press, 1991), 73–75.

12. Walter Benjamin, "On Some Motifs in Baudelaire," in *Illuminations: Essays and Reflections* (New York: Schocken Books, 1986).

13. Occasionally, I also utilize the expression "middle sectors."

14. See Pierre Bourdieu, *Practical Reason: On the Theory of Action* (Cambridge: Polity, 1998). "What the worker eats, and especially the way he eats it, the sport he practices and the way he practices it, his political opinions and the way he expresses them," Bourdieu argues, "are systematically different from the industrial owner's corresponding activities." Bourdieu, *Practical Reason*, 8.

15. Bourdieu, *Practical Reason*, 12.

16. About this growing homogenization of the middle classes, see Jorge Graciarena, *Poder y clases sociales en América Latina* (Buenos Aires: Paidós, 1972), 204.

17. Tucumán, however, did undergo important structural transformations. The shuttering of eleven of its twenty-seven sugar mills in 1966 produced a structural

dislocation in the province, and by the end of the decade, both social conflicts and their repression had worsened severely. About the closing of the sugar mills, see Roberto Pucci, *Historia de la destrucción de una provincia: Tucumán 1966* (Tucumán: Del pago chico, 2008). For a general history of Tucumán, see Carlos Páez de la Torre, *Historia de Tucumán* (Buenos Aires: Plus Ultra, 1987).

18. Susana Torrado, "Estrategias de desarrollo, estructura social y movilidad," in *Una historia social del siglo XX*, ed. Susana Torrado (Buenos Aires: Edhasa, 2007), 41.

19. Torrado, *Estructura social de la Argentina* (Buenos Aires: De la Flor, 1994). A part of this growth in the independent or self-employed sector is explained by the precarious position of salaried labor.

One Political Culture

1. With the concept of sensibility, I refer to the complex of feelings and ideas that make up a particular subjectivity. I have preferred to use this concept here—and not that of ideology—since I want to emphasize the weight of the emotional over the political.

2. See Carlos Altamirano, "Estudio preliminar," in *Bajo el signo de las masas (1943–1973)* (Buenos Aires: Ariel, 2001), especially 19–49.

3. See Juan Carlos Portantiero, "Clases dominantes y crisis política en la Argentina actual," in *El capitalismo argentino en crisis*, ed. Oscar Braun (Buenos Aires: Siglo XXI, 1973), and Portantiero, "Economía y política en la crisis argentina: 1958–1973," *Revista Mexicana de Sociología* 39, no. 2 (April–June 1977): 531–65.

4. Some authors argue that the middle class itself, as a social identity that was known and recognized by those claiming to be its members, developed as a reaction to the rise of Peronism. See, for example, Enrique Garguin, "'Los argentinos descendemos de los barcos': The Racial Articulation of Middle-Class Identity in Argentina (1920–1960)," *Latin American and Caribbean Ethnic Studies* 2, no. 2 (September 2007): 161–84; and Ezequiel Adamovsky, *Historia de la clase media argentina: Apogeo y decadencia de una ilusión, 1919–2003* (Buenos Aires: Planeta, 2009), especially 349–78.

5. Maurice Halbwachs, *The Collective Memory* (New York: Harper and Row, 1980), see especially 128–57.

6. About this topic, see Jorge Graciarena, "Clases medias y movimiento estudiantil: El reformismo argentino: 1918–1966," *Revista Mexicana de Sociología* 33, no. 1 (January–March 1971): 61–100.

7. Bruno Filliol, a Peronist student leader at the Universidad Nacional de Tucumán in the 1970s, remembering the student assemblies of that time, recounted: "We had a pet, one of the good leaders would come and he always came with the pet. And he took the pet to the meetings. Who were the pets? A mason, a construction worker, someone representative of the working class. [. . .] What sons of bitches! How are they going to bring this guy to talk, who doesn't even know how to talk?" This type of testimony leads us to doubt that the activists could break away from the class

prejudice that considered that formal education and greater material and cultural resources were sufficient conditions to establish their superiority.

8. See, for example, Oscar Terán, *Nuestros años sesentas* (Buenos Aires: Punto Sur, 1991); Carlos Altamirano, "La pequeña burguesía, una clase en el purgatorio," in *Peronismo y cultura de izquierda* (Buenos Aires: Siglo XXI, 2011), 99–127; and Juan Carlos Torre, "A partir del Cordobazo," *Estudios*, no. 4 (July–December 1994): 15–24. The radicalization of Catholicism in certain youth sectors was a fundamental ingredient of the general political process. After the Vatican II Council, the Catholic Church at the global level began a transformation that was very important in Latin America. The conference of Latin American bishops in Medellín in 1968 deepened this change and pushed many priests to a deep commitment with the dispossessed. In Argentina this process translated into the formation of the Movement of Priests for the Third World (Movimiento de Sacerdotes para el Tercer Mundo; MSTM), which would have great influence on the Catholic youth. On MSTM, see Jimmie Dodson, "Religious Innovation and the Politics of Argentina: A Study of the Movement of Priests for the Third World" (PhD diss., Indiana University, 1973). On the nexus between Catholics and Marxists, see Beatriz Sarlo, *La batalla de las ideas* (Buenos Aires: Ariel, 2001), 53–57.

9. CIMS, "Estudio de la opinión pública sobre imágenes del presidente y la Revolución," *Estudio No.* 47, 1967 (Colecciones Especiales y Archivos, Universidad de San Andrés, Argentina). The categories used to designate the social classes are those of CIMS. The methodology used was multiple-stage probabilistic (interview with José Enrique Miguens, September 24, 2009, Buenos Aires). The samples covered forty-five routes with four hundred interviewees in Capital Federal, forty-three routes with four hundred interviewees in greater Buenos Aires metropolitan area, twenty routes with two hundred interviewees in Rosario, and eighteen routes with two hundred interviewees in Córdoba. The interviews were conducted in participants' homes. The sampling was designed by the Rosario Statistical Institute (Instituto Estadístico de Rosario). See also "¿Valió la pena hacer la Revolución?," *Panorama*, no. 58 (March–April 1968): 36–43.

10. CIMS, "Estudio de la opinión pública sobre imágenes del presidente y la revolución."

11. Rosario and the greater Buenos Aires metropolitan area were equidistant from both cities, where the presidential approval rating reached 44.5 percent and 42 percent, respectively. CIMS, "Estudio de la opinión pública sobre imágenes del presidente y la revolución."

12. "Encuestas: Dos años de Onganía," *Primera Plana*, no. 287 (June 25–July 1, 1968): 20–22.

13. See a detailed analysis of this issue in Sebastián Carassai, "Ni de izquierda ni peronistas, medioclasistas. Ideología y política de la clase media argentina a comienzos de los años setentas," *Desarrollo Económico* 205 (April–June 2012): 95–117.

14. José Enrique Miguens, "Las interpretaciones intelectuales del voto peronista: Los prejuicios académicos y las realidades," in *Racionalidad del peronismo: Perspectivas*

internas y externas que replantean un debate inconcluso, ed. José Enrique Miguens and Frederick Turner (Buenos Aires: Planeta, 1988), 209–32.

15. Data constructed from the INDEC, "Censo Nacional de Población, Familias y Viviendas 1970: Resultados obtenidos por muestra; Total del país" (Buenos Aires: INDEC, 1970), table no. 1, "Población total, por grupo y años simples de edad según sexo," 19–20. The 1970 census revealed that the country had aged in comparison to past decades. In that year, 7 percent of the population was over sixty-five years old. See Nélida Redondo, "Composición por edades y envejecimiento demográfico," in *Población y bienestar en la Argentina del primero al segundo Centenario: Una historia del siglo XX*, ed. Susana Torrado (Buenos Aires: Edhasa, 2007), 2:139–75. A United Nations comparison of the 1970 census results with other countries' data established that the average per capita annual growth rate was situated among the areas with the slowest growth in the world." "El por qué de nuestro presente y cómo será nuestro futuro," *Gente*, no. 282 (December 17, 1970).

16. Data constructed from the INDEC, "Censo Nacional de Población, Familias y Viviendas 1970: Resultados obtenidos por muestra; Total del país" (Buenos Aires: INDEC, 1970), table no. 9, "Población de 5 años y más, por sexo, grupo y años simples de edad según nivel de instrucción," 33. This 8.22 percent included both those who had finished their university studies ("university and superior level complete") and those who had not done so ("university and superior level incomplete"). If the next age bracket (twenty-five to twenty-nine years old) is included, the percentage of the population that was in the universities or some institution of higher learning falls to 7.95 percent.

17. In these elections, the Popular Revolutionary Alliance (Alende-Sueldo) obtained 7.43 percent, the Socialist Workers' Party (Coral-Sciappone) 0.62 percent, and the Popular Left Front (Ramos-Silvetti) 0.41 percent of the vote. It should be remembered that the leader of the largest leftist party, Oscar Alende, came from Radicalism and in 1958 rose to the government of Buenos Aires province as a candidate of the Intransigent Radical Civic Union, Frondizi's party. Although in 1972 he founded a party that situated him on the left of the political spectrum, he was more of a classic "committee politician." Abelardo Ramos, leader of a more radical left-wing position, declared that Alende represented those who wanted "prosperity without revolution" and who wanted to make "an omelette without breaking the eggs." For this Left, Alende was "a decent and moderate man. It wasn't good for him to pose as a revolutionary." "Jorge Abelardo Ramos: Alguien tiene que perder," *Análisis-Confirmado*, no. 510–397 (January 23–29, 1973): 50.

18. Rodolfo Pandolfi, "El voto de los argentinos," *Análisis-Confirmado*, no. 616–394 (January 2–8, 1973): 10–16.

19. Santiago Bergadá, Guillermo Fretes, and Juan Ramos Mejía (Jr.), "Universidad: Muchos estudiantes pueden pagar," *Carta Política*, no. 37 (November 1976): 52–53.

20. The remaining 50.5 percent was divided in the following way: the Radical Civic Union (Unión Cívica Radical) (Balbín-Gamond) 21.29 percent, the Popular

Federalist Alliance (Alianza Popular Federalista) (Manrique-Martínez Raymonda) 15.17 percent, the Popular Revolutionary Alliance (Alianza Popular Revolucionaria) (Alende-Sueldo) 7.56 percent, the Federal Republican Alliance (Alianza Republicana Federal) 2.96 percent, the New Force Party (Nueva Fuerza) (Chamizo-Ondarts) 2 percent, the Democratic Socialist Party (Partido Socialista Democrático) (Ghioldi-Balestra) 0.93 percent, the Socialist Workers' Party (Partido Socialista de los Trabajadores) 0.63 percent, and the Popular Left Front (Frente de Izquierda Popular) 0.41 percent. Even if it is true that each of these forces got the majority of their support from the middle and upper classes, their ideological character disproves the alleged leftward shift of the middle classes. Taken together, the left-wing fronts took less than 10 percent of the votes. On the contrary, more than 40 percent belonged to center and center-right forces.

21. Although they later withdrew, Sánchez Sorondo's Movement for a National Revolution (Movimiento por la Revolución Nacional), two Christian parties, and even the Argentine Peoples' Union (Unión del Pueblo Argentino) founded by ex-president Aramburu, who overthrew Perón in 1955 and was later assassinated by the Montoneros in 1970, initially participated in the electoral front.

22. La Opinión, July 13, 1973, 5. If the March 1973 votes are divided by support for parties that, in some way, symbolized the continuation of the Argentine Revolution, it could be said that 80 percent of the electorate voted for change and not continuity. This percentage is obtained by adding together the votes obtained by the FREJULI (49.59 percent), the UCR (21.3 percent), the Popular Revolutionary Alliance (7.43 percent) and various Left factions (1 percent). The remaining 20 percent voted for the Popular Federalist Alliance (15.17 percent) led by Manrique, a former minister of the Argentine Revolution; the Federal Republican Alliance (2.96), whose candidate Ezequiel Martínez enjoyed the support of General Lanusse; or the New Force party (2 percent), founded by Álvaro Alsogaray, who was associated with the general economic orientation of the deposed regime. It should not be overlooked that this "continuity" cluster drew its support mainly from the middle and upper classes of the population. Manrique's electoral discourse "rejected ideological rhetoric and called for a search for efficient solutions, appealed to the common sense of the middle classes, and set up a political operation with the electorate with strong liberal populist components." Oscar Landi, "La tercera presidencia de Perón: gobierno de emergencia y crisis política." Revista mexicano de sociología 40, no. 4 (December 1978): 1363.

23. Manuel Mora y Araujo and Peter Smith, "Peronism and Economic Development: The 1973 Elections," in Juan Perón and the Reshaping of Argentina, ed. Frederick Turner and José Enrique Miguens (Pittsburgh: University of Pittsburgh Press, 1983), 175.

24. Mora y Araujo and Smith, "Peronism and Economic Development," 176. Indeed, the economy minister's first measures implemented the program developed by the Hour of the People (La Hora del Pueblo)—a multiparty grouping created in late 1970 that included Peronism, the Radical Civic Union of the People, and the

Argentine Socialist, Popular Conservative, and Bloquista political parties—in addition to some documents produced together by the CGT and the CGE in 1972.

25. "Vicente Solano Lima: ¿Amigo o enemigo?," *Confirmado*, no. 393 (May 15–21, 1973): 11.

26. These words belong to Carlos Altamirano, "Peronismo y cultura de izquierda," in *Peronismo y cultura de izquierda* (Buenos Aires: Siglo XXI, 2011), 63.

27. See Edgardo Catterberg, *Argentines Confront Politics: Political Culture and Public Opinion in the Argentine Transition to Democracy* (Boulder, CO: Rienner, 1991), 76.

28. See, for example, the previously cited CIMS study that asked the population to choose between the rebellious and centrist currents of the movement. While 60 percent selected the latter, only 19 percent preferred the former (while the rest preferred not to respond). Considering only Peronist sympathizers, both percentages rose to 66.3 percent and 24.3 percent, respectively. At any rate, the leftist faction represented a minority. CIMS, "Pronóstico electoral de las elecciones presidenciales: Resumen de las conclusiones de la encuesta realizada y algunas recomendaciones que surgen," *Estudio No. 112* [O.P. 32] (Colecciones Especiales y Archivos, Universidad de San Andrés, Argentina).

29. Using statistical regression analysis, three researchers made estimates for the percentage of each occupational/employment category that supported Peronism in the 1946 and March 1973 elections. The analysis proved that, first, while in 1946, 74 percent of workers supported Peronism and 26 percent other parties; in March 1973, the respective percentages were 84 percent and 16 percent. Second, it determined that the percentage of nonworkers that supported Peronism decreased, although only slightly. In 1946, 25 percent of nonworkers supported Perón and in March 1973, 22 percent did so. Despite this, the composition of worker and non-worker support within the Peronist vote remained in a relatively stable relationship. This is because in 1946, the working class represented 56 percent of total voters, while in 1973 it only represented 46 percent. See Darío Cantón, Jorge Raúl Jorrat, and Eduardo Juárez, "Un intento de estimación de las celdas interiores de una tabla de contingencia basado en el análisis de regresión: El caso de las elecciones presidenciales de 1946 y marzo de 1973," *Desarrollo Económico* 63 (October–December 1976): 395–417.

30. Luis González Esteves and Ignacio Llorente, "Elecciones y preferencias políticas en Capital Federal y Gran Buenos Aires: El 30 de octubre de 1983," in *La argentina electoral*, ed. Natalio Botana et al. (Buenos Aires: Sudamericana, 1985), 47. Something similar was established with respect to the centrist parties.

31. Peronism's multiclass character in 1973 was not homogeneous in all areas of the country. Strictly speaking, as Mora y Araujo proposed, in the zones defined as "central" (those most developed industrially), Peronism closely resembled a workers' party, given that it was based on the working class and in the unions. In the zones defined as "peripheral" (those less developed industrially), its bases of support increased to nonworker and unorganized, rural and semi-urban sectors of the lower or "popular" classes, who were in many cases historically represented by

traditional conservatism. Having reached the government for the first time thanks primarily to the working-class vote, in 1950 Peronism managed to establish an alliance between working-class sectors (from the industrialized zones) and "popular"/ lower-class sectors (from the peripheral zones). This double social base was essentially unmodified in 1973. Manuel Mora y Araujo, "Las bases estructurales del peronismo," in El voto peronista: Ensayos de sociología electoral argentina, ed. Manuel Mora y Araujo and Ignacio Llorente (Buenos Aires: Sudamericana, 1980), 397–440.

32. Manuel Mora y Araujo, "Populismo, laborismo y clases medias (Política y estructura social en la Argentina)," Criterio 1755–56 (1977): 17.

33. The 1970 census classified 45.2 percent of the population as working-class (both salaried and independent) and 9.1 percent as marginal. Data referring to the social structure can be consulted in Susana Torrado, "Estrategias de desarrollo, estructura social y movilidad," in Una historia social del siglo XX, ed. Susana Torrado (Buenos Aires: Edhasa, 2007), 31–67. See also Susana Torrado, Estructura social de la Argentina (Buenos Aires: de la Flor, 1994).

34. José Enrique Miguens, "The Presidential Elections of 1973 and the End of an Ideology," in Juan Perón and the Reshaping of Argentina, ed. Frederick Turner and José Enrique Miguens (Pittsburgh: University of Pittsburgh Press, 1983), 147–70.

35. Félix Luna, "El futuro del peronismo: El estudio de su ser," Carta Política, no. 14 (summer 1975): 21.

36. Tulio Halperín Donghi, La larga agonía de la Argentina peronista (Buenos Aires: Ariel, 1994), 61–62.

37. La Opinión, July 4, 1974.

38. See Rodolfo Terragno, "Perón y Balbín no entraron en una componenda," Clarín, September 12, 2010.

39. In reality, it represented more than a paradox. Both Cámpora and his running mate, Solano Lima, came from conservative ranks. Indeed, as one analyst wrote, "for the leftists, the Cámpora–Solano Lima ticket conceals a return to the regime of the 1930s: in both candidates they see traces of 'patriotic fraud'"; Jorge Lozano, "El necesario repliegue militar," Panorama, no. 295 (December 21–27, 1972): 12. That the Peronist left led the campaign that would carry this ticket to victory remains paradoxical.

40. A provincial election that demonstrated the distance that existed between these middle classes and militant electoral formulas was held in Córdoba, the vanguard of the social uprisings. There, Radicalism achieved its best electoral result in the entire country (42 percent), and FREJULI, which had Atilio López, a radicalized worker leader, at the head of its formula, could not break the 50 percent barrier— the exhortations to cast blank ballots trumpeted by the far-left were insignificant. Córdoba was the clearest expression of the fact that in the central provinces (economically developed, with a significant presence of both industrial workers and the middle classes), Peronism continued to be a party with a primarily working class base. See Osvaldo Tcherkaski, "El FREJULI obtuvo el voto expectante de los obreros pero alejó a la clase media," La Opinión, April 1, 1973, 10–11.

41. "Perón-Montoneros y FAR: Los tramos más importantes," El Descamisado, no. 17 (September 11, 1973): 4.

42. See Rodolfo Pandolfi, "Juventud: obediencia o rebeldía," Carta Política, no. 11 (spring 1974): 14–15.

43. Cámpora's principal virtue, both for Perón and for himself, was his seamless subordination to the general's designs. The first verses of the "Chamamé de Cámpora," a song composed for his campaign, read: "He is a sincere and loyal man / always loyal to the general / Cámpora is a Peronist / like one can't be any more [Peronist]." El Descamisado, no. 2 (May 29, 1973): 5. In his message to the candidates of the Justicialist Liberation Front (FREJULI) on January 20, 1973, Héctor Cámpora said: "I will rise to the government by virtue of the mandate that you know [. . .] I have received this mandate because of a personal characteristic that, among other things, has characterized my entire life [. . .] I will speak to you, above all, about loyalty. Total, unconditional loyalty to my movement. Total, unconditional loyalty to my true friends. I consider that the greatest of these is General Juan Perón and I have been loyal to him during his government and during his exile. I add the special loyalty that a leader deserves to this personal loyalty." Héctor Cámpora, "Mensaje de las Pautas Programáticas," in Cómo cumplí el mandato de Perón (Buenos Aires: Quehacer Nacional, 1975), 9. His running mate, Vicente Solano Lima, also expressed his submission to Perón's designs. "In regard to me," Solano Lima declared only days before being sworn in, "I not only accept the three fundamental ideas of Justicialism: I also accept Peronism's methodology to put them into practice, I accept Peronism's verticalism as the spinal cord of the Justicialist Front, and I am in complete solidarity with the leader of Peronism, General Juan Perón." "Vicente Solano Lima: ¿Amigo o enemigo?," Confirmado, no. 393 (May 15–21, 1973): 18. Also see the CIMS poll that establishes that, in January 1973, Cámpora was, for Peronist voters, the one who best represented General Perón, distantly followed by Rucci and the 62 Organizations. CIMS, "Pronóstico electoral de las elecciones presidenciales."

44. Andrés Zavala, "Con una mayor inserción en la clase media el Frente intenta consolidarse," La Opinión, February 6, 1973.

45. "Cámpora-Lima: La fórmula de la discordia," Panorama, no. 295 (December 21–27, 1972): 14.

46. See, for example, Rodolfo Terragno, "Cámpora buscó fortalecer su posición con un discurso para no peronistas," La Opinión, April 10, 1973, 1; and "Anatema contra los neoperonistas y seducción para la clase media," La Opinión, April 13, 1973.

47. In fifteen districts, FREJULI did not attract a sufficient amount of votes to avoid a runoff. In almost all of these cases, FREJULI won the second round.

48. See, for example, the speech that Cámpora delivered to the nation from Mendoza on Sunday, April 8, 1973. Los Andes, April 9, 1973.

49. See "En su gira, Cámpora trata de captar a los sectores de la clase media," La Opinión, April 10, 1973.

50. In an early work, Mora y Araujo proposed the existence of three political forces: one populist, one labor-oriented, and one middle-class. After establishing

that 1973 Peronism mostly relied on the populist and labor political forces, he indicated that the middle-class political force, whose electoral behavior was primarily oriented toward non-Peronist options, included other smaller forces, such as that constituted by "intellectual and highly educated sectors of the urban middle classes, who are prone to recurring nationalist and leftist political expressions." Mora y Araujo, "Populismo, laborismo y clases medias," 14.

51. Heriberto Kahn, "Los vaivenes dentro del poder," *Carta Política*, no. 12 (spring 1974): 12.

52. The rapprochement between Perón and Balbín had begun well before 1973. In regard to this, see the article "Un peronismo balbiniano," *Primera Plana*, no. 400 (September 29, 1970): 16–17, and the interview with Balbín in the same issue, "Balbín: Los custodios de las siglas," 18–19. In 1970, over the period of six months, Jorge Daniel Paladino—Perón's delegate in Argentina and the secretary of the Peronist movement—met with Radical leaders. Perón, who by this point considered the Radical Party (UCR) a "popular force," had written to Balbín that he was "emaciated" and that he wanted to seek a "national union" based on an accord between Peronism and Radicalism. See the testimony of Enrique Vanoli, ex-president of the UCR's National Committee, in the documentary *Décadas: 1970*, directed by Otelo Borroni and Roberto Vacca, 1986. About Perón's attempts to organize a joint formula with Radicalism, including for the March 1973 elections, in which he could not be a candidate, see Wayne Smith, "El diálogo Perón-Lanusse," in *Racionalidad del peronismo: Perspectivas internas y externas que replantean un debate inconcluso*, ed. José Enrique Miguens and Frederick Turner (Buenos Aires: Planeta, 1988), 117–66. Also see Perón's speech opening the 1974 congressional sessions, an unequivocal testament to the unprecedented understanding that had been achieved between Radicals and Peronists. "Before reading the message of the Executive branch," Perón said on that day, "I would like to present in my name, the deepest gratitude to the legislators, who have made possible the approval of laws that were absolutely indispensable. In doing so, I would like to pay tribute to the senators and deputies of the opposition, who with a highly patriotic attitude have not expressed opposition but rather a permanent collaboration with the Executive branch which is appreciated in the highest terms." "Discurso del presidente Perón ante la Asamblea Legislativa al inaugurar las sesiones ordinarias," www.mrperon.com.ar. This was also the speech in which Perón announced, in words that would become famous, the change in epoch with respect to the 1950s. If at that point there was nothing better for a Peronist than another Peronist, in 1974, "we have thus started the time in which for an Argentine, there is nothing better than another Argentine." Shortly before his death, in the same rally where the radicalized wings of his movement withdrew from the Plaza de Mayo, insulted by their leader, Perón once again thanked the cooperation of all of the political parties, particularly emphasizing the UCR. The final seal on this unprecedented understanding that was reached between Perón and the traditional party of the middle classes came from the leader of the Radicals. After Perón's death, in a speech whose last words still endure in the collective

memories of the middle classes, Balbín closed his speech saying: "this old adversary bids farewell to a friend." "Discurso del Dr. Ricardo Balbín despidiendo los restos de Perón en el Congreso Nacional," July 4, 1974, http://www.oratoriaconsulting .com.ar/discursos/balbin.pdf.

53. About the conversations between Perón and the MID, see the interesting interview in which Rogelio Frigerio, the most lucid of the men surrounding Frondizi, speaks about the numerous conversations he held with Perón in Madrid. "Cara a cara con Rogelio Frigerio: De Frente contra el Acuerdo," *Confirmado*, no. 348 (February 15–21, 1972): 12–16. A political analyst attributed the Justicialist leader's interest in meeting with Frigerio to the belief that, for Perón, Frondizi was who best "interpreted the middle class." "Gran Acuerdo: Un ministro en el laberinto," *Panorama*, no. 248 (January 25–31, 1972): 13.

54. See "El teniente de Perón," *Panorama*, no. 212 (May 18–25, 1971): 9–10.

55. "Informe Licastro: Por qué Perón presidente," *Panorama*, no. 325 (August 2–8, 1973): 15.

56. Some examples: Arturo Jauretche, a polemicist associated with Peronism, declared in 1969 that Peronism and anti-Peronism were simply "names" and that the choice between one and the other was a "false choice." "The reality," Jauretche argued, "is in the national and colonialist tendencies," identifying liberalism with the latter of these. "Arturo Jauretche: 'Este gobierno es un suplente,' " *Panorama*, no. 103 (April 15–21, 1969): 15. The "liberalism-nationalism" antinomy even divided the Argentine Revolution. In 1968, *Panorama* affirmed that "the government has a liberal wing (its economics) and a nationalist wing (its politics)." "Y usted: ¿Por qué es opositor?," *Panorama*, no. 83 (November 26–December 2, 1968): 8. Shortly thereafter, Onganía tried to situate himself as a synthesis of both currents. "It is not coincidental," he said, "that both liberals and nationalists are equally represented in my government." "¿Qué hará Onganía en 1969?," *Panorama*, no. 90 (January 14–20, 1969): 7. For some observers, this diagnostic was also valid for the various sectors that made up the country: "as in the rest of society," an analyst wrote, "the military officials choose between one of two lines: the liberal or the national." "1970: Año político," *Panorama*, no. 140 (December 30, 1969–January 5, 1970): 11. Father Milan Viscovich, one of the priests who founded and led the Movement of Priests for the Third World (Movimiento de Sacerdotes para el Tercer Mundo) (MSPTM), also considered that there was a national and a liberal wing in the church, as in other institutions and social sectors. "Entre Perón y el 'Che': Adónde va el nacionalismo," *Panorama*, no. 148 (February 24–March 2, 1970): 6. In terms of the revolutionary/counterrevolutionary antinomy, one can see the declaration of ex-president Arturo Frondizi (who, while justifying as many other politicians did the 1966 coup that overthrew Illia, in 1969 was in the ranks of the critics of Onganía's government). Shortly before the Cordobazo, Frondizi indicated that "the central point of political action today is the struggle of the revolution against the counterrevolutionary forces. This struggle completely transcends the limits of those that govern and those that are governed. One struggles for and against revolution from the highest

positions of government and from the governed sectors—whether they consider themselves to be in the opposition or not—and an absolutely similar confrontation occurs." "Frondizi propone una salida," *Panorama*, no. 102 (April 8–14, 1969): 13. Everything seems to indicate that, by the beginning of the 1970s, the Peronism/anti-Peronism antimony had lost intensity.

57. See IPSA POLL # 1972-OP010: ELECTIONS (computer file), Roper Center for Public Opinion Research, Research Study ARIPSA 1972-OP010 Version 3, Institute IPSA, SA (producer), 1972 (Storrs, CT: Roper Center for Public Opinion Research, University of Connecticut (distributor), 2006), question 12. This poll was conducted in January 1972, covering two hundred subjects on the national level through face-to-face interviews.

58. "Una encuesta oficial," *Panorama*, no. 306 (March 8–14, 1973): 17. The survey involved 14,104 interviews in twenty-one cities in the country. More than 70 percent of those interviewed belonged to the middle classes. To perform the segmentation by social class, the firm that conducted the study took the monthly income of respondents as its indicator.

59. See "La elección y las minorías," *Panorama*, no. 307 (March 15–21, 1973): 18.

60. According to the Audience Verification Institute (Instituto Verificador de Audiencias) this program reached forty rating points at its maximum. The IPSA firm, whose measurement was significantly lower (an average of 27.5 rating points), showed that the greatest audience was concentrated in the middle class (32.4 points, compared with 25.8 in the upper class and 20.1 in the lower class). See "La clase media fue el principal oyente del diálogo con el líder justicialista," *La Opinión*, September 6, 1973.

61. The expression is Perón's; he used it with representatives of the Peronist Youth on September 8, 1973.

62. Perón, "Mensaje dirigido al pueblo argentino desde el Salón Glanco la Casa de Gobierno," June 12, 1974. www.jdperon.gov.or/1945/10/discursos/.

63. Perón, "Mensaje dirigido al pueblo argentino desde los balcones de la Casa de Gobierno." members.libreopinion.com/justicalismo/discursos/peron/12_6_74.htm.

64. Luna, "El tercer Perón," *Panorama*, no. 331 (September 20–26, 1973): 36.

65. In 1973, Perón said, in a phrase that remained, together with many others, forever associated with his thought: "Everything to its proper extent and harmoniously" (*"Todo en su medida y armoniosamente"*). *Gente* magazine selected it as its "phrase of the year," as a "synthesis of action and prudence at the same time." "'73 ¡Qué año! 365 días con la lupa de 'Gente,'" *Gente*, no. 445 (January 31, 1974). Undoubtedly, a large segment of public opinion liked this Perón, including *Gente* magazine, which was by no means leftist.

66. See Silvia Sigal and Eliseo Verón, "Perón: Discurso político e ideología," in *Argentina, hoy*, ed. Alain Rouquié (Buenos Aires: Siglo XXI, 1982), 151–205.

67. "Discurso del General Perón en la CGT," November 2, 1973, http://www.libre opinion.com/members/justicalismo/libros/peron/jdp_comorg_3.htm.

68. It should be remembered that the economic leadership in the Peronist government, from May 25, 1973, until October 21, 1974, rested in the hands of José Ber Gelbard, leader of the General Economic Confederation (Confederación General Económica) (CGE), the employers' union that brought together small and medium-sized businesses. For a study about this Peronist economy minister, see María Seoane, El burgués maldito: Los secretos de Gelbard, el último líder del capitalismo nacional (Buenos Aires: Sudamericana, 2003).

69. "Discurso del General Perón en la CGT," November 2, 1973, http://www.libre opinion.com/members/justicialismo/libros/peron/jdp_comorg_3.htm.

70. Perón's speech, May 1, 1974, http://www.elortiba.org/1may074.html.

71. See Halperín Donghi, La larga agonía de la Argentina peronista, 64.

72. In addition to FREJULI, only three other electoral forces presented themselves for this election: the Radical Civic Union, the Popular Federalist Alliance, and the Socialist Workers Party. The 38 percent that these political forces obtained together were divided in the following manner: 24.42 percent for the UCR, 12.19 percent for the APF, and 1.52 percent for the PST.

73. However, it should be noted that these elections demonstrated a "diminished civic fervor contrary to that shown in the previous campaign which concluded on March 11th." "Los primeros 70 días de un nuevo proceso," Panorama, no. 331 (September 20–26, 1973): 8. In a sense, this decrease in vigor exuded the low intensity of the hopes that were aroused by the Perón-Perón formula for wide sectors of the middle classes.

74. Some analysts of those days became excited about this Perón "leader of the community as a whole" precisely because they believed Perón's approach toward the middle classes as its opposite; in other words, the middle classes' approach toward Perón. See, for example, Alonso, "La confluencia de la clase media y los trabajadores es un motor para el cambio," La Opinión, October 16, 1973. Reality would soon demonstrate that the large majority of the middle classes would continue to have all kinds of reservations about Peronism. Some of these reservations or fears were covered by the journalism of the period. See, for example, "Una declaración de Calabró apacigua las inquietudes de sectores de clase media," La Opinión, April 3, 1973, about the commitment of the elected governor of the province of Buenos Aires to not rename the provincial capital "Eva Perón"—a practice that angered a majority of the middle classes.

75. It should be remembered that a significant part of activist youth increased the radicalization of their positions. In the democratic period, for example, days before the elections that would make Perón president with 62 percent of the votes, the young activists of Base Peronism (Peronismo de Base) asked their leaders for weapons, chanting the slogan "we want knives, we want knives" at one of their rallies. In response to a speaker's comment that the system won't give it to them, they responded, "We're going to snatch [steal] them, we're going to snatch them." See "La sangre derramada está siendo negociada," Militancia, no. 15 (September 20,

1973): 11. The slogan "we want knives" ("*queremos fierros*") was the response of the rally attendees to the Peronist leader Envar El Kadri's statement that "we are the people's army, the workers, united, organized, and armed."

76. Although he was never able to put it into practice, it was Perón's declared intention to form a State Council that would advise the president, formed from the most representative leaders of the different political parties.

77. Heriberto Kahn, "El poder va hacia el centro," *La Opinión*, September 2, 1973, 1.

78. Indeed, if one rereads the press of the left-wing Peronist activist groupings, it can be seen that, from the Ezeiza massacre onward, each time that they wanted to include Perón's phrases or thoughts that favored their point of view, they had to turn to stock phrases and documents prior to his definitive return to the country.

79. Jorge Lozano, "La patria infantil," *Carta Política*, no. 1 (winter 1974): 13.

80. Félix Luna, "Perón, antes y ahora," *Carta Política*, no. 1 (winter 1974): 21.

81. When opening the congressional sessions in 1974, shortly after affirming "for an Argentine there is nothing better than another Argentine," Perón made a description of the country that was as contrary to reality as it was consistent with his intent to underline the isolation of the radicalized youth. "Fortunately," Perón said, "the time in which we live and where we are inevitable protagonists, finds us Argentines as united as we were in the most fruitful periods of our history. It is a true miracle that we can now discuss and disagree amongst ourselves, think in different ways and judge different solutions to be valid, having arrived at the conclusion that beyond the disagreements, the fate of the Homeland belongs to all of us equally, as it contains the fate of every one of us, of our present and our future. Our Argentina is pacified." "Discurso del presidente Perón ante la Asamblea Legislativa." If Argentines were at peace with one another and their different sectors were discussing and disagreeing amongst themselves in a civilized fashion, those who were not doing so could only be characterized as maladjusted. Perón said it thusly: "Those that attempt to impede the consolidation of an order imposed by the peaceful revolution that we proposed and the majority of Argentines accepted are agents of disorder. Those who try, uselessly, to promote violence as an alternative to our irrevocable purpose of achieving our own peaceful development are agents of chaos [. . .] We will overcome subversion. We will isolate the violent and the maladjusted." In line with both the military discourse of the Argentine Revolution and with what would follow in his wife's government, in the same speech Perón described this violence as something that came from abroad and was foreign to the national spirit. "We do not ignore that violence also comes from outside our borders," Perón indicated, "by means of a calculated sabotage of our irrevocable decision to free ourselves from any hint of colonialism." Maladjusted and at the service of foreign ideologies, the radicalized youth were thus isolated from "the majority of Argentines," coming from no one less than the man who always fulfilled the role of "eternal father" to the different groups that formed his movement, in addition to being the president of the nation. The fate of the "maladjusted" was, in this way, set.

82. Indeed, a certain sector of the revolutionary activists saw an attempt to "de-Peronize the country" in this Justicialist government, even with Perón alive. See "¿Hay comandos parapoliciales?," *Militancia*, no. 35 (February 21, 1974): 10. Perón's project of mobilizing the "silent majority" of the youth, which was not represented by either the revolutionary tendency or by Julio Yessi's sector—theoretically associated with the movement's Superior Council (Consejo Superior)—was a step in this direction. Perón sought to balance the weight of the radicalized sectors within his movement by attempting to register youth that were not necessarily Peronist, but were certainly not radicalized. See Cámara, "¿Quién se quedará con la llave?," *Panorama*, no. 340 (November 22–28, 1973): 4–5.

83. For the official voice of the Peronist Youth see, for example, "Tenemos ahora a nuestros peores enemigos dentro del movimiento," El Descamisado, no. 6 (June 26, 1973): 6–7. For Perón's view, see the speech that he made after the events of Ezeiza, the day of his definitive return to the country (reproduced in "Lo que dijo Perón," El Descamisado, no. 6 (June 26, 1973): 30) or what he pronounced to the CGT in November of that same year, where he directed his barbs at the "infiltrators" in his movement. "El discurso del general," El Descamisado, no. 26 (November 13, 1973): 4–5. Nobody knew that "the issue is within the movement" better than the Peronists themselves, as the editor of this activist publication affirmed after the assassination of the CGT's general secretary. "Ante la muerte de Rucci," El Descamisado, no. 20 (October 2, 1973).

84. Oscar Landi, "Sobre lenguajes, identidades y ciudadanías políticas [1981]," in "Crisis y lenguajes políticos," Estudios CEDES 4, no. 4 (1982): 36–37.

85. It was also Oscar Landi who first observed that the petty and middle bourgeoisie (referring to the business sector) began to distance themselves from the economic leadership as soon as they saw that, given that the state's capacity for maneuver was reduced at the productive, commercial, and financial levels, they did not find the sufficient support to reconvert them. See Oscar Landi, "La tercera presidencia de Perón: Gobierno de emergencia y crisis política," Revista Mexicana de Sociología 40, no. 4 (October–December 1978): 1397.

86. Interview with Ítalo Luder, "El justicialismo debe recuperar a la clase media," La Opinión, January 6, 1976. Also see "Encuesta: ¿Qué tendría que ocurrir en la Argentina en 1976? Pero, ¿qué piensa usted que va a ocurrir?," Extra, no. 127 (January 1976): 24–26.

87. In 1956, in a text titled *The Other Face of Peronism*, the writer Ernesto Sabato narrated an autobiographical scene that would later become famous and transform into a symbol of the anti-Peronists' blindness to the social phenomenon that Perón's rise represented. Meeting with upper-class families in a house in the northern city of Salta, "on that night in September '55," Sabato wrote, remembering the jubilation with which he received the news of Perón's overthrow, "while the doctors, landowners, and writers loudly celebrated the fall of the tyrant in the living room, I saw that in a corner of the pantry, the two Indian women who worked there had their eyes soaked with tears." Ernesto Sabato, El otro rostro del peronismo (Buenos

Aires: n/e, 1956), 40. "Many millions of workers and dispossessed" cried through these two women. Peronism had another face and not only the one seen by the most affluent sectors of society.

88. About this, see the description of the "literary explosion" and the "ideological euphoria of the student body" that followed the Liberating Revolution, described from the perspective of a defender of Peronism in Agustín Ferraris, *Pido la palabra: Contestando a Martínez Estrada, Mario Amadeo y Ernesto Sabato* (Buenos Aires: Capricornio, 1957), 3–6.

89. The expression "hour of freedom" belongs to Tulio Halperín Donghi, from a famous article published in the issue that *Sur* magazine dedicated to "national reconstruction," in response to the fall of Peronism. Tulio Halperín Donghi, "La historiografía argentina en la hora de la libertad," *Sur*, no. 237 (1955): 114–21.

90. For example, the Ezeiza massacre, which confronted different Peronist factions, provoked memories of this sort among different interviewees. "Let them kill each other," Claudio Mastrángelo remembered that he thought when he learned of the confrontation. Ema Mateo remembered having thought something similar about the conflict between the Montoneros and the Triple A: "For me, let them all kill each other! What is it to me? I don't feel sorry for them. Let them feel sorry, but I, particularly, am not interested in them."

91. She could not have voted for Frondizi because the presidential election occurred when she was only sixteen years old. She could perhaps have voted for Frondizi's candidates in the 1960 legislative elections.

92. For example, with the candidates that won with the ALIANZA coalition in 1999, for whom two of the three voted.

93. For example, in the 1973 elections, the Cámpora-Solano Lima electoral formula received 1,529 votes, against 1,038 for the Popular Federalist Alliance and 219 for the Radical Civic Union. *La Voz de Correa*, March 15, 1973.

94. About the life of Eva Duarte before she became Eva Perón, see Beatriz Sarlo, *La pasión y la excepción* (Buenos Aires: Siglo XXI, 2003), 29–88, and the bibliographical references alluded to in this text. The author does not doubt the will/necessity of the regime in erasing Eva's past, which was unsuccessful in artistic terms and doubtful in moral terms—for the standards of the period.

Excursus I Waiting for Violence

1. "¿Los argentinos perdieron la imaginación?," *Panorama*, no. 94 (February 11–17, 1969): 9.

2. "¿Todo tiempo futuro será mejor?," *Panorama*, no. 89 (January 7–13, 1969): 32.

3. Heriberto Kahn, "Estudiantes. Violencia. Revolución," *Confirmado*, no. 148 (April 18, 1968): 25–27. That same year, *Panorama* asked itself why Herbert Marcuse, a key theoretical referent for the student rebellions in Europe and the United States, did not resonate among Argentine students, politicians, and intellectuals. "Mar-

cuse: ¿El nuevo profeta de la izquierda?," *Panorama*, no. 73 (September 17–23, 1968): 14–16.

4. "Así las vio el periodismo," *Gente*, no. 182 (January 16, 1969).

5. "¿Todo tiempo futuro será mejor?," *Panorama*, no. 89 (January 7–13, 1969): 32.

6. Those who consider the 1960s guerrilla experiences to be important emphasize their character as historical predecessors of the groups who would shake public opinion with greater force in the following decade. Peter Waldmann, however, has maintained that "their existence and actions did not have any political or social resonance in the country." Peter Waldmann, "Anomia social y violencia," in *Argentina, hoy*, ed. Alain Rouquié (Buenos Aires: Siglo XXI, 1982), 208.

7. María Matilde Ollier, *Golpe o revolución: La violencia legitimada, Argentina 1966–1973* (Buenos Aires: Eduntref, 2005), 61–62.

8. The first characterization belongs to an editorial titled "La legitimidad de la represión," *La Capital*, June 28, 1969. The second belongs to "Editorial: Salir de la trampa," *Análisis*, no. 445 (September 23–29, 1969): 23.

9. For a chronicle of the events in Tucumán in 1969, see "La 'guerrilla urbana' en Tucumán," *Noticias*, December 29, 1969, 4.

10. "Dos frentes contra Onganía," *Panorama*, no. 110 (June 3–9, 1969): 9.

11. "1969: Historia de un año que cambió en un mes," *Panorama*, no. 139 (December 23–29, 1969): 10.

12. "La violencia asistió a la cita," *Panorama*, no. 110 (June 3–9, 1969): 6–8.

13. Mariano Grondona, "Por la Nación," *Primera Plana*, no. 184 (June 30, 1966): 3.

14. "Argentina pregunta: El momento político, la violencia, huelgas, inquietud," *Gente*, no. 218 (September 25, 1969).

15. "Con las velas desplegadas," *Panorama*, no. 114 (July 1–7, 1969): 6.

16. "1970: Año político," *Panorama*, no. 140 (December 30, 1969–January 5, 1970): 11.

17. "Tiempo de violencia," *Análisis*, no. 472 (March 31–April 6, 1970): 10.

18. Tomás Eloy Martínez, "Editorial," *Panorama*, no. 192 (December 29, 1970–January 4, 1971), 3.

19. "Desbordamiento extremista," *La Capital*, July 6, 1970.

20. "Balance de un año que concluye," *La Gaceta*, December 31, 1970, 6.

21. The first quote belongs to Mariano Grondona, "Los argentinos ante la violencia," *Gente*, no. 358 (June 1, 1972): 32, and the following quotes to "El peronismo hacia el gobierno: Responde Mariano Grondona," *Gente*, no. 403 (April 12, 1973): 15–16 (emphasis in original).

Two Social Violence (1969–1974)

1. "Estudiantes: Los muertos mandan," *Panorama*, no. 108 (May 20–26, 1969): 6–7.

2. "Nordeste: La paz de los fusiles," *Panorama*, no. 109 (May 28–June 2, 1969): 13.

3. "El ex gobernador analiza el Cordobazo," *Panorama*, no. 122 (August 26–September 1, 1969): 10.

4. Juan Carlos Agulla, *Córdoba: Mayo de 1969: Diagnóstico social de una crisis* (Buenos Aires: Editel, 1969), 37.

5. CIMS, "Problemas universitarios," *Estudio Nro. 30* (1967) (Colecciones Especiales y Archivos, Universidad de San Andrés, Argentina). The categories are those of CIMS.

6. "Dos Años de Onganía," *Primera Plana*, no. 287 (June 25–July 1, 1968): 22. The denominations correspond to the A&C (Analistas de Empresas y Consultores de Dirección/Business Analysts and Management Consultants).

7. See, for example, Juan Carlos Agulla, *Córdoba: Mayo de 1969*; Francisco Delich, *Crisis y protesta social: Córdoba, mayo 1969* (Buenos Aires: Signos, 1970); Roberto Roth, *Los años de Onganía* (Buenos Aires: de la Campana, 1981); and James Brennan and Mónica Gordillo, *Córdoba rebelde: El Cordobazo, el clasismo y la movilización social* (Buenos Aires: de la Campana, 2008).

8. Channel 10 was inaugurated on July 9, 1966, on the occasion of President Onganía's visit to the city for the 150th anniversary of independence.

9. The daily newspaper *El Pueblo*, directed by one of the sons of the García Hamilton family, was never able to go beyond an audience of a small minority of the provincial capital's society.

10. "La conveniente moderación," *La Gaceta*, May 21, 1969.

11. "Que cese la violencia," *La Gaceta*, July 3, 1969, 6.

12. "Volver a la normalidad," *La Gaceta*, November 22, 1970, 6.

13. "Buscar puntos conciliables," *La Gaceta*, November 29, 1970, 6.

14. "Las memorias de Agapito Chancalay," *La Gaceta*, August 20, 1970.

15. "Las memorias de Agapito Chancalay," *La Gaceta*, October 22, 1970.

16. An example of this position can be seen in the editorial the paper devoted to the March 1971 events in Córdoba, where, on the one hand, it criticized the decision of the national government of designating a governor challenged by the people of Córdoba, and, on the other, called upon demonstrators to abandon violence. "Córdoba, epicentro de la violencia," *La Gaceta*, March 17, 1971, 6.

17. "La muerte de un estudiante," *La Gaceta*, June 25, 1972, 6.

18. See, for example, editorials from May 28, 1969, "Una inútil y peligrosa violencia," and March 14, 1971, "Violencia en Córdoba."

19. In "Terrorismo: Buenos días, agente . . . ," *Panorama*, no. 158 (May 5–11, 1970): 12, a typical reference to the "amazement of the silent majority" in the face of the attacks of "subversive commandos" can be seen. An allusion to "the majority currents of the citizenry, obviously moderate" can be found in "Terror en el vacío," *Análisis*, no. 472 (March 31–April 6, 1970): 23.

20. "Editorial: Salir de la trampa," *Análisis*, no. 445 (September 23–29, 1969): 23.

21. "Sin guión, sin plan," *Análisis*, no. 433 (July 1–7, 1969): 23.

22. "Que el ruido no nos aturda," *Gente*, no. 206 (July 3, 1969).

23. "Gobierno, ¿qué quieren las Fuerzas Armadas?," *Panorama*, no. 161 (May 26–June 1, 1970): 10.

24. "Cartas: Violencia," *Panorama*, no. 131 (October 28–November 3, 1969).

25. *Panorama* magazine, for example, was already speaking of a "party of violence" in 1970, referring to different groups who carried out violent actions. "El terrorismo: Avatares del personaje del año," *Panorama*, no. 192 (December 29, 1970–January 4, 1971): 19.

26. *Análisis*, no. 534 (June 8–14, 1971), 21.

27. "Gobierno: La estrategia de aproximación indirecta," *Panorama*, no. 214 (June 1–7, 1971): 9.

28. Marías, a disciple of José Ortega y Gasset, had great prestige in Argentina. In 1970, his lectures in the San Martín Theater in Buenos Aires were reproduced for the great number of people that were not able to enter the theater. That year, he also participated in a television series broadcast by *Teleonce*. See "Su mejor alumno," *Análisis*, no. 482 (June 9–15, 1970): 50–52.

29. "Diálogo de Julián Marías con dos jóvenes izquierdistas," *Gente*, no. 308 (June 17, 1971): 84–86.

30. "Esta semana," *Panorama*, no. 185 (November 10–16, 1970): 3. Víctor Massuh's book was called *La libertad y la violencia*. In the middle of the decade, he published another book in which he affirmed: "Nihilism is a terrorist bomb placed in the contemporary culture to make it explode into a thousand pieces. [. . .] Nihilism seeks to be alone with destruction, in its state of maximal purity." Víctor Massuh, *Nihilismo y experiencia extrema* (Buenos Airess: Sudamericana, 1975), 123.

31. "La vida como partido," *Carta Política*, no. 37 (November 1976): 11. On November 2, 1976, Massera declared: "Here and all over the world today, those who are in favor of death and those who are in favor of life are in struggle."

32. "Violencia indiscriminada," *La Capital*, October 19, 1969.

33. "Desenfreno de violencia y represión," *La Capital*, June 25, 1969.

34. "Ante la dolorosa situación," *La Capital*, September 19, 1969.

35. "Ante la violencia desenfrenada," *La Capital*, March 17, 1971.

36. "Informe sobre subversión," *La Capital*, December 8, 1971.

37. Bores was the only person present in the documentary prepared for this research who enjoyed the approval of all the respondents.

38. Between 1957 and 1993, Tato Bores filmed twenty-nine televised series.

39. Bores's programs were broadcast on Channel 11 and 13 in Buenos Aires, Channel 10 in Tucumán, and Channel 3 in Rosario (which reached Correa) in the early 1970s.

40. Tato Bores and Carlos Ulanovsky, *Tato: Memorias inéditas y biografías del Actor Cómico de la Nación* (Buenos Aires: Emecé, 2010), 278.

41. "¿Qué pasa con Tato Bores?," *Gente*, no. 270 (September 24, 1970): 33–34.

42. "En busca del rating para el 13," *Análisis-Confirmado*, no. 633–411 (May 1–7, 1973): 48.

43. "El retorno del humor político," *Somos*, no. 103 (September 8, 1978): 68–69.

44. The declaration refers to *Poor Tato*, one of his theater series from the 1970s. Bores and Ulanovsky, *Tato: Memorias inéditas*, 74.

45. *Gente*, no. 421 (August 16, 1973): 58.

46. Bores and Ulanovsky, *Tato: Memorias inéditas*, 253–63. "The only one who didn't find me funny was Perón," Bores declared in an interview, "to the degree that in 1974, he sent me out to freeze." Documentary *Tato Bores: Actor Cómico de la Nación*, directed by Sergio Frías and Gustavo Desplats. In this same film, it is mentioned that the official who intervened in Channel 13 in 1974 alleged that Bores's program "was a program that only represented minorities." Four years later, during the military dictatorship, he remembered this episode. In an empty studio, fighting off nightmares of the past, Tato said: "All this for making a joke about the green eyes of don José López Strega," an allusion to Perón's minister of social welfare, José López Rega. "El retorno del humor político," *Somos*, no. 103 (September 8, 1978): 68–69.

47. His relevance was acknowledged by the political powers. In June 1980, the interior minister Albano Harguindeguy, in a conversation with female journalists, affirmed that "the household today is penetrated more and more by the media, both radio and television, and their influence on public opinion is so great that today we don't have lunch or dinner with our family but rather with the television, today we have lunch with Mirtha Legrand and dinner with Tato Bores." Quoted in Carlos Ulanovsky, Marta Merkin, Juan José Panno, and Grabriela Tijman, *Días de radio: Historias de la radio argentina* (Buenos Aires: Espasacalpe, 1996), 355.

48. The scriptwriter was Pedro Pernías, who went by the pseudonym of Jordán de la Cazuela. The Tato–de la Cazuela duo reached a rating of 35 points, one of the highest of the different series produced by the humorist throughout his entire career.

49. Jordán de la Cazuela (Pedro Pernías), *Tato y yo* (Buenos Aires: Baesa, 1974), 133–36. Unless noted otherwise, all quotes belong to this monologue.

50. The scriptwriter for this series continued to be Jordán de la Cazuela.

51. De la Cazuela, *Tato y yo*, 139–43. Unless noted otherwise, all quotes belong to this monologue.

52. About how these womens' price control commissions operated, see the interesting article "¡Van a cobrar lo que Cámpora dijo, ni un peso más!," *El Descamisado*, no. 3 (June 5, 1973): 5.

53. De la Cazuela, *Tato y yo*, 223–27. Unless otherwise noted, all the quotes belong to this monologue.

54. The scriptwriter that year was Aldo Cammarota.

55. "Tato analiza situaciones provinciales," *Panorama*, no. 362 (May 16–22, 1974): 64–65.

56. "Rosario: La capital del miedo," *Panorama*, no. 109 (May 27–June 2, 1969): 14–16.

57. "Rosario: La capital del miedo," *Panorama*, no. 109 (May 27–June 2, 1969): 14–16.

58. "Legitimidad de la represión," *La Capital*, June 28, 1969.

59. The characterization of the political activists is from Beatriz Sarlo, *La pasión y la excepción* (Buenos Aires: Siglo XXI, 2003), 134.

60. The Tucumanazo was a student revolt that began with a demand to stop the closing of the university cafeteria and developed into a rebellion led by students.

61. Hugo Foguet, *Pretérito Perfecto* (Buenos Aires: Legasa, 1983), 43.

62. "Dos frentes contra Onganía," *Panorama*, no. 110 (June 3–9, 1969): 10.

63. *Susana Mancuso's Diary*, San Miguel de Tucumán, 1972. Author's files.

64. *Susana Mancuso's Diary*, San Miguel de Tucumán, 1972. Author's files.

65. *La Gaceta*, June 29, 1972.

66. Until 1974, student enrollment did not stop growing in the three universities mentioned. In that year, the Universidad de Buenos Aires had 166,215 students, the Universidad Nacional de Rosario 25,043, and the Universidad Nacional de Tucumán 18,903. In 1975, the Universidad de Buenos Aires saw its enrollment decrease to 152,863 students, and this tendency continued until 1980, when only 108,387 students were enrolled. In Tucumán and Rosario the downward tendency started in 1976 and finished in 1982, with 17,984 students enrolled in Rosario and 16,045 in Tucumán. Statistics from the Ministry of Education of the nation of Argentina were provided by the secretary of university policies at the request of the author.

67. Pandolfi, "Estudiantes: Rebeldes, revolucionarios o guerrilleros," *Confirmado*, no. 279 (October 21–27, 1970): 24–30.

68. The 1972 university census showed the following results: 9.6 percent of students' parents had high incomes, 64 percent had middle incomes, and 20 percent did not answer. Only 6.3 percent of students were children of low-income parents (foremen, specialized workers, and unspecialized workers). Santiago Bergadá, Guillermo Fretes, and Juan Ramos Mejía (Jr.), "Universidad: Muchos estudiantes pueden pagar," *Carta Política*, no. 37 (November 1976): 52–53.

69. "Universidad: El pulso del cambio," *Análisis*, no. 453 (November 18–24, 1969): 20.

70. "El treinta por ciento de los alumnos votó en los comicios realizados en los centros," *La Opinión*, November 12, 1972, 13.

71. See, for example, Juan Carlos Agulla, "La universidad problema," *Confirmado*, no. 260 (June 10–16, 1970): 44–46; Heriberto Kahn, "El desafío estudiantil," *Confirmado*, no. 246 (March 4–10, 1970): 20–22; Editorial, "¿Qué hacer con la universidad?," *Análisis*, no. 557 (November 19–25, 1971): 12–13.

72. See the interview with eight university students in "Estudiantes: Rebeldes, revolucionarios o guerrilleros," *Confirmado*, no. 279 (October 21–27, 1970): 24–30.

73. "Nuevo presidente de FUA: No somos los de antes," *Panorama*, no. 140 (December 30, 1969–January 5, 1970): 9.

74. Beatriz Sarlo, *La batalla de las ideas (1943–1973)* (Buenos Aires: Ariel, 2001), 74–76.

75. On the question of the university in the 1960s, see Silvia Sigal, *Intelectuales y poder en la década del sesenta* (Buenos Aires: Punto Sur, 1991).

76. "Hablan los jóvenes: Lecciones para adultos," *Panorama*, no. 249 (February 1–7, 1972): 34–37. All quotes in this paragraph come from this article.

77. "Dirigentes universitarios: Después del desborde," *Panorama*, no. 109 (May 27–June 2, 1969): 17.

78. "Estudiantes: Rebeldes, revolucionarios o guerrilleros," *Confirmado*, no. 279 (October 21–27, 1970): 24–30.

79. See Carlos Altamirano, "Montoneros," *Punto de vista* 19, no. 55 (1996): 1–9. On the relationship between Catholics and Marxists, see Sarlo, *La batalla de las ideas*, 53–57.

80. "Violencia," *Confirmado*, no. 272 (September 2–8, 1970): 10.

81. "Violencia," *Panorama*, no. 210 (May 4–10, 1971): 7.

82. Several days after the Cordobazo, Frondizi declared that "popular violence is the response to the violence which comes from above," referring to deficient salaries, taxation pressures, and the denationalization of the economy. "¿Qué les pasa a los argentinos?," *Panorama*, no. 111 (June 10–16, 1969): 7.

83. "Los jóvenes, el país y el mundo," *Gente*, no. 247 (April 16, 1970): 20–23.

84. See, for example, "La nueva generación," *Claudia*, no. 160 (September 1970); "Los jóvenes preguntan: ¿Cuánto cuesta estar de novio?," *Gente*, no. 277 (November 12, 1970); "¿De qué se habla hoy en la familia?," *Gente*, no. 305 (May 27, 1971); and "El país visto con ojos jóvenes," *Gente*, no. 333 (December 9, 1971): 68–70.

85. Some of these series were *Ruido Joven*, *Gente Joven* (Channel 7, 1970), led by Raquel Satragno (Pinky) and Emilio Ariño; *El poder joven* (Channel 7, 1971), led by Aguirre Mencía; *Adelante, juventud* (Channel 7, 1971–75), led by Ángel Magaña and Clarisa Gerbolés; *Peña Juvenil* (Channel 11, 1971), led by Professor Bonamino; *Alta Tensión* (Channel 13, 1970–71), led by Fernando Bravo; *Jóvenes en acción* (Channel 7, 1973), led by Oscar Schiaritti; *Música en libertad* (Channel 9, 1973), led by Leonardo Simons; and *Música Joven* (Channel 9, 1975), with Emilio Disi and Mónica Jouvet.

86. "La impunidad de los famosos," *Militancia*, no. 16 (September 27, 1973): 36.

87. His series *Tiempo Nuevo* was promoted as "the program created and led by Bernardo Neustadt for a healthy, vital youth!" *Análisis*, no. 472 (March 31–April 6, 1970).

88. *El profesor hippie*, Fernando Ayala (director), Aries Cinematográfica Argentina, 1969.

89. A majority of the interviewees reacted favorably to Sandrini's scenes in the documentary. This reaction included explicit support for the values expressed in his films. The support for these values also existed at the time, even in official strata. Proof of this is that the secretary of press and publications of the Peronist government named Sandrini as an artistic advisor for Argentine television in 1975. Carlos Ulanovsky, Silvia Itkin, and Pablo Sirvén, *Estamos en el aire: Una historia de la televisión en la Argentina* (Buenos Aires: Planeta, 1999), 345.

90. In the town of Correa, for example, the weekly outing of most middle-class families was to go to the town movie theater.

91. See the following films, belonging to this period (1969–74): among those starring Sandro, *Quiero llenarme de ti* (1969) and *Gitano* (1970), directed by Emilio Vieyra; *Muchacho* (1970), *Siempre te amaré* (1971), and *Destino de un capricho* (1972), directed by Leo Fleider; and *El deseo de vivir*, directed by Julio Saraceni. Among those

starring Palito Ortega, *Corazón contento* (1969), *Viva la vida* (1969), *Los muchachos de mi barrio* (1970), *Aquellos años locos* (1971), *La familia hippie* (1971), *Muchacho que vas cantando* (1971), *La sonrisa de mamá* (1972), *Me gusta esa chica* (1973), and *Yo tengo fe* (1974), all directed by Enrique Carreras. Among those starring Luis Sandrini, in addition to the already mentioned saga, directed by Fernando Ayala, were *Pimienta y Pimentón* (1970) and *Mi amigo Luis* (1972), directed by Carlos Rinaldi; *Pájaro loco* (1971), directed by Lucas Demare; and *Hoy le toca a mi mujer* (1973), directed by Enrique Carreras. Among those starring Sabú, *Vuelvo a vivir, vuelvo a cantar* (1971), directed by Julio Saraceni; and *El mundo que inventamos* (1973), directed by Fernando Siro. Among those starring Donald, *En una playa junto al mar* (1971), directed by Enrique Salaberry; *Siempre fuimos compañeros* (1973), directed by Fernando Siro; and *Un viaje de locos* (1974), directed by Rafael Cohen. One can also see, with other starring actors, Julio Porter's *El mundo es de los jóvenes* (1970); Leo Fleider's *Arriba juventud!* (1971); and Fernando Siro's *Este loco, loco Buenos Aires* (1973). This sort of film production continued throughout the entire decade and, paradoxically, ended up being associated with el Proceso. However, the characteristics attributed to the cinema of the last dictatorship (mediocre, moralizing, apolitical, and promilitary) were already present in the films that preceded it.

92. Directed by Leo Fleider, the film *Piloto de pruebas* (1972) presented two models of youth, both of which were indifferent to political questions. Of two candidates for a position on a car racing team, one of them is responsible, hardworking, and incapable of cheating, while the other embodies all the possible social vices (he is a womanizer, irresponsible, and willing to do anything to achieve his goal). The most striking part of the movie, however, is a scene three minutes long where a musical group, unrelated to the plot, sings and dances to a song on a boat with the actors present. The subject of the song is the desperate wish for a peaceful world, attributed to the youth. The lyrics read: "Peace! What people need is peace! / the whole world cries out for peace! / but first you have to understand / that you should start with your own house / because there are those that throw the stone and then hide their hand / and there are those that never remember that we are human. [. . .] Peace!, the youth cry out for peace! [. . .] And the war cries advance like poison / Killing all those that want to be good / Silencing the peoples' voice with shrapnel. [. . .] Peace!"

93. "La Creación," *Gente*, no. 480 (May 16, 1974).

94. "Las izquierdas en la Argentina: División en torno al peronismo y a la violencia," *Panorama*, no. 66 (July 30–August 5, 1968): 12.

95. "Crítico pájaro la juventud," *Análisis*, no. 458 (December 23–29, 1969): 43.

96. Contemporary press observers noted these characteristics. "No mastermind has appeared as of yet in the police reports concerning the terrorist groups," wrote Roberto Aizcorbe, "and if there exists a common denominator for the activists, it is first that of youth, and then that of belonging to the upper-middle class." "Argentina en la tormenta: ¿Anarquía o Democracia?," *Panorama*, no. 172 (August 11–17, 1970): 55. Two years later James Neilson wrote that "both here as in other countries,

the majority of the terrorists are rather well-educated middle-class youth." James Neilson, "El cautivante guerrillero de rifle y boina," *Buenos Aires Herald*, December 22, 1972, reprinted in J. Neilson, *La vorágine argentina* (Buenos Aires: Marymar, 1979), 23–24.

97. See also Beba Balvé and Beatriz Balvé, *El '69: Huelga política de masas* (Buenos Aires: Contrapunto, 1989), 16–17.

98. See, for example, Bores's 1971 monologues. De la Cazuela, *Tato y yo*, 37–40.

99. *La Voz de Correa*, November 27, 1969.

100. *La Voz de Correa*, November 25, 1982.

101. *La Voz de Correa*, June 26, 1969.

102. *La Voz de Correa*, December 31, 1970.

103. *La Voz de Correa*, December 14, 1972.

104. *La Voz de Correa*, July 29, 1971.

105. A partial exception is Alberto Monti, a young town secretary in the administration of Ángel Bellochi (1973–1976), who was tied to Justicialist sectors in the province of Santa Fe and was town president on various occasions after the return of democracy, alternating in the position with two of his relatives. He was later a representative and a provincial senator. The Monti are "the" political and Peronist family in Correa. However, in the 1970s, his active participation did not go down the radicalized route.

106. Channel 7 was available in Correa from 1961 on, and Rosario's Channel 5 and Channel 3 from their launch dates, in 1964 and 1965, respectively.

107. This information comes from my interview with their ex-leader, Alberto Ponce. August 30, 2009.

108. "El partido que tiene mayor peso en el país," *Panorama*, no. 62 (July 2–8, 1968): 6.

Three Armed Violence (1970–1977)

1. Juan Carlos Marín, "Acerca de la relación poder-saber y la relación saber-poder. (La razón de la fuerza o la fuerza de la razón)," Study Series No. 34, CICSO, 1978.

2. Prudencio García, *El drama de la autonomía militar* (Madrid: Alianza, 1995), 58–65 about the Triple A, and 53–58 about the guerrillas.

3. García, *El drama de la autonomía militar*, 440. In February 1975, the executive branch of the government issued an order, decree 261, "to neutralize and/or annihilate the actions of subversive elements acting in the Province of Tucumán." In October of the same year, this order was extended to the entire nation through decree 1711. On January 21, 1974, Perón himself had declared that "annihilating the terrorist criminal as soon as possible is a task for all of us who wish for a just, free, and sovereign homeland." Quoted in Liliana de Riz, *Retorno y derrumbe* (Mexico City: Folios, 1981), 68.

4. "Cuando la violencia intensifica su ritmo, como en el último mes de marzo, cobra dos víctimas por cada día," *La Opinión*, April 9, 1975, 10.

5. "Atención, argentinos: Esta es la nota más dolorosa del año," *Gente*, no. 543 (December 18, 1975).

6. René Girard, *La violencia y lo sagrado* (Buenos Aires: Anagrama, 1983), especially 9–45.

7. The middle classes who were not directly affected by state repression have clearer memories of guerrilla actions than those committed by armed right-wing groups, such as the Triple A. The latter, however, is remembered as a fundamental element of the chaos and anarchy that the period before el Proceso is associated with.

8. Guillermo O'Donnell, *Bureaucratic Authoritarianism: Argentina, 1966–1973, in Comparative Perspective* (Berkeley: University of California Press, 1988), 308.

9. The Spanish-language version consulted is Guillermo O'Donnell, *El Estado Burocrático Autoritario (1966–1973)* (Buenos Aires: Universidad de Belgrano, 1982), 464. In the English-language version (cited in note 8), the index is found on page 309.

10. O'Donnell, *Bureaucratic Authoritarianism*, 308.

11. See Frederick Turner, "The Study of Argentine Politics through Survey Research," *Latin American Research Review* 10 (1975): 73–116.

12. This questionnaire can be examined in: POLITICS/BUSINESS (computer file), Roper Center for Public Opinion Research, Research Study ARIPSA 1972-OP039 Version 3, Institute IPSA, SA (producer), 1972 (Storrs, CT: Roper Center for Public Opinion Research, University of Connecticut [distributor], 2006). The questionnaire also included the options "other (specify)," "don't know," and "no answer."

13. POLITICS/BUSINESS, question 24. The rest of those interviewed opted for other responses, but none of these exceeded 1.3 percent. Eighteen percent did not respond.

14. Roberto Pereira Guimarães, "Understanding Support for Terrorism," in *Juan Perón and the Reashaping of Argentina*, ed. Frederick Turner and José Enrique Miguens (Pittsburgh: University of Pittsburgh Press, 1983), 220.

15. Pereira Guimarães, "Understanding Support for Terrorism," 200.

16. Turner, "The Study of Argentine Politics," 92–93.

17. "José Enrique Miguens: Los secretos de la opinión pública," *Análisis-Confirmado*, no. 627–405 (March 20–26, 1973): 50; and "El duro golpe de las encuestas," *Análisis-Confirmado*, no. 626–404 (March 13–19, 1973): 14–17. See other comments in *Gente*, no. 412 (June 14, 1973): 96; and *Esquiú*, May 6, 1973.

18. There were four urban areas considered by the CIMS studies: Capital Federal, the greater Buenos Aires metropolitan area, Rosario, and Córdoba. To structure the social categories (upper class, upper-middle class, lower-middle class, and lower class), the studies established four indicators of socioeconomic level: education, employment, housing location, and employment of domestic workers. A score was assigned to every respondent for each variable, and, according to the result obtained from their sum, they were placed in one of the four social categories mentioned. In some of his studies Miguens segmented the classes differently. Instead of "upper"

and "lower" middle classes, he divided them into "upper middle class," "intermediate or middle middle class," and "lower middle class."

19. CIMS, "Estudio de opinión pública sobre: Medida de las insatisfacciones, y del apoyo que tiene el functionamiento del sistema existente," Estudio No. 100 (Colecciones Especiales y Archivos. Universidad de San André. 1972. The quotations of this section come from this report.

20. In 1971, not only the conservative media but a majority called these groups "subversives," "guerrillas," "terrorists," or "extremists" (less frequently "seditious" or "delinquents") without distinctions. The activist youth themselves chanted in 1973, "Yes, yes, sirs, I am a terrorist / I am a terrorist from the heart / I put the bomb, I light the fuse, I run a block and hear the explosion." "La historia del Viva Perón—Perón Vuelve," El Descamisado, no. 21 (October 9, 1973): 4–5, and no. 22 (October 16 1973): 10–11. Although this chant came from the period of the Peronist resistance, in the context of the rise of the guerrilla organizations, it implied support for their armed actions. "Terrorism" and "subversion" formed part of everyday vocabulary to the degree that even Quino's popular comic Mafalda used the terms.

21. This is 1.35 percent more than the average of the population.

22. CIMS, "Actitudes de la población urbana frente al terrorismo político, frente al terrorismo político," in Opiniones generales desde la O.P. 10 a la O.P. 24, Estudio No. 105 (Colecciones Especiales y Archivos. Universidad de San Andrés, Argentino), 252–65.

23. In October 1969, an Argentine student carried out the first hijacking of an airplane to Havana. The fear that this type of crime could spread can be seen in "Nueve días de octubre," Panorama, no. 129 (October 14–20, 1969): 9.

24. However, the press was aware of a sector of society that desired that terrorism be combated with the utmost severity from the very beginning of the guerrilla experience. When the Revolutionary Armed Forces (Fuerzas Armadas Revolucionarias) (FAR) took over the city of Garín, mortally wounding Corporal Fernando Sulling, Panorama magazine wrote that, in response to this act, "once again Argentine opinion is divided as it was before June 8th (the date of Onganía's fall): for some it is a question of applying a firm hand. [. . .] For others, it's about opening the game and calling elections." "Terrorismo: Vivir se puede, pero no dejan," Panorama, no. 171 (August 4–10, 1970): 11.

25. "Los argentinos ante la violencia," Gente, no. 358 (June 1, 1972): 32.

26. The CIMS survey conducted in January 1973 established that only 2.4 percent of the population thought that the Montoneros and FAR best represented Perón. CIMS (Centro de Investigaciones Motivacionales y Sociales), "Pronóstico electoral de las elecciones presidenciales: Resumen de las conclusiones de la encuesta realizada y algunas recomendaciones que surgen," Estudio No. 112 [O.P. 32] (Colecciones Especiales y Archivos, Universidad de San Andrés, Argentina).

27. "Personaje del año: El argentino medio," Panorama, no. 244 (December 28, 1971–January 3, 1972): 28–31. All the testimonies cited come from the same article.

28. The "Gran Acuerdo Nacional" was the name that General Lanusse gave to his project to find a political exit from the de facto regime.

29. Alejandro Lanusse, *Mi testimonio* (Buenos Aires: IEA, 1977), 10–11.

30. "Sondeos a los anónimos," *Análisis*, no. 531 (May 18–24, 1971): 40.

31. The sensibility of the middle class toward inflation and housing was reflected in a survey conducted by A&C in 1968. In larger proportion than other sectors, the middle class recognized the "Argentine Revolution" government's anti-inflation plan and measures relating to rent and housing. See "Dos Años de Onganía," *Primera Plana*, no. 287 (June 25–July 1, 1968): 20–22.

32. Quino, *Panorama*, no. 201 (March 2–8, 1971): 74.

33. "Personaje del año: El argentino medio," *Panorama*, no. 244 (December 28, 1971–January 3, 1972): 28–31.

34. Robert Clyde Allen, *Speaking of Soap Operas* (Chapel Hill: University of North Carolina, 1985).

35. The soap opera was first broadcast in March 1972 and finished in December of the following year, with an average close to thirty rating points (each point meant twelve thousand television sets tuned in). The series was so successful that Channel 13 rebroadcast it in 1979. Additionally, it obtained recognition from the entertainment industry: in 1973 it won the Martín Fierro prize for the best program of its genre. Its main character "attained popularity with the speed of lightning." Diego Baracchini, "Éxito. . . . . . y otras intoxicaciones," *Claudia*, no. 197 (October 1973): 57–59. At the end of 1973, *Gente* selected the author of the series as the "television man of the year" because with this series he "made us happy, made us cry, excited us." *Rolando Rivas, Taxi Driver* was, according to this magazine, "a program that captured the attention of even the most skeptical and disdainful" and "made the factory of tears run at full speed the day of its farewell." " '73 ¡Qué año! 365 días con la lupa de 'Gente,' " *Gente*, no. 445 (January 31, 1974).

36. In addition to portraits of Perón and Evita, painted slogans on doorways and walls that alluded to "uncle" Cámpora or to the electoral slogans of 1973, and references to union problems related to the Taxi Drivers Union, the soap opera incorporated the forms of 1970s politics. There were kidnappings, ransom requests, bombings, escapes, and assassinations. The critic Enrique Raab wrote that "Alberto Migré's soap opera brings with it other ideological innovations: the class struggle, stealthily presented with the relation between Rolando and Mónica Helguera Paz, takes on involuntarily realistic characteristics." "La intimidad de los demás," *Panorama*, no. 325 (August 2–8 1973): 82. Another soap opera from the same period included among its characters a young man who horrified his mother with his "subversive" appearance. It was titled *Stories of Mom and Dad* (*Historias de mamá y papá*) (Channel 9) and featured Eduardo Rudy. In September 1973, a month before the Peronist government would intervene in the television channels, a sort of (politically) committed soap opera was attempted, which had little impact. Its name was *Contrafrente*, its creator was Julián Carreño, and it was broadcast by the official channel (7).

37. "La guerrilla en la televisión," *El Descamisado*, no. 1 (May 22, 1973): 15.

38. Alberto Migré himself declared that his aspiration was to "attract equally all

the members of the family." Alicia Creus, "Televisión: Lágrimas y lucha de clases," *Panorama*, no. 326 (August 16–22, 1973): 46–48. This goes back to an older tradition in radio plays, e.g., *Los Pérez García*.

39. *Rolando Rivas, taxista*, Channel 13 and Proartel, 1972, chapter 3.

40. *Rolando Rivas, taxista*, chapter 14.

41. The quotes pertain to *Rolando Rivas, taxista*, chapter 3.

42. Rolando's taxi driver friends referred to Quique as a "rich guy," "a flower of a bum," and someone that "lived off Rolando's expense" before learning of his death (chapters 12 and 13). Once he was dead, his wife affirmed that he always treated Rolando like "a pack mule who paid for everything, up to his cigarettes" (chapter 14).

43. See *Rolando Rivas, taxista*, chapter 38.

44. "The life of Helguera Paz for the life of Enrique Rivas," said the police officer explaining the logic that drove the guerrilla group to assassinate the businessman, an equation also inspired by the political realities of those times. *Rolando Rivas, taxista*, chapter 31.

45. *Rolando Rivas, taxista*, chapter 10.

46. *Rolando Rivas, taxista*, chapter 10.

47. *Rolando Rivas, taxista*, chapter 11.

48. *Rolando Rivas, taxista*, chapter 31.

49. *Rolando Rivas, taxista*, chapter 11.

50. *Rolando Rivas, taxista*, chapter 12.

51. *Rolando Rivas, taxista*, chapter 12.

52. Much later, speaking to the priest from his childhood school about his emotional conflicts, he once again asked a similar question: "Father, why has it become so difficult to live? Why is everything, eh, everything from buying an apple to finding a partner [so hard]? Everything: politics, soccer, even chess. [. . .] There is a sort of aggression, a sort of intolerance, a sort of cruel desire to hurt ourselves instead of being happy." *Rolando Rivas, taxista*, chapter 29.

53. *Rolando Rivas, taxista*, chapter 38.

54. Nora Mazzioti, *Conversaciones con Alberto Migré: "Soy como de la familia"* (Buenos Aires: Sudamericana, 1993), 81.

55. *Rolando Rivas, taxista*, chapter 44.

56. *Rolando Rivas, taxista*, chapter 45.

57. *Rolando Rivas, taxista*, chapter 44.

58. *Rolando Rivas, taxista*, chapter 45. Another dialogue in which he speaks about the difficult national situation can be seen in chapter 51, when Eduardo Borocotó, a well-known doctor, gets in Rolando's taxi, and tells him, worried, that doctors were leaving the country.

59. *Rolando Rivas, taxista*, chapter 76.

60. The political violence of the 1970s was named in this way at an early stage by the most varied and dissimilar political and social actors. I will cite some examples, all from 1970 and 1971. In regard to the modification of Law 18,701 which established the death penalty, Levingston and Lanusse's justice minister, Jaime Perriaux,

justified its necessity to the press, claiming that it was necessary in order to fight against the "new type of criminals" who "do not hesitate to commit grave acts: armed robberies, extortion, kidnappings, and murders. [. . .] Our society is in grave danger. We are facing a war. We are at war." "Habla el ministro Perriaux: Por qué tenemos pena de muerte," *Gente*, no. 296 (March 25, 1971): 24. *Confirmado* magazine published an article titled "The Stage of the Dirty War," which was devoted to the "alarming toll of the last 10 days—5 police officers and 6 guerrillas dead." In the article, "the struggle between the security forces and the insurrectional organizations" was characterized as a "dirty war—in military terms—that began in mid-1969." "Subversión: La etapa de la guerra sucia," *Confirmado*, no. 334 (November 9, 1971): 14. The Private University Union (Sindicato de Universidades Privadas), which depended on the Unionist University Confederation (Confederación Sindical Universitaria), distributed a pamphlet which affirmed: "The year is now over. Let the enemy prepare themselves. Next year we will put an end to the homosexuality propagated by Marxist theology. We will demolish the theft institutionalized by Jesuit phariseeism. We will not accept dialogue with the deceitful businessmen of culture. They will have to accept the dialogue of justice. They fall under the force of the truth. To the bureaucracy: War. To lies: War. To theft: War. And the war will come with bullets." *Primera Plana*, no. 460 (November 23, 1971): 17. After assassinating Osvaldo Sandoval, deputy chief of political affairs of the federal police, the Alejandro Baldú brigade of the Argentine Liberation Forces (Fuerzas Argentinas de Liberación) (FAL) justified the crime, affirming: "this is a just war, a revolutionary war. The repression has increasingly become a dirty war." "Guerrilla: Claves para Crystabel," *Panorama*, no. 187 (November 24–30, 1970): 10. In June 1971, after kidnapping the English consul Sylvester in Rosario, the People's Revolutionary Army (ERP) declared in a communiqué that it considered "a civil war inevitable," and that, moreover, it believed that it had already begun. "Los guerrilleros de la estrella roja," *Panorama*, no. 214 (June 1–7, 1971): 10.

61. The Teleonce (Channel 11) and Telenoche (Channel 13) news programs in the early 1970s frequently made references in their reporting about the foreignness of the guerrillas and about the population's surprise in regard to guerrilla actions.

62. "Caso Aramburu: ¿La eclosión de un tercer frente?," *Panorama*, no. 162 (June 2–8, 1970): 10.

63. See also "Si no llega la luz verde hay esquinas peligrosas," *Panorama*, no. 223 (August 3–9, 1971): 8–9, where, in response to the bombing of the Rosario Golf Club, the magazine warned that "both the right and the ultra-left are lighting the bonfires of ideological war to bombard the so-called GAN [the Great National Agreement/Gran Acuerdo Nacional]. The majority of Argentines, obviously, will remain on the sidelines of this battle."

64. "Caso Sallustro (II): Ningún plazo expira al mediodía," *Panorama*, no. 257 (March 28–April 3, 1972): 13–14.

65. "Caso Sallustro (II): Ningún plazo expira al mediodía," *Panorama*, no. 257 (March 28–April 3, 1972): 13–14.

66. Mariano Grondona, "La violencia," *Gente*, no. 351 (April 13, 1972): 18.

67. For non-Peronist sectors of the middle classes, the assassination of Aramburu seems to have been equally reprehensible.

68. *La Voz de Correa*, July 1, 1971.

69. *La Voz de Correa*, May 18, 1972.

70. Only one person remembered having supported not only this assassination but also other assassinations of military officials and businessmen. This support, however, was not based on political-ideological agreement with the armed groups. In response to my question of "what perception did you have of the guerrillas in those years?" Ricardo Montecarlo (a medical student who was not active politically within the Universidad Nacional de Tucumán during the early 1970s) responded: "I accept the guerrillas as guerrillas. But not their political ideas. In terms of trying to confront the dictatorship, the guerrilla movement seemed correct to me, right? They had to give the Army and the government a slap, strike them. I think that this must have been the only way to protest. I agree more with the guerrillas in the mountains than with the urban guerrillas. The urban guerrillas I didn't see so well because they had killed innocent people, no? I agreed more with the guerrillas in the mountains." The "slap" that the army needed to receive did not, however, translate to support for the revolutionary cause. Ricardo also mentioned that the guerrilla violence ended up going out of control. "We were living in a situation of tremendous insecurity," he commented about the period of Isabel's government, "and you don't know who was going to go down [. . .]. Here there were mistakes. They were uncontrolled, they went too far, both the guerrillas and the Armed Forces. More the Triple A than the Armed Forces. [. . .] It was out of control, both sides went out of control."

71. "Contra el país y la voluntad popular," *La Gaceta*, April 5, 1973.

72. "Las memorias de Agapito Chancalay," *La Gaceta*, September 16, 1971. See also the column from November 11, 1971.

73. For a similar declaration from the paper's editorial section, see "Vigencia del crimen político," *La Gaceta*, August 28, 1970, 4. This emphasis on society's responsibility for the violence would disappear after 1971.

74. Agapito Chancalay, "Gubay, che 72," *La Gaceta*, December 31, 1972.

75. "Un agravio contra nosotros mismos," *La Gaceta*, February 15, 1971, 4.

76. Months before, similar actions were carried out at the Monument to the Flag in the city of Rosario. *La Capital* declared that "no link can exist between a population like our own, characterized by its hardworking spirit, committed to general and individual development, and these agents that attempt to sow anarchy, unsuccessfully and without support." "Atentados agraviantes," *La Capital*, July 28, 1970.

77. POLITICS/BUSINESS (computer file). Roper Center for Public Opinion Research, Study ARIPSA1972-OP039 Version 3. Institute IPSA, SA [producer], 1972. Storrs, CT: Roper Center for Public Opinion Research, University of Connecticut (distributor), 2006, question 25.

78. Of subjects, 2.47 percent opted not to answer this question.

79. Of respondents, 2.06 percent answered that they had "other" motives, dis-

tributed in the following form: "liberate Argentina, improve the country" (0.88 percent), "seek their own benefit" (0.63 percent), and "seek the good of the people" (0.55 percent).

80. "Caso Sallustro (II): Ningún plazo expira al mediodía," *Panorama*, no. 257 (March 28–April 3, 1972): 13–14.

81. This was also true in state discourse. In 1971, the justice minister asserted that subversive crime was "almost the flipside of the common criminal: we have boys and girls whose ages range between 20 and 28 years old, well educated, frequently university students, and, in some cases, members of prominent families." "Habla el ministro Perriaux: Por qué tenemos pena de muerte," *Gente*, no. 296 (March 25, 1971): 24.

82. Landrú, *Gente paqueta* (Buenos Aires: Orion, 1972), 54–55.

83. *El Burgués*, no. 7 (July 21, 1971). With President Perón reminding the Peronist left that its leaders came from the upper classes, the union movement was the enemy. In a letter that accused the Peronist guerrillas of being Marxists and murderers, the Peronist Unionist Youth (Juventud Sindical Peronista) described Firmenich and Quieto, the leaders of Montoneros and FAR, respectively, as "two adventurers, mercenaries born in the very source of the oligarchy that has already been defeated by the People." "Agravian al pueblo y ofenden a Perón," *La Razón*, October 22, 1973.

84. Jorge Lozano, "La patria infantil," *Carta Política*, no. 1 (winter 1974): 13.

85. James Neilson, "Contra la tendencia a la anarquía," *The Buenos Aires Herald*, March 15, 1974, 47, reprinted in J. Neilson, *La vorágine argentina* (Buenos Aires: Marymar, 1979), 46–48. Less thoughtfully, he also called them "leftist terrorist gangs" and "deserters, thirsty for blood" and compared them with the fanatics who sympathized with Hitler.

86. Bernardo Neustadt, "¿Se preguntó Ud: Cuántas Ana María González hay?," *Gente*, no. 571 (July 1, 1976): 76–77.

87. Bullrich reflected on the cultural role of the Argentine middle classes. "We have an admirable, patient, long-suffering, studious, hard-working middle class," she affirmed in an interview, "for me, the boom of the Argentine novel was created by the middle class because these people read a lot, they inform themselves, they love art, and many times they've made sacrifices to buy a painting." Interview with Silvina Bullrich, "Virtudes y defectos de los argentinos," *Gente*, no. 685 (September 7, 1978): 58. See also "Con la actuación estelar de Borges, Mujica Láinez y Silvina Bullrich," *Somos*, no. 127 (February 23, 1979): 47. Moreover, like the majority of bestselling authors, Bullrich wrote for the middle class. Months before publishing *Mal Don*, in response to the question "Who do you write for?" Bullrich responded: "I write for Argentines and, among them, primarily for students, women, and some professionals"; she believed that her success stemmed from the fact that her books "speak of what I have inside me and what 24 million Argentines have inside them;" because of this, "the country" read her. "La increíble y larga historia de Silvina Bullrich y su oficio desalmado," *Claudia*, no. 186 (November 1972): 71–72. Writing from

a critical perspective, Kado Kostzer and Marcial Berro agreed that Bullrich wrote for the middle classes. "Whether you like it or not, she dominates," they wrote in 1971, "the art of making a certain side (the least difficult) of literature accessible to a small and not-so-small bourgeoisie that demonstrates an eagerness to cultivate themselves, although they do not always put the corresponding effort into this." "Bullrich: El best-seller de la playa," *Panorama*, no. 198 (February 9–15, 1971): 50.

88. "La opinión pública y su veredicto actual," *La Opinión*, December 30, 1973, 14. Between July 1973, the date of the novel's release, and February 1974, the publisher reprinted two editions of twenty thousand and ten thousand copies, respectively. . . . Bullrich maintained a significant level of public exposure throughout all of the 1970s and even the 1980s. In 1977, *Gente* magazine selected her as one of its people of the year. To justify this choice, the magazine wrote: "Silvina Bullrich. The best-selling writer. The country reads her. The world praises her." "Las 77 caras del '77," *Gente*, no. 648 (December 22, 1977). Her success, however, found no echo among scholarly critics or politically committed sectors (see Alberto Speratti, "Reportajes frustrados: Silvina Bullrich," *Humor* (November 1978): 60–61).

89. Silvina Bullrich, *Mal Don* (Buenos Aires: Emecé, 1973), 82.

90. Bullrich, *Mal Don*, 82–85.

91. "All these chalets [in Punta del Este], all these immense towers that have shot up have Punta as their 'stage set,' but all that it takes (from the first scoop to the first artisan) comes from Maldonado. All this inspired *Mal Don* a little. I tried to demonstrate that we live in an evolving society and that the grandson of a Maldonado housewife can grow up to be a banker. From this I inferred that any form of social resentment is unjustifiable." "Recorra Punta del Este con Silvina Bullrich," *Gente*, no. 604 (February 17, 1977): 17–18.

92. On the topic, Carlos Etecheverría, who was a young Buenos Aires man employed in a bank in the 1970s, remembered: "In general, terrorism was not looked upon positively. Well, that was logical. Imagine—today I live in an apartment tower where 204 people live. I wouldn't live in this building during the period of the dictatorship. It's that simple. People moved! When they learned that a colonel lived on the fifth floor, for fear of being blown through the air because you didn't know what the hell that colonel was doing and you didn't know where the bomb would be coming from. [. . .] It was totally normal that you could be waiting for a bus, and then, suddenly, a bomb would explode fifty meters away. Then, hell, we didn't live so peacefully."

93. http://members.fortunecity.com/foroverdad/listadoatentad.htm.

94. The same attack against the police bus was also evoked by other people in the town.

95. "Carta: Terrorismo," *Panorama*, no. 181 (October 13–19, 1970): 4. Several months before, the magazine itself had spoken of a "Homeland in danger" due to terrorism and appealed to all citizens to fight against it. "One thing is certain," *Panorama* wrote after the takeover of the city of Garín by the Revolutionary Armed Forces (*Fuerzas Armadas Revolucionarias*) (FAR), "the security forces are impo-

tent against the surprise. It would be right to declare that the Homeland is in danger and mobilize every citizen in the labor of civic vigilance against violence. Each person needs to choose to defend the system, the citizenry needs to shake off inertia." "Terrorismo: Vivir se puede, pero no dejan," *Panorama*, no. 171 (August 4–10 1970): 11.

96. This vision is not limited to nonactivist sectors. Humberto Saldaña, an activist and student leader in the Engineering School of the Universidad Nacional de Tucumán, and political prisoner from 1975 to 1981, made an observation that coincided with Claudio's. "I believe that in the 1970s," Humberto commented, "a very large part of society was politicized. But not only because of politics, but also because it was in fashion. You would flirt with a girl, and if you didn't know what was happening in the university cafeterias, where your university life took place . . . [you wouldn't get anywhere]. And the form of dialogue, of interacting, was this. . . ."

97. Rodolfo Pandolfi, "Estudiantes: Rebeldes, revolucionarios o guerrilleros," *Confirmado*, no. 279 (October 21–27, 1970): 24.

98. Norma is referring to the ERP's failed attempt to take over the 601 Viejo Bueno weapons depot, in the Buenos Aires municipality of Monte Chingolo in December 1975. The newspapers reported a minimum of one hundred casualties over the next several days. See "Pasarían de 100 los extremistas muertos," *La Nación*, December 26, 1975, and "100 Muertos: Ataque subversivo a unidad del ejército," *Última Hora*, December 24, 1975. Although it turned out that there were no more than fifty guerrillas killed, the episode undoubtedly had a great impact on public opinion. About this act, see Gustavo Plis-Sterenmerg, *La batalla de Monte Chingolo* (Buenos Aires: Planeta, 2006).

99. The closest to this vision that can be found in the press of the time are some declarations of guerrillas' relatives that, upon discovering that someone in their family was implicated in an armed action, suspected that they had been manipulated. See "Mi hijo Firmenich," *Gente*, no. 261 (July 23, 1970): 16. In the phase where he confronted his own youthful followers, Perón also accused the guerrilla leaders of having contaminated them. The youth were portrayed as "tricked" and "led by people who did not deserve this leadership," who "don't support either the country or its people but rather the cunning of evil." "El discurso del general," *El Descamisado*, no. 26 (November 13, 1973): 4–5.

100. "It is possible that this impressive [death] toll of the episode in Monte Chingolo, both known and unknown," *Criterio* editorialized, "produced a feeling of relief among many people: one hundred dead are one hundred fewer enemies, and the more the better, no matter what the manner of the death may have been." "La guerra y la paz," *Criterio*, no. 1731–1732 (January 22, 1976): 4. Several months later, the *Buenos Aires Herald* made a similar commentary. "Many people, moreover, who are respectable," wrote Neilson, "believe that the leftists, whether they be bomb-throwing activists or spacey idealists, deserve the death penalty. Needless to say, they do not call for this to be written in the penal code, but they do accept the violent deaths of leftists with total equanimity. They are horrified if the person killed

did not have a known political affiliation. If a leftist is murdered, however, then this is enough for an explanation, the killing is understandable. This type of mentality seems to have gained much ground in Argentina in recent times." James Neilson, "Civilizacion y salvajismo," *Buenos Aires Herald*, May 28, 1976, reprinted in J. Neilson, *La vorágine argentina* (Buenos Aires: Marymar, 1979), 66–68.

101. This reading was "made official" and not created, since a genealogy of this theory reveals that the characterization of the radicalized political struggle in terms of two types of violence or even two terrorisms in conflict was present since the beginning of the 1970s. Unlike commonly thought, the "theory of the two demons" did not originate in the state and impose itself on civil society. Part of the press and even the first human rights organizations shared this characterization of armed violence. I have elaborated on this argument in "La violencia 'de los dos lados.' Hacia una genealogía de la teoría de los dos demonios (1969–76)," mimeo, 2014. See also Hugo Vezzetti, *Pasado y presente: Guerra, dictaduro y sociedad en la Argentina* (Buenos Aires: Siglo XXI, 2003).

102. "Cinco opiniones sobre la violencia en Argentina," *Panorama*, no. 172 (August 11–17, 1970): 57.

103. "Los argentinos ante la violencia," *Gente*, no. 358 (June 1, 1972): 22.

104. "¿De qué hablan hoy los argentinos?," *Gente*, no. 463 (June 6, 1974): 108–11.

105. The survey covered a thousand cases, half of which were in Capital Federal and the other half in Avellaneda, Ciudadela, San Martín, Martínez, and San Isidro. "Random sampling" methodology was used. Unfortunately, the magazine that published the poll did not mention which company conducted it. See "El cambio, según la opinión pública," *Extra*, no. 131 (May 1976): 14–15.

106. Of the subjects, 16 percent did not respond.

Four State Violence (1974–1982)

1. Juan E. Corradi, Eldon Kenworthy, and William Wipfler, "Argentina de hoy: Un régimen de terror. Informe sobre la represión desde julio de 1973 hasta diciembre de 1974," documentary supplement to "Argentina 1973–1976: The Background to Violence," by J. E. Corradi, E. Kenworthy, and W. Wipfler, appearing in the LASA Newsletter, Latin American Studies Association, September, 1976, 25–27.

2. Corradi, Kenworthy, and Wipfler, "Argentina 1973–1976: The Background to Violence," LASA Newsletter, Latin American Studies Association, September, 1976.

3. Corradi, Kenworthy, and Wipfler, "Argentina de hoy: Un régimen de terror," 1, 11.

4. See, for example, the following testimony. The witness "stated that he had been driven, blindfolded, to a certain site where he was tortured from the 9th [May 1974]: 'I believe that the first time they used two cattle prods at the same time, because of the frequency and consistency that they passed them everywhere, especially the lips and testicles.' After calling him a 'Montonero son of a bitch,' they put his head in a plastic bag, keeping it there until he began to suffocate. 'They threatened me, say-

ing that they had my wife and had all already raped her. At that moment, I went into cardiac arrest, from which they brought me out by massaging my heart.'" Corradi, Kenworthy, and Wipfler, "Argentina de hoy: Un régimen de terror," 54.

5. Corradi, Kenworthy, and Wipfler, "Argentina de hoy: Un régimen de terror," 114, 138, 140, 163–66, 212–13, and 220–21.

6. Corradi, Kenworthy, and Wipfler, "Argentina 1973–1976: The Background to Violence," 13, 15, 26–27.

7. See Inés Izaguirre, "El problema y la historia de la investigación," in I. Izaguirre and collaborators, *Lucha de clases, guerra civil y genocidio en la Argentina (1973–1983)* (Buenos Aires: Eudeba, 2009), 20.

8. The idea of throwing corpses in the river or throwing live people from helicopters or airplanes, however, were already mentioned in LASA's report. Corradi, Kenworthy, and Wipfler, "Argentina de hoy: Un régimen de terror," 234–42, 247–48.

9. As an example, see the news article about more than fifty disappearances and detentions reported to the Federal Court in the Criminal section and Correctional no. 4 by Dr. Daffis René Niklison: "Piden ubicar a detenidos o desaparecidos," *La Opinión*, September 5, 1975. Also see "Secuestros: La normalidad de lo anormal," *Primera Plana*, no. 452 (September 28, 1971): 14; and "Fue denunciada la desaparición de otras seis personas," *La Opinión*, December 17, 1974.

10. See, for example, "Así se fue moviendo la conspiración," *El Descamisado*, no. 9 (July 17, 1973): 10.

11. Rafael Braun, "Contra la tortura," *Criterio*, no. 1644 (May 25, 1972): 269–70.

12. The quote is from Paco Urondo in his comment about the premiere of Augusto Boal's *Torquemada*. "La tortura, elemento inherente a sistemas políticos dominantes," *La Opinión*, July 4, 1972.

13. In July 1973, the documentary *Informes y testimonios* premiered in Buenos Aires, about the tortures suffered by political prisoners during the "Argentine Revolution," made by alumni of the film department of the Escuela Superior de Bellas Artes of the Universidad Nacional de La Plata. "Impresionante documental sobre la tortura en el país," *La Opinión*, July 26, 1973, 30. A year before, the artist Luis Pazos exhibited in the Art and Communication Center his work *Project for a Monument for the Disappeared Political Prisoner*, which consisted of a figure of a black coffin, without any name identified. A reproduction can be seen in "Las obras de la revolución," *Primera Plana*, no. 496 (August 1, 1972): 51. In 1971, the jury of the Second National Contest of Visual Investigations gave the Grand Prize of Honor of the Second National Fine Arts Exhibition to the work *Made in Argentina*, from the fine artists Ignacio Colombres and Hugo Pereyra, which consisted of a large box made of transparent acrylic, inside of which was a broken human figure whose hands and feet were tied together with ropes, tangled up in an electric cable that ended with a cattle prod at the side of the box, with a voltage regulator included. The description can be seen in "Censura y picana eléctrica," *Militancia*, no. 23 (November 15, 1973): 41. During 1973 and 1974, the cast of the Payró Theater presented Eduardo Tato Pavlovsky's play *El señor Galíndez*, which denounced, as the author remembered years later, "a new social

monstrosity: torture as an institution." *Página 12*, October 28, 1994. The advertisement that announced this work asked, "Is torture a profession?" *Militancia*, no. 14 (September 13, 1973): 51. The play was performed in the Payró Theater in Buenos Aires; a tour in the interior provinces of the country included Rosario and Tucumán, among other cities.

14. For a study of this organization, see Ignacio González Janzen, *La triple A* (Buenos Aires: Contrapunto, 1986).

15. "La ofensiva de la derecha," *Militancia*, no. 17 (October 4, 1973): 3. Also see "Orden de matar," *Militancia*, no. 22 (November 8, 1973): 13; and "¿Hay comandos policiales?," no. 35 (February 21, 1974): 10. Similar allegations can be found in another newspaper of Peronist activism; see "La policía de Calabró tortura peronistas," *El Descamisado*, no. 41 (February 26, 1974): 22–24.

16. "La ofensiva de la derecha," *Militancia*, no. 17 (October 4, 1973): 3.

17. "Adonde vamos," *Militancia*, no. 34 (February 7, 1974): 6.

18. *Militancia*, no. 32 (January 24, 1974): 6.

19. "Entre la definición y la violencia," *Militancia*, no. 35 (February 21, 1974): 4–9. Since his return to the country, Perón had defined himself against the expectations of the leftist sectors of his movement. In August 1973, he promised to apply the full force of the law to the "ultra-left," and, he said, "we aren't afraid to be outside of the law either." Rodolfo Terragno, *El peronismo de los 70: De Cámpora a Isabelita (I)* (Buenos Aires: Capital Intelectual, 2005), 50.

20. The designations of Alberto Villar as a deputy chief of the Federal Police and officer Luis Margaride as chief of the Federal Security Superintendency were a symbol of the repressive hardening of the state. The military summary trials for repressive abuses committed in Córdoba that weighed on the former and the general indignation that the latter aroused for having been the symbol of the moralizing vocation of Onganía's government were brushed aside by the Peronist government. The point was to give a clear signal to the combative sectors of their movement that the state decision to repress was firm. The activist youth understood this when, doubling the bet on the first anniversary of Cámpora's election victory, they chanted, "Montonero, the people ask you, we want Villar and Margaride's heads." "Palabras de Firmenich," *Militancia*, no. 37 (March 14, 1974): 38–42.

21. "Discurso del General Perón en la CGT," November 2, 1973, http://www.libre opinion.com/members/justicialismo/libros/peron/jdp_comorg_3.htm (my emphasis).

22. Heriberto Kahn, "La existencia del otro yo," *Carta Política*, no. 13 (spring 1974): 14.

23. Jorge Lozano, "La prueba de la violencia," *Carta Política*, no. 3 (winter 1974): 3.

24. "Carta de la dirección," *Carta Política*, no. 24 (fall 1975): 1.

25. Various political leaders shared this diagnosis. Rafael Martínez Raymonda, one of the main leaders of the Democratic-Progressive Party, asserted in 1975 that "never before have the people unanimously had the sensation that the ground beneath their feet has disappeared. . . . We are invaded by the anguish of feeling

that we are in the most absolute vacuum." "Todavía hay salida. . . ." Extra, no. 122 (August 1975): 17. Rogelio Frigerio, a developmentalist, declared in early 1976 that "we have to reconstruct not only the government, but also the State, which is in a process of decomposition. The state apparatus has to recover the monopoly of force that the subversive groups dispute today. They have to achieve an operational consistency that they lack now." "Encuesta: ¿Qué tendría que ocurrir en la Argentina en 1976? Pero, ¿qué piensa usted que va a ocurrir?," Extra, no. 127 (January 1976): 30. Perón himself had declared in 1974, justifying the hardening of the penal code, that "the citizens no longer have the security that the State has the obligation to give them." These declarations were even published in general interest and women's magazines. See, for example, "Para usted que quiere saber: Así se reformó el código penal para combatir la violencia," Para Ti, no. 2692 (February 11, 1974): 4–5.

26. Carlos Floria, "Sobre los reaccionarios," Carta Política, no. 12 (spring 1974): 24.

27. A survey conducted between March 27 and April 2, 1976, in Buenos Aires and its surrounding metropolitan area determined that 78 percent of respondents judged that the recently deposed government "lacked effectiveness." Only 9 percent believed that it was capable, and 13 percent abstained from responding. Seventy-one percent declared that they were in favor of the intervention and only 12 percent opted for critical responses. "El cambio, según la opinión pública," Extra, no. 131 (May 1976): 14–15. There were one thousand people consulted, five hundred in Buenos Aires city and five hundred in the metropolitan area.

28. See Tulio Halperín Donghi, La larga agonía de la Argentina peronista (Buenos Aires: Ariel, 1994), 93–94.

29. See Serge Moscovici, Social Representations: Explorations in Social Psychology (New York: New York University Press, 2001), 47, 72, 158–59.

30. Between 1930 and 1976, only Justo and Perón—in his first period—finished their legal mandates.

31. "Tácticas del miedo," La Opinión, January 2, 1976. The paramilitary terror under the Peronist government was labeled as "genocidal" by about fifteen civil associations. See "¿Quién rinde cuenta de los culpables?," La Opinión, January 30, 1976.

32. During the death rattles of the military regime installed in 1976, Peter Waldmann wrote that when the coup occurred, Argentines "had been accustomed in the meantime to the new situation in such a way that terror only drew their attention when they had some relation to the victim. The guerrillas were, if not the only, the principal cause of this change in mentality." Peter Waldmann, "Anomia social y violencia," in Argentina, hoy, ed. Alain Rouquié (Buenos Aires: Siglo XXI, 1982), 206–48.

33. Some media sources made explicit the existence of what I call an "inertial structure." In response to the decision of the director of the Buenos Aires Herald to flee the country because of threats, Confirmado wrote that "at some point, we will have to return to a situation in which episodes like Mr. [Robert] Cox's are nothing short of unimaginable. Of course, here habit is important, and the fact is that, after a decade of violence, our capacity to be shocked has been dulled, the necessity to live pushes

us forward and we tend to underestimate that which, seen from other latitudes, is alarming." "Caso Cox: Las dos visiones," *Confirmado*, no. 519 (December 13, 1979): 5.

34. Rodolfo Walsh's famous letter to the military government, written on the first anniversary of the coup d'état, captures the emergence into the open of the secret task forces when it affirmed that "the 3A is now the 3 Arms [different branches of the military], and the Junta that you preside over is not the guardian over the balance of 'violences of a different sign' nor the just referee between 'two terrorisms,' but rather the very source of the terror that has lost its way and can only babble its discourse of death." Rodolfo Walsh, "Carta abierta de Rodolfo Walsh a la Junta Militar," in R. Walsh, *El violento oficio de escribir. Obra periodística (1953–1977)* (Buenos Aires: de la Flor, 2008), 433.

35. See "El primer ex gobernador condenado," *Gente*, no. 566 (May 27, 1976). Judged by a Special Military Tribunal, the Peronist ex-governor Enrique Cresto was found guilty of the crime of "possession of arms and explosives." The title of the article reflected the sensation that the military government wanted to transmit to the population quite well: the verdict was the first of a series that promised to be more extensive, something that excited part of the society. In June 1976, *Gente* conducted interviews on board a taxi with middle-class citizens (an economist, an architect, a designer, a law student, and a publicist). Several of these interviewees mentioned that they hoped that the new authorities would imprison those who had governed the country before March 24. "¿Quiere saber lo que piensa la gente? Maneje un taxi y entérese," *Gente*, no. 568 (June 10, 1976).

36. This judgment still survives in the memories of the middle classes. There were a variety of memories and judgments of Perón, Lanusse, and even Videla. This was not the case for Isabel and her government.

37. Ernesto Sabato, "La argentina de este minuto," *Extra*, no. 129 (March 1976): 14–15.

38. The bombings and armed actions of the guerrillas did not disappear, but their operational capacity decreased enormously. Although the military government continued playing up the "subversive threat," the character of the armed acts that the guerrilla organizations carried out after March 24, 1976, indicated weakness instead of strength. They only served to give the military government a justification for its repression. Terror was slowly becoming the monopoly of the state.

39. "Editorial," *Cuestionario*, no. 36 (April 1976).

40. Walter Benjamin, "Theses on the Philosophy of History," in *Illuminations*, ed. and intro. Hannah Arendt, trans. Harry Zohn (New York: Harcourt, Brace and World, 1968; reprint: Schocken, 1969; 1992 reprint: Thesis VII), 253–64.

41. See, for example, "Editorial: Comenzó la contrarrevolución," *Confirmado*, no. 415 (December 1976): 6–7; and "El horizonte político," *Criterio*, no. 1757–1758 (February 24, 1977): 54. The case of *Criterio* is interesting because it was not by a pro-government magazine. It criticized the military government on its education and economic policies. However, in regard to the fight against the guerrillas as such, it accepted the military cause without many nuances, as did the majority of the media.

42. Beatriz Sarlo has called attention to this point in *Tiempo pasado: Cultura de la memoria y primera persona* (Buenos Aires: Siglo XXI, 2005).

43. At the beginning of 1976 the National Statistics and Census Institute (Instituto Nacional de Estadísticas y Censos) (INDEC) indicated that, considering only the year 1975, the cost of living had risen 353 percent. Salaries in January 1976 were the lowest they had been in fifteen years. For the press, the Rodrigazo meant the death of the middle class. "The middle class was sentenced to death on June 2nd," a journalist asserted, "and the sentence has been carried out. [. . .] The middle class has died." Horacio Chaves Paz, "El proletariado de cuello blanco ha reemplazado a la clase media," *La Opinión*, November 27, 1975, 17. Also see the series of articles that this newspaper published under the title "Requiem for the Middle Class" on June 28, 1975, each of which argued that the middle class had been battered beyond repair from different points of view. Also see "Se hunde la clase media," *Para Ti*, no. 2776 (September 22, 1975): 68–71.

44. Slavoj Žižek, *El sublime objeto de la ideología* (Buenos Aires: Siglo XXI, 2003), 64.

45. Michael Taussig, "*Maleficium*: State Fetishism," in *The Nervous System* (New York: Routledge, 1992), 111–140.

46. Taussig, "*Maleficium*: State Fetishism," 132.

47. Taussig, "*Maleficium*: State Fetishism," 132.

48. Taussig, "*Maleficium*: State Fetishism," 116 (emphasis in original).

49. I derive this idea from the Lacanian formula *le sujet supposée savoir*. Jacques Lacan, *The Four Fundamental Concepts of Psycho-analysis* (New York: W. W. Norton, 1978). So just as psychoanalytic transference is only possible when the patient assumes that the analyst is a subject who knows, so too must citizens assume that the state knows in order for a social order to be effective.

50. "Slowly, almost so that we didn't realize it was happening," affirmed Massera, "a machine of horror was unleashing its iniquity over the unsuspecting and the innocent, amid the disbelief of some, the complicity of others, and the astonishment of many." See COMA 13: *Del Cordobazo a Malvinas: Trece años de historia en imágenes*, part 2 (1975–1982).

51. This conviction constantly appears in all three sites studied. He who wasn't "in anything strange," he who wasn't "involved," he who wasn't "in the mess" or didn't have "anything to hide" was safe. I will soon go back to this.

52. Gustavo Maíño, a young man of twenty-four in Buenos Aires in 1976, was even more emphatic: "my sense toward the police and the security forces is that they were always my enemies. [. . .] It's like, I'm not with these guys [referring to the guerrillas], but these other guys [referring to the security and police forces] are against me," he said, remembering how he perceived the very presence of the police or military. A few months after the beginning of el Proceso, *Confirmado* devoted its cover article to analyzing the different challenges that the government faced, indicating the possibility that the youth would become one of them. The youth under el Proceso, according to this magazine, found themselves "in a sharpened climate of repression of everything that expresses its spontaneity [. . .], with its political

activity prohibited simultaneously inside and outside the classroom, with its religious activity [considered] suspicious and almost illegal when it goes beyond mere liturgy, [and] with a tendency to consider any activity subversive that was not clearly anti-subversive (how does one participate in 'anti-subversive activities'?) Examples of these activities would be: organizing camps, letting one's beard grow, loving, psychoanalyzing oneself, et cetera." "Los frentes de tormenta," *Confirmado*, no. 412 (September 1976): 20–23.

53. I call all the allusions to a subject that is not the one narrating and, if they include it, do so only in an undefined way "impersonal." I call "personal" the "I" register and occasionally the "we" when it refers to a reduced, defined collective that includes the speaker.

54. According to one newspaper, "practically 90 percent of Argentines talk about the imminence of a coup d'état." "Visión del país frente al golpe," *La Opinión*, March 20, 1976, 11.

55. See chapter 2 about her participation in an independent student group.

56. Martin Heidegger, *Being and Time: A Translation of Sein und Zeit*, trans. Joan Stambaugh (New York: State University of New York Press, 1996), 118–19.

57. Heidegger, *Being and Time: A Translation of Sein und Zeit*, 119.

58. Heidegger, *Being and Time: A Translation of Sein und Zeit*, 119.

59. Heidegger, *Being and Time: A Translation of Sein und Zeit*, 120.

60. Heidegger, *Being and Time: A Translation of Sein und Zeit*, 120.

61. "Caducaron los permisos para portar armas," *La Capital*, August 1, 1976.

62. "Aclaración oficial sobre armas civiles," *La Capital*, August 22, 1976.

63. See *Auto Club*, a magazine where sports occupied an important place. Until 1976, *Auto Club* included dozens of advertisements for guns and munitions, often in the same issue. After the coup, the magazine reduced, modified, or cancelled these types of ads in its pages.

64. See the April 9, 1976, editions of *Clarín* and *La Razón*.

65. "It was outrageous," the manufacturer declared; "sometimes human beings make mistakes. This is why one should have the possibility of rectifying one's mistakes." "No al 'guerrillero,'" *Gente*, no. 563 (May 6, 1976). This magazine had devoted an article to the subject, which warned that "the country is also being killed with a toy gun." "Un caso a favor: El fusil guerrillero no se fabrica más," *Gente*, no. 561 (April 22, 1976): 68–69.

66. The government advertising campaigns came from the civil society as well as from the state. "Defend Your Argentina," organized by *Para Ti* magazine in 1978, is emblematic for the impact it had and the intensity with which it involved the middle classes. It consisted of postcards with images of the country so that "every Argentine woman and her family can respond to the ferocious anti-Argentina campaign unleashed in Europe and the United States in her own handwriting," a campaign that denounced the violation of human rights by the military dictatorship. *Para Ti*, no. 2925 (July 31, 1978): 82. The "Defend Your Argentina" campaign was supported by many celebrities. Mirtha Legrand, a film actress of the 1940s and 1950s who in

the 1970s became a key figure on Argentine television—and who presented herself as a representative of the middle class (see Diego Baracchini-Mirtha Legrand, "Mirtha Legrand almuerza con Mirtha Legrand," *Claudia*, no. 191 [April 1973]: 50–53)—declared on her program on Channel 13: "the initiative seems splendid to me [. . .] I am sure that it will have enormous repercussions and the gentlemen who run the anti-Argentina campaign will be asking themselves a lot of questions from today on." It also received similar support from radio or television hosts Julio Lagos, Victor Sueyro, Fernando Bravo, Héctor Larrea, Bernardo Neustadt, and Miguel Ángel Merellano. "Entre nosotras: La Argentina está bien defendida," *Para Ti*, no. 2925 (July 31, 1978): 19. In 1979, the same magazine installed street kiosks in Buenos Aires, Córdoba, and Mendoza so that people could write their testimonies about the "real Argentina" to the members of the Inter-American Commission on Human Rights who were visiting Argentina. See "Las argentinas le escriben a la Comisión de Derechos Humanos," *Para Ti*, no. 2985 (September 24, 1979): 80.

67. *Gente*, no. 619 (June 2, 1977).

68. *Gente*, no. 648 (December 22, 1977).

69. " 'Corto' pero bueno," *Carta Política*, no. 43 (May 1977): 88.

70. *Somos*, no. 45 (July 29, 1977); and *Confirmado*, no. 420 (May 1977).

71. A commercial film also made a comical allusion to the DGI and its pursuit of tax evaders. In *Mi mujer no es mi señora* (directed by Hugo Moser, 1978), the director of an advertising agency (Alberto Olmedo) rejected an actor selected for a men's cologne saying: "the guy who sees this ad should be convinced that, if he uses this cologne, he will be chased by beautiful women. But look at the guy you brought me! This guy . . . not even the tax authorities will chase him!"

72. "El evasor es el culpable de esta campaña," *Gente*, no. 663 (April 6, 1978).

73. "A Usted le deben," *Gente*, no. 673 (June 15, 1978).

74. "Señalar al culpable," *Gente*, no. 676 (July 6, 1978).

75. "Las reglas del juego," *Gente*, no. 685 (September 7, 1978).

76. A few months after Peronism's return to power, the Ministry of the Interior complemented the modification of the law of possession of weapons and explosives with an identification campaign of kidnappers carried out by the public. Through the publication of photographs of those arrested and accused of kidnapping, the government sought to thus make society committed to its struggle against "subversion." See "Decretos sobre tenencia de armas y explosivos y difusión de solicitadas," *La Opinión*, August 5, 1973, 1.

77. "Para repartir mejor," *Confirmado*, no. 438 (May 25, 1978).

78. "Antihéroes," *Gente*, no. 677 (July 13, 1978).

79. "La gran familia," *Gente*, no. 686 (September 14, 1978).

80. "Los demás," *Gente*, no. 682 (August 17, 1978).

81. "Sabotaje," *Gente*, no. 679 (July 27, 1978).

82. "Sólo para delincuentes," *Gente*, no. 680 (August 3, 1978).

83. "Juego prohibido," *Gente*, no. 689 (October 5, 1978).

84. "Con el almanaque a favor," *Confirmado*, no. 442 (June 22, 1978).

85. "Bajo la lupa," *Gente*, no. 689 (October 5, 1978).

86. "Jaque mate," *Gente*, no. 700 (December 21, 1978).

87. "Hecha la trampa . . . hecha la ley," *La Capital*, August 31, 1978.

88. "Reflexionando," *Gente*, no. 688 (September 28, 1978).

89. "En defensa propia," *Gente*, no. 687 (September 21, 1978).

90. "Su marido en peligro," *Gente*, no. 684 (August 31, 1978).

91. "Sin respuesta," *Gente*, no. 689 (October 5, 1978).

92. "Los caminos de la razón," *Criterio*, no. 1764 (May 26, 1977): 253.

93. "No a corruptos y a subversivos," *La Capital*, May 30, 1977, 1–2.

94. Author's emphasis.

95. James Neilson, "Cómo no combatir al marxismo," *Buenos Aires Herald*, August 24, 1977, reproduced in J. Neilson, *La vorágine argentina* (Buenos Aires: Marymar, 1979), 99–101.

96. "Por qué hicimos las tarjetas," *Para Ti*, no. 2930 (September 4, 1978): 3.

97. Oscar Landi, "Cultura y política en la transición a la democracia," *Crítica y utopía latinoamericana en ciencias sociales*, no. 10–11:76.

98. The survey was conducted in Buenos Aires, the greater Buenos Aires metropolitan area, and central points of the interior provinces of the country. See *La Semana*, no. 367 (December 14, 1983): 36–42, 75.

99. Thirty-nine percent mentioned "education," 26 percent "union democracy," 23 percent "the restructuring of the Armed Forces," 19 percent a "greater respect for human rights," and 12 percent a "flourishing economy."

100. Edgardo Catterberg, *Argentines Confront Politics: Political Culture and Public Opinion in the Argentine Transition to Democracy* (Boulder, CO: Rienner, 1991), 77. The survey covered eighteen hundred cases in the districts of Buenos Aires, the greater Buenos Aires metropolitan area, Córdoba, Rosario, and Mendoza. A three-stage probabilistic technique was used.

101. "Low-formal" includes, fundamentally, workers in the formal sectors and "low-informal" poor sectors and informal workers, to which marginal citizens are added. Disapproval of the 1973–76 Peronist government reached 64 percent for the former and 59 percent for the latter.

102. "El gran plebiscito de *Gente*," *Gente*, no. 850 (November 5, 1981). The poll consisted of a questionnaire published in the magazine that 1,042 readers responded to voluntarily.

103. The Alfonsín government, however, often accompanied references to state violence with mentions of guerrilla violence, which was not only judged to be reprehensible but also viewed as preceding the state violence. Indeed, before signing decree 158/83, which ordered the trials of the three military juntas that governed during el Proceso, Alfonsín signed decree 157/83, which allowed for the indictment of guerrilla leaders. In 1985, his interior minister, Antonio Tróccoli, prefaced the televised broadcast of the *Nunca más* program—which broadcast excerpts of the trials of the military officials—by affirming "but what you are about to see is only one aspect of the drama of violence in Argentina. The other face, the other aspect,

started when subversion and terrorism erupted on Argentina's beaches, fed from distant borders, from remote lands, with a handful of men who, possessing a political project notoriously rooted in terror and with a deep messianic vocation, wanted to occupy power by force and violence and ended up unleashing an orgy of blood and violence and the deaths of people and institutions." Television program *Nunca más*, broadcast by Argentina Televisora Color (ATC), April 22, 1985. Tróccoli stated, as Horacio Jaunarena, another Alfonsín-era minister, would later tell, that the Radical government would also conduct a *Nunca más* of the Montoneros. "Una decisión política que soportó todas las presiones," *Clarín*, September 24, 2010.

104. See Sebastián Carassai, "Antes de que anochezca: Derechos humanos y clases medias en Argentina antes y en los inicios del golpe de Estado de 1976," *América Latina Hoy* 54 (April 2010): 69–96. See also Inés González Bombal, "Nunca más: El juicio más allá de los estrados," in Carlos Acuña et al., *Juicio, castigos y memorias: Derechos humanos y justicia en la política argentina* (Buenos Aires: Nueva Visión, 1995).

Excursus II A Model Kit

1. James Neilson, *En tiempo de oscuridad* (Buenos Aires: Emecé, 2001), 20.

Five Desire and Violence (1969–1975)

1. CIMS, "Estudio de opinión pública sobre: Medida de las insatisfacciones y del apoyo que tiene el funcionamiento del sistema existente," *Estudio Nro. 100* (Colecciones Especiales y Archivos, Universidad de San Andrés, Argentina). All the statistics mentioned in this paragraph come from this source.

2. POLITICS/BUSINESS (computer file), Roper Center for Public Opinion Research, Study ARIPSA 1972-OP039 Version 3, Institute IPSA, SA (producer), 1972 (Storrs, CT: Roper Center for Public Opinion Research, University of Connecticut (distributor), 2006). Achieving order or change "at all costs" as well as making "profound and accelerated" transformations were the responses of approximately 40 percent of those surveyed. The gradualist options earned the support of only a minority of respondents. A total of 2,138 people were interviewed in the entire country. This survey did not divide its results by social class.

3. For an analysis of official policies regarding mass media during much of the 1970s, see Héctor Schmucler and Margarita Zires, "El papel ideológico de los medios de comunicación: Argentina 1975, La crisis del lopezrreguismo," in *Comunicación y Cultura* 5 (Mexico City: Nueva Imagen, 1978), 119–78; and Heriberto Muraro, "La comunicación masiva durante la dictadura militar y la transición democrática en la Argentina, 1973–1986," in *Medios, transformación cultural y política*, ed. Oscar Landi (Buenos Aires: Legasa, 1987), 13–57. Also see, in this last compilation, Oscar Landi, "Medios, procesos culturales y sistema político," 89–133.

4. Consulting audiovisual sources in Argentina is not easy. However, analysts emphasize the importance of the print media market over the audiovisual market

in the advertising business of the 1970s. See "Periodismo: La revancha de las revistas," *Confirmado*, no. 393 (May 15–21, 1973): 30–32. In 1976, newspapers and magazines received 40 percent of the total amount allocated to advertising in the country, which was higher than the 32 percent that television received. "Inversiones en publicidad y promoción durante 1976," *Gente*, no. 643 (November 17, 1977).

5. Edgar Morin, "La industria cultural," in Theodor Adorno and E. Morin, *La industria cultural* (Buenos Aires: Galerna, 1967), 23.

6. See Stuart Hall's classic text, "Encoding-Decoding," in *Culture, Media, Language* (London: Hutchinson, 1980), 129–139; and W. Russell Neuman, *The Future of the Mass Audience* (Cambridge: Cambridge University Press, 1991). Referring to Latin America, see Juan Franco's pioneering essay, "What's in a Name? Popular Culture Theory and Its Limitations," in *Studies in Latin American Popular Culture*, no. 1 (1982): 5–14.

7. Morin, "La industria cultural."

8. Some of these products could have transcended the scope of the middle classes. This should not lead us to lose sight of the fact that they were conceived, designed, and promoted with a specific social audience in mind.

9. Influenced by Umberto Eco's *Apocalípticos e integrados ante la cultura de masas* and by the Frankfurt School, this researcher denounced the dehumanization to which society was submitted by consumption. Beyond that, de Behar's work is a faithful testimony to the centrality that advertising acquired during the late 1960s in countries such as Uruguay and Argentina. "One smokes, drinks, dresses, loves, speaks, and thinks like the 'star' of the day," de Behar wrote; "the most cherished values of our civilization are derived from the stunning blonde model who, among other superfluities, insinuates delights spilling foam from a beer pitcher; of the audacious and aggressive young man who dominates all kinds of people and properties thundering through a new epic with the throttle of his motorcycle clearly identifiable; of the sophisticated lady who has freed herself from social convention only by smoking the best cigarette." Lisa Block de Behar, *El lenguaje de la publicidad* (Buenos Aires: Siglo XXI, 1976), 15.

10. Anibal Ford and Jorge B. Rivera, "Los medios masivos de comunicación en la Argentina," in A. Ford, J. B. Rivera, and E. Romano, *Medios de comunicación y cultura popular* (Buenos Aires: Legasa, 1985), 29. By 1973, 16 agencies dominated the advertising market, 60 percent of them foreign and mixed enterprises and 40 percent of them national. In total, they registered for 150 trillion old pesos. Alejandro Horowicz, "Creciente expectativa entre las agencias de publicidad por las reglas que definan el futuro juego económico," *La Opinión*, November 24, 1973. The advertising industry in Argentina was primarily divided between subsidiaries of American companies, such as McCann-Erickson, J. Walter Thompson, and Grant Adv., managed by Argentine professionals, and local companies, such as Yuste, Eter, Pueyrredón Propaganda, Gowland, De Luca, and Nexo Publicidad. See Laura Podalsky, *Specular City: Transforming Culture, Consumption, and Space in Buenos Aires, 1955–1973* (Philadelphia: Temple University Press, 2004), 213–21.

11. About the television advertising business in the early 1970s, see Heriberto Muraro, *Neocapitalismo y comunicación de masa* (Buenos Aires: Eudeba, 1974), 213–39.

12. Cámara Argentina de Anunciantes, "Estudio de la inversión publicitaria en la República Argentina, 1960–1972" (Buenos Aires: Cámara Argentina de Anunciantes, 1974). This study was conducted during the second half of 1973 and was disseminated through a press conference held in January 1974. The survey, the first of its kind in the country, was a good indicator of the importance of advertising investment in the beginning of the 1970s. Another symptom of this importance was the creation of technical agencies supporting advertising businesses in the interior provinces of the country, which were sponsored by the Argentine Chamber of Advertisers from 1973 on.

13. Cited in Muraro, "Neocapitalismo y comunicación de masa," 223.

14. In 1973, there were 270 dailies and 4,100 newspapers in the country, as well as ninety-four radio stations. See "Documento histórico: Lea, entérese, esto es nuestro país," *Gente*, no. 395 (February 15, 1973).

15. Ford and Rivera, "Los medios masivos de comunicación en la Argentina," 24. See also "Educación y medios de comunicación en América Latina," *Crisis*, no. 40 (August 1976): 10–11.

16. Ford and Rivera, "Los medios masivos de comunicación en la Argentina," 33–37. The 1975 crisis hit the magazine world hard. In 1974, the total circulation volume of magazines was 340 million copies.

17. "GENTE," *Militancia*, no. 14 (September 13, 1973): 24–25.

18. "Reflexiones sobre la propaganda," *Primera Plana*, no. 496 (August 1, 1972): 30.

19. Armando Alonso Piñeiro, *Breve historia de la publicidad argentina (1801–1974)* (Buenos Aires: Alzamor, 1974), 94–95. At the beginning of the 1970s, according to Piñeiro, advertising professionals had attained an "absolute comprehension of the time in which we lived, to catch the spiritual necessities of the people."

20. Significantly, advertising directed toward the same target audience in the United States (*Newsweek* and *Life*), France (*Paris Match*), and Germany (*Der Spiegel*), which in many senses shared a similar aesthetic to Argentine advertising, did not appeal to weapons or violent metaphors, at least between 1969 and 1975.

21. Alonso Piñeiro, *Breve historia de la publicidad argentina*, 69.

22. See Alonso Piñeiro, *Breve historia de la publicidad argentina*, appendix 2, 247–58.

23. Alonso Piñeiro, *Breve historia de la publicidad argentina*, 71. See also the "Declaración sobre publicidad agresiva," in *Memoria y Balance* (Buenos Aires: Cámara Argentina de Anunciantes—CAA, 1970), and "Comisión intersocietaria para comerciantes de televisión," in *Memoria y Balance* (Buenos Aires: CAA, 1973).

24. "Publicidad: La consigna es no agredir," *Panorama*, no. 384 (November 13–19, 1974): 27. For this businessman, advertising needed to return to natural and human values because "we are all distressed."

25. Advertisements can be seen as a social space in which the beliefs and values of a society are expressed. Around 1920, for example, children smoked cigarettes in

Argentine advertisements. This does not mean that advertising imposed smoking on children, but rather that it developed from the existence of this phenomenon and used it to communicate content. See Alberto Borrini, *El siglo de la publicidad (1898–1998): Historias de la publicidad gráfica argentina* (Buenos Aires: Atlántida, 1998), 52.

26. About the most important advertising agencies of the period, see Alonso Piñeiro, *Breve historia de la publidad Argentina*; and Borrini, *El siglo de la publicidad*, 8–11.

27. Throughout the 1970s, Monzón was one of the most important and famous Argentine public figures. His image symbolized the "macho" Argentine man, and he was presented like this on various occasions. In 1973, for example, *Gente* magazine chose him as its "superman of the year." " '73 ¡Qué año! 365 días con la lupa de 'Gente,' " *Gente*, no. 445 (January 31, 1974).

28. "Monzón se entrena para vivir," *Gente*, no. 375 (September 28, 1972): 58.

29. "Monzón y . . . ," *El Gráfico*, no. 2658 (March 23, 1971): 31.

30. "Las venganzas del Beto Alonso," *El Gráfico*, no. 2815 (September 18, 1973).

31. "Un matrimonio de gente linda," *Gente*, no. 181 (January 9, 1969).

32. "No . . . Ustedes no entienden. Yo estoy en otra cosa," *Gente*, no. 482 (October 17, 1974).

33. See Pierre Bourdieu, *Distinction: A Social Critique of the Judgement of Taste* (Cambridge, MA: Harvard University Press, 1984), especially 260–67.

34. *El Gráfico*, no. 2583 (April 9, 1969).

35. *El Gráfico*, no. 2705 (August 10, 1971).

36. *El Gráfico*, no. 2901 (May 14, 1975).

37. *Auto Club*, no. 68 (January–February 1973). Various advertisments incited children to demand a specific rifle or shotgun from their parents. The sports magazine *Aire y Sol* promoted one of its issues with a boy holding a rifle, ready to fire. *La Capital*, April 30, 1973.

38. *El Gráfico*, no. 2586 (April 29, 1969). Annan De Lujo made the same association using cartoons; two men drawn with big smiles were showing off colorful shirts, as one of them held a shotgun. *El Gráfico*, no. 2602 (August 19, 1969).

39. *Panorama*, no. 385 (November 19–25, 1974).

40. *Auto Club*, no. 54 (September–October 1970); *Gente*, no. 324 (October 7, 1971).

41. *Gente*, no. 328 (November 4, 1971).

42. *El Gráfico*, no. 2588 (May 13, 1969).

43. *El Gráfico*, no. 2590 (May 27, 1969).

44. *La Capital*, July 4, 1969; *Panorama*, no. 110 (June 3–9, 1969): 27; *Panorama*, no. 112 (June 17–23, 1969): 63; *Confirmado*, no. 207 (June 5–11, 1969): 27; *Análisis*, no. 429 (June 3–9, 1969): 47.

45. "Estas noticias son un balazo," *La Capital*, August 11, 1972; and *La Capital*, October 5, 1973. "A Gun for Every Occasion" was the slogan for the Ítalo Gra brand of revolvers, *Auto Club*, no. 69 (March–April 1973). Also see advertisements for Bersa revolvers in *El Gráfico*, no. 2667 (November 17, 1970), and in *Auto Club*, no. 62 (January–February 1972): 70; the Bagual revolvers, supposedly the "best for self-defense," in *Auto Club*, no. 73 (March–April 1972): 133; Diana guns, in *Auto Club*, no. 68 (Janu-

ary–February 1973); and more than thirty ads for gun vendors, manufacturers, servicers, and distributors in *Auto Club*, no. 69 (March–April 1973).

46. "Ante la violencia," *Auto Club*, no. 63 (March–April 1972): 16–18. Fabricaciones Militares and two gun businesses (Armería Italiana and La Triestina) sponsored the issue.

47. *Noticias*, December 11, 1969, 11; *La Capital*, July 5, 1970; *La Capital*, July 12, 1970, 28; *La Capital*, March 7, 1971; "Seguridad sin seguro," *La Capital*, August 18, 1972.

48. *Noticias*, February 24, 1970.

49. *Noticias*, August 1, 1969.

50. *La Capital*, August 3, 1969, 2.

51. "Tirar, precisamente," *Análisis*, no. 479 (May 19–25, 1970): 40.

52. About this concept, see Bourdieu, *Distinction*, 97–168.

53. "Road Test Peugeot 504 E," *Corsa*, August 22–28, 1972, 21–28.

54. *Gente*, no. 389 (January 4, 1973): 64; *Claudia*, no. 190 (March 1973): 113; *Panorama*, no. 297 (January 4–10, 1973): 49; *Análisis-Confirmado*, no. 518 and 396 (January 16–22, 1973).

55. *Para Ti*, no. 228 (December 4, 1969): 83. El *Gráfico* promoted itself using a pistol shooter, with gun and magazine in hand, surprised by the precision of the publication's journalists. El *Gráfico*, no. 193 (April 3, 1969).

56. "¡Abajo la violencia! ¡Viva el matrimonio!," *Para Ti*, no. 2539 (March 8, 1971): 65.

57. "Cuero: El asalto del año," *Claudia*, no. 142 (March 1969): 76–93; "A la caza, a la pesca, y a la moda," *Para Ti*, no. 2555 (June 1971): 48–51; "Éxito 71: La gamuza," *Claudia*, no. 167 (April 1971): 154–57; "Disparen sobre el tricot . . . ," *Claudia*, no. 225 (March 1976): 52–59.

58. *Gente*, no. 203 (June 12, 1969).

59. *La Capital*, October 26, 1969.

60. Quino, *Todo Mafalda* (Buenos Aires: De la Flor, 1997).

61. "Decretos sobre tenencia de armas y explosivos y difusión de solicitadas," *La Opinión*, August 5, 1973, 1.

62. "Una mirada desde adentro de la vidriera," *Gente*, no. 513 (May 22, 1975).

63. For an analysis of Mussolini's maxim "*vivere pericolosamente*," see Christopher Duggan, *A Concise History of Italy* (Cambridge: Cambridge University Press, 1994), chapter 8.

64. Miss Ylang's ads can be seen in *Claudia*, nos. 143, 144, 153 (April 1969, May 1969, February 1970); FlooCrem's ads in *Claudia*, nos. 146, 149 (July 1969, October 1969); Leila's ad in *Para Ti*, no. 2491 (April 6, 1970): 86; and Festival's ad in *Para Ti*, no. 2462 (September 25, 1969).

65. *Análisis*, no. 577 (May 5–11, 1970).

66. *Gente*, no. 483 (December 13, 1973).

67. *Gente*, no. 206 (July 3, 1969): 67.

68. *Gente*, no. 308 (June 17, 1971): 50.

69. *Gente*, no. 408 (May 17, 1973).

70. *La Capital*, April 15, 1973, and April 28, 1973.

71. *Gente*, no. 501 (February 27, 1975).

72. *El Gráfico*, no. 2793 (April 17, 1973).

73. Some of these advertisements can be seen in *El Gráfico*, no. 2607 (September 23, 1969): 33; *Claudia*, no. 153 (February 1970); and *Confirmado*, no. 220 (September 3–9, 1969).

74. *El Burgués*, no. 31 (June 21, 1972): 9.

75. *Gente*, no. 479 (September 26, 1974).

76. *La Capital*, May 29, 1973.

77. *Panorama*, no. 388 (December 10–16, 1974), and *Panorama*, no. 387 (December 3–7, 1974).

78. *Gente*, no. 486 (November 14, 1974).

79. Carlos Ulanovsky, *1951–1976: Televisión Argentina, 25 años después* (Buenos Aires: Hachette, 1976), 112. The soundtrack to the soap opera analyzed in chapter 3, *Rolando Rivas, Taxi Driver*, related love to violence. Its chorus rang: "Rolando and Mónica, love, love, love, sweet and violent."

80. "Crítico pájaro la juventud," *Análisis*, no. 458 (December 23–29, 1969): 44.

81. Roland Barthes, "Myth Today," in *Mythologies* (New York: Hill and Wang, 1972). See especially 109–12.

82. *La Capital*, July 22, 1970.

83. *La Capital*, February 10, 1972.

84. *Noticias*, June 28, 1969.

85. *La Capital*, November 23, 1969.

86. Landrú, *Gente paqueta* (Bueno Aires: Orion, 1972), 29.

87. *La Capital*, June 2, 1971.

88. *La Capital*, July 22, 1971.

89. See the cover of *Panorama*, no. 349 (January 24–30, 1974).

90. *Auto Club*, no. 62 (January–February 1972).

91. New Force advertisements can be seen in *El Gráfico*, no. 2719 (November 16, 1971), and in *Para Ti*, no. 2587 (February 7, 1972).

92. *Satiricón*, no. 3 (January 1973).

93. *La Capital*, November 5, 1969.

94. *La Capital*, November 9, 1969, 7.

95. *El Gráfico*, no. 2648 (July 7, 1970).

96. *La Capital*, June 14, 1971. An image of this advertisement is presented in the next section in Figure 5.39.

97. *La Capital*, July 27, 1969, 15.

98. *Análisis*, no. 446 (September 30–October 6, 1969).

99. *Gente*, no. 208 (July 17, 1969).

100. *Gente*, no. 479 (September 26, 1974).

101. *Gente*, no. 366 (July 27, 1972).

102. *La Capital*, December 15, 1969.

103. See *Satiricón*, no. 1 (November 10, 1972): 1.

104. According to IPSA, in 1970 the "Los Campanelli" program (Channel 13) was among the most-watched series of that entire year, occasionally garnering higher ratings than those of important soccer matches. "Los programas más vistos," *Gente*, no. 234 (January 15, 1970).

105. *Noticias*, August 1, 1969.

106. *Para Ti*, no. 2628 (November 20, 1972).

107. *La Capital*, June 12, 1973.

108. *El Gráfico*, no. 2793 (April 17, 1973).

109. *Gente*, no. 471 (August 1, 1974).

110. *Panorama*, no. 356 (March 21–27, 1974); *Claudia*, no. 202 (March 1974): 62.

111. *Gente*, no. 521 (July 17, 1975).

112. *Noticias*, June 12, 1975.

113. *El Burgués*, no. 35 (August 16, 1972); no. 40 (October 25, 1972); no. 19 (January 5, 1972); no. 30 (June 7, 1972).

114. *Confirmado*, no. 201 (April 24–30, 1969).

115. *Corsa*, no. 227 (August 25–31, 1970); *Gente*, no. 266 (August 27, 1970): 90.

116. *Confirmado*, no. 478 (October 14–20, 1970). Castro was also a figure used in advertising. See for example, the advertisement for Toshiba's "revolutionary photocopiers," which affirmed that "the traditional systems no longer work ." *Primera Plana*, no. 496 (August 1, 1972).

117. *Panorama*, no. 380 (October 8–14, 1974).

118. Another term that took on an unprecedented positive meaning was "violent." See *Gente*, no. 194 (April 10, 1969): 68–69, and the advertisement for Chinon camcorders in *Claudia*, no. 155 (April 1970).

119. "Informe 'al día' para entender a los jóvenes de hoy," *Gente*, no. 535 (October 30, 1975): 68.

120. A reproduction of this ad can be found in "Reflexiones sobre la propaganda," *Primera Plana*, no. 496 (August 1, 1972): 30.

121. "Andrés Percivale, Mister éxito 1975," *Gente*, no. 533 (October 9, 1975).

122. "Gibran mata mil," *Gente*, no. 535 (October 30, 1975).

123. *La Capital*, July 11, 1974.

124. Carlos Ulanovsky, "El oportunismo de la TV dirigió con humor el triunfo del Frejuli," *La Opinión*, March 16, 1973, 1.

125. "Con los argentinos que 'matan' en Mónaco," *Gente*, no. 483 (October 24, 1974).

126. *El Gráfico*, no. 2921 (October 1, 1975).

127. "El adiós de un gran campeón: Se fue como llegó: ¡Matando!," *El Gráfico*, no. 2837 (February 19, 1974).

128. James Neilson, "El cautivante guerrillero de rifle y boina," *The Buenos Aires Herald*, December 22, 1972, reproduced in J. Neilson, *La vorágine argentina* (Buenos Aires: Marymar, 1979), 24.

129. "La tarde en armas," *Confirmado*, no. 381 (October 3–9, 1972): 42.

130. Interview with Héctor Solanas, in Alonso Piñeiro, *Breve historia de la publici-*

dad argentina, 228. In the same interview, Solanas situated the Bonafide ad among his company's "memorable campaigns" and defined advertising as "part of the daily literature of a people." It "reflects what a people is and how it feels," especially in Argentina, where "our way of being is full of spice. Our advertising is a little bit like we are, it's acute, it's subtle." Solanas, in a clear expression of the conception of advertising that took shape toward the end of the 1960s, argued that "one must understand, once and for all, that now we don't sell things, we sell states of being." Alonso Piñeiro, *Breve historia de la publicidad argentina*, 228, 230, 238.

131. This advertisement can be seen in the documentary, COMA 13: *Del Cordobazo a Malvinas: Trece años de historia en imágenes*, part 1 (1969–1974). In 1971, Bonafide announced the continuation of this spot. Once again, Grimau eliminated the speaker that asked him for a candy, but this time he pressed a button that opened the floor where the person who spoke to him was standing, causing him to fall into an abyss.

132. The "Code of Ethics for Television Commercials," approved in 1968 by three associations connected to this industry, established that "narration or staging of acts that imply a direct apologia for crime shall be avoided." In 1970, a commission that was composed of representatives of these associations objected to certain commercials and ordered their modification, in the majority of cases for "attitudes or insinuations of a sexual nature." Bonafide's ad, however, was not objected to. Instead, the commision affirmed that "the film does indicate an intensification of subjects that include scenes of violence, and in accordance with the Ethical Norms for Television Commercials, we do not offer comments." The commission, moreover, praised the wit, ingenuity, creativity, and originality of the ad, as well as the actor's performance. See appendix 3 (documentary appendix), in Alonso Piñeiro, *Breve historia de la publicidad argentina*, 278–84.

133. Another indicator of this naturalization of violence is seen in Heriberto Muraro, *La publicidad* (Buenos Aires: Acción, 1976), the first critical book about the advertising business in Argentina. Muraro denounces the connections between advertising and consumer ideology and the use of psychoanalysis to increase sales but ignores the question of violence.

134. Carlos Ulanovsky, "¿Muerto Olmedo se acabó la rabia?," *Cuestionario*, no. 38 (June 1976): 60.

135. See "Las obras de la revolución," *Primera Plana*, no. 496 (August 1, 1972): 50–51. The full proclamation declared: "Five propositions for Latin American art: 1) Make art into a tool to raise awareness of the present. 2) Liberate our colonized culture, opposing it a counterculture of violence. 3) Find an opening toward the People as the only means of integrating art with reality. 4) Create from the borders inward. 5) Love our own culture with the most ferocious of loyalties; hate the dominant cultures with the most implacable hatred. Because only ferocity will makes us free."

136. Hannah Arendt, *On Violence* (New York: Harcourt, Brace and World, 1969).

137. Pierre Bourdieu, *Practical Reason: On the Theory of Action* (Cambridge: Polity, 1998).

138. See Bourdieu, *Distinction*, 471.

139. On the issue of the banalization of violence, see André Duarte, Christina Lopreato, and Marion Brepohl de Magalhães (orgs.), *A banalização da violência: A atualidade do pensamento de Hannah Arendt* (Río de Janeiro: Relume Dumará, 2004).

140. Arendt, *On Violence*.

141. Metaphors of seduction were also used to promote the sale of firearms, where the guns seduced instead of women. See "Una línea en silueta," *La Capital*, August 11, 1972.

142. About the concepts of "denotation" and "connotation," see Roland Barthes, *Elements of Semiology* (New York: Hill and Wang, 1968), 89–104.

143. See "La mujer argentina: ¿Libre o esclava?," *Panorama*, no. 176 (September 8–14, 1970): 25.

144. *El Gráfico*, no. 2617 (December 2, 1969): 73.

145. *Para Ti*, no. 2436 (March 17, 1969): 57.

146. *La Capital*, June 14, 1971.

147. For a view of women (from the middle class and, generally, university students) in this cultural transformation on the plane of gender at the time, see "Víctimas, competidoras," *Análisis*, no. 472 (March 31, 1970). In this article, various women, including the young sociologist Silvia Sigal and the singer Marikena Monti, dialogue about the new feminine roles in contrast with the traditional ones. The article is illustrative not only of the newness but also of the limitations that characterized this process.

148. Klaus Theweleit, *Male Fantasies* (Minneapolis: University of Minnesota, 1987), 70–79.

149. *Para Ti*, no. 2491 (April 6, 1970), and *Claudia*, no. 157 (June 1970).

150. Because of space limitations, I prefer to concentrate my analysis on the images reprinted here. However, it should also be noted that there were other combinations of sex and violence. See, for example, the 1971 advertisements from Orea, another pantyhose company. *Gente*, no. 299 (April 15, 1971); *Gente*, no. 303 (May 13, 1971); *Gente*, no. 308 (June 17, 1971); and *Para Ti*, no. 2442 (April 28, 1969): 47.

151. *Para Ti*, no. 2679 (November 12, 1973): 26.

152. See Lacan's seminar "Desire, Life, and Death," *El seminario de Jacques Lacan: El Yo en la teoría de Freud y en la técnica psicoanalítica (1954–1955)* (Barcelona: Paidós, 1983), 331–51.

153. Jacques Lacan, *The Four Fundamental Concepts of Psycho-analysis* (New York: W. W. Norton, 1978), 257.

154. Alexandre Kojève, *La dialéctica del amo y del esclavo en Hegel* (Buenos Aires: Fausto, 1999), 12.

155. See Lacan, *The Four Fundamental Concepts of Psycho-analysis*, 263–76.

156. In his study of ideology, Žižek asks: "What happens with desire after we

'traverse' fantasy?" The response comes not from Žižek himself but from Lacan: "Lacan's answer, in the last pages of his *Seminar XI*, is drive, ultimately the death drive: 'beyond fantasy' there is no yearning or some kindred sublime phenomenon, 'beyond fantasy' we find only drive, its pulsation around the *sinthome*." Slavoj Žižek, *The Sublime Object of Ideology* (London: Verso, 1999), 123–24.

157. "Perhaps we have no other instincts except libidinal ones," wrote Freud in 1920. Sigmund Freud, *Beyond the Pleasure Principle* (London: Hogarth and the Institute of Psychoanalysis, 1961), especially 38–55.

158. Hugo Vezzetti, *Sobre la violencia revolucionaria* (Buenos Aires: Siglo XXI, 2009), 131.

159. See, for example, the Perro Mundo comic strip from the humorist Heredia in the daily *La Nación*.

160. Jorge B. Rivera, "Historia del humor gráfico argentino," in A. Ford, J. B. Rivera, and E. Romano, *Medios de comunicación y cultura popular* (Buenos Aires: Legasa, 1985), 124.

161. *Análisis*, no. 464 (February 2–9, 1970): 4.

162. *Análisis*, no. 509 (December 15–21, 1970): 4.

163. *Análisis*, no. 521 (March 9–15, 1971): 4.

164. *Panorama*, no. 312 (April 19–25, 1973).

165. *Panorama*, no. 319 (June 7–13, 1973): 66.

166. Born in 1972, *Satiricón* reached a distribution of 100,000 copies in little time and by March 1974 was publishing 250,000. In September of that year, the publication was closed by Peronist censorship. See Rivera, "Historia del humor gráfico argentino," 133–34.

167. *Satiricón*, no. 5 (March 5, 1973): 11.

168. *Satiricón*, no. 5 (March 5, 1973): 23.

169. *Satiricón*, no. 6 (April 3, 1973): 55.

170. Fontanarrosa, *¿Quién es Fontanarrosa?* (Buenos Aires: de la Flor, 1973).

171. *Panorama*, no. 385 (November 19–25, 1974): 66.

172. Quino, *Todo Mafalda*, 250.

173. *Panorama*, no. 331 (September 20–26, 1973): 46.

174. *Panorama*, no. 389 (December 17–23, 1974): 66. "The boys" ("*los muchachos*") was a term associated with Peronist activists in political language.

175. *Crisis*, no. 11 (March 1974): 35.

176. Landrú, *Gente paqueta*, 65.

177. Vides Almonacid, *Goyito*, published in *El Pueblo*, 1973. Archivo Almonacid.

178. Almonacid, *Goyito*, published in *El Pueblo*, 1974. Archivo Almonacid.

179. Ulanovsky, *1951–1976: Televisión Argentina*, 81; and "¿Muerto Olmedo se acabó la rabia?," *Cuestionario*, no. 38 (June 1976): 60. After this episode, the program was pulled. Olmedo returned to television during the following year with his children's character, Capitán Piluso, and a year after that began with "Olmedo 78."

180. The film *Las turistas quieren guerra*, directed by Enrique Salaberry (1977).

181. Arendt, *On Violence*, 72.

182. See, for example, *La Gaceta*, "Cada día, más violencia," September 13, 1970, 6; "Normalizar la vida Argentina," *La Gaceta*, March 26, 1973; "Los locos, locos días," *Análisis*, no. 466 (February 17, 1970); "Personaje del año: El argentino medio," *Panorama*, no. 244 (December 28, 1971–January 3, 1972): 28–31; "Agresividad conductiva," *Auto Club*, no. 70 (May–June 1973); and "Agresividad sin ideas en ciertos ciclos televisivos," *La Opinión*, January 3, 1973.

183. Landrú, *Gente paqueta*, 52.

184. "Alfredo Alcón, la necesidad del riesgo," *Confirmado*, no. 341 (December 28, 1971–January 3, 1972): 30.

185. A conflict that involved Correa residents and those of Bustinza, another town in the area, earned the adjectives "extraordinary" and "barbarous" from the daily paper of the neighboring city of Cañada de Gómez. This newspaper spoke of the "urban guerrilla warfare in Bustinza between residents of Correa and Bustinza" and of "barricades on the streets" to trap the "invaders" and reported that "finally the police took control of the band of guerrillas that carried out the almost incredible war between Bustinza and Correa, which seemed more like an action story than an event that could have happened between us . . ." "Bárbaro: Guerra entre Correanos y Bustinceros," *La Estrella de la Mañana*, March 31, 1970, 4.

186. "Para salir del infierno," *Carta Política*, no. 7 (winter 1974): 4.

187. See, for an example, the extra issue of *El Descamisado* that the Montoneros published after their event in the Atlanta stadium, on March 11, 1974.

188. Bourdieu, *Distinction*, especially chapter 8.

189. "Rodolfo Puiggrós: El nuevo peronismo en la universidad," *Nuevo Confirmado*, no. 394 (June 12–18, 1973): 17.

190. See, for example, the declaration of the minister of foreign relations of the military dictatorship, César Augusto Guzzetti, in an interview with *La Opinión*, where he affirms that "the social body is contaminated by a sickness that is consuming its insides and is forming antibodies" and that, "as the government controls and destroys the guerrillas, the action of the antibody is going to disappear," implicitly justifying what was then called "the terrorism of the Right." Neilson, "Murder Most Natural?," *Buenos Aires Herald*, October 12, 1976.

Conclusions

1. We lack a study that has attempted to precisely identify the meaning of calling oneself "leftist" in this historical-political context. Many elements imply that thinking of oneself as "leftist" in the early 1970s could mean a wide range of things. It is worth citing how Héctor Alterio, one of the most acclaimed and important actors of 1972, defined himself politically, during a period of intense courtship between intellectual and cultural sectors and the Left. "Do you define yourself politically?" asked the journalists; "I'm from the Left," the actor responded, "but I'm neither socialist nor communist. I am someone who has an attitude toward life, a dynamic attitude that is defined by every moment in front of everyone. No party forces me to think

in one way or another." "Héctor Alterio: Un hombre sobre el escenario," *Claudia*, no. 187 (December 1972): 89.

Epilogue

1. However, the October 1983 elections provided some novelties. The truly important changes did not relate to the middle classes, but rather to the "popular" and working-class sectors, who for the first time in thirty-eight years divided their vote between Peronism and Radicalism. In these elections, in minority but in any case unprecedented proportions, "popular" and, above all, skilled-worker sectors (whom electoral sociology refers to as the "low structured sectors") redirected their traditional vote for Peronism toward the Radical candidate. See Edgardo Catterberg, "Las elecciones del 30 de octubre de 1983: El surgimiento de una nueva convergencia electoral," *Desarrollo Económico* 25, no. 98 (July–September 1985): 259–67. This author indicates that, unlike the past when working-class parents transmitted their electoral behavior to their children (and both voted for Peronism), in 1983, the opposite occurred; "the children transmitted their values and their disenchantment with Peronism to their elders, many of whom were former Peronist voters," and both voted for the Radicals (266). In any case, what is certain is that Radicalism came to power with an unprecedented amount of traditionally Peronist votes. In some provinces such as Jujuy—traditionally Peronist, like the majority of the provinces in the North—the UCR obtained ten times more votes in 1983 than it had won ten years earlier. Across the entire country, Peronism, which in March 1973 had attracted virtually 50 percent of votes, won less than 40 percent ten years later.

2. About the Radical Party and its traditional representation of the middle classes in the society, see the classic study by David Rock, *Politics in Argentina, 1890–1930: The Rise and Fall of Radicalism* (Cambridge: Cambridge University Press, 1975).

3. If one pays more attention to the ideological preferences than the party orientation of the vote, the size of the segment of the middle classes with sympathies toward the left does not seem to have changed significantly with respect to ten years earlier. In 1984, the Gallup Company asked one thousand Argentines to situate themselves from left to right in the political spectrum. Without mentioning parties, simply declaring their ideological inclinations, the results showed that 15 percent of the population (the Gallup report did not present the results disaggregated by social class) situated themselves on the "left" or the "center-left." See Marita Carballo, "Cambios en actitudes y valores políticos de la sociedad argentina en la última década," *Gallup Argentina*, no. 3 (1984):5. The question with a similar purpose that CIMS had posed in 1973, whose results I showed in chapter 1, gave results that were compatible with this Gallup study. Although we do not know for sure, it is realistic to assume that a majority of the 15 percent that situated themselves on the left or center-left of the political spectrum in 1984 came from the middle classes, as it did ten years before.

4. The terrible judgment that society retained of the last Peronist government

contributed to the degree of the Radical triumph. "Clearly, in light of the election results," Edgardo Catterberg wrote in his analysis of the 1983 elections, "the most influential image for the electoral behavior of the population was the negative perception of the second Peronism [1973–1976], which displaced the positive perception of the first Peronism." Catterberg, "Las elecciones del 30 de octubre de 1983," 264.

5. These polls were conducted in the country's most important urban centers (Buenos Aires, greater Buenos Aires, Córdoba, Rosario, and Mendoza) in May and June 1983. The first covered seventeen hundred cases and the second eighteen hundred cases. For all of the polls, a three-stage probabilistic sampling was used. See Edgardo Catterberg, *Argentines Confront Politics: Political Culture and Public Opinion in the Argentine Transition to Democracy* (Boulder, CO: Rienner, 1991), 76.

6. This study defined the position on the social ladder according to the occupational category of the voters. The survey on which it was based was conducted between November 1983 and January 1984, with five hundred voters in Capital Federal and La Matanza County. Darío Cantón, *El pueblo legislador: Las elecciones de 1983* (Buenos Aires: Centro Editor de América Latina, 1986).

7. Mora y Araujo has indicated that the Radical vote that did not come from the middle classes was related to the growth of the self-employed sector in the 1970s. A majority of those in this sector, without being middle class, "maintain middle-class expectations, perceive their surroundings as the middle class does, and in many aspects behave like a middle-class person. This particularly occurs in the electoral domain." Manuel Mora y Araujo, "La naturaleza de la coalición alfonsinista," in *La argentina electoral*, ed. AA.VV. (Buenos Aires: Sudamericana, 1985), 95.

8. Mora y Araujo showed that the part of Alfonsín's vote that came from outside his party came from people who in 1973 had opted for the center-right. He thus defined Alfonsín's coalition as being "predominantly center-right" while affirming the supremacy of its middle class component. Mora y Araujo, "La naturaleza de la coalición alfonsinista," 89–107.

9. Catterberg, *Argentines Confront Politics*, 16. Ten percent did not answer the question.

10. Carballo, "Cambios en actitudes y valores políticos de la sociedad argentina en la última década," *Gallup Argentina*, no. 3 (1984):26. Twelve percent did not answer.

11. Perón's message from the balcony of the Casa Rosada to a crowd in the Plaza de Mayo, August 31, 1955.

Appendix 1 Case Selection

1. Eduardo Zalduendo, *Las desigualdades económicas entre las regiones de Argentina* (Buenos Aires: n.p., 1973), Introducción. In terms of population density, in 1970 the first group represented 37 percent of the population, the second 45.7 percent, and the third 17.3 percent. Also see Alejandro Rofman, *Desigualdades regionales y concentración económica (el caso argentino)* (Buenos Aires: Siap-Planteos, 1974).

2. In the 1970s census, Buenos Aires recorded a population of 2,972,453 inhabi-

tants (over eight million counting its suburbs). In 1980, this reduced slightly to 2,922,829 inhabitants (almost ten million including the suburbs). INDEC (National Statistics and Census Institute [Instituto Nacional de Estadísticas y Censos]), "Población según los censos nacionales de 1895 a 2001, por provincia ordenadas por la cantidad de población en 2001," http://www.indec.gov.ar/default.htm. In 1970, the city of Tucumán had a population of 308,826 inhabitants, and a decade later, in 1980, this rose to 395,373. INDEC, Censo Nacional de Población y Vivienda 1980: Serie B: Características generales: Provincia de Tucumán (Buenos Aires: INDEC, 1980), 14 and 15. The town of Correa had a total population of 4,646 inhabitants in 1970 (3,441 in the urban area and 1,205 in rural areas). In 1980, the total population had grown to 5,370, and the process of urbanization had deepened. La Voz de Correa, December 29, 1970, and November 27, 1980.

Appendix 2 Sources

1. La Capital sold an average of 77,462 copies between 1969 and 1982. La Gaceta sold an average of 73,927 copies in Tucumán. In the case of the city of Buenos Aires, I privileged weekly, biweekly, or monthly political magazines, because their analysis tends to be deeper than that of newspapers and because they had great influence on public opinion. Panorama sold sixty thousand copies per printing and Primera Plana over thirty thousand. There are no official statistics for other newspapers. Circulation Verification Institute (Instituto Verificador de Circulaciones) provided data to the author. Two of these magazines briefly merged to create Análisis-Confirmado, and one of these appeared for some time with a different name, Nuevo Confirmado.

2. About the newpaper La Nación, see Ricardo Sidicaro, La política mirada desde arriba: Las ideas del diario La Nación (1909–1989) (Buenos Aires: Sudamericana, 1993).

3. This newspaper is the source that researchers tend to favor when analyzing the first half of the 1970s. Although it was read by an "enlightened" and primarily Buenos Aires–centered minority, I also consider it, although I do not focus on it. About this newspaper, see Abrasha Rotenberg, Historia confidencial: La Opinión y otros olvidos (Buenos Aires: Sudamericana, 1999); about its editor, see Graciela Mochkofsky, Timerman: El periodista que quiso ser parte del poder (1923–1999) (Buenos Aires: Sudamericana, 2004).

4. In 1978, general interest magazines almost doubled in sales compared to those in second place, the comics. Of the 116,521,682 copies sold in eight months, 32,052,762 belonged to the general interest category. See "Estadísticas," Gente, no. 698 (December 7, 1978).

5. Gente magazine sold an average of 277,045 copies weekly between 1969 and 1982, reaching a peak of 360,000 in 1974. Circulation Verification Institute (Instituto Verificador de Circulaciones) provided data to the author. Somos magazine, from the same publisher, reported fifty thousand issues sold weekly in July 1977. "Las revistas en cifras," Gente, no. 633 (September 8, 1977).

6. According to the Atlántida publisher, in 1969, 9,723,441 copies of El Gráfico

were printed, an average of 810,286 copies monthly. *Gente*, no. 245 (April 2, 1970). Its competitor *Goles* averaged 74,000 copies. *Autoclub* magazine was distributed free to all members of the Argentine Automobile Club (Automóvil Club Argentino). Its January–February 1972 edition had a circulation of almost 600,000 copies. The rest of the months of that year exceeded this amount, reaching a peak of 625,000 copies in November–December. *Autoclub*, no. 68 (January–February 1973).

7. *Para Ti* sold a yearly average of 147,974 copies during the period studied, with a peak of almost 250,000 issues in 1974. *Claudia* sold a yearly average of 109,000 during this same period, but its sales volume varied much more than that of other magazines. For example, in 1969, it sold 160,811 copies; in 1982, only 54,418. Circulation Verification Institute (Instituto Verificador de Circulaciones) provided data to the author.

8. *Humor* magazine was a success. It was released in 1978 with 156,238 copies sold during that year, leaped to more than half a million copies the following year, increased to two million in 1980, and by 1982 had reached four million copies sold per year. Andrea Matallana, *Humor y política: Un estudio comparativo de tres publicaciones de humor político* (Buenos Aires: Eudeba, 1999).

Adamovsky, Ezequiel. *Historia de la clase media argentina: Apogeo y decadencia de una ilusión, 1919–2003*. Buenos Aires: Planeta, 2009.

Adorno, Theodor. "A Portrait of Walter Benjamin." In T. Adorno, *Prisms*. Cambridge, MA: MIT Press, 1997.

Agulla, Juan Carlos. *Córdoba: Mayo de 1969; Diagnóstico social de una crisis*. Buenos Aires: Editel, 1969.

Allen, Robert Clyde. *Speaking of Soap Operas*. Chapel Hill: University of North Carolina Press, 1985.

Alonso Piñeiro, Armando. *Breve historia de la publicidad argentina (1801–1974)*. Buenos Aires: Alzamor, 1974.

Altamirano, Carlos. "Estudio preliminar." In *Bajo el signo de las masas (1943–1973)*, 17–96. Buenos Aires: Ariel, 2001.

Altamirano, Carlos. "Montoneros." *Punto de vista* 19, no. 55 (1996): 1–9.

Altamirano, Carlos. "La pequeña burguesía, una clase en el purgatorio." In *Peronismo y cultura de izquierda*, 99–127. Buenos Aires: Siglo XXI, 2011.

Arendt, Hannah. *Eichmann in Jerusalem: A Report on the Banality of Evil*. New York: Viking, 1963.

Arendt, Hannah. *On Violence*. New York: Harcourt, Brace and World, 1969.

Balvé, Beba, and Beatriz Balvé. *El '69: Huelga política de masas*. Buenos Aires: Contrapunto, 1989.

Barthes, Roland. *Elements of Semiology*. New York: Hill and Wang, 1968.

Barthes, Roland. "Myth Today." In *Mythologies*, 109–59. New York: Hill and Wang, 1972.

Benjamin, Walter. "On Some Motifs in Baudelaire." In *Illuminations: Essays and Reflections*. Edited and introduction by Hannah Arendt. Translated by Harry Zohn. New York: Harcourt, Brace and World, 1968. Reprint Schocken, 1969. Reprint 1992, 155–94.

Benjamin, Walter. "Theses on the Philosophy of History." In *Illuminations: Essays and Reflections*. Edited and introduction by Hannah Arendt. Translation by Harry Zohn.

New York: Harcourt, Brace and World, 1968. Reprint Schocken, 1969. Reprint 1992, 253–64.

Block de Behar, Lisa. *El lenguaje de la publicidad*. Buenos Aires: Siglo XXI, 1976.

Bores, Tato, and Carlos Ulanovsky. *Tato: Memorias inéditas y biografías del Actor Cómico de la Nación*. Buenos Aires: Emecé, 2010.

Borrini, Alberto. *El siglo de la publicidad (1898–1998): Historias de la publicidad gráfica argentina*. Buenos Aires: Atlántida, 1998.

Bourdieu, Pierre. *Distinction: A Social Critique of the Judgement of Taste*. Cambridge, MA: Harvard University Press, 1984.

Bourdieu, Pierre. *Practical Reason: On the Theory of Action*. Cambridge: Polity, 1998.

Buck-Morss, Susan. *The Dialectics of Seeing: Walter Benjamin and the Arcade Project*. Cambridge, MA: MIT Press, 1991.

Bullrich, Silvina. *Mal Don*. Buenos Aires: Emecé, 1973.

Cámara Argentina de Anunciantes. "Comisión intersocietaria para comerciantes de televisión." In *Memoria y Balance*. Buenos Aires: CAA, 1973.

Cámara Argentina de Anunciantes. "Declaración sobre publicidad agresiva." In *Memoria y Balance*. Buenos Aires: Cámara Argentina de Anunciantes—CAA, 1970.

Cámara Argentina de Anunciantes. "Estudio de la inversión publicitaria en la República Argentina, 1960–1972." Buenos Aires: Cámara Argentina de Anunciantes, 1974.

Cámpora, Héctor. "Mensaje de las Pautas Programáticas." In *Cómo cumplí el mandato de Perón*. Buenos Aires: Quehacer Nacional, 1975.

Cantón, Darío. *El pueblo legislador: Las elecciones de 1983*. Buenos Aires: Centro Editor de América Latina, 1986.

Cantón, Darío, Jorge Raúl Jorrat, and Eduardo Juárez. "Un intento de estimación de las celdas interiores de una tabla de contingencia basado en el análisis de regresión: El caso de las elecciones presidenciales de 1946 y marzo de 1973." *Desarrollo Económico* 16, no. 63 (October–December 1976): 395–417.

Carassai, Sebastián. "Antes de que anochezca: Derechos humanos y clases medias en Argentina antes y en los inicios del golpe de Estado de 1976." *América Latina Hoy* 54 (April 2010): 69–96.

Carassai, Sebastián. "La violencia 'de los dos lados': Hacia una genealogía de la teoría de los dos demonios (1969–1976)," mimeo, 2014

Carballo, Marita. "Cambios en actitudes y valores políticos de la sociedad argentina en la última década." *Gallup Argentina*, no. 3 (1984).

Catterberg, Edgardo. *Argentines Confront Politics: Political Culture and Public Opinion in the Argentine Transition to Democracy*. Boulder, CO: Rienner, 1991.

Catterberg, Edgardo. "Las elecciones del 30 de octubre de 1983: El surgimiento de una nueva convergencia electoral." *Desarrollo Económico* 25, no. 98 (July–September 1985): 259–67.

Corradi, Juan E., Eldon Kenworthy, and William Wipfler. "Argentina de hoy: Un regimen de terror; Informe sobre la represión desde julio de 1973 hasta diciembre de 1974." Documentary supplement to "Argentina 1973–1976: The Background to

Violence," by J. E. Corradi, E. Kenworthy, and W. Wipfler, appearing in the LASA Newsletter, Latin American Studies Association, September 1976, 25–27.

Corradi, Juan E., Eldon Kenworthy, and William Wipfler. "Argentina 1973–1976: The Background to Violence," LASA Newsletter, Latin American Studies Association, September 1976.

de la Cazuela, Jordán. *Tato y yo.* Buenos Aires: Baesa, 1974.

Delich, Francisco. *Crisis y protesta social: Córdoba, mayo 1969.* Buenos Aires: Signos, 1970.

de Riz, Liliana. *Retorno y derrumbe.* Mexico City: Folios, 1981.

Dodson, Jimmie. "Religious Innovation and the Politics of Argentina: A Study of the Movement of Priests for the Third World." PhD diss., Indiana University, 1973.

Duarte, André, Christina Lopreato, and Marion Brepohl de Magalhães, eds. *A banalização da violência: A atualidade do pensamento de Hannah Arendt.* Río de Janeiro: Relume Dumará, 2004.

Duggan, Christopher. *A Concise History of Italy.* Cambridge: Cambridge University Press, 1994.

Ferraris, Agustín. *Pido la palabra: Contestando a Martínez Estrada, Mario Amadeo y Ernesto Sábato.* Buenos Aires: Capricornio, 1957.

Foguet, Hugo. *Pretérito Perfecto.* Buenos Aires: Legasa, 1983.

Fontanarrosa, Roberto. *¿Quién es Fontanarrosa?* Buenos Aires: de la Flor, 1973.

Ford, Anibal, and Jorge B. Rivera. "Los medios masivos de comunicación en la Argentina." In *Medios de comunicación y cultura popular,* edited by Ford, Rivera, and Eduardo Romano, 33–37. Buenos Aires: Legasa, 1985.

Franco, Juan. "What's in a Name? Popular Culture Theory and Its Limitations." *Studies in Latin American Popular Culture,* no. 1 (1982): 5–14.

Freud, Sigmund. *Beyond the Pleasure Principle.* London: Hogarth and the Institute of Psychoanalysis, 1961.

García, Prudencio. *El drama de la autonomía militar.* Madrid: Alianza, 1995.

Garguin, Enrique. " 'Los argentinos descendemos de los barcos': The Racial Articulation of Middle-Class Identity in Argentina (1920–1960)." *Latin American and Caribbean Ethnic Studies* 2, no. 2 (September 2007): 161–84.

Girard, René. *La violencia y lo sagrado.* Buenos Aires: Anagrama, 1983.

González Bombal, Inés. "Nunca más: El juicio más allá de los estrados." In *Juicio, castigos y memorias: Derechos humanos y justicia en la política argentina,* edited by AA.VV., 193–216. Buenos Aires: Nueva Visión, 1995.

González Esteves, Luis, and Ignacio Llorente. "Elecciones y preferencias políticas en Capital Federal y Gran Buenos Aires: El 30 de octubre de 1983." In *La argentina electoral,* edited by AA.VV. Buenos Aires: Sudamericana, 1985.

González Janzen, Ignacio. *La triple A.* Buenos Aires: Contrapunto, 1986.

Gordillo, Mónica, and James Brennan. *Córdoba rebelde: El Cordobazo, el clasismo y la movilización social.* La Plata: De la Campana, 2008.

Graciarena, Jorge. "Clases medias y movimiento estudiantil: El reformismo argentino, 1918–1966." *Revista Mexicana de Sociología* 33, no. 1 (January–March 1971): 61–100.

Graciarena, Jorge. *Poder y clases sociales en América Latina*. Buenos Aires: Paidós, 1972.

Halbwachs, Maurice. *The Collective Memory*. New York: Harper and Row, 1980.

Hall, Stuart. "Encoding-Decoding." In *Culture, Media, Language*, 129–39. London: Hutchinson, 1980.

Halperín Donghi, Tulio. "La historiografía argentina en la hora de la libertad." *Sur*, no. 237 (1955): 114–21.

Halperín Donghi, Tulio. *La larga agonía de la Argentina peronista*. Buenos Aires: Ariel, 1994.

Heidegger, Martin. *Being and Time: A Translation of Sein und Zeit*. Translated by Joan Stambaugh. New York: State University of New York Press, 1996.

Izaguirre, Inés. "El problema y la historia de la investigación." In *Lucha de clases, guerra civil y genocidio en la Argentina (1973–1983)*, edited by Ines Izaguirre, 15–22. Buenos Aires: Eudeba, 2009.

Kojève, Alexandre. *La dialéctica del amo y del esclavo en Hegel*. Buenos Aires: Fausto, 1999.

Lacan, Jacques. "Desire, Life, and Death." In *El seminario de Jacques Lacan: El Yo en la teoría de Freud y en la técnica psicoanalítica (1954–1955)*, 331–51. Barcelona: Paidós, 1983.

Lacan, Jacques. *The Four Fundamental Concepts of Psycho-analysis*. New York: W. W. Norton, 1978.

Landi, Oscar. "Crisis y lenguajes políticos." *Estudios* CEDES 4, no. 4 (1982): 36–37.

Landi, Oscar. "Medios, procesos culturales y sistema político." In *Medios, transformación cultural y política*, 89–133. Buenos Aires: Legasa, 1987.

Landi, Oscar. "La tercera presidencia de Perón: Gobierno de emergencia y crisis política." *Revista Mexicana de Sociología* 40, no. 4 (October–December 1978): 1353–410.

Landrú. *Gente paqueta*. Buenos Aires: Orion, 1972.

Lanusse, Alejandro. *Mi testimonio*. Buenos Aires: IEA, 1977.

Marín, Juan Carlos. "Acerca de la relación poder-saber y la relación saber-poder. (La razón de la fuerza o la fuerza de la razón)." *Serie de Estudios*, no. 34, CICSO, 1978.

Massuh, Victor. *Nihilismo y experiencia extrema*. Buenos Aires: Sudamericana, 1975.

Matallana, Andrea. *Humor y política: Un estudio comparativo de tres publicaciones de humor político*. Buenos Aires: Eudeba, 1999.

Mazzioti, Nora. *Conversaciones con Alberto Migre: "Soy como de la familia."* Buenos Aires: Sudamericana, 1993.

Miguens, José Enrique. "Las interpretaciones intelectuales del voto peronista: Los prejuicios académicos y las realidades." In *Racionalidad del peronismo: Perspectivas internas y externas que replantean un debate inconcluso*, edited by Miguens and Frederick Turner, 209–32. Buenos Aires: Planeta, 1988.

Miguens, José Enrique. "The Presidential Elections of 1973 and the End of an Ideology." In *Juan Perón and the Reshaping of Argentina*, edited by Frederick Turner and Miguens, 147–70. Pittsburgh: University of Pittsburgh Press, 1983.

Mochkofsky, Graciela. *Timerman: El periodista que quiso ser parte del poder (1923–1999)*. Buenos Aires: Sudamericana, 2004.

Mora y Araujo, Manuel. "Las bases estructurales del peronismo." In *El voto peronista: Ensayos de sociología electoral argentina*, edited by Mora y Araujo and Ignacio Llorente, 397–440. Buenos Aires: Sudamericana, 1980.

Mora y Araujo, Manuel. "La naturaleza de la coalición alfonsinista." In *La argentina electoral*, edited by AA.VV. Buenos Aires: Sudamericana, 1985.

Mora y Araujo, Manuel. "Populismo, laborismo y clases medias (Política y estructura social en la Argentina)." *Criterio*, no. 1755–56 (1977): 9–20.

Mora y Araujo, Manuel, and Peter Smith. "Peronism and Economic Development: The 1973 Elections." In *Juan Perón and the Reshaping of Argentina*, edited by Frederick Turner and José Enrique Miguens, 171–88. Pittsburgh: University of Pittsburgh Press, 1983.

Morin, Edgar. "La industria cultural." In *La industria cultural*, edited by Theodor Adorno and Morin, 7–20. Buenos Aires: Galerna, 1967.

Moscovici, Serge. *Social Representations: Explorations in Social Psychology*. New York: New York University Press, 2001.

Muraro, Heriberto. "La comunicación masiva durante la dictadura militar y la transición democrática en la Argentina, 1973–1986." In *Medios, transformación cultural y política*, edited by Oscar Landi, 13–57. Buenos Aires: Legasa, 1987.

Muraro, Heriberto. *Neocapitalismo y comunicación de masa*. Buenos Aires: Eudeba, 1974.

Muraro, Heriberto. *La publicidad*. Buenos Aires: Acción, 1976.

Neilson, James. *En tiempo de oscuridad*. Buenos Aires: Emecé, 2001.

Neilson, James. *La vorágine argentina*. Buenos Aires: Marymar, 1979.

Neuman, W. Russell. *The Future of the Mass Audience*. Cambridge: Cambridge University Press, 1991.

O'Donnell, Guillermo. *Bureaucratic Authoritarianism: Argentina, 1966–1973, in Comparative Perspective*. Berkeley: University of California Press, 1988.

O'Donnell, Guillermo. *El Estado Burocrático Autoritario (1966–1973)*. Buenos Aires: Universidad de Belgrano, 1982.

Ollier, María Matilde. *Golpe o revolución: La violencia legitimada, Argentina 1966–1973*. Buenos Aires: Eduntref, 2005.

Páez de la Torre, Carlos. *Historia de Tucumán*. Buenos Aires: Plus Ultra, 1987.

Pellettieri, Osvaldo. "El teatro de Ricardo Monti (1970–2000): La resistencia a la modernidad marginal." In *Teatro (Tomo II): Ricardo Monti*, 9–79. Buenos Aires: Corregidor, 2000.

Pereira Guimarães, Roberto. "Understanding Support for Terrorism." In *Juan Perón and the Reshaping of Argentina*, edited by Frederick Turner and José Enrique Miguens, 189–222. Pittsburgh: University of Pittsburgh Press, 1983.

Portantiero, Juan Carlos. "Clases dominantes y crisis política en la Argentina actual." In *El capitalismo argentino en crisis*, edited by Oscar Braun. Buenos Aires: Siglo XXI, 1973.

Portantiero, Juan Carlos. "Economía y política en la crisis argentina: 1958–1973." *Revista Mexicana de Sociología* 39, no. 2 (April–June 1977): 531–65.

Pucci, Roberto. *Historia de la destrucción de una provincia: Tucumán 1966*. Tucumán: Del pago chico, 2008.

Quino. *Todo Mafalda*. Buenos Aires: De la Flor, 1997.

Redondo, Nélida. "Composición por edades y envejecimiento demográfico." In *Población y bienestar en la Argentina del primero al segundo centenario: Una historia social del siglo XX*, edited by Susana Torrado, 2:139–75. Buenos Aires: Edhasa, 2007.

Rivera, Jorge B. "Historia del humor gráfico argentino." In *Medios de comunicación y cultura popular*, edited by Anibal Ford, Jorge B. Rivera, and Eduardo Romano. Buenos Aires: Legasa, 1985.

Rock, David. *Politics in Argentina, 1890–1930: The Rise and Fall of Radicalism*. Cambridge: Cambridge University Press, 1975.

Rofman, Alejandro. *Desigualdades regionales y concentración económica (el caso argentino)*. Buenos Aires: Siap-Planteos, 1974.

Romero, Luis Alberto. "La violencia en la historia argentina reciente: Un estado de la cuestión." In *Historizar el pasado vivo en América Latina*, edited by Anne Pérotin-Dumon, 1–137. Santiago: Universidad Alberto Hurtado, Centro de Ética, 2007. http://etica.uahurtado.cl/historizarelpasadovivo/es_contenido.php.

Rotenberg, Abrasha. *Historia confidencial: La Opinión y otros olvidos*. Buenos Aires: Sudamericana, 1999.

Roth, Roberto. *Los años de Onganía*. Buenos Aires: de la Campana, 1981.

Sabato, Ernesto. *El otro rostro del peronismo*. Buenos Aires: n.p., 1956.

Sarlo, Beatriz. *La batalla de las ideas (1943–1973)*. Buenos Aires: Ariel, 2001.

Sarlo, Beatriz. *La pasión y la excepción*. Buenos Aires: Siglo XXI, 2003.

Sarlo, Beatriz. *Tiempo pasado: Cultura de la memoria y primera persona*. Buenos Aires: Siglo XXI, 2005.

Schmucler, Héctor, and Margarita Zires. "El papel ideológico de los medios de comunicación: Argentina 1975, La crisis del lopezrreguismo." In *Comunicación y Cultura* 5:119–78. Mexico City: Nueva Imagen, 1978.

Seoane, María. *El burgués maldito: Los secretos de Gelbard, el último líder del capitalismo nacional*. Buenos Aires: Sudamericana, 2003.

Sidicaro, Ricardo. *La política mirada desde arriba: Las ideas del diario La Nación (1909–1989)*. Buenos Aires: Sudamericana, 1993.

Sigal, Silvia. *Intelectuales y poder en la década del sesenta*. Buenos Aires: Punto Sur, 1991.

Sigal, Silvia, and Eliseo Verón. "Perón: Discurso político e ideología." In *Argentina, hoy*, edited by Alain Rouquié, 151–205. Buenos Aires: Siglo XXI, 1982.

Smith, Wayne. "El diálogo Perón-Lanusse." In *Racionalidad del peronismo: Perspectivas internas y externas que replantean un debate inconcluso*, edited by José Enrique Miguens and Frederick Turner, 117–66. Buenos Aires: Planeta, 1988.

Taussig, Michael. "*Maleficium*: State Fetishism." In *The Nervous System*. New York: Routledge, 1992.

Terán, Oscar. *Nuestros años sesentas*. Buenos Aires: Punto Sur, 1991.

Terragno, Rodolfo. *El peronismo de los 70: De Cámpora a Isabelita (I)*. Buenos Aires: Capital Intelectual, 2005.

Theweleit, Klaus. *Male Fantasies*. Minneapolis: University of Minnesota Press, 1987.

Torrado, Susana. "Estrategias de desarrollo, estructura social y movilidad." In *Población y bienestar en la Argentina del primero al segundo centenario: Una historia social del siglo XX*, 1:31–68. Buenos Aires: Edhasa, 2007.

Torrado, Susana. *Estructura social de la Argentina*. Buenos Aires: de la Flor, 1994.

Torre, Juan Carlos. "A partir del Cordobazo." *Estudios* 4 (1994): 15–24.

Turner, Frederick. "The Study of Argentine Politics through Survey Research." *Latin American Research Review* 10 (1975): 73–116.

Ulanovsky, Carlos. *1951–1976: Televisión Argentina, 25 años después*. Buenos Aires: Hachette, 1976.

Ulanovsky, Carlos, Silvia Itkin, and Pablo Sirvén. *Estamos en el aire: Una historia de la televisión en la Argentina*. Buenos Aires: Planeta, 1999.

Ulanovsky, Carlos, Marta Merkin, Juan José Panno, and Grabriela Tijman. *Días de radio: Historias de la radio argentina*. Buenos Aires: Espasacalpe, 1996.

Vezzetti, Hugo. *Pasada y presente: Guerra, dictadura y sociedad en la Argentina*. Buenos Aires: Siglo XXXI, 2003.

Vezzetti, Hugo. *Sobre la violencia revolucionaria: Memorias y olvidos*. Buenos Aires: Siglo XXI, 2009.

Viñas, David. "Talesnik: Denuncia y compasión de la clase media," preface to Ricardo Talesnik, *Cien veces no debo*. Buenos Aires: Talía, 1972, 5–6.

Waldmann, Peter. "Anomia social y violencia." In *Argentina, hoy*, edited by Alain Rouquié, 206–48. Buenos Aires: Siglo XXI, 1982.

Walsh, Rodolfo. "Carta abierta de Rodolfo Walsh a la Junta Militar." In *El violento oficio de escribir: Obra periodística (1953–1977)*. Buenos Aires: de la Flor, 2008.

Zalduendo, Eduardo. *Las desigualdades económicas entre las regiones de Argentina*. Buenos Aires: n.p., 1973.

Žižek, Slavoj. *The Sublime Object of Ideology*. London: Verso, 1999.

cacionales y Sociales; CIMS), 21–22, 52, 105–7, 205–6, 284n9, 284n11, 287n28, 305n18, 306n26, 334n3
Centro Editor de América Latina (CEAL), 176
Cerain, Marta, 211, 214
Chaco (province), 12, 54, 277
Chamizo, Julio, 228, 231, 286n20
Chancalay, Agapito [pseud. for Demetrio Oliva), 54, 74–75, 138
channels (TV). *See* television channels
Charrúa y Cía.: advertisement, 235
Chile, 50, 88, 153, 155
China, 85, 162
Chubut (province), 277
Citroën Argentina company: advertisement, 218–19
City of the Children (La Ciudad de los Niños), 64
civil superstition, 159–70
Codevilla, Pablo, 110
Cohen, Rafael, 303n91
Colegio Nacional Florentino Ameguino, Cañada de Gómez, 191–92
Colombres, Ignacio, 315n13
COMA 13. *Del Cordobazo a Malvinas. Trece años de historia en imagines*, 6–7, 18, 34–36, 41, 85, 92, 129–30, 136, 164–65, 168–70, 173, 195–97, 201–2, 243, 282n11, 302n89, 319n50, 330n131
communism, 11, 13, 40, 69, 102, 248, 333n1
Córdoba (city), 6, 21, 48, 52, 55–56, 58, 64, 68–69, 79, 89, 94, 99, 103, 105–8, 146, 155, 164, 205, 277, 284n9, 298n16, 305n18, 320n66, 322n100, 335n5
Córdoba (province), 49, 79, 80, 121, 124, 146, 228–29, 288n40, 316n20
Cordobazo, 48–52, 56, 68–69, 77, 91–94, 97, 291n56, 298n16, 302n82
Correa, 6, 8, 15, 35, 39, 41–45, 57, 68, 82, 89–90, 97–100, 128, 130, 134–35, 137, 143, 145–46, 159, 163–64, 172, 174, 176, 190–91, 194, 202, 228, 230, 264, 274,

277, 279, 299n39, 302n90, 304nn105–6, 333n185, 336n2
Corrientes (province), 51, 277
Cortázar, Julio, 44, 158
Cosak: men's dress pants advertisement, 180, 215, 217
Cox, Robert, 317n33
Creedence Clearwater Revival, 99
Crespi Seco: wine advertisement, 256
Cresto, Enrique, 318n35
Crisis of 2001, Argentina, 195, 267
Cruz, Luis, 36
Cuba, 20, 85, 135, 172

de Gaulle, Charles, 101
De Luca advertising company, 324n18
de Triana, José, 282
de Vries, Peter, 2
Delon, Alain, 218
Demare, Lucas, 303
Democratic-Progressive Party (Partido Demócrata Progresista), 43, 45, 316n25
Democratic Socialist Party (Partido Socialista Democrático), 286
Desplats, Gustavo, 300n46
developmentalism, 13, 20, 23, 28, 33, 39, 43, 191, 316n25
Disi, Emilio, 302n85
Dodge 1500: advertisement, 215
Donald (singer), 82, 303n91

Eco, Umberto, 324n9
Economic Commission for Latin America (Comisión Económica para América Latina; CEPAL), 267
Egypt, 162
Eichmann, Adolf, 203
elections: 1973 elections (March), 10, 22–25, 27, 29, 31, 105, 241, 253, 256–57, 268, 286n22, 287n29, 290n52, 293n73, 334n1; 1973 elections (September), 24, 26, 29–32, 293n75; 1983

Viola, Roberto, 203
violence, 242–44
Viscovich, Milan, 291n56
Vitess hairspray: advertisement, 225, 239

Walsh, Rodolfo, 318n34
Warsaw ghetto, 158
Wash Lan Oro, cleaning product for wool
   fabrics: advertisement, 245–46
working-class, 2, 6–7, 9, 14–15, 17–18,
   20–22, 24–26, 28, 31, 35, 52, 60, 75, 91,

155, 283n7, 287n29, 287n31, 288n33,
   288n40, 334n1
World War I, 247

Yankee imperialism, 87
Yrigoyen, Hipólito, 9, 202
Yuste advertising company, 324n10

Zecchin, Dimma, 228
Žižek, Slavoj, 160, 331n156